The IDG Books Strategies® Advantage

We at IDG Books Worldwide created *Workflow Strategies* to meet your growing need for quick access to the most complete and accurate computer information available. Our books are not long-winded manuals or dry reference tomes. In each book, expert authors help you understand new technology and teach you how to evaluate its usefulness for your needs.

The authors of IDG books are uniquely qualified to give you expert advice as well as to provide insightful tips and techniques not found anywhere else. Our authors maintain close contact with end users through feedback from articles, training sessions, e-mail exchanges, user group participation, and consulting work. Because our authors know the realities of daily computer use and are directly tied to the reader, our books have a strategic advantage.

Our authors have the experience to approach a topic in the most efficient manner, and we know that you, the reader, will benefit from a "one-on-one" relationship with the author. Our research shows that readers make computer book purchases because they want expert advice. Because readers want to benefit from the author's experience, the author's voice is always present in an IDG book.

You will find what you need in this book whether you read it from cover to cover, section by section, or simply one topic at a time. As a computer user and emerging technology user, you deserve a comprehensive resource of answers. We at IDG Books Worldwide are proud to deliver that resource with *Workflow Strategies*.

Brenda McLaughlin
Senior Vice President and Group Publisher
Internet: YouTellUs@idgbooks.com

WORKFLOW STRATEGIES®

WORKFLOW STRATEGIES®

by James G. Kobielus

IDG BOOKS WORLDWIDE, INC.
AN INTERNATIONAL DATA GROUP COMPANY

Foster City, CA ◆ Chicago, IL ◆ Indianapolis, IN ◆ Southlake, TX

Workflow Strategies®

Published by
IDG Books Worldwide, Inc.
An International Data Group Company
919 E. Hillsdale Blvd.
Suite 400
Foster City, CA 94404

Library of Congress Catalog Card No.: 96-080031

ISBN: 0-7645-3012-7

Printed in the United States of America

10 9 8 7 6 5 4 3 2 1

1QBCM/RU/QS/ZW/FC

Distributed in the United States by IDG Books Worldwide, Inc.

Distributed by Macmillan Canada for Canada; by Contemporanea de Ediciones for Venezuela; by Distribuidora Cuspide for Argentina; by CITEC for Brazil; by Ediciones ZETA S.C.R. Ltda. for Peru; by Editorial Limusa SA for Mexico; by Transworld Publishers Limited in the United Kingdom and Europe; by Academic Bookshop for Egypt; by Levant Distributors S.A.R.L. for Lebanon; by Al Jassim for Saudi Arabia; by Simron Pty. Ltd. for South Africa; by Pustak Mahal for India; by The Computer Bookshop for India; by Toppan Company Ltd. for Japan; by Addison Wesley Publishing Company for Korea; by Longman Singapore Publishers Ltd. for Singapore, Malaysia, Thailand, and Indonesia; by Unalis Corporation for Taiwan; by WS Computer Publishing Company, Inc. for the Philippines; by WoodsLane Pty. Ltd. for Australia; by WoodsLane Enterprises Ltd. for New Zealand. Authorized Sales Agent: Anthony Rudkin Associates for the Middle East and North Africa.

For general information on IDG Books Worldwide's books in the U.S., please call our Consumer Customer Service department at 800-762-2974. For reseller information, including discounts and premium sales, please call our Reseller Customer Service department at 800-434-3422.

For information on where to purchase IDG Books Worldwide's books outside the U.S., please contact our International Sales department at 415-655-3172 or fax 415-655-3295.

For information on foreign language translations, please contact our Foreign & Subsidiary Rights department at 415-655-3021 or fax 415-655-3281.

For sales inquiries and special prices for bulk quantities, please contact our Sales department at 415-655-3200 or write to the address above.

For information on using IDG Books Worldwide's books in the classroom or for ordering examination copies, please contact our Educational Sales department at 800-434-2086 or fax 817-251-8174.

For authorization to photocopy items for corporate, personal, or educational use, please contact Copyright Clearance Center, 222 Rosewood Drive, Danvers, MA 01923, or fax 508-750-4470.

 is a trademark under exclusive license to
IDG Books Worldwide, Inc.,
from International Data Group, Inc.

ABOUT IDG BOOKS WORLDWIDE

Welcome to the world of IDG Books Worldwide.

IDG Books Worldwide, Inc., is a subsidiary of International Data Group, the world's largest publisher of computer-related information and the leading global provider of information services on information technology. IDG was founded more than 25 years ago and now employs more than 8,500 people worldwide. IDG publishes more than 275 computer publications in over 75 countries (see listing below). More than 60 million people read one or more IDG publications each month.

Launched in 1990, IDG Books Worldwide is today the #1 publisher of best-selling computer books in the United States. We are proud to have received eight awards from the Computer Press Association in recognition of editorial excellence and three from *Computer Currents'* First Annual Readers' Choice Awards. Our best-selling *...For Dummies*® series has more than 30 million copies in print with translations in 30 languages. IDG Books Worldwide, through a joint venture with IDG's Hi-Tech Beijing, became the first U.S. publisher to publish a computer book in the People's Republic of China. In record time, IDG Books Worldwide has become the first choice for millions of readers around the world who want to learn how to better manage their businesses.

Our mission is simple: Every one of our books is designed to bring extra value and skill-building instructions to the reader. Our books are written by experts who understand and care about our readers. The knowledge base of our editorial staff comes from years of experience in publishing, education, and journalism — experience we use to produce books for the '90s. In short, we care about books, so we attract the best people. We devote special attention to details such as audience, interior design, use of icons, and illustrations. And because we use an efficient process of authoring, editing, and desktop publishing our books electronically, we can spend more time ensuring superior content and spend less time on the technicalities of making books.

You can count on our commitment to deliver high-quality books at competitive prices on topics you want to read about. At IDG Books Worldwide, we continue in the IDG tradition of delivering quality for more than 25 years. You'll find no better book on a subject than one from IDG Books Worldwide.

John Kilcullen
President and CEO
IDG Books Worldwide, Inc.

Eighth Annual Computer Press Awards ≥1992

Ninth Annual Computer Press Awards ≥1993

Tenth Annual Computer Press Awards ≥1994

Eleventh Annual Computer Press Awards ≥1995

IDG Books Worldwide, Inc., is a subsidiary of International Data Group, the world's largest publisher of computer-related information and the leading global provider of information services on information technology. International Data Group publishes over 275 computer publications in over 75 countries. Sixty million people read one or more International Data Group publications each month. International Data Group's publications include: ARGENTINA: Buyer's Guide, Computerworld Argentina, PC World Argentina; AUSTRALIA: Australian Macworld, Australian PC World, Australian Reseller News, Computerworld, IT Casebook, Network World, Publish, Webmaster; AUSTRIA: Computerwelt Osterreich, Networks Austria, PC Tip Austria; BANGLADESH: PC World Bangladesh; BELARUS: PC World Belarus; BELGIUM: Data News; BRAZIL: Annuário de Informática, Computerworld, Connections, Macworld, PC Player, PC World, Publish, Reseller News, Supergamepower; BULGARIA: Computerworld Bulgaria, Network World Bulgaria, PC & MacWorld Bulgaria; CANADA: CIO Canada, Client/Server World, ComputerWorld Canada, InfoWorld Canada, NetworkWorld Canada, WebWorld; CHILE: Computerworld Chile, PC World Chile; COLOMBIA: Computerworld Colombia, PC World Colombia; COSTA RICA: PC World Centro America; THE CZECH AND SLOVAK REPUBLICS: Computerworld Czechoslovakia, Macworld Czech Republic, PC World Czechoslovakia; DENMARK: Communications World Danmark, Computerworld Danmark, Macworld Danmark, PC World Danmark, Techworld Denmark; DOMINICAN REPUBLIC: PC World Republica Dominicana; ECUADOR: PC World Ecuador; EGYPT: Computerworld Middle East, PC World Middle East; EL SALVADOR: PC World Centro America; FINLAND: MikroPC, Tietoverkko, Tietoviikko; FRANCE: Distributique, Hebdo, Info PC, Le Monde Informatique, Macworld, Reseaux & Telecoms, WebMaster France; GERMANY: Computer Partner, Computerwoche, Computerwoche Extra, Computerwoche FOCUS, Global Online, Macwelt, PC Welt; GREECE: Amiga Computing, GamePro Greece, Multimedia World; GUATEMALA: PC World Centro America; HONDURAS: PC World Centro America; HONG KONG: Computerworld Hong Kong, PC World Hong Kong, Publish in Asia; HUNGARY: ABCD CD-ROM, Computerworld Szamitastechnika, Internetto online Magazine, PC World Hungary, PC-X Magazin Hungary; ICELAND: Tolvuheimur PC World Island; INDIA: Information Communications World, Information Systems Computerworld, PC World India, Publish in Asia; INDONESIA: InfoKomputer PC World, Komputek Computerworld, Publish in Asia; IRELAND: ComputerScope, PC Live!; ISRAEL: Macworld Israel, People & Computers/Computerworld; ITALY: Computerworld Italia, Macworld Italia, Networking Italia, PC World Italia; JAPAN: DTP World, Macworld Japan, Nikkei Personal Computing, OS/2 World Japan, SunWorld Japan, Windows NT World, Windows World Japan; KENYA: PC World East African; KOREA: Hi-Tech Information, Macworld Korea, PC World Korea; MACEDONIA: PC World Macedonia; MALAYSIA: Computerworld Malaysia, PC World Malaysia, Publish in Asia; MALTA: PC World Malta; MEXICO: Computerworld Mexico, PC World Mexico; MYANMAR: PC World Myanmar; NETHERLANDS: Computer! Totaal, LAN Internetworking Magazine, LAN World Buyers Guide, Macworld Netherlands, Net, WebWereld; NEW ZEALAND: Absolute Beginners Guide and Plain & Simple Series, Computer Buyer, Computer Industry Directory, Computerworld New Zealand, MTB, Network World, PC World New Zealand; NICARAGUA: PC World Centro America; NORWAY: Computerworld Norge, CW Rapport, Datamagasinet, Financial Rapport, Kursguide Norge, Macworld Norge, Multimediaworld Norge, PC World Ekspress Norge, PC World Nettverk, PC World Norge, PC World ProduktGuide Norge; PAKISTAN: Computerworld Pakistan; PANAMA: PC World Panama; PEOPLE'S REPUBLIC OF CHINA: China Computer Users, China Computerworld, China InfoWorld, China Telecom World Weekly, Computer & Communication, Electronic Design China, Electronics Today, Electronics Weekly, Game Software, PC World China, Popular Computer Week, Software Weekly, Software World, Telecom World; PERU: Computerworld Peru, PC World Profesional Peru, PC World SoHo Peru; PHILIPPINES: Click!, Computerworld Philippines, PC World Philippines, Publish in Asia; POLAND: Computerworld Poland, Computerworld Special Report Poland, Cyber, Macworld Poland, Networld Poland, PC World Komputer; PORTUGAL: Cerebro/PC World, Computerworld/Correio Informático, Dealer World Portugal, Mac*In/PC*In Portugal, Multimedia World; PUERTO RICO: PC World Puerto Rico; ROMANIA: Computerworld Romania, PC World Romania, Telecom Romania; RUSSIA: Computerworld Russia, Mir PK, Publish, Seti; SINGAPORE: Computerworld Singapore, PC World Singapore, Publish in Asia; SLOVENIA: Monitor; SOUTH AFRICA: Computing SA, Network World SA, Software World SA; SPAIN: Communicaciones World España, Computerworld España, Dealer World España, Macworld España, PC World España; SRI LANKA: Infolink PC World; SWEDEN: CAP&Design, Computer Sweden, Corporate Computing Sweden, Internetworld Sweden, it.branschen, Macworld Sweden, MaxiData Sweden, MikroDatorn, Natverk & Kommunikation, PC World Sweden, PCaktiv, Windows World Sweden; SWITZERLAND: Computerworld Schweiz, Macworld Schweiz, PCtip; TAIWAN: Computerworld Taiwan, Macworld Taiwan, NEW ViSiON/Publish, PC World Taiwan, Windows World Taiwan; THAILAND: Publish in Asia, Thai Computerworld; TURKEY: Computerworld Turkiye, Macworld Turkiye, Network World Turkiye; UKRAINE: Computerworld Kiev, Multimedia World Ukraine, PC World Ukraine; UNITED KINGDOM: Acorn User UK, Amiga Action UK, Amiga Computing UK, Apple Talk UK, Computing, Macworld, Parents and Computers UK, PC Advisor, PC Home, PSX Pro, The WEB; UNITED STATES: Cable in the Classroom, CIO Magazine, Computerworld, DOS World, Federal Computer Week, GamePro Magazine, InfoWorld, I-Way, Macworld, Network World, PC Games, PC World, Publish, Video Event, THE WEB Magazine, and WebMaster; online webzines: JavaWorld, NetscapeWorld, and SunWorld Online; URUGUAY: InfoWorld Uruguay; VENEZUELA: Computerworld Venezuela, PC World Venezuela; and VIETNAM: PC World Vietnam.   10/1/96

To my wonderful wife, Egidia, who helped me squeeze this project into the crazy contours of our life together

To my rambunctious children, Jason and Sonya, who flowed, flew, and fluttered through my home office during the many months I worked on this book

To the beautiful rhythm of a well-tuned workplace

Acknowledgments

To IDG Books for publishing me

To Ellen Camm at IDG Books for plucking me out of thin air and asking me if I wanted to write a book (guess what my answer was)

To *Network World* for giving me a slot on their editorial calendar and a prime space (right next to the cartoon) on their op/ed page for many years running; many of the ideas presented in this book got their first try-out in the pages of that fine periodical

To Gray Somerville, a natural-born workflow designer if I ever saw one — keep at it — rule the world — your struggles mirror mine

To Patrick J. McGovern, who made this book possible.

Benediction

AND SO IT FLOWS
Starts and fits and somehow it works.
Pieces and bits and blood on the pages.
Rush and push and squeeze it between times.
Scream and stream and give it a name.

(poem copyright 1997, James Kobielus)

Foreword

James Kobielus has delivered an easy-to-digest, well-thought-out examination of a complex subject — workflow technology, the engine powering some of the most provocative corporate reengineering success stories.

To his credit, he doesn't fall into the trap that some technology authors do — getting so caught up in the subject matter that, by the end, they have convinced themselves that technology solves everything.

Workflow tools, after all, are only as powerful as the processes that they are called on to facilitate. Typically those processes are overhauled as the tools are brought in, meaning the technology amplifies the effect of the new rules of order.

Workflow is not a quick fix and may, in fact, accelerate the deterioration of badly reasoned or otherwise flawed processes. That makes *Workflow Strategies* a must-have strategic planning guide for technical and nontechnical managers alike looking to reap sustainable competitive advantage out of workflow investments.

John Dix

Editor, *Network World*

Contents at a Glance

Contents

INTRODUCTION

What Makes a Well-managed Business in the Nineties?

Workflow management systems, intranets, and all the other technologies in the world won't help a poorly managed business in a slow-growing or declining market.

Workflow management — the automated routing of documentation and tasks — is a tool for helping well-managed businesses run better. If your business fundamentals aren't strong, you probably need stronger medicine, such as a corporate turnaround consultant or a thorough reexamination of your business strategies.

Savvy management will recognize in workflow a powerful tool for streamlining and speeding up fundamental business processes. Couple workflow with *intranets* — internal corporate enterprise networks based on World Wide Web and Internet technologies — and you have a powerful environment for the collaboration of many people across diverse business functions, great distances, and several time zones.

So ask yourself, while exploring the workflow market, what sort of company you want to be. How do you measure success? What management structure and processes are needed for corporate success? What information technologies and applications should you use to support reengineered business processes?

When the Work Flows Smoothly, and Otherwise

Visualizing a well-run workplace is not hard to do. You know a successful enterprise when you see it, even if you're not sure how it got that way or how long it will stay on the ball.

A prosperous, well-run business flows smoothly and pulses with its own distinctive rhythm (see Figure I-1). The company's management, staff, contractors, and suppliers all seem to be pulling in the same direction. People work feverishly hard but always have an extra burst of energy for new challenges. They don't let bureaucratic obstacles stand in the way of getting the job done. Even the dumpiest work environment takes on a luster of purposeful activity.

Figure I-1
A prosperous, well-run business flows smoothly and pulses with its own distinctive rhythm.

These days, however, it's too easy for companies to lose the magic touch seemingly overnight. Process reengineering is an ongoing concern for many enterprises, because internal work rhythms can easily slip out of sync with today's volatile competitive environment. Business processes and management approaches that worked beautifully last year may have become an impediment to flexibility and growth. Companies miss out on potential sales when new product designs take too long to flow from research and development to manufacturing. Customers jump to the competition when their calls for help are met constantly with delays or incoherent responses.

"The chump-to-champ-to-chump cycle used to be three generations," according to late MCI Chairperson William McGowan, as quoted by management consultant Tom Peters in his 1992 book *Liberation Management: Necessary Disorganization for the Nanosecond Nineties*[1]. "Now it's about five years." Peters notes with a touch of humility that some of the exemplar companies featured in his and Robert H. Waterman, Jr.'s 1982 bestseller *In Search of Excellence* have since been "desconstructed by competitors."

Is There a Secret Weapon for Sustainable Competitive Advantage?

More often than not, a hot company's success is due to subtle process innovations — procedures that last year's market leader cannot easily copy. Competitors scratch their heads and ask how they are supposed to duplicate the upstart's special teamwork, organization, preparedness, or chemistry. How, they ask, was our cross-town rival able to ship its new product in half the time expected? How were its engineers able to virtually eliminate out-of-box defects while our own products remain notoriously buggy? How did they come up with that sleek, sharp, intuitive new design? How were their international sales people able to win over our long-time Brazilian customer, even though we've been in business three times as long as the rival? How could they underprice us and still stay in business?

Increasingly, the winner's secret weapon is an effective application of information technologies to internal processes. Management books and trade publications are full of case studies of companies that have used information technology to achieve their competitive advantage. The dominant firm's killer app could be as simple and mundane as an intranet-based Web bulletin board on which all interested parties share experiences and insights on a product design issue. It could also be a shared competitive intelligence database that roving salespeople can access and update, either through the Internet, dial-up terrestrial modem connections, or wireless data communications networks, such as the new generation of personal communications services. Or it could be a concurrent-engineering workflow application that speeds the flow of engineering change requests and associated documentation through research and development.

Sustainable competitive advantage lies in a firm's ability to use information technologies to respond rapidly to new challenges by modifying internal processes and external links to customers, distributors, and suppliers. This method is a core tenet of most management philosophies these days. A typical formulation is in Don Tapscott and Art Caston's 1993 book *Paradigm Shift: The New Promise of Information Technology*[2]:

> "A shift is occurring in the nature of organizations. The corporation of old simply does not work anymore. Business transformation enabled by information is required to succeed in the new environment. The new enterprise is dynamic and can respond quickly to changing market conditions. It has a different structure — flatter and team-oriented — eliminating bureaucratic hierarchy. It is based on commitment rather than control. Business processes are streamlined for productivity and quality. The new enterprise is open and networked."

What Is Workflow Management?

Workflow management systems let you anchor these grand ideals in real-world business applications with clear paybacks. These systems are for managers who are serious about business-process reengineering.

Most workflow products support two basic functions. First, they provide tools for mapping out business-process models, which may be defined as sets of routes, roles, and rules for the movement of documentation and tasks. Second, they implement process models through linkages with a company's computer networks, shared databases, e-mail systems, and other applications, so that information can flow through the organization at a controlled, monitored pace.

One typical workflow user is the U.S. Department of Energy's Sandia National Laboratories. Sandia uses Action Technologies' Web-based workflow environment, Metro, to eliminate routing delays and paper handling on travel requests and access-badge requests, and it has plans to implement future workflow applications for shop-floor automation, purchase requisitions, employee transfer processing, and expense reporting. Action Metro allows Sandia's 8,000 employees to retrieve new work items from across the laboratory's intranet through their existing Netscape Navigator browsers, which run on Windows PCs, Apple Macintoshes, and UNIX workstations. Action's workflow server integrates with many pieces of Sandia's intranet infrastructure, including the Netscape Commerce Server, Sybase database on a UNIX file server, SQL Server database on a Microsoft Windows NT server, and Legacy human-resources, financial, and purchasing systems on an IBM mainframe. Sandia's systems analysts use Action's graphical flowcharting tool to map out workflow routes and business rules.

Diverse, Dynamic Market for Workflow Management Solutions

Action Technologies is one of dozens of vendors preparing workflow products for various network platforms, applications, and price points. Workflow industry solutions range from simple forms-routing tools to full-blown production systems supporting complex process models. Web- and intranet-based workflow products are a fast growing segment of the market, as are workflow tools that integrate with popular groupware products (such as IBM/Lotus Development Corporation's popular Notes) and application suites (such as Microsoft Office and BackOffice). Workflow prices range from less than $200 per user for some messaging-based workflow products, to between $15,000 – 25,000 per server or host computer for production workflow products. Quoted software prices will greatly understate the total sum of money the average network or information systems manager will wind up spending on workflow applications. Custom application development and integration (much of which is performed by high-priced consultants and resellers) will chew up the larger portion of the average workflow budget.

Workflow products have evolved beyond their original vertical-market focus on document-image processing, which has long been popular with financial, insurance, and engineering users. A growing number of workflow applications will route almost any file, including ASCII text, computer-aided design (CAD) drawings, word-processing documents, spreadsheets, databases, graphics, scanned images, and electronic forms.

The lines between workflow, groupware, document management, database management, and project management applications continue to blur. Most workflow products access server- or host-based file, document, and database management systems. Files relating to a particular task can often be routed as a linked *folder* and presented to recipients as a list of pending action items. Multiple versions of a particular document can be tracked by server-based document management systems. After a process is complete, the contents of a form can be written to shared corporate databases.

Used properly, workflow management systems can be powerful tools for reinventing your organization as a more flexible, efficient, customer-focused competitor. The flip side, however, is that they can also hard-wire bad processes and hasten your company's competitive decline if implemented without proper application planning and organizational redesign. Investments in workflow tools will come to naught unless accompanied by an ongoing, well-thought-out, broad-based corporate commitment to procedural innovation.

You don't have to bet the company on any one vendor's workflow product. In fact, you may not have to spend a dime on new software, if you take advantage of simple workflow capabilities in existing software. Major application suites (such as Microsoft Office and Lotus SmartSuite) allow you to route files from within desktop applications (such as word processors and spreadsheets) to one or more recipients. These suites typically wrap an e-mail *envelope* around the file and deliver it as an attachment to the recipient's e-mail inbox. This capability is often known as *messaging-enabled workflow*.

As your workflow needs grow in sophistication, you may choose to graduate up to mail-enabled or Web-enabled electronic-forms routing products. These products allow you to define an electronic form that gets routed via the corporate e-mail system or intranet. Inputted data fields are entered automatically into corporate databases at the end of the workflow. These products also allow you to send forms data through facsimile, paging, or wireless data networks.

As your company embarks on complex business-process reengineering projects, you'll want to explore production workflow systems. Many production workflow applications descend from established imaging-based workflow products or from text-based document management and retrieval products. These applications automate complex business processes that vary little from case to case, similar to a white-collar assembly line. They support high-volume transaction processing, shared document repositories, and sophisticated document and task tracking. Some applications also allow you to radically collapse sequential workflows by providing customer service representatives with a wide range of operational data when fielding customer inquiries or taking purchase orders.

See Figure I-2.

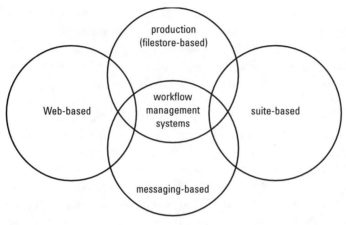

Figure I-2
Workflow management systems can be grouped into four categories — production, messaging-based, Web-based, and suite-based, with significant overlap among them.

When Should You Implement Workflow Applications on Intranets and the Internet?

Workflow applications have traditionally been hosted on intranets, which may be defined broadly as internal corporate networks supporting a wide range of telecommunications protocols and services. All the case studies presented in Chapter 14 concern intra-organizational applications. However, you may regard *electronic data interchange* — the long-established industry practice of electronically transmitting purchase orders, invoices, and other structured business documents to trading partners — as a form of interorganizational workflow.

One of the most startling business phenomena of the mid-90s has been the rapid development of World Wide Web-based intranets, hand in hand with the mass-market commercialization of the Internet. Naturally, companies are considering implementing workflow applications on their Web-based intranets, and a wide range of solutions is emerging to support these requirements. Company workflows are protected from hackers by security gateways known as *firewalls*. Users can participate in workflows through their existing Web browsers (such as Netscape Navigator or Microsoft Internet Explorer), accessing remote information via underlying telecommunications protocols and services such as Transmission Control Protocol/Internetwork Protocol (TCP/IP), HyperText Transfer Protocol (HTTP), and Multipurpose Internet Messaging Extensions (MIME).

Companies should eagerly explore the market for Web-based workflow tools, but not automatically assume that their intranets are the most appropriate platform for these applications. Many workflows are limited to a single workgroup, facility, or campus environment, making Web-based solutions, which are typically oriented toward wide-area network environments, an overkill approach.

With regard to wide-area workflows, you may find that your company's distributed document databases, messaging systems, groupware, and desktop application suites provide a more feature-rich, flexible environment for complex workflows. Lotus Notes, Microsoft Exchange, and other messaging-based groupware environments support sophisticated workflow features accessible to anybody with a local-area network (LAN) account and e-mail box.

How Will This Book Enhance Your Skills as a Business or Technical Manager?

With the aid of this book, you'll have no problem finding commercial workflow solutions suited to your requirements, network environment, and budget.

Chances are, however, that you won't select the right product if you don't first have a clear understanding of your company's requirements. In addition, you won't implement the product effectively if you don't identify business processes that could benefit from technology-enabled applications. And your workflow applications will probably die on the vine if company staff refuses to use them, considering them cumbersome, counterproductive, and inefficient.

In particular, consult your management information systems (MIS) staff before you invest in a particular workflow solution. The burden will fall on your MIS staff to develop and support workflow applications, and they may prefer to work with a particular vendor's development environment, such as those provided by Microsoft, IBM/Lotus, Novell, and Netscape. Because many commercial workflow and groupware solutions are also application development platforms, you should think twice before requiring MIS to change over to unfamiliar tools just to get your new automated business process off the ground.

Workflow Strategies is a business book that will help you think through all these issues before investing precious corporate resources on workflow applications.

This book illustrates the technical backbone behind the often fuzzy concept of business-process reengineering. It shows the average business reader how to start from a small-scale workflow pilot and scale up as appropriate to a complex, enterprise-wide information routing and tracking system. The focus is always on the bottom line: illustrating how workflow applications can help you increase the speed, flexibility, and efficiency of your business processes.

Workflow Strategies is aimed at two groups of readers.

Nontechnical management: Business professionals who have a basic understanding of computer and telecommunications concepts and are responsible for business-process reengineering within their organizations.

Technical management: Information systems and telecommunications professionals who have a basic understanding of management issues and are responsible for application planning and process redesign within their organizations.

This book provides concrete guidelines that describe how managers should evaluate, select, implement, and administer workflow management systems. Corporate case studies of successful workflow implementations are presented. The chapters discuss workflow functionality, survey commercial solutions, define evaluation criteria, and lay out guidelines for business-process reengineering to realize a payback from investments in workflow management tools.

Where Do You Find the Answers to Your Questions?

Deciding which type of workflow management system is right for your business and which tools to implement it with is an overwhelming task if considered in one big chunk. To help you better understand the key stages of the decision making process, this book is organized into five parts:

Part I — Strategic Vision: The Workflow Paradigm

This part discusses why managers should explore workflow solutions as tools for increasing organizational efficiency, productivity, flexibility, and competitive advantage. The reader is taken on a quick tour of modern management and business-process reengineering theories from authors such as Tom Peters, Michael Hammer, and James Champy. The conundrum of declining white-collar productivity in the face of rapid computerization is examined. Following this is a discussion of the strategic potential of technology-enabled collaboration environments in the post-modern, knowledge-based economy. Workflow management tools as a specific subset of information technologies is defined.

The three chapters in Part I raise strategic business issues that should guide your company's selection, implementation, and use of workflow management products:

- Chapter 1 provides you with guidelines for identifying and prioritizing strategic business processes that could benefit from application of workflow management systems. It summarizes the major cultural, regulatory, and technological trends shaping the business environment. It presents thumbnail sketches of today's most popular management theories, which clutter the bookshelves and mindspace of corporate America. This book is strictly agnostic as to the relative merits of various gurus' teachings. It is aimed to show you how to use workflow tools to shoot for whatever ideal corporate structure and processes — that is, hierarchical, decentralized, or something in between — you want.

- Chapter 2 provides you with guidelines for developing business justifications for workflow/reengineering projects. The discussion in this chapter will make you ponder whether workflow management or any other information technology application can make a difference in your company's competitive posture. At the economy-wide level, researchers have yet to find significant correlations between the amount of money a company invests in information technologies and that company's sales, market share, productivity, or competitive strength. At the grass-roots level, however, many researchers can point to case studies of companies that have gained an unquestioned competitive boost from a specific application of networks and computers. This chapter is aimed at getting you to focus at the micro level on fitting workflow applications to particular business processes while also considering the big-picture issue of how workflow-enabled processes make your company better able to compete.

- Chapter 3 presents a framework for mapping workflow applications to your business requirements. This chapter provides a high-level, conceptual perspective on the application of workflow technologies. It will also help you to distinguish workflow products based on general capabilities and applicability. This chapter is written to show you how to compare and contrast workflow products based on their support for three principal collaborative dimensions: platform, structure, and media. Each real-world workflow application must conform to the user's requirements for network and computing platforms, management and process structures, and communications and application media.

Part II — Technology Primer: Workflow System Architectures and Standards

This part presents a primer on the architectural components of a workflow management system, which includes process-definition tools, enactment services, client applications, invoked applications, and administration and monitoring tools. It describes the four types of commercial workflow products: 1) production workflow, 2) messaging-based workflow, 3) Web-based workflow, and 4) suite-based workflow. Following that is a detailed discussion of the many technologies that provide the application infrastructure for automated workflows, including image management, database management, document management, electronic messaging, and intranet services.

The three chapters in Part II provide a primer on the workflow management technologies incorporated in today's commercial products:

- Chapter 4 presents a detailed primer on the technical architecture of workflow systems, employing the reference model and standard terminology proposed by the Workflow Management Coalition (WfMC), a broad-based vendor consortium. The reader is shown how workflow process models are built with various flowcharting tools and methodologies. Workflow standards proposed by the WfMC and Microsoft are discussed.

- Chapter 5 describes the four types of workflow technologies on the market: production workflow, messaging-based workflow, Web-based workflow, and suite-based workflow. This latter category represents the future of distributed computing, in which workflow capabilities will be embedded within all desktop applications rather than stand alone. Suite-based applications provide convenient document-routing capabilities to the mass market, typically using messaging and/or Web transport options.

■ Chapter 6 discusses the enterprise networking application infrastructure needed to support workflow solutions. The chapter discusses workflow-relevant technologies and standards in such areas as image processing, database management, document management, object management, product data management, electronic messaging, directory services, Internet/intranet services, and electronic commerce.

Part III — Market Survey: Workflow Solutions For Serious And Casual Business Users

This part provides a general survey or overview of workflow management products available at the time of publication in each of the categories just described. Brief vendor profiles and product overviews are presented for the most noteworthy solutions. Workflow product development strategies are presented for the largest, most influential software vendors, including Action Technologies, FileNet, IBM/Lotus, JetForm, Novell, Microsoft, and Wang Laboratories.

The four chapters in Part III present a survey of leading production workflow, messaging-based workflow, Web-based workflow, and suite-based products available at the time of publication. The products featured run from high-end, complex, multimedia workflow systems to simple document-routing applications. There is something in this book's market survey (Chapters 7-10) to appeal to workflow users of all stripes — from serious to casual.

The market survey is organized as follows:

■ Chapter 7 surveys the production workflow market, focusing on the following vendors (in alphabetical order): Action Technologies, Autodesk, BancTec, FileNet, IA, IBM/Lotus Development, InConcert, Keyfile, ViewStar, and Wang Laboratories.

■ Chapter 8 surveys the messaging-based workflow market, focusing on Banyan Systems, IBM/Lotus Development, JetForm, Microsoft, and Novell.

■ Chapter 9 surveys the Web-based workflow market, focusing on Action Technologies, Documentum, OpenText, Reach Software, Ultimus, Wang, and WebFlow.

■ Chapter 10 surveys the workflow-enabled application environment market, focusing on Digital Equipment, IBM/Lotus Development, Microsoft, and Novell.

The focus is on the workflow industry's leading brand-name vendors and products. Each vendor profile provides a brief corporate background, product overview, and discussion of strategic business alliances and directions. In-depth profiles are presented for workflow vendors that meet many or all of the following criteria in their respective market segments: horizontal application focus; significant market share; innovative technical approach; standards-based product architecture; strategic business alliances; and broad international sales, distribution, and reseller channels.

Obviously, vendor hotlists can grow obsolete rapidly, especially in a dynamic, entrepreneurial market such as workflow. Almost overnight, mergers, consolidations, divestitures, and alliances can eliminate some familiar company names and bring others to the fore. Nevertheless, the brand names featured in these four chapters have fundamental strengths that should translate into staying power in the fast-changing workflow marketplace.

Just as important, the vendors highlighted in these four chapters represent the leading edge of the workflow industry. These companies are pacesetters, implementing new standards, architectures, alliances, and applications that are driving the evolution of the workflow market.

Part IV — Evaluation And Implementation Guidelines: Realizing Organizational Payback From Workflow

This part presents management guidelines for evaluating, planning, acquiring, implementing, and administering workflow applications within small and large organizations. The section is organized according to the following phases in the life of a workflow project: project planning and justification, operations review and analysis, market survey and product selection, application development and implementation, and user training and support.

The six chapters in Part IV present management guidelines for justifying, planning, evaluating, acquiring, implementing, and administering workflow applications.

- Chapter 11 provides tips on justifying corporate investments in workflow management systems. Your ability to win support for a workflow redesign/reengineering project depends on many factors, including the project's mission impact, size, scope, complexity, risk, and cost. Having a solid cost-benefit analysis and an enthusiastic, highly placed management sponsor couldn't hurt your chances.

- Chapter 12 lays out steps for rethinking current workflows to define innovations that can be enabled or facilitated with workflow systems. This is where your workflow-reengineering project team rolls up its collective sleeves and begins to block out your new process at a high level. You had better have a clear idea of your target workflow before you invest in a commercial workflow management system.

- Chapter 13 provides criteria to use in surveying and evaluating commercial workflow products and providers. With close to a hundred workflow products on the market, you will need clear criteria and priorities to avoid falling prey to information overload and *analysis paralysis* when shopping for a solution.

- Chapter 14 presents recent case studies of companies that have applied workflow technologies successfully. It's important, before you plunge into a high-stakes workflow-reengineering project, to see how workflow tools fit into living, breathing organizations. My goal for this chapter will be to help you learn from others' experiences with workflow-reengineering projects, technologies, and applications.

■ Chapter 15 describes how to implement and administer automated workflow applications. This is where you use process-definition, forms-design, and various programming and integration tools to build a real live workflow application. You will then be ready to introduce your application to actual end users, preferably in a controlled fashion with opportunities for user feedback and continued refinement. The chapter also discusses how to train and support workflow users to gain the full benefits of the technology, ensure grass-roots acceptance, and minimize work disruption. End-user comfort and understanding is critical to the success of any process redesign. It becomes increasingly important in this new age of workflow-enabled applications, in which much of the responsibility for process-redesign and dynamic rerouting falls to users themselves.

■ Chapter 16 helps you to anticipate and address the human impacts of implementing workflow applications in your organization.

Part V — Appendixes

This part provides supplementary material that will help round out your understanding of workflow technologies discussed in the book. It consists of the following appendices:

■ Appendix A: Workflow System Resources. This section provides a compressive listing of vendor, products, consultants, researchers, standards organizations, and publications in the workflow and business-process-reengineering markets.

■ Appendix B: Workflow Management Coalition — The Workflow Reference Model. This section reprints the Workflow Management Coalition's seminal reference model document, first published in 1994, which forms part of the conceptual backbone of this book.

■ Appendix C: Notes. This section compiles citations of all external books and other publications referenced in the preparation of this book.

■ Appendix D: Glossary — Workflow Lingo Laid Bare. This section provides definitions of terminology in the workflow industry and related technologies that are used in the book and which might not be familiar to the average business reader.

PART I

Strategic Vision
The Workflow Paradigm

his part discusses why managers should explore workflow solutions as tools for increasing organizational
efficiency, productivity, flexibility, and competitive
advantage. The reader is taken on a quick tour of modern management and business-process reengineering theories from
authors such as Tom Peters, Michael Hammer, and James
Champy. The conundrum of declining white-collar productivity in the face of rapid computerization is examined. Following
this is a discussion of the strategic potential of technology-
enabled collaboration environments in the post-modern,
knowledge-based economy. Workflow management tools as a
specific subset of information technologies is defined.

CHAPTER ONE

FORMULATING A STRATEGIC MANAGEMENT VISION

Workflow, Business-Process Reengineering, and the Ever-changing Competitive Landscape

Workflow management systems are catalysts for goal-oriented business transformation. To identify potential applications of workflow tools, you must first comprehend the far-reaching changes taking place in today's global economy and society. This chapter provides you with the strategic management vision needed to understand the business relevance and applications of your investment in workflow technologies.

Modern Business Drivers

One of the clichés of modern thinking is that we're in the grips — or on the brink — of a complete, pervasive, radical change in many, if not all, spheres of life. Crack open almost any popular management book, and you're likely to find the word *revolution* in the title or on the first page. Many authors have taken to waving the red flag of *revolution* — business, technological, cultural, and otherwise — simply to be noticed in the cluttered marketplace of ideas.

We may or may not be on the cusp of a new world order, conveniently timed to coincide with the approaching millennium, but there is a kernel of truth in all this revolution-mongering. Any way you look at it, the world economy is changing rapidly through the convergence of many powerful trends (see Table 1-1).

TABLE 1-1: MODERN BUSINESS DRIVERS

TREND	DISCUSSION
Cultural	Speed, service, and customization have become imperatives for modern business. Life everywhere is moving at a faster pace. The mass market has disintegrated into countless specialized niches, as consumers increasingly demand products and services tailored to their particular needs and tastes. Ethnic, cultural, and other demographic minorities are asserting their identities more forcefully. The growth of international media, travel, immigration, and intermarriage has spawned a new generation with a global outlook.
Regulatory	Free-market capitalism has become the model for national economic development the world over, most notably in the former Soviet empire and bloc. Governments everywhere are privatizing formerly nationalized industries and retreating from overt microregulation of the economy. Continental free-trade zones that have emerged in Europe and North America seem likely to expand geographically, steadily bringing the curtain down on import tariffs, quotas, and other trade barriers. Industries that were once regarded as *natural monopolies* (such as telecommunications and parcel delivery) are now hotbeds of competition.
Technological	We live in an increasingly media-rich environment — on the job, at home, in our cars, and even in the great outdoors. Most of us are never far from terminals of some sort — phone, computer and modem, pager, fax, TV, radio, and so on — and the reassuring, nonstop connectedness they provide. Mobile communications and computing technologies allow us to carry our virtual offices with us to wherever the work may be. Distributed computer networks — most notably, the Internet and World Wide Web — have permeated the business world, delivering instantaneous operational statistics and market intelligence. Increasingly, the Web browser is becoming the universal client for accessing information throughout the Internet, as well as within company-specific intranets. The pace of commerce has quickened with the rapid introduction of electronic data interchange and automated funds transfer networks, which support a form of interorganizational workflow management.

Change-driven second-guessing goes a long way toward explaining the boom market for management books.

Business Transformation as Abiding Concern

Faced with so much change, modern managers naturally question whether the old ways of doing business are still relevant. This change-driven second-guessing goes a long way toward explaining the boom market for management books. It's not entirely coincidental that the current management mania caught fire in 1982 upon the publication of Tom Peters and Robert H. Waterman's landmark *In Search of Excellence.* That was also the year in which IBM released its first PC and *Time* magazine named the computer its "Man of the Year." Radical new tools spur people to search for radical new ways to manage and use them. When the road to the future is unclear, people eagerly snatch up any available roadmap, even one that is highly speculative.

Workflow management — as an overall paradigm, rather than a discrete set of technologies — is central to many management books. It is addressed — explicitly or implicitly — under such topics as business-process reengineering, intra- and inter-organizational linkages, organizational structure, just-in-time management, value-chain analysis, and electronic data interchange. The focus is usually on business processes that either work well and should be emulated, or not very well and should be discarded or avoided. Information technologies are usually discussed as an integral *enabler* for these processes, facilitating workflows of a sequential, concurrent, or complex nature.

Management Visions Galore

One common theme in most of today's management books is that hierarchical workflows — in other words, the traditional corporate command, reporting, and review chain — lack the speed and flexibility necessary for success in today's business world. Most management thinkers call for workflows that are more streamlined, nonbureaucratic, decentralized, parallel, team-oriented, and customer-driven. They use different buzzwords to describe the same vision of the flexible, reconfigurable, distributed, empowered enterprise (see Table 1-2).

TABLE 1-2: MANAGEMENT VISIONS

VISION	DESCRIPTION
Business Reengineering	Post-industrial corporations built around the idea of reunifying production tasks into coherent business processes[1]
Cluster Organization	Multidisciplinary project teams working together on a semipermanent basis[2]
Dancing Elephants	Large companies surviving in the competitive arena by learning how to behave like small companies, establishing flexible project-oriented management structures, moving quickly to take advantage of opportunities, and cultivating close, responsive customer relationships[3]
Extended Enterprise	Enterprise that uses information technology to implement high-performance team structures, function as integrated businesses despite considerable business-unit autonomy, and reach out and develop new relationships with external organizations[4]
Human Networking	Dynamic coalescence of people with diverse skills into transient project teams[5]
Necessary Disorganization	Dynamic construction of networks of small, self-contained elements, units, and businesses[6]

(continued)

TABLE 1-2: MANAGEMENT VISIONS (*continued*)

VISION	DESCRIPTION
Networked Organization	Highly decentralized enterprise that relies on contractors, suppliers, and consultants to perform many or most functions[7]
Perpetual Organization	Organization that can take the form of any structure, based upon market demands at the moment[8]
Relational Organization	Organization defined not by fixed structures but by ease of relationships[9]
Value Chain	Organization modeled as interrelated series of activities that each add value, directly or indirectly, to finished goods and services[10]
Virtual Corporation	Amorphous organization with permeable and continuously changing interfaces between internal functions, as well as between the company proper and external suppliers, distributors, and customers[11]

Workflow Management Tools for Process Reengineering

All of these management visions are worth considering, and you may find that one aligns closely with your core business philosophies and addresses your most pressing competitive challenges. Your decision to adopt one or another of these frameworks is as much an act of faith as analysis.

A central theme of *this* book is that you can find productive uses for workflow management tools in your organization without having to endorse these or any other popular management philosophy. Workflow tools can help your company be a better centralized bureaucracy — if that's the structure that seems best — or a better decentralized web. Most workflow tools are essentially value-neutral. They have potential uses — and misuses — within most types of organization.

You should consult popular management texts when mapping out your company's workflow strategy, if for no other reason than to identify candidate business processes that could benefit from workflow tools. Today's management thinkers have many provocative ideas and interesting case studies but, unfortunately, often come up short on concrete guidelines. The average management reader is looking (more or less) for a cookbook approach to improving his or her business. Many management gurus come off a bit like restaurant critics, praising the few exquisite entrees they've encountered and lamenting the scarcity of good cooks in the world. All the while, you simply want somebody to help you become a better cook.

So, how do you get down to the business of reengineering your organization's workflows? Start by sniffing out the problems, inefficiencies, and weak points in existing processes. A good three-step approach to this task is to define and name recurring processes, identify areas that don't meet specified performance criteria, and prioritize the troublespots you want to fix.

Identifying Candidate Processes for Reengineering

You may want to call on business-process consultants to help you get started with workflow reengineering, but proceed with caution. You'll need to firm up your reengineering priorities before you call on consultants. Outsiders, for all their expertise, probably won't understand your business problems half as well as your staff — and they may run up quite a hefty tab looking for problems to fix. Bring in consultants only when you've narrowed down reengineering priorities to a short list of potential projects with well-defined objectives, and for which in-house expertise is lacking.

Workflow reengineering starts with something as simple as compiling a list of fundamental business processes in your organization. One useful approach for identifying potential workflow applications, presented by Hammer and Champy[12], is to define recurring processes and give them names that express their beginning and end states (and imply multiple intermediate tasks). A manufacturing company, for example, might use this technique to generate the following list of fundamental business processes (see Table 1-3).

TABLE 1-3: FUNDAMENTAL BUSINESS PROCESSES

PROCESS	BEGINNING AND END STATES
Budget Preparation	Forecast to allocation
Product Planning	Analysis to authorization
Product Development	Concept to specification
Manufacturing Ramp-Up	Specifications to retooling
Sales	Prospect to order
Fulfillment	Order to delivery
Payment	Order to remittance
Procurement	Requirements to receipt
Service	Inquiry to resolution
Problem	Manifestation to clearance

The beauty of this technique is that it defines processes at a high functional level —
that is, broad functions that must be performed in order for the business to survive —
but does not constrain you to fulfilling these functions with existing procedures. For
example, you may recognize that technical problems with your products must be
cleared as soon as they manifest themselves (better yet, be prevented from happening in
the first place), but this doesn't necessarily require fielding a large service force. You
may reengineer the trouble-support function to emphasize remote monitoring and
diagnostics, preventive maintenance, upfront user training, and hot-swappable on-site
spare parts.

> *Today's dynamic environment demands that you treat reengineering*
> *not as a one-time activity, but as a continuing culture.*

After you establish a high-level business model, you will want to use it as the basis
for ongoing, continuous workflow reengineering. Today's dynamic business and technological environment demands that you treat reengineering not as a one-time activity
but as a continuing culture of innovation and refinement. Another reason not to rely
too heavily on process-reengineering consultants is that you will need to cultivate these
analytical skills in-house to sustain just such a business culture.

Don't let this year's reengineered workflow degenerate into next year's hidebound
business process.

Diagnosing sick processes

After you and your colleagues have identified the candidate workflows at a high level,
you should be able to sniff out those that are not performing well. At this point, you
will need to be explicit about the symptoms you're using to diagnose sick processes.
You should start with the old perennial criteria (see Table 1-4).

TABLE 1-4: PROCESS DIAGNOSTIC CRITERIA

CRITERION	DISCUSSION
Speed	You know a business process is broken when it consistently takes too long to produce the desired result. Protracted processes are the *squeaky wheel* that gets first grease in many corporate reengineering projects, because they often affect external stockholders who aren't shy about voicing their displeasure. Customers ask why it takes three days and several rounds of telephone tag to get answers to simple service requests. Distributors ask why it takes the manufacturer twice as long as competitors to develop new products. Suppliers ask why it takes two months to authorize a simple contract modification.

CRITERION	DISCUSSION
Cost	You may need to do some investigative work to identify cost problems stemming from process inefficiencies, as opposed to those resulting from resource constraints or lack of bargaining clout. Some of the warning signs include excessive labor-hours billed (legitimately) to simple tasks, accumulation of costly inventories and work-in-process, and frequent routing of *no brainer* service requests to high-priced technical personnel. To track down cost problems to their source, your firm needs good accounting and auditing systems.
Accuracy	Chronic accuracy problems with company documentation are almost never due to individual negligence or incompetence. People make data-entry mistakes, but organizations are supposed to guard against these through such built-in preventive and corrective processes as training, guidelines, inspections, verifications, reviews, and audits. Inaccuracies may also stem from a company's faulty processes for keeping scattered manual or electronic files consistent and up-to-date.
Quality	Companies must provide quality products from the get-go, which requires development processes founded on pervasive customer input, concurrent engineering, and shared responsibility. You're practically asking for quality problems if you dispense with such critical processes as structured user interviews, cross-disciplinary design reviews, rapid prototyping, focused beta testing, and ongoing configuration control.
Customer Satisfaction	Customer satisfaction is a paramount consideration in most companies (except for exceptional creatures such as government agencies and legal monopolies). Any process that generates a steady stream of customer complaints, trouble reports, and defections is candidate number one for reengineering. If company staff involved in the process have only a shaky grasp of customer requirements and concerns, they are prime candidates for reeducation. Be wary of any process that provides customers with little opportunity to define their requirements up front or review work-in-progress. Under these conditions, you're likely to shoot yourself in the foot when the customer finds that you've spent precious time and money developing the wrong solution for the wrong problem. You're also likely to lose the customer.
Flexibility	Rigid procedures, no matter how well-intentioned, are likely to produce absurd results under exceptional circumstances. Every process should contain *manual override* procedures, under which each employee is encouraged to take the most direct, sensible course of action (such as handcarrying necessary documentation rather than relying on interoffice mail), even if it goes against standard procedures. If the bureaucratic straightjacket depicted in Scott Adams' comic strip Dilbert seems uncomfortably close to your company, you should think about building some ad-hoc wiggle-room into your business processes. Of course, staff must always be prepared to explain and justify their actions after the fact.

Prioritizing workflow-reengineering projects

After your reengineering team has identified processes that could benefit from work-flow management solutions, you'll want to produce a *top ten* list of high-priority feasible projects. Of course, this may be easier said than done. After a thorough company-wide process review, you may be tempted to throw up your hands and exclaim, "It's all broken, so where on earth do I start?" Explore the following approaches for prioritizing workflow-reengineering projects (see Table 1-5).

TABLE 1-5: APPROACHES FOR PRIORITIZING PROCESS
REENGINEERING PROJECTS

PRIORITIZATION APPROACH	DISCUSSION
Critical Success Factors	The critical success factor (CSF) approach starts with management consensus on competitive differentiators that contribute to the company's success or, if not present, to its decline. CSFs are usually expressed in general terms, such as the performance criteria discussed in Table 1-4: speed, cost, accuracy, quality, customer satisfaction, and flexibility. After your management team has ranked CSFs by importance, you can prioritize workflow projects according to whether they address one or more of these *hot buttons*. Sometimes, the paramount CSF is indisputable, such as speed (if you're in the overnight parcel-delivery business), cost (if you're a discount auto-parts store), accuracy (if you translate foreign-language legal documents for corporate customers), quality (if you cater gourmet food for ritzy cultural functions), and customer satisfaction (if you have only one, very demanding, very fickle client). Typically, though, your management team will settle on two or more CSFs that are equally important and should be addressed in any process redesign effort. Paul A. Strassmann, former assistant U.S. defense secretary for corporate information management, provides a good overview of CSF consensus-building techniques in the 1988 book *Measuring Business Value of Information Technologies*[13].
Strategic Imperatives	This prioritization approach starts with an assessment of your company's strategic positioning vis-à-vis competitors, customers, distributors, and suppliers. Strategic imperatives may include, per Peter G.W. Keen's discussion in his 1988 book *Competing in Time*[14], such considerations as operational necessity, defensive necessity, and competitive opportunity. An aggressive, risk-taking company would probably rank competitive opportunities ahead of defensive and operational necessities when prioritizing workflow-reengineering projects. A reengineering project may represent a competitive opportunity if it improves your electronic communications with key distributors or customers and in the process makes it more expensive or less convenient for them to do business with the competition. Defensive necessity characterizes almost any workflow and reengineering project that focuses on CSFs (such as speed and cost) because these projects are usually an effort to hold onto one's existing competitive advantage. An operational necessity is any project that helps you to simply catch up with the basic level of service in your industry (such as an insurance company installing a document-imaging workflow system to streamline claims processing, long after its competitors had implemented similar systems).

PRIORITIZATION APPROACH	DISCUSSION
Core Competencies	This approach focuses on corporate competencies or functions that add the most value to your products and services. If your corporate strength is in product development, you may want to focus on projects designed to streamline, standardize, and control the flow of product data from concept to design to manufacturing. If you're a highly regarded technical-book publisher, you may focus on workflow projects that speed up internal manuscript routing and revision while enforcing editorial and graphics standards. If service is the core value of your business, you may concentrate on putting yourselves in customers' shoes as they experience what Tom Peters calls the *unfolding process* of consuming your product or service[15]. Airlines that pride themselves on customer service operate under process-oriented standards for such things as "how long baggage handlers should take to unload a plane, how quickly reservations clerks should answer their phones, and how fast maintenance crews should finish cleaning an aircraft so it will be ready for the next flight," report William H. Davidow and Bro Uttal in their 1989 book *Total Customer Service: The Ultimate Weapon*[16]. By focusing reengineering efforts on core competencies, you'll be strengthening those operations with which your company is most closely identified in the eyes of customers, staff, and the general public.

Put Problem Before Solution

Study your company's current business processes and what ails them in some depth before you invest serious resources in workflow solutions. Focus first on processes that are fairly well defined and for which the benefits are likely to outweigh the costs and short-term work disruption associated with reengineering. This method allows you to demonstrate the value of workflow management applications and secure corporate support and funding for reengineering over the long term.

Keep an open mind as to what type of redesigned process — hierarchical, decentralized, or some creative blend — will best serve your company's business goals and objectives. Workflow applications can be designed to support whatever new processes make business sense. Don't feel that you have to radically *flatten* your organizational structure just because some high-paid consultant says it's the *third wave* thing to do.

Above all, don't try to fit the process-reengineering problem to the information technology solutions you currently have at hand. A well-managed enterprise finds or builds the most appropriate workflow solutions for its requirements and paves its own road to success.

Of course, before you invest in a workflow-reengineering project, you must sell the idea to management, who may not fully understand or support what you're trying to do. Selling them on workflow is the topic of the next chapter.

Summary

This chapter gave guidelines for identifying and prioritizing strategic business processes that could benefit from the application of workflow management systems. It summarized trends shaping business and offers sketches of today's management theories.

CHAPTER TWO

JUSTIFYING WORKFLOW APPLICATIONS

Status-Quo Inertia, Payback Calculations, and the "White-Collar Productivity Paradox"

Workflow-reengineering projects are controversial in many companies, because they often upset old, established ways of doing business. Justifying investments in workflow management applications in the face of steady opposition from the status quo can be difficult. To develop a strong business case for workflow tools, you should be aware of the challenges in measuring paybacks from this or any other application of information technologies. This chapter provides you with tips and techniques for justifying workflow investments.

Information Technologies and Corporate Productivity

In the last ten years, one of the hottest management topics has been the *white-collar productivity paradox*. This topic refers to management researchers' inability to find significant statistical correlations between the size of corporate investments in information technologies and companies' sales, market share, productivity, and competitive position. Fueling the ongoing furor is a recent study by the economics department of banking firm Morgan Stanley[1], which stated that white-collar productivity has been essentially flat for the past 30 years, rising only 10 percent from 1962 to 1992, while blue-collar productivity increased 140 percent over the same period.

Productivity debate questions basic tenets

What's disturbing about this apparent economy-wide stagnation in white-collar productivity is that it casts serious doubt on three sacrosanct assumptions of the late 20th century:

- That society's massive investments in information technologies have boosted our overall living standards

- That knowledge workers are the primary source of value-added productive inputs in the modern economy

- That there is an inherent connection between information technology utilization and corporate success

Increasing the productivity of knowledge workers is the greatest challenge for modern managers, according to longtime management consultant Peter Drucker. As paraphrased by Tapscott and Caston[2], Drucker argues that "productivity will dominate management thinking for many decades. It will ultimately determine the competitive performance of companies, the quality of life in every industrialized nation, and the very fabric of society."

Technology success stories belie gloom

Countering this big-picture gloominess is a steady stream of media-propagated success stories describing how particular companies achieved market share, productivity, and profitability through focused applications of information technology. As Peter G.W. Keen notes in *Competing in Time*[3], "The figure of a 15 – 20 percent improvement in productivity occurs again and again in reports of information technology: improvements in productivity from office technology, reductions in head count of corporate staff, reductions in inventories, and cuts in manufacturing cost." Of course, you must remind yourself that many positive case studies are the self-serving output of network managers patting themselves on the back, vendors trying to market products, and magazine feature writers scraping for *feel good* stories that won't alienate advertisers.

Information technology is not a yellow brick road to corporate success.

Technology payback accrues to savvy management

Nobody denies that applications of computers and networks have indeed resulted in impressive productivity gains for many companies. However, it's becoming clear that information technology is not a yellow brick road to corporate success and that the critical issue is how technology is managed and used.

The lackluster high-level productivity picture may be due to an even split between companies that know how to manage their technology assets and those that haven't a clue. As Michael Borrus of the Berkeley Roundtable on the International Economy put it[4], "It simply isn't good enough to spend money on new technology and then use it in old ways. I suspect that for every company using computers right, there is one using it wrong — and the two negate each other."

Technology itself may be part of the problem, for several reasons. First, companies struggle to integrate a jungle of computers, networks, and software and get users up to speed on them, neutralizing any productivity gains the technologies may help them realize. Second, users, daunted by the technology's complexity (or intrigued by its sophistication), spend inordinate amounts of time playing around with it, as opposed to doing their jobs. Third, people learn one set of technologies, standards, and products when along comes wave after wave of new solutions driving familiar solutions to the brink of extinction.

Under these free-wheeling conditions, even market-leading environments such as Windows (desktops), Novell NetWare (LANs), and Lotus Notes (groupware) quickly begin to look like dinosaurs, fending off evolutionary challenges from technologies such as the Internet, Web browsers, and intranet-based collaboration tools. Meanwhile, users are caught in the crossfire, forced to upgrade or change out technologies faster than they would wish, never having enough time to fully integrate existing tools into their workstyles.

Despite these countervailing forces, it is possible to ward off the productivity paradox and profit from workflow technology. Companies must reorganize their processes, practices, staffing, and competitive positioning to maximize their return from new technologies. Supporting this guideline is research by the Strategic Planning Institute on Management Productivity of Information Technology, cited by Strassmann[5].

"The level of information technology expense does not directly relate to management productivity. Businesses using large amounts of information technology do not deliver results superior to firms using lesser amounts of information technology.

"If the ratio of management expenses (for example, overhead costs) to value-added is substantially above the average, no amount of computerization will deliver improved productivity. It seems that excessive overhead staffs cannot benefit from computerization without first simplifying their work.

"Companies that are subject to fundamental strategic hardships such as low market share, heavy capitalization, and an inferior product quality cannot remedy these conditions principally through computer-aided management.

"Computers will not make a badly managed business better. The expenses for computerization and the increased rigidity of computer-managed procedures are likely to accelerate the decline of incompetent management.

"Computers may reduce information-processing costs. However, any paperwork added by new legislation will diminish information-worker productivity, regardless of how efficiently work is carried out.

"Companies most likely to benefit from computer investments are those that have simplified their management, focused on improved quality, reduced their assets, and introduced innovative ways of delivering value-added to customers. Such companies also obtain additional benefits from reduced administrative costs. Strategically sound organizations benefit from computers. They have more than twice the amount of computer expense, per capita, than companies with a low level of productivity."

Traditional productivity measures and well-structured workflows

Many experts have criticized macroeconomic productivity studies because traditional measures — geared to industrial processes with their rigid structures and discrete outputs — are a poor indicator of productivity in knowledge-based administrative, professional, and creative work. "[T]o have a significant impact on the business, tasks must be repetitive," say N. Dean Meyer and Mary E. Boone in their 1987 book, *The Information Edge*[6]. "It is of little value to make someone twice as efficient at a task that he performs only once a year. Most executives, managers, and professionals do not produce measurable outputs, their inputs are unclear, and their jobs are not routine. Therefore, productivity measures do not apply."

Guidelines for Justifying Workflow-Reengineering Projects

Actually, traditional productivity measures do apply to many workflow management applications, because workflow tools' primary purpose is usually to speed up, streamline, and control repetitive business processes. Workflow environments encourage knowledge workers to add greater structure — in the form of routing lists, receipt notifications, version controls, and the like — to traditionally "loosey-goosey" procedures. Many knowledge-based companies could benefit from a greater awareness of the routine workflows that inform (or hamper) their daily operations.

To sell a workflow project to an unsympathetic status quo, stress revenues to be generated, costs reduced, errors eliminated, and time saved.

Stress quantifiable benefits

Workflow tools also provide the ability to monitor the performance of networked processes, along such parameters as elapsed process time, queuing delays, queue sizes, cumulative hours spent on a task, and number of tasks initiated or cleared per person per unit of time.

The most persuasive business justifications are built on quantifiable payback calculations. To sell a workflow project to an unsympathetic corporate status quo, you will need to stress the revenues to be generated, costs reduced, errors eliminated, and time saved from a process redesign. The more concrete your proposal — specifying the tasks and functional linkages to be redesigned — the better. And the more cost-effective your proposal the better. Consequently, it's a good idea to stress the extent to which your workflow application will integrate with existing corporate technology assets, such as PCs, file servers, databases, e-mail systems, and directories services.

See Chapter 14 for case studies of organizations that have derived quantifiable payoffs from workflow applications.

Allow for flexibility and other intangibles

Although you must allow for flexibility and other intangibles, you must not go too far and apply exclusively quantitative measurements to all process redesigns. Organizational processes span the spectrum from structured to unstructured. You will also have to factor *soft* benefits (such as flexibility, quality, and customer satisfaction) into a full-blooded workflow business case.

Most value-added management work (for example, decision making, coordination, and team building) takes place in semistructured or unstructured contexts such as project meetings, informal conversations, or e-mail. Evaluating a business manager only by the number of case folders that pass across her virtual desk is a bit like judging a master chef by the number of dinners he serves on any given day. "From an organizational perspective," say Meyer and Boone [7], "flexibility and effectiveness grow increasingly important as our organizational, economic, political, and social environments become more volatile and complex. Optimizing individual managerial tasks may lock them in with detailed procedures . . . just when organizational flexibility is most needed. Thus, a focus on managerial efficiency alone is likely to create only minor productivity gains."

Semistructured processes are supported by a growing number of workflow products, through the ability to support dynamic, midprocess document rerouting. In addition, e-mail-based workflow tools usually allow nonprogrammers to design simple routing procedures, encouraging more users to design *ad hoc* workflows to facilitate transfer of a single document on a single occasion. The accent with such applications is on user-driven flexibility to redefine processes on the fly, rather than pump a greater number of routine documents through a predefined, structured process.

Many companies also turn to *groupware* products (such as Lotus Notes) to support unstructured and semiunstructured collaboration. Notes and similar products provide data-rich work environments built around such capabilities as mail-enabled applications, asynchronous discussion groups, shared databases, distributed document libraries, and computer conferencing — with some electronic forms and other workflow features thrown in for good measure.

Users Ultimately Determine Tools' Benefits

Obviously, the more diverse the applications and unpredictable their ultimate uses, the more difficult it is to formulate a valid cost-benefit justification for a groupware (or workflow) application suite. End users will find many creative applications for workflow and groupware tools in everyday operations. The ultimate impact of transformative technologies can scarcely be forecast to any great detail.

"Technologies will be justified based on whether they enable organizations to restructure on a continuing basis and empower their workers," says Thomas M. Koulopoulos in his 1995 book *The Workflow Imperative* [8].

The Human Factor of Process Redesign

A human productivity cost exists in all this never-ending organizational redesign. Every new process represents new work styles, procedures, and rhythms that must be learned by many people spanning, in many cases, many workgroups at many sites. Conversely, it represents a whole suite of old procedures that must be unlearned and forgotten.

Remain sensitive to the human dislocations that may result from a process redesign. You should be careful to temper management expectations regarding near-term paybacks from a workflow system, because it may take some time for staff to relearn their jobs to accommodate a redesigned process.

Always involve staff in the critical task of redesigning processes to meet corporate-level business objectives. Stress that redesigned processes need not throw anybody out of a job — rather, they should free up human efforts to be reinvested in more profitable activities.

Reengineered business processes will fail unless staff understand them and are committed to seeing them succeed. Workflow solutions don't completely automate business processes — they primarily give employees a more structured, streamlined environment for carrying them out.

After you have sold your management and staff on the need for workflow reengineering, you will need to involve them in the complex task of mapping out new business processes that will be *workflow-enabled*, which is the topic of the next chapter.

Summary

Chapter 2 provided guidelines for developing business justifications for workflow-reengineering projects. The discussion makes you ponder whether workflow management can make a difference in your company's competitive posture.

CHAPTER THREE

MAPPING OUT A WORKFLOW-ENABLED ORGANIZATION

Technology Platforms, Management Structures, and Collaboration Media

W orkflow applications can be tailored to the precise contours of your corporate processes, systems, and culture. To define the workflow solution that best fits your requirements, you should look at your organization with fresh eyes, unconstrained by its current structure and processes, but mindful of the political difficulties associated with abandoning current processes entirely and starting fresh. This chapter presents an organizing framework — a new workflow paradigm — to help you design workflow applications to meet your requirements and address strategic business concerns.

What Is a Workflow?

Every long journey demands a roadmap. Before reengineering the corporation (or some small piece of it), you and your colleagues will need a template for visualizing the potential power of workflow technologies to transform your business.

Most fundamentally, you will need to agree on a definition of *business process* (also known as *workflow*). A good starting point is the definition found in *The Reengineering Handbook: A Step-by-Step Guide to Business Transformation* by Raymond L. Manganelli and Mark M. Klein[1].

"A process . . . is an interrelated series of activities that convert business inputs into business outputs."

Manganelli and Klein define three types of activities of which business processes are composed (see Table 3-1).

TABLE 3-1: TYPES OF ACTIVITIES IN BUSINESS PROCESSES

ACTIVITY TYPE	DISCUSSION
Value-Adding	These business activities bring shape, substance, and coherence to the end product and are the ones that matter most to the consumer. Within workflow environments, they correspond to productivity applications (for example, electronic forms readers, computer-aided design, and spreadsheets) that are automatically invoked by the system to facilitate each step in the processing of a work item.
Hand-Off	These business activities move work across functional, departmental, or organizational boundaries. Within a workflow environment, they correspond to the underlying utility or network — generally a distributed file system or e-mail backbone — used to pass work items from user to user.
Control	These activities control hand-offs across boundaries. Within a workflow environment, they correspond to the various techniques used to design and execute automated routing procedures and track the current location and status of work items.

Workflow can be defined as the flow of information and control in a business process. Workflows may be sequential in design, involving hand-offs from person A to person B, then from person B to person C. They may be parallel, in which case person A hands off copies of the same item to persons B and C at the same time. A concurrent process is a parallel process in which persons B and C must hand off the item to another person at the same time. In addition, there are conditional workflows, in which person A hands off to either person B or C depending on some condition — for example, routing all purchase orders greater than $10,000 to person B.

Software developers can intuitively grasp this concept of workflow as a transfer of information and control, because their job is to define an analogous sort of flow — one that executes within the confines of a particular computer or computerized device.

A workflow application is a different animal from the run-of-the-mill desktop application.

Defining Your Workflow Requirements Functionally

A workflow application is a completely different animal from the run-of-the-mill desktop application.

Workflow processes may be thought of — according to my discussion in *The Rapport Messaging Review*[2] — as activities taking place in three-dimensional *collaborative space*, consisting of the dimensions of *platform*, *structure*, and *media*. (See Table 3-5 later in the chapter.) Defining workflow requirements in these precise terms helps you to quickly narrow the range of commercial solutions to a manageable short list. It also helps you to understand how technology-enabled workflows complement and extend traditional nonautomated workflows.

Platform

The collaborative platform refers to the geographic, physical, and technological environment in which work is performed — in other words, the means of production and distribution.

Most real-world workflows consist of activities that are either completely manual or are automated to varying degrees. Consequently, the platform for most business processes is a blend of many technologies, based in varying degrees on flesh and bone, brick and mortar, tool and die, pen and paper, and bits and bytes. These technologies are the building blocks underlying any business process.

When you install a workflow management system in your organization, you're tipping the balance in favor of increased automation, for good or ill. Unless you plan to replace all employees with obedient robots, you'll need to think through how your new (semi-) automated workflow meshes into and supports your company's culture. Every enterprise's computing and networking infrastructure creates its own special (or execrable) collaboration platform. One risk you run is creating an office environment where people feel they have no control over the pace of work and suspect they are being monitored and manipulated by unseen technocrats.

You may find it useful to frame your workflow platform requirements in the terms described in Table 3-2.

Structure

The collaborative structure consists of the organizational apparatus and controls used to define, coordinate, and track workflows.

Workflow management (an organizational discipline that may or may not rely on computers and networks) may be defined as the ability to support structured routing and tracking of documents, folders, and other information throughout a workgroup or enterprise. *Structured routing* is routing according to the fundamental controls that define your corporate structure, including the chain of command, policies, operating procedures, project plans, schedules, budgets, and standard practices. In a company's information technology environment, the collaborative structure resides in the total of automated information systems that implement and enforce organizational controls.

TABLE 3-2: COLLABORATIVE PLATFORM

PLATFORM COMPONENTS	DISCUSSION
User Terminals	What types of shared, desktop, or portable terminal equipment (e.g., desktop phone, cellular phone, computer and modem, fax, and pager) and application software is available to workflow participants?
Operating Environments	What operating systems (e.g., Windows 95, Apple Macintosh, Sun Solaris, and IBM AIX), network operating systems (e.g., Novell NetWare, Banyan Vines, and Windows NT Advanced Server), distributed file and database systems (e.g., Network File System, and World Wide Web), e-mail transports (e.g., cc:Mail, Simple Mail Transfer Protocol, and X.400 Message Handling Service), directory services (e.g., Novell NetWare Directory Service, and X.500 Directory Services), and communications protocols (e.g., Transmission Control Protocol/Internetwork Protocol, and Sequenced Packet Exchange/Internetwork Packet Exchange) are used to provide application services to workflow participants over the network?
Networks	What departmental, corporate, public, and international communications facilities (e.g., local-area networks, integrated services digital network lines, private branch exchanges, virtual private networks, packet-switched networks, dial-up asynchronous connections, very small aperture terminals, cellular phone networks, and packet radio networks) are used to physically connect workflow participants to each other and to various application resources?
Geographic Range	How widely are workflow participants and the requisite information-processing resources scattered across the map?
Mobility	How extensively do workflow participants move or roam during execution of the business process?

Every workgroup's own mix of shared in-house and commercial productivity applications (for example, accounting, budget tracking, project planning, group scheduling, and status reporting) imposes its own special collaboration structure. These systems store and maintain the records upon which the business is managed. They provide the formats within which project plans are developed, schedules established, resource requests made, assignments distributed, progress reported, and issues resolved. Try to deviate from a course of action recorded in one of these official business systems, and you'll run up against a wall of institutionalized opposition.

Frame your workflow structural requirements according to the types of controls — routes, roles, and rules — that must be supported, as described in Table 3-3.

TABLE 3-3: COLLABORATIVE STRUCTURE

STRUCTURE COMPONENTS	DISCUSSION
Routes	Every organization has a dominant routing path (hierarchical, peer-to-peer, or some creative blend). Workflow management applications are predicated upon the notion of prespecified routing paths. A document's route (e.g., sequential, parallel, conditional) may be specified on the fly by its originator. Alternately, the standard route for a routine business document may be defined within a visual process map — a flowchart — by a master process architect, usually the supervisor or manager of a function. Typically, document recipients have limited ability to stop workflows or modify routing paths. In this regard, you can contrast workflow with traditional e-mail systems, which allow recipients to forward messages to anybody they want.
Roles	Workflow structures are also characterized by people's defined roles in the routing process, such as originator, reviewer, editor, and approval authority. A workflow program may allocate read/write privileges based on the recipient's workgroup or position in the organization. Recipients may have different views of the same document and be allowed to input or modify different fields.
Rules	Document routing and handling procedures may be defined to any level of detail, depending on the business rules specified in the workflow process model. One rule may limit the range of values that can be input into a particular document field. Another rule may invoke a spreadsheet application to facilitate complex calculations within a particular document section. Yet another rule may generate an e-mail notification to the document originator when all necessary management approvals have been secured.

Media

In a workflow, collaborative media consist of the work product and all raw and semifinished materials — including information and communications inputs — used to give the product shape, substance, and coherence. Media are the things that flow in a workflow, within the context of a technological platform and organizational structure.

Workflow management systems support one broad category of collaborative media — those that can be reduced to digital bits and transmitted over communications networks. This makes workflow management systems a potentially near-total collaborative environment for any white-collar or service organization (such as a book publisher) wherein the end product and most inputs consist primarily of information (such as data files, conference calls, voice mails, e-mail messages, graphics, and faxes). Workflow tools are also applicable to firms that produce durable goods (for example, test/measurement equipment manufacturer) and provide personal services (for example, catering contractor), but can only manage part of the total workflow, and can only partially control the critical collaborative processes, those that take place off-line.

Every workflow management system pulls in its distinctive blend of information from the desktop, local server, intranet, Internet, and elsewhere.

Every enterprise has its own distinctive blend of collaboration media, shaped in part by the extent and sophistication of its information technology platform. Take inventory of all the user terminals, operating environments, and services available to your users (for example, desk phone, cellphone, fax, desktop computer, laptop computer, pager, videoconference system, and Internet/intranet browser), and you've begun to glimpse the true dimensions of your company's collaborative media.

Every workflow management system pulls in its own distinctive blend of information types and formats from the desktop, local server, intranet, Internet, and elsewhere. You should define your workflow media requirements in the following terms presented in Table 3-4.

How Do You Zero In on Workflow Solutions That Broadly Meet Functional Requirements?

After you parse your workflow requirements according to these criteria, determining the most appropriate commercial solutions shouldn't be too hard.

You can use these three collaborative dimensions — platform, structure, and media — to distinguish between the four types of workflow management systems currently on the market: production, messaging-based, Web-based, and suite-based solutions. (See Table 3-5.)

The fundamental difference between these workflow technologies lies in their divergent platforms. Production workflow systems — the traditional core of the market — revolve around shared filestores, which typically include server-based image, document, and database management systems. Messaging-based workflow systems, as their name implies, route files over users' e-mail systems. Web-based workflow solutions route files over the World Wide Web. Suite-based solutions are tied to particular vendors' groupware or desktop application suites, such as Lotus Notes or Microsoft Exchange.

Other differences between these workflow technologies are highlighted in Table 3-5 and discussed at great length in Parts II and III.

TABLE 3-4: COLLABORATIVE MEDIA

MEDIA COMPONENT	DISCUSSION
Information-Base Sharing Media	Organizational life revolves around an ever-growing pile of shared documents, records, files, databases, directories, designs, images, and other information objects, including those stored on Internet and intranet Web sites. Workflow applications ensure that updates to the corporate information base are made in a standardized, controlled fashion. They enable documents to be generated in prescribed formats, populated with standard data values, routed through appropriate personnel, and written to shared filestores or databases at workflow's end. They also allow files to be organized into folders, cases, and compound objects, and searched by keywords and other attributes.
Messaging Media	Messages are the most flexible, feasible, convenient collaboration media in today's virtual economy. Proliferating messaging options include e-mail, voice mail, facsimile, paging, bulletin boards, electronic forms, and electronic data interchange. Almost every Internet/intranet Web includes links to e-mail services, so that you can send messages to the site's owner/administrators. You'll almost never find all workflow participants in the same place at the same time, which makes it necessary to use messaging to share project information. Workflow management systems use messaging systems either to transport documents or notify people of the current location or status of a workflow item.
Conferencing Media	Many people prefer to do their most focused, detail-intensive, time-critical collaboration in conference settings. A conference may be as mundane as a hasty conversation in somebody's office, a chance hallway encounter, or a call on the phone. Increasingly, companies are investing in systems to support multipoint conference calls, full-motion videoconferences, computer screen sharing, and chat sessions. Few workflow management systems support real-time conferencing, being more oriented toward asynchronous, store-and-forward processes. However, it's perfectly possible to write a workflow rule that launches a computer-conferencing application at several desktops simultaneously and requests that scattered users work on the same document at the same time. Workflow application designers are limited only by their vision.

TABLE 3-5: COMPARISON OF WORKFLOW TECHNOLOGIES BY COLLABORATIVE PLATFORM, STRUCTURE, AND MEDIA

WORKFLOW SYSTEM TYPE	COLLABORATIVE PLATFORM	COLLABORATIVE STRUCTURE	COLLABORATIVE MEDIA
PRODUCTION	Access through wide range of popular user terminals and operating environments Require a desktop inbox specifically for workflow items Span local- and wide-area networks supporting underlying filestores Application development tools oriented toward complex folder, compound-document, and forms design by MIS	Complex process models Visual process flowcharting, mapping, and modeling tools Server-based workflow control	Filestore-based information-sharing architecture Distributed or centralized file, document, data, image, and/or object base Multidocument folder routing to workflow-specific inbox Logical routing through transfer of access privileges Messaging links for user notifications and reminders
MESSAGING-BASED	Access through wide range of popular user terminals and operating environments Place workflow items in users' existing e-mail inboxes Span local and wide area networks supporting underlying e-mail Application development tools oriented to complex or simple mail-based forms design by MIS or users	Simple process models Routing-list process definition Client-based workflow control	Message-store based information sharing architecture Distributed or centralized message stores Physically route documents as file attachments over users' existing e-mail systems Oriented towards routing of electronic forms
WEB-BASED	Access through wide range of popular user terminals and operating environments supporting Web browsers	Complex and simple process models Visual process flowcharting, mapping, and modeling tools	Web-server-based information-sharing architecture Distributed or centralized file, document, data, image, and/or object base

WORKFLOW SYSTEM TYPE	COLLABORATIVE PLATFORM	COLLABORATIVE STRUCTURE	COLLABORATIVE MEDIA
WEB-BASED *(continued)*	Span wide-area, HTTP-based Web intranets or Internet Place workflow items in special inboxes accessed with users' Web browsers Application development tools oriented to Web-based forms design by MIS	Client- or server-based workflow control	Document routing to workflow-specific inbox Logical routing through transfer of access privileges Messaging links for user notifications and reminders
SUITE-BASED	Accessed through user terminals and operating environments supported by particular groupware or desktop application suites Place workflow items in users' existing e-mail inboxes under those suites Span local and wide-area networks supported by underlying suites Application development tools oriented to complex or simple mail-based forms design by MIS or users	Simple or complex process models Routing-list or visual flowchart process definition Client or server-based version control	Message-store or filestore-based information sharing architecture Distributed or centralized message and filestores Physically route documents as file attachments over users' existing e-mail systems, or route logical access privileges Oriented towards routing any desktop or server file

Guidelines for Workflow-enabled Process Redesign

After examining the potential of today's workflow products, you may be tempted to *reinvent* your company from scratch — but be careful. The point of workflow management is not to exercise all the nifty features built into commercial software. Rather, your primary concern should be on mapping out an optimal process redesign, given your business requirements and constraints.

After you've identified general parameters for a new business process, you're ready to begin conceptualizing a technology-enabled workflow solution. You may take any of several approaches in mapping an optimal process redesign and defining the appropriate workflow application: minimizing process time, maximizing value-added process content, or maximizing flexibility at the initial point of customer contact.

Minimize process time

Time is the principal indicator by which most business processes are evaluated and is a strong proxy for many other things that matter. Chronically late shipments often correlate with angry customers, low-quality products, error-plagued billing, inflexible bureaucracy, and high overhead. Workflow applications allow you to compress time by defining routes and rules that affect process variables. Table 3-6 presents general guidelines and examples for minimizing process time.

TABLE 3-6: GUIDELINES FOR MINIMIZING PROCESS TIME

GUIDELINE	EXAMPLE
Reduce the number of participants in a process	Allow a customer service representative to prepare a more complete, detailed service order by pulling relevant client information from multiple databases in a single transaction
Reduce the maximum completion time of each task	Automatically prompt or notify each workflow participant of approaching due dates
Reduce the time needed to transfer work between tasks	Use e-mail-enabled workflow rather than postal-mail or manual hand-off procedures
Reduce the time that work is queued awaiting start	Automatically escalate items that have sat in someone's workflow inbox more than a few days
Increase the number of tasks running in parallel	Speed merchandise delivery by submitting an order, automatically checking inventories, generating shipment orders, generating production back-orders for out-of-stock items, and notifying customers of delivery dates

Maximize value-added process content

The customer pays directly for value — embodied in the shape, substance, and coherence of your product or service — and not for your internal control and hand-off processes (however necessary they may be for ensuring value). Workflow applications enable you to eliminate unnecessary control and hand-off processes and to squeeze out the manual, paper-bound components in those that remain. Table 3-7 provides guidelines and examples for how you might maximize value-added process content in your workflow.

Maximize flexibility at the initial point of customer contact

Most value-added staff inputs should be provided at the point of first customer contact, which former Scandinavian Airlines president Jan Carlzon has referred to as the "moment of truth"[3]. This guideline is derived from the first two, in that it entails minimizing process time while maximizing value-added staff inputs. First impressions make a big difference in whether you'll hold onto customers or lose them to competitors.

TABLE 3-7: GUIDELINES FOR MAXIMIZING VALUE-ADDED PROCESS CONTENT

GUIDELINE	EXAMPLE
Apply standard workflow routes, roles, and rules automatically to each new case	Automatically route every e-mailed electronic purchase request through the same standard review chain, with alternate routing activated only when data fields in the request form cross predefined thresholds (e.g., dollar value) or are flagged as exceptional (e.g., requires expedited consideration due to urgent time-critical business matter)
Launch appropriate applications, formats, stylesheets, and business rules at a user's desktop upon receipt of a task	Automatically load the appropriate HTML form, with mandatory fields and input constraints activated, when a work item is downloaded into the user's Web browser from a particular path on a particular intranet Web site
Provide participants with immediate, on-line access to all information bases (e.g., documents, records, files, databases) and expert personnel needed to complete their tasks	Design document search/retrieval, database query, and messaging buttons, dialog boxes, and other links into the workflow application, so that needed information and assistance is no more than a mouse-click away
Ensure steady task flow through all necessary corporate reviews, inspections, and approvals	Set up a workflow routing procedure that automatically reroutes or escalates an item that has sat in someone's inbox for more than a day or two
Enable continual tracking and notification of work location and status by all impacted parties	Provide all workflow participants with access to a status tracking database, and/or send e-mail notifications to alert them to critical events (e.g., an item was rejected and returned to its originator for rework)
Eliminate the material, processing, transport, storage, and retrieval costs associated with paper documentation	Scan and index all paper documentation as soon as it enters the workflow; send the original to an off-site archival facility

Your first point of contact — a salesclerk, service representative, or World Wide Web site — should have the flexibility to address most customer questions regarding products, prices, warranties, shipment dates, and other critical concerns. Consequently, you may want to design workflows that are more immediate (that is, collapsed, compressed, and concurrent) than sequential, focusing on the customer at the point of inquiry, sale, service, or consumption. Table 3-8 provides guidelines and examples that show how you might achieve this ideal.

TABLE 3-8: GUIDELINES FOR MAXIMIZING FLEXIBILITY AT THE INITIAL POINT OF CUSTOMER CONTACT

GUIDELINE	EXAMPLE
Provide multiple access options	Go where the customer is and allow access to your workflow environment through whatever terminals and communications options are most appropriate (e.g., telephone, mobile computer, wireless network, facsimile, paging, voice messaging, electronic data interchange, e-mail, and World Wide Web). A well-designed workflow flows from the source of business requirements, which usually means the customer
Capture customer data only once	After customer data has been captured by your first point of contact, that data should inform every subsequent step in the workflow. One of the more effective methods of capturing customer data is through an on-line electronic form, which can be routed throughout the process. Bar-code scanning is a convenient way to link the customer or product with that data at each step in the workflow.
Support distributed transaction processing	The customer interface should be able to complete as much of a transaction as possible in a single session, by means of on-line quotation, order entry, credit checking, and inventory-lookup applications. Customer reps should have immediate access to as many applications and databases as are necessary to close the transaction, or at least prepare it well for the next workflow step.
Enable ad-hoc flexible workflow	The first point of contact should be able to define an ad-hoc workflow that directly supports the customer's requirements, regardless of whether it conforms to standard operating procedures. One of the secrets behind superior customer service, say many management consultants, is empowering the first point of contact to *own* the customer relationship and marshall corporate resources to meet customer requirements.

Milestones for Workflow-Reengineering Projects

After you have clarified the conceptual parameters of workflow-enabled process redesign within your company, you're ready to establish a formal workflow-reengineering project. This is where you roll up your sleeves and dive into the turf-conscious, meeting-intensive world of process reengineering. The workflow-reengineering project plan should include the following critical activities and milestones:

- Gain high-level corporate sponsorship for the workflow-reengineering project
- Prepare a formal business justification and cost/benefit analysis
- Review existing policies, procedures, and forms
- Flowchart the proposed process redesign
- Survey and select commercial workflow management solutions, as well as consultants, system integrators, and value-added resellers
- Develop and integrate application components
- Roll out a limited pilot application

- Roll out full-scale workflow implementation
- Train users on the new workflow application and revised policies, procedures, and forms

These workflow evaluation, implementation, and administration activities are discussed at great length in Part IV, which also contains case studies of organizations that have implemented workflow applications successfully.

Summary

This chapter presented a framework for mapping workflow applications to your business requirements.

Now that you've mapped out your workflow requirements and reengineered process at a high level, you're ready to explore the inner workings of commercial workflow management solutions. This is the focus of Part II, which details the general architecture of workflow management systems; explains the architectural distinctions between production, messaging-based, Web-based, and suite-based network application environments; and describes the sophisticated application infrastructure, including image and database management technologies, needed to support full-blooded workflow management solutions. Part III presents in-depth profiles of leading vendors in each of the principal workflow market segments, companies whose offerings you should begin to explore in earnest.

PART II
Technology Primer
Workflow System Architectures and Standards

This part presents a primer on the architectural components of a workflow management system, which includes process definition tools, enactment services, client applications, invoked applications, and administration and monitoring tools. It describes the four types of commercial workflow products: 1) production workflow, 2) messaging-based workflow, 3) Web-based workflow, and 4) suite-based workflow. Following that is a detailed discussion of the many technologies that provide the application infrastructure for automated workflows, including image management, database management, document management, electronic messaging, and intranet services.

CHAPTER FOUR

WORKFLOW REFERENCE MODEL

Workflow technology is mature enough to have developed a distinctive architectural approach that cannot be reduced neatly to any one of its constituent technologies. A useful framework for understanding it is provided by the *Workflow Management Coalition (WfMC)*, which published its Workflow Reference Model in 1994. Per the WfMC's model, workflow management systems may be deconstructed into the following five high-level functional subsystems presented in Table 4-1 (though, as Chapter 5 points out, real-world workflow systems implement these functions in very different ways).

Figure 4-1 depicts these components within the context of WfMC's workflow reference model. The model fits most closely to the traditional architecture of production workflow products, but it's also useful for understanding the design and functionality of messaging-based workflow, Web-based workflow, and suite-based workflow tools. It describes the superset of high-end functionality toward which those other three market segments are migrating (while, concurrently, production workflow products migrate toward greater interoperability with messaging, Web, and suite platforms).

TABLE 4-1: WORKFLOW REFERENCE MODEL FUNCTIONAL
SUBSYTEMS

FUNCTIONAL SUBSYTEM	DEFINITION
Process-Definition Tools	Software that supports development of computerized process representations, including both the automated and manual process components
Workflow Enactment Services	Software that provides a run-time environment for initiating, executing, sequencing, and controlling instances of a process definition, adding work items to user worklists and invoking application tools as necessary
Workflow Client Applications	Software that allows workflow participants to interact with workflow enactment services in order to sign on and off the service, initiate processes, display worklists, invoke applications, and access workflow-relevant, application, and control data
Invoked Applications	Software that is launched by the workflow enactment service, according to the process definition, to initiate or execute an activity
Administration and Monitoring Tools	Software that supports real-time surveillance, control, configuration, and optimization of workflow execution

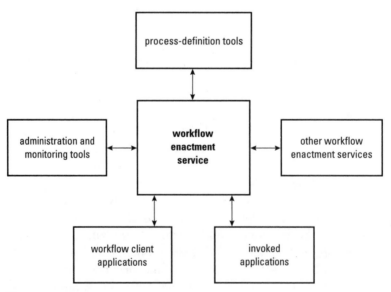

Figure 4-1
The WfMC reference model.

To discover how the WfMC reference model's five functional subsystems interoperate, the best approach is to examine each one in depth. The following discussions use the WfMC's Reference Model as a starting point, while, in many instances, providing additional information and clarification of topics that were only partially developed in the Coalition's draft document.

Process-Definition Tools

One of the first things you look for in a workflow product is a user-friendly tool for defining business processes. Indeed, you may not even turn to a workflow product for this capability. Many computer-aided software engineering (CASE) and business-process reengineering (BPR) tools allow you to build detailed process definitions — also called process models — using flowcharts, entity-relationship (E-R) diagrams, scripting languages, or other modeling paradigms.

Process-definition tools enable users to specify the routes, roles, and rules — the collaborative structure, per Chapter 3 — used to initiate and control workflows. Within production workflow environments, process definitions are executed at *run time* by the workflow enactment service, which functions as a master enforcer and coordinator of distributed processes. A process definition specifies automated activities, such as application launching and event notification; it also specifies human-driven activities, such as conditional routing, which may be based on inputs into an on-screen form field.

Workflow, CASE, and BPR tool vendors need not use the same flowcharting or scripting approaches. Indeed, vendors will continue to compete vigorously in these areas, introducing easier, more intuitive tools to bring the average business analyst or user up to speed on workflow application development. (A comparison of vendors' process-definition approaches is presented later in this section.) Ideally, one vendor's process-definition tool would be able to generate a logical process representation that can be interpreted accurately by other vendors' workflow enactment services. This would allow users the flexibility to acquire workflow development and application products from different vendors, using *best-of-breed* technology for each workflow system component. Traditionally, users have been limited to using the process-definition capabilities bundled with their run-time workflow environment — or manually converting a process model generated with one vendor's tool into a format to be interpreted by another's run-time environment.

Alternative commercial process-modeling techniques

Process-modeling tools allow you to transform bright new business-process ideas into detailed routing and processing instructions understood by the product's workflow enactment service. The same workflow may be defined in many different ways, depending on the modeling paradigm. Your decision to select one workflow product over its competitors may come down to the relative merits of their graphical process-modeling and flowcharting tools.

You can identify several alternative process-modeling techniques in today's workflow, BPR, and simulation tools. These techniques are presented in Table 4-2.

TABLE 4-2: PROCESS-MODELING TECHNIQUES

PROCESS-MODELING TECHNIQUE	DEFINITION/DESCRIPTION
Address-Driven Modeling	This approach models processes as routing paths between predefined users, positions, or groups in the organizational structure. The process map has nodes that represent recipients' network addresses (or proxy addresses that may be translated to users' actual addresses at process run-time). See Figure 4-2 for an illustration of an address-driven process map.
Decision-Chain Modeling	This approach models processes as chains of milestones and associated manual decision points, such as *review resume* (milestone) and *interview/do not interview* (associated decision point). See Figure 4-3 for an illustrative decision-chain process map. This technique associates project milestones with roles or individual users.
Event-Flow Modeling	This approach models processes as chains of manual events, such as human decisions, and automated events, such as routing, collecting, printing, faxing, and archiving documents. This approach allows workflow logical dependencies to be depicted in great detail. See Figure 4-4 for an illustrative event map.
Milestone-Document Modeling	This approach models processes as sets of associated milestones, documents, roles, and dependencies in a single process map, in which the necessary electronic forms, reference documents, and user-provided documents can be identified and associated with particular milestones and users. (See Figure 4-5.)
Resource-Utilization Modeling	This approach models processes within the context of the organizational structure and provides a strong basis for resource estimation. (See Figure 4-6.) It decomposes a process into linked subprocesses and activities, each of which is associated with a particular timeframe as well as human, equipment, and other material resources. The figure shows how a particular process phase, when exploded, can be viewed as a set of linked activities, any one of which can be further exploded to reveal the resources employed in that activity. Activity time and cost may be modeled explicitly, making it possible to view the impact of process redesigns on business schedules and profitability. A simulated process can be stopped at any time to determine the current activity and workload associated with any resource.

PROCESS-MODELING TECHNIQUE	DEFINITION/DESCRIPTION
Throughput Modeling	This approach models processes as sets of activities that involve flows, accumulations, and rules for transforming inputs into outputs. (See Figure 4-7.) This approach has a strong operations analysis spin and is oriented to maximizing the throughput of an end-to-end process. This approach supports modeling both the physical and informational media in a process.
Transactional Modeling	This approach, implemented in Action Technologies, Inc.'s Action Workflow System, models processes as complex transactions involving customers, performers, and conditions of satisfaction (including scheduling constraints) for the process as a whole, as well as for each milestone activity within the process. For example, the originator of a purchase request may be regarded as the ultimate customer in the procurement process, the vendor's shipping clerk as the ultimate performer, and timely delivery of the specified solution as the overall condition of satisfaction. Each person in the workflow may be regarded as the performer with respect to prior individuals and customers with respect to subsequent individuals. Each process milestone (e.g., submit order, obtain management approval, and ship product) will have associated scheduling and acceptance conditions, which allow participants to reject procurement documentation or return it with comments, suggestions, and revisions. Once these functional roles, milestones, and conditions have been identified, Action's framework dictates that each milestone be broken into four phases with associated activities (see Figure 4-8 for a graphical illustration of Action's modeling paradigm): preparation (customer or performer proposes work to be done by the performer); negotiation (customer or performer may or may not enter into a cycle of offers and counteroffers, though eventually, they agree on the work to be performed); performance (performer performs the work, reporting progress and, eventually, completion); and acceptance (customer evaluates the work performed, declaring satisfaction or dissatisfaction, possibly returning the work to the performer to be done over; ultimately, the customer may accept or reject the work; if the work is accepted, the process moves to the next milestone). Ultimately, a final process map will be prepared that may contain a combination of sequential, parallel, concurrent, and conditional workflows. An example of such a map, which can drive a run-time enactment service provided by Action, is presented in Figure 4-9.

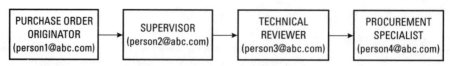

Figure 4-2
Address-driven process modeling.

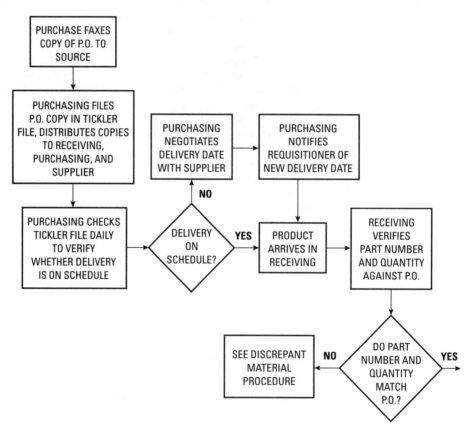

Figure 4-3
Decision-chain process modeling.

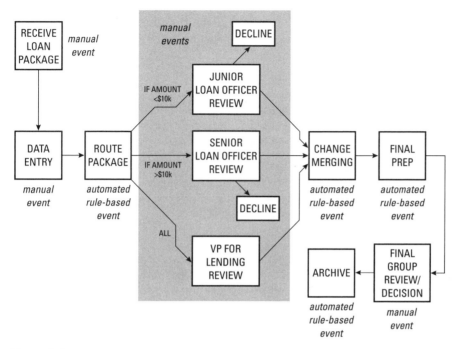

Figure 4-4
Event-flow process modeling.

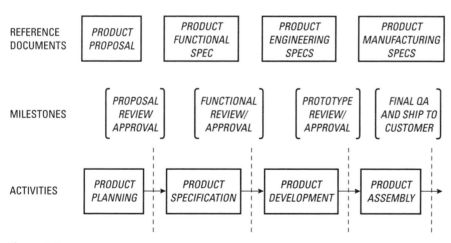

Figure 4-5
Milestone-document process modeling.

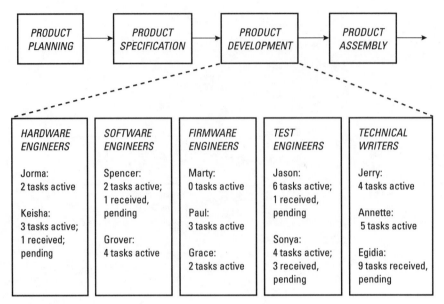

Figure 4-6
Resource-utilization process modeling.

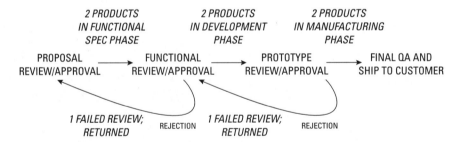

Figure 4-7
Throughput process modeling.

Figure 4-8
Transaction process modeling (Action Technologies Paradigm).

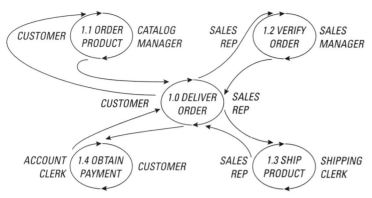

Figure 4-9
Transaction process modeling (Representative Process Map with Action Technologies Framework).

Principal business-process parameters underlying a workflow application

These alternate modeling approaches, in spite of their differences, can all be described with some basic workflow concepts and terminology, which underlie the basis for the WfMC's proposed standard process-definition interchange format. The WfMC has formulated a *meta-model* or *general process model* (see Figure 4-10) that specifies basic entities and relationships involved in simple workflows. The Coalition may periodically extend the meta-model to support more complex workflows. Vendors are free to define extensions that support interchange of workflow application parameters above and beyond those mapped out within the meta-model.

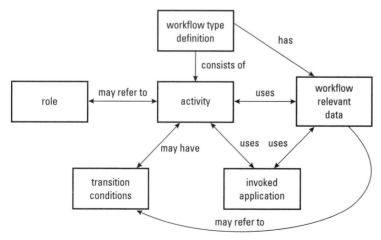

Figure 4-10
Process-definition meta-model (Workflow Management Coalition).

Business-process analysts should familiarize themselves with the concepts introduced in the WfMC's meta-model, because these are the principal parameters to be specified in designing a workflow application. The most general process parameters, outlined in Draft 1.1 of the Workflow Reference Model, are workflow type, activity, role, transition conditions, workflow-relevant data, and invoked applications. You will encounter these parameters or equivalent functionality and terminology when you try to set up and design a business process with your chosen workflow tool, so it's important to familiarize yourself with this material.

WORKFLOW TYPE

When defining a new workflow, an analyst must first define its general parameters, which distinguish the workflow from all other business processes managed by the workflow system. The attributes that must be defined include the process' name, version number, initiation and termination conditions, and security and audit conditions. These may be defined as follows (see Table 4-3).

TABLE 4-3: WORKFLOW-TYPE ATTRIBUTES

ATTRIBUTE	DEFINITION/DESCRIPTION
WORKFLOW NAME	Each process definition should have an alphanumeric identifier that designates it uniquely to the workflow enactment service, as well as other identifiers, generated by the enactment service, that apply to each run of the process. It's up to each organization to define its own internal workflow nomenclature conventions. However, it might be helpful to give processes names that indicate whether they are special cases or subprocesses of more general procedures. For example, purchasing process — personal computers could be defined as a special twist on the general purchasing process. Likewise, purchasing process — personal computers — functional specification would be a subprocess. Companies might find it useful to organize process definitions in a hierarchical directory structure — such as that defined by the X.500 naming standard — that clearly indicates relations of nesting and inheritance. See Figure 4-11 for an illustration of how workflow-type definitions can be arranged in an X.500 directory structure. You might also find it useful to provide processes with plain-English names, making it easy for users to designate processes for the purposes of reviewing, modifying, and monitoring.
VERSION NUMBER	No process definition can survive unmodified for long in today's business world. Version-numbering conventions should reflect an ongoing corporate effort to control and track changes to its business processes. Process version numbers might conform to the software industry's x.x numbering scheme or indicate the date and time the process was modified.
INITIATION CONDITIONS	The process definition must describe the conditions under which the enactment service will initialize a workflow and launch into the first activity. Initiation conditions can be whatever you as the workflow designer want them to be, but generally they fall into the six categories — application login, document origination, document submission, document receipt, event-driven, and time-driven — presented next.

ATTRIBUTE	DEFINITION/DESCRIPTION
Application login	The user logs into the workflow application, which initiates a new process. An application is launched, the appropriate on-screen form is presented, a new task reference number is automatically generated, and the appropriate routing list is generated, either up front or in response to input data fields.
Document origination	The user retrieves a blank electronic form from the departmental workflow server. This action automatically generates a unique reference number and starts up a new process, creating a process log before the completed document or case folder has been routed to its first recipient.
Document submission	The originator clicks on a document or case folder's send button, signaling to the enactment service that a workflow is being created and requesting application of the appropriate process model, routing list, and reference number.
Document receipt	A document or case folder is received or deposited at a particular server, volume, directory, or path, signaling to the enactment service to initiate a new workflow.
Event-driven	A process is automatically initiated in response to a database event (e.g., inventory of particular item dropping below reorder threshold), system event (e.g., trouble report from branch-office server), or other real-time phenomena being monitored by an external application in communication with the workflow enactment service. The appropriate document or case folder is routed to the appropriate people, depending on the nature of the event.
Time-driven	A process is automatically initiated at a prespecified time, recurring time interval, or elapsed time since termination of a prior process. A document or case folder is automatically originated, populated with information from various databases, and routed to the appropriate personnel.
TERMINATION CONDITIONS	The process definition must describe the conditions under which the enactment service will terminate a workflow, notify the appropriate personnel, and archive process data to the appropriate storage systems. Termination conditions generally fall into these categories: cycle back to originator, receipt of final approval, transmission to final recipient, event-driven, and time-driven. See the following entries for more details on each.
Cycle back to originator	A process is terminated when a document or case folder is returned to the person who originated it. Typically, this person has the authority to approve the final version of the case folder and decide on its subsequent disposition.
Receipt of final approval	A process is terminated when the final person in the routing cycle, not the originator, has explicitly approved the document or case folder. Typically, this would result in updates being made to corporate databases, notifications being sent to appropriate personnel, and authorization of some corporate action.
Transmission to final recipient	A process is terminated when the final recipient has received a document or case folder. Ultimate approval or disposition of the case by this person would fall outside the scope of the automated workflow.

(continued)

TABLE 4-3: WORKFLOW-TYPE ATTRIBUTES *(continued)*

ATTRIBUTE	DEFINITION/DESCRIPTION
Event-driven	A process is terminated when some event — being monitored by an external application in communication with the workflow enactment service — either occurs, fails to occur as expected, or stops occurring.
Time-driven	A process is terminated at a prespecified time, recurring time interval, or elapsed time since initiation of the process.
SECURITY CONDITIONS	The process definition must describe the conditions under which process participants will be authenticated, authorized for various functions, and provided with workflow control and application data. Security conditions generally address authentication, process-definition privileges, process-initiation privileges, data-access controls, and data backup, archive, and restoration controls. See the following entries for details on each.
Authentication	Users may authenticate themselves to the workflow enactment service using the time-honored ID/password combo or a more sophisticated scheme involving smart cards, digital signatures, or biometrics such as fingerprints and voiceprints. Various workflow software components may authenticate each other by exchanging digital signatures encrypted with their respective private keys. Equipment and paper documents involved in the process may be authenticated using bar codes.
Process-definition privileges	Some users may be allowed to define new processes, modify existing processes, or dynamically reroute those currently active. Generally, the privileges of originating, modifying, or deleting process definitions are reserved for senior administrators in most user organizations, in which case the bulk of users can only review and participate in workflow scripts developed by others.
Process-initiation privileges	Some users may be allowed to initiate or activate processes that have already been defined, while others may be barred from doing so. Corporate departments, positions, and personnel differ widely in the types of administrative actions they can authorize. For example, only designated personnel in each department may initiate purchase requests.
Data-access controls	Depending on their need to know, users may or may not be allowed to view data files describing the current status of an executing process. The workflow system would limit users' access to distributed application data, using security capabilities of the underlying network operating system. Even process administrators may be prevented from modifying or deleting data describing current or past processes, in order to preserve a complete audit trail for legal purposes.
Data backup, archive, and restoration controls	Process and application data may be backed up and archived at various intervals. If the data changes constantly and is extremely critical to business operations, it may be backed up incrementally by the workflow system in conjunction with third-party utility programs. In many situations, however, daily backups would be sufficient. Backed-up data might need to be restored quickly to restart a process, in which case it would best be kept in on-line disk subsystems. Otherwise, it could be backed up to near-line optical jukeboxes or off-line tape drives.

ATTRIBUTE	DEFINITION/DESCRIPTION
AUDIT CONDITIONS	The process definition must describe the conditions under which process definitions and the details of active workflows will be logged for audit purposes. Audit trails of processes may be required for legal reasons, to investigate security problems, or evaluate the timeliness, efficiency, and effectiveness of the business process. Audits may be performed either by professional auditing firms or by internal management and staff. Management needs to be sensitive to employee privacy concerns in handling audit information, so as not to give the appearance of engaging in workplace monitoring for frivolous or sinister reasons. Audit conditions generally fall into the categories of events, detail, frequency, and path. Descriptions of each parameter are as follows.
Events	The process administrator determines the types of workflow events to be logged. The system could be set up to log every time a process definition is originated, modified, or deleted, including the responsible parties. Processes could be logged every time they are initiated, advanced to the next participant, and terminated. Every file access, update, and deletion could be logged. Failed authentications might flag potential security breaches.
Detail	The process administrator must determine how much detail to include each time a process event is logged. Logs can be terse, simply including the time and reference number for each entry, or provide an extended textual description of the event.
Frequency	Process logs may be updated in real time, as events occur, or at periodic intervals, recording a summary of the current state of the executing workflow.
Path	Logged entries may be routed to various paths: to a printer, terminal screen, disk, or, if associated with an important business matter or serious security breach, to an administrator's pager.

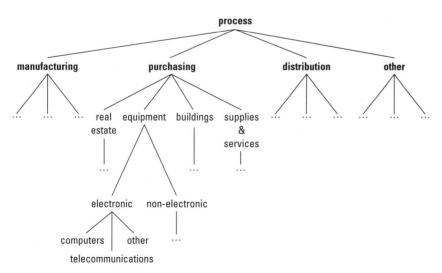

Figure 4-11
Workflow-type definitions arranged in a hierarchical directory structure.

ACTIVITY

After the name, type, and other general attributes of the workflow are defined, the analyst begins to build the process by defining each of its constituent activities. The attributes that apply to each activity in a process definition are its name, type, pre- and post-activity conditions, and scheduling constraints. These attributes may be defined as follows (see Table 4-4):

TABLE 4-4: ACTIVITY ATTRIBUTES

ATTRIBUTE	DEFINITION/DESCRIPTION
ACTIVITY NAME	Each activity definition should have a unique name that defines it unambiguously to the workflow enactment service and to users. An activity definition (or name) is regarded as a modular object, in computer terminology, to be used multiple times in a single process definition, as well as in many distinct process definitions. For example, you might define a standard technical review activity that allows the person performing that activity to redline and annotate a document but not edit it. This activity might be used several times, by different participants, within a particular workflow, and represent a standard activity in many corporate workflows. As noted previously in regards to process-definition names, an activity's name should indicate whether it's a special case or subset of a more general activity, for example, independent cost evaluation — optical storage subsystem could be defined as a technology-specific variant on the standard independent cost evaluation that is required on all storage subsystems above a certain dollar threshold.
ACTIVITY TYPE	Each activity definition must indicate whether the activity belongs to a more general class of activities — an activity type — from which it would presumably inherit various attributes and conditions. For example, company policy may dictate that all independent cost evaluations be performed in a specified spreadsheet model, which could be launched on the user's desktop at the time he or she begins the activity. The activity type would also indicate whether the activity is a single work item (sometimes called an atomic activity) or is a proxy for a subprocess (i.e., group of interdependent activities with common process entry and exit points). Subprocesses might nest several levels deep in a master process definition, a phenomenon that could be indicated in the activity-type field.
PRE-ACTIVITY CONDITIONS	These are the conditions under which the enactment service launches into a particular activity. If it's the first activity in the process, the conditions may be that the process as a whole be instantiated and that the appropriate user log onto the system. If it's any other activity, the pre-activity conditions could be start-to-start (parallel or concurrent), event-to-start (conditional), or finish-to-start (sequential). See the following entries for more details on each of these conditions. See Figure 4-12 for a comparative illustration of parallel, concurrent, conditional, and sequential processes.
Start-to-start	This condition requires that two or more activities sharing a common predecessor activity be initiated at the same time. If the activities also share a common successor activity, this would be known as a *parallel process*. If, in addition, the activities must end at the same time, the process would be referred to as *concurrent*.

ATTRIBUTE	DEFINITION/DESCRIPTION
Event-to-start	This condition requires that some specified event occur in a predecessor activity in order to launch into the current activity. If the process could take alternate routes depending on the character of the triggering event, the process would be referred to as *conditional.* The triggering event could be retrieval of a particular document or entry of a particular value into a particular database field. The triggering event may or may not cause the immediate termination of the predecessor.
Finish-to-start	This condition requires that one or more predecessor activities terminate in order for the current activity to start. Workflows comprised of finish-to-start activity dependencies are referred to as *sequential* or *serial processes.*
POST-ACTIVITY CONDITIONS	This is the flip side, obviously, of pre-activity conditions. It refers to the conditions that trigger the enactment service to terminate an activity and that actions are taken immediately after the activity has terminated. If the activity is the last in the process, the triggering condition may be approval of a particular document, and subsequent actions would be termination of the process and archiving of process-relevant data. If it's any other activity, the post-activity conditions might be start-to-finish, finish-to-start, or finish-to-finish. See the following entries for more details on each of these conditions.
Start-to-finish	This condition requires that a successor activity commence before the current one may terminate.
Finish-to-start	This condition requires that the current activity terminate before a successor may commence.
Finish-to-finish	This condition requires that parallel activities terminate at the same time, constituting a concurrent process.
SCHEDULING CONSTRAINTS	Activity scheduling and timing are among the most critical workflow optimization parameters. The required maximum or minimum timing of an activity may be specified in great detail, according to the parameters of in-queue time, processing time, and out-queue time. See the following entries for more details.
In-queue time	This parameter specifies the time that a particular case, folder, or document may remain in a user's workflow inbox before being retrieved for active processing.
Processing time	This parameter specifies the time that a work item may remain in use, after initial retrieval by a particular recipient, before completion.
Out-queue time	This parameter specifies the time that a completed work item may remain in a user's workflow outbox before forwarding to the next user. Many production workflow applications route items automatically upon completion, but some may be set up to allow users to hold onto completed documents temporarily to double-check work or avoid overloading the next person in the routing chain.

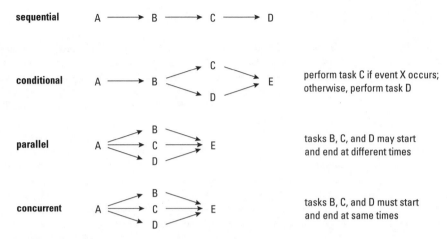

Figure 4-12
Four types of workflow.

ROLE

After the workflow's activities and scheduling parameters are defined, each activity must be associated with particular organizational roles that will perform it. Eventually, a workflow administrator will associate these roles, in turn, with particular individuals in the organizational structure, but, in classic workflow process definition, the roles are initially defined in functional terms. The attributes that apply to each workflow participant's role in the process definition are name, authentication field, organizational entity, and capabilities. These attributes may be defined as follows (see Table 4-5).

TABLE 4-5: ROLE ATTRIBUTES

ATTRIBUTE	DEFINITION/DESCRIPTION
NAME	Each workflow participant (or group of participants) must be specified by a unique name, which may be a personal name, job title, or description of responsibilities within the context of a workflow-enabled process. The name may also serve as the participant's login ID to the workflow application. Companies should think twice before *hard-wiring* personal names into a workflow application. Using job titles or proxy names preserves process administrators' flexibility to assign new people to existing roles. The enactment service will map a person's actual name, network address, or other personal designator to his or her workflow role at process run-time.
AUTHENTICATION FIELD	This field would be occupied by a role-specific password if password authentication is being used. Otherwise, it might contain pointers to a user's public-key certificate, voiceprint, or other digital tokens associated with the applicable authentication scheme.

ATTRIBUTE	DEFINITION/DESCRIPTION
ORGANIZATIONAL ENTITY	This describes the relevant project, workgroup, location, department, or company associated with a participant's role in the workflow. A hierarchical X.500 *relative distinguished name* may be employed to describe someone's relative position in the corporate structure. Typically, a participant would inherit workflow-relevant capabilities from his or her organizational entity.
CAPABILITIES	This describes a person's authorized capabilities along three dimensions — process definition, work item, and workflow. See the following entries for details.
Process definition	Users may be authorized to originate, review, revise, approve/disapprove, or delete process definitions or segments thereof.
Work item	Users may be authorized to originate, review, revise, approve/disapprove, or delete work items or components thereof.
Workflow	Users may be authorized to suspend workflows in process. They may also be allowed to monitor the location and status of workflows in process and/or those already complete.

TRANSITION CONDITIONS

After defining roles within the workflow, the analyst must specify transition conditions, which determine whether, when, and how an executing workflow advances to the next automated or manual activity. Transition conditions fall into three categories: flow conditions, execution conditions, and notification conditions, the attributes of which are presented in Table 4-6.

TABLE 4-6: TRANSITION CONDITION ATTRIBUTES

ATTRIBUTE	DEFINITION/DESCRIPTION
FLOW CONDITIONS	These define the conditions under which a work item is automatically transferred to the next user in the process. They may be regarded as synonymous with the pre- and post-activity conditions described in Table 4-4.
EXECUTION CONDITIONS	These define the conditions or context within which a work item is processed within a particular activity. This is a critical set of parameters, because it defines the work performed — hence, value added — at each step of the workflow. Execution conditions include the application tools invoked, information objects presented, and file access, input, and manipulation controls applied at each activity. See the following entries for more details.

(continued)

TABLE 4-6: TRANSITION CONDITION ATTRIBUTES *(continued)*

ATTRIBUTE	DEFINITION/DESCRIPTION
Application tools invoked	In accepting a new work item, the user may automatically launch the appropriate applications, such as a spreadsheet or CAD package, needed to complete that activity. You will need to have a deep understanding of the work performed in each activity, as well as the type of staff performing it, in order to specify which tools to invoke, when, and for whom. For example, you may specify that a particular spreadsheet — the corporate standard — be invoked when budget proposals reach financial analysts' desktops. Or you might tweak that rule to indicate that financial analyst A will get his preferred spreadsheet, while financial analyst B will get her preferred spreadsheet. You can tailor these application invocation rules precisely to the idiosyncrasies of your organization. If your workflow application is Web-enabled, you could download Java applets as needed to support user analysis on new tasks for which his or her local applications are not appropriate.
Information objects presented	In launching an application, the user automatically retrieves and displays the directory, folder, file, or other information object to be processed. The file may be converted from a format understood by the prior activity's application to one compatible with the application currently invoked. Workflow applications can be truly multimedia, pulling text, graphics, scanned images, video and audio clips, and any other information from the user's PC, LAN server, or any place on the corporate intranet or worldwide Internet.
File access, input, and manipulation controls applied	Users may be prevented from retrieving information not needed to complete the task. Input controls — such as auto field entry, mandatory field entry, and pick-list selection — would be applied to maintain data integrity and validity. System controls would prevent unauthorized modification and deletion of workflow-relevant information.
NOTIFICATION CONDITIONS	These describe the conditions under which workflow events automatically trigger notifications to various users. Process administrators and document originators are the usual recipients of notifications. Any event can be set up to trigger notifications, but they are usually required to acknowledge delivery, receipt, forwarding, and final approval of routed work items. See Figure 4-13 for an illustration of notifications that might be sent in a typical procurement workflow.

WORKFLOW-RELEVANT DATA

Workflow-relevant data is user-input application data that is read directly by the workflow enactment service to trigger routing and execution rules. For example, some fields in an electronic purchase-request form may be used to trigger routing rules specifying that certain technical and purchasing specialists need to review the document. Other application data is not read directly by the enactment service and does not figure into routing decisions.

Workflow analysts, in addition to defining the workflow-relevant data fields and database, also need to define the following attributes associated with such data (see Table 4-7).

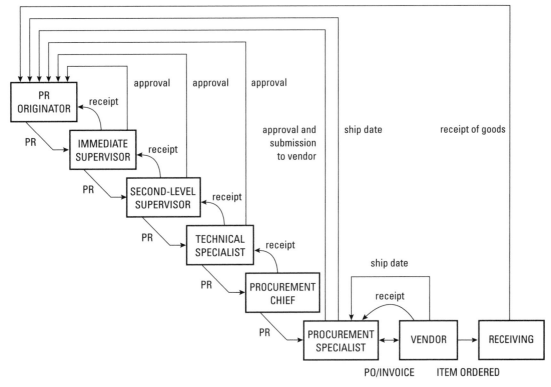

Figure 4-13:
Notifications in a typical procurement workflow.

TABLE 4-7: WORKFLOW-RELEVANT DATA ATTRIBUTES

ATTRIBUTE	DEFINITION/DESCRIPTION
NAME	This specifies the unique name by which a workflow-relevant data object, such as an electronic business form, will be designated to the enactment service. The name will be used in process definitions to define rules triggered by that object. For example, the *estimated cost* field in a purchase request will figure into the routing rule: *if estimated cost is greater than $100,000, route PR to chief financial officer.*
TYPE	This specifies the originating application, file format, and internal structure of the data object — attributes that will be used to trigger transition rules. For example, the type *Microsoft Excel 3.0 spreadsheet with three worksheets and embedded links to Microsoft Access database file* could be used in a complex rule such as *transfer linked files together, launch corresponding applications in tandem, open database file before spreadsheet, and display the second worksheet.*
PATH	This specifies the server, volume, directory, filename, and range of the workflow-relevant data object. These attributes ensure that the enactment service will be able to locate data objects precisely in order to execute transition rules correctly.

INVOKED APPLICATION

Analysts will also have to specify the applications that are invoked or launched automatically by the workflow system to access, modify, and output workflow-relevant data. The attributes that apply to an invoked application in a process definition are as follows (see Table 4-8).

TABLE 4-8: INVOKED APPLICATION ATTRIBUTES

ATTRIBUTE	DEFINITION/DESCRIPTION
NAME	This specifies the unique name and version of the commercial or in-house application.
TYPE	This specifies whether the invoked application is a word processor, spreadsheet, database management system, image processing system, computer-aided design tool, or some other type of software tool.
EXECUTION PARAMETERS	This specifies the conditions that will cause applications to be invoked and de-invoked in an activity. An application can be invoked at the start of an activity, in mid-activity (in response, for example, to user inputs), or at its conclusion. Factors that determine which application is invoked would include the nature of the activity and preference of the participant.
PATH	This specifies the machine, volume, directory, and filename of application executables.

Process-definition summary

Although all these definitions and conditions may seem overwhelming at first, such details will help you select the best process-modeling tools for your requirements. Just as a good financial analyst, well-versed in underlying concepts and relationships, can master a new spreadsheet program in no time, a business-process analyst, acquainted with basic workflow concepts, should be able to delve right into a new workflow product without too much difficulty.

The enactment service is a master traffic cop for workflow applications.

Workflow Enactment Services

Workflow enactment services put process definitions into motion. Depending on the workflow solution you choose, enactment services may be implemented as stand-alone, run-time workflow environments, or as value-added workflow capabilities layered on top of existing corporate document, database, and image management systems.

In either case, per the WfMC's Workflow Reference Model, the enactment service's core functions are as follows:

■ Initiate, execute, schedule, and control actual workflows in accordance with process definitions

■ Sign users on and off the system

■ Authenticate users

■ Add, modify, and delete items in users' workflow inboxes (also known as *worklists*)

■ Invoke external applications

■ Retrieve application files

■ Maintain run-time workflow control status data

■ Facilitate workflow control, administration, and audit

■ Archive process definition, workflow control, workflow relevant, and workflow application data

The enactment service is a master traffic cop for workflow applications. It manages an application's run-time transitions between the states described in Table 4-9. See Figure 4-14 for an illustration of a workflow application as a *state transition machine*.

TABLE 4-9: STATE TRANSITIONS OF A WORKFLOW ENACTMENT SERVICE

PROCESS STATE	DEFINITION
INITIATED	A run-time process instance has been created, based on a predefined process definition, but the process has not fulfilled the conditions (e.g., time/date and user logins) needed to start execution.
RUNNING	The process instance has started execution but not yet fulfilled the conditions needed to enter into the first activity and create a work item.
ACTIVE	The process instance is executing, one or more process activities have been started, and a work item has been created.
SUSPENDED	The process instance is executing, and activities have been started but are currently inactive pending issuance of a resume or restart command.
TERMINATED	The process instance has been stopped and deleted before its normal completion.
COMPLETED	The process instance has fulfilled all conditions for completion.

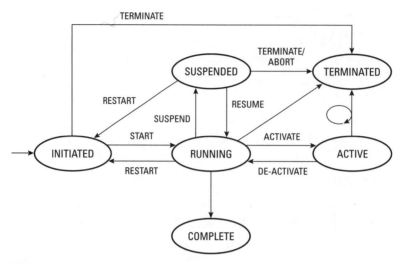

Figure 4-14
Workflow state transitions managed by the enactment service
(Workflow Management Coalition).

The enactment service also maintains all lower-level network and system interfaces, which need not directly concern the operations and business analysts who prepare high-level process definitions.

Workflow engines

The enactment service is composed of one or more *workflow engines*, which are software programs installed on network servers. Workflow engines may be configured within the enactment service using a centralized or distributed approach (per Figure 4-15).

The centralized approach involves installing the workflow engine, workflow process definition, workflow control data, workflow-relevant data, workflow applications data, and worklist handler on a single server.

The distributed approach, on the other hand, involves installing these software and application files on different servers, based on some network mechanism for run-time file sharing and transfer. Workflow engines may be installed on several servers communicating over local- and wide-area networks. When a workflow application is distributed across multiple engines, process definitions and run-time control data will need to be shared across the network. This information may be centralized on a single engine, replicated across all engines, or partitioned selectively among engines. It may be pre-installed on distributed engines prior to workflow initiation or transferred to them at process runtime.

In a distributed configuration, workflow application processes may be partitioned across engines based on any of the following factors (see Table 4-10).

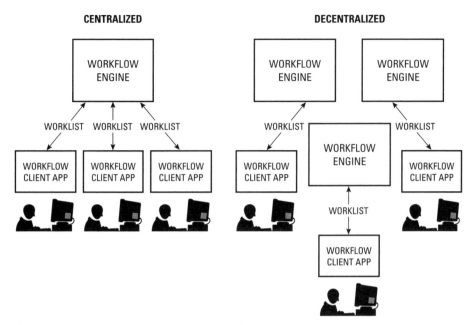

Figure 4-15
Alternative workflow enactment service configurations (Workflow Management Coalition).

TABLE 4-10: WORKFLOW APPLICATION PARTITIONING FACTORS

PARTITIONING FACTOR	DESCRIPTION
PROCESS TYPE	Workflow processes are often administered by different functional departments. Companies may establish policies requiring that departments run their own processes or segments of enterprise-wide processes on their servers. Purchasing-related processes might be set up to execute only on the procurement department's servers, application development workflows on MIS' engines, and so on.
ACTIVITIES	Activities associated with particular applications or files may be dedicated to engines controlling access to those resources.
ROLES	Processes and activities performed by particular users may be run on workflow engines in those users' departments or locations. This avoids the need to transfer process definitions and data to those sites at process runtime.
INVOKED APPLICATIONS	Software-licensing restrictions may require that some applications run only on particular servers. In these cases, it may be necessary to configure those applications to run with the workflow engines installed on those servers.
WORKFLOW-RELEVANT DATA	Workflow-relevant databases may not be replicable or distributable to multiple servers. Consequently, it would be necessary to dedicate database management systems to run in conjunction with co-located workflow engines.

Different processes may execute on different workflow engines within a single vendor's environment, or across two or more vendors' environments. Interoperability between different enactment services might conform to any of the scenarios described in Table 4-11 (and depicted in Figure 4-16).

TABLE 4-11: WORKFLOW ENACTMENT SERVICE INTEROPERABILITY SCENARIOS

SCENARIO	DESCRIPTION
CHAINED	This involves transfer of work items from enactment service A (at activity A4) to service B (at activity B1), with control of the process being transferred entirely to service B. In this scenario, processes are divided into discrete subprocesses, no enactment service controls more than one subprocess, and each service surrenders control completely to the next one when its subprocess is complete.
HIERARCHICAL	This involves transfer of work items from service A (at activity A3) to service B (at activity B1), with control of the process being returned to service A (at activity A3) when the process managed by service B has completed. In this scenario, the subprocess controlled by service B is nested entirely as an activity within service A.
PEER-TO-PEER	This involves transfer of work items between service A and service B, with control of the process flip-flopping back and forth between the services. In this scenario, processes are divided into activities that are managed in alternating turns by the various enactment services, and the same service may manage multiple distinct, noncontiguous subprocesses and activities.
PARALLEL SYNCHRONIZED	This involves no transfer of synchronization messages (but no work items) between service A (at activity A3) and service B (at activity B4). In this scenario, processes may execute independently and in parallel under different enactment services, synchronizing through message exchange at predefined activities or events.

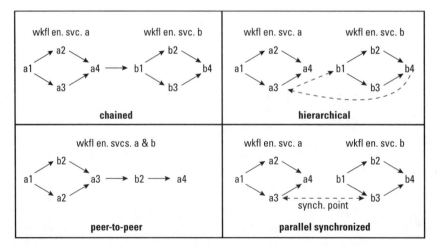

Figure 4-16
Workflow enactment service interoperability scenarios.

Interoperability between different workflow enactment services would require interchange of formatted process definition and control data, per the following functions (see Table 4-12).

TABLE 4-12: INFORMATION INTERCHANGE REQUIRED FOR WORKFLOW ENACTMENT SERVICE INTEROPERABILITY

INTEROPERABILITY FUNCTION	DESCRIPTION
DEFINITION	Defining a common object-naming scheme across enactment services
	Defining common process objects and attributes across enactment services
EXCHANGE	Exchanging definitions of processes or selected subprocesses and activities between enactment services
	Exchanging workflow control data between enactment services
	Exchanging workflow-relevant data between enactment services
	Exchanging workflow application data between enactment services
CONTROL	Transferring process control between enactment services
	Initiating, suspending, restarting, and terminating processes, subprocesses, and activities on other enactment services
	Synchronizing interdependent tasks across multiple enactment services
	Supporting common administration and monitoring functions across enactment services

Under the WfMC's reference model, these interoperability functions may be supported in gateway software installed on any or all of the communicating enactment services, or through APIs provided by one or more of the services.

Workflow client applications

Workflow client applications are a critical component of your overall workflow application, because they control the look, feel, and content of users' interaction with the enactment service. Workflow client applications may be custom-built user-interface software or simply existing desktop applications that have been retrofitted to issue function calls to server-resident workflow enactment services.

Per the WfMC Reference Model, user functions supported by workflow client applications include:

- Providing user access to a workflow inbox, which incorporates a *worklist handler* that displays worklist items retrieved from the enactment service

- Signing on and off an enactment service

- Requesting initiation of process instances

- Invoking the appropriate application when a work item is opened

- Accessing workflow relevant, application, and control data and organizing it into on-screen cases, folders, and documents

- Creating, modifying, and deleting process definitions and instances (supervisory users only)

Client application controls

The core client function is display and manipulation of items in the workflow inbox. In principle, a workflow inbox functions much like an e-mail inbox, displaying a list of pending work items assigned by the enactment service and opening and closing items in response to user commands. Depending on the application, worklists typically display the following information (see Figure 4-17 for an illustrative worklist display):

- List of work items (sorted by time of arrival, priority, process type, process instance, or other criteria; the list may represent multiple activities on a single process instance, across two or more process instances, and/or across two or more workflow engines)
- Name, type, status, creation date, and originator of each work item
- Role and privileges of the current user with respect to the item
- Required completion or due date

DOODAD CORPORATION ADMINISTRATIVE PROCESS WORKLIST				
FILE	**OPTIONS**	**FILTER**	**ACTIONS**	**HELP**
PRIORITY	*STATUS*	*SUBPROCESS/TASK*	*CREATED*	*ORIGINATOR*
TOP	*ITEM OPEN*	*PURCHASE/REVIEW*	*11/13/96*	*KIM J*
PRIORITY	ORIGINATOR	TASK NAME	PRIVILEGES	DUE DATE
TOP	*KIM J.*	*PURCHASE/REVIEW*	*READ/COMMENT*	*11/14/96*
ROUTINE	*CHRIS M.*	*PURCHASE/REVIEW*	*READ/COMMENT*	*11/17/96*
ROUTINE	*RALPH B.*	*PURCHASE/REVIEW*	*READ/COMMENT*	*11/20/96*
ROUTINE	*PETER K.*	*TIMESHEET/APPROVE*	*APPROVE/REJECT*	*11/13/96*
ROUTINE	*GAYLA S.*	*PROPOSAL/REVIEW*	*READ/WRITE/EDIT*	*12/01/96*

Figure 4-17
Typical worklist/inbox.

Depending on the controlling process definition, users may have a great deal or precious little latitude in worklist manipulation. Client applications may support the user-driven, process-driven, or some hybrid worklist-manipulation models. In the user-driven model, users may be allowed to select which of several presented items they will work on, which they will defer, and which they will forward or refuse. Alternately, in the process-driven model, the workflow enactment service may present only one item at a time to each user, requiring activity completion before the next item is presented. The enactment service may be set up to withdraw and reassign items that have sat unopened in a user's inbox beyond a prespecified time interval. Or the enactment service may be able to distribute items among users in order to balance workloads across a workgroup.

Client-engine communications

Workflow application developers have some flexibility in deciding where to install the client application, worklist handler, and worklist. The WfMC Reference Model describes four alternative architectures for communication between workflow client applications and workflow engines (described in Table 4-13 and depicted in Figure 4-18).

TABLE 4-13: ALTERNATIVE WORKFLOW CLIENT-TO-ENGINE COMMUNICATIONS ARCHITECTURES

ARCHITECTURE	DESCRIPTION
Host-based	In this scenario, the client application, worklist handler, worklist, and workflow engine all reside on a central host computer, which the user accesses from a dumb terminal or terminal-emulating workstation.
Shared Filestore	This scenario places the client application and worklist handler on the user's workstation and the workflow engine is on a central computer. Worklists are maintained on a shared file system that is network-accessible to both the application and engine.
Electronic Mail	This scenario places the client application and worklist handler on the user's workstation and the workflow engine on a central computer. Worklist items are delivered to users in e-mail messages.
Procedure Call	This scenario places the client application and worklist handler on the user's workstation, and the worklist and work engine on a central computer. Worklists are accessed by the client through *remote procedure calls (RPCs)*, which are a programming technique for distributing application modules across multiple networked devices.

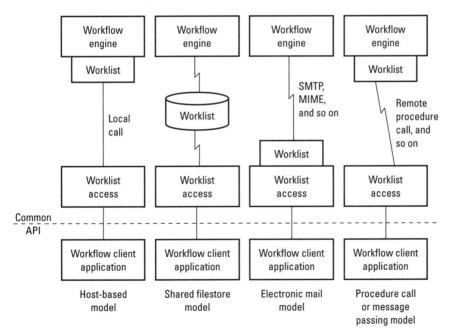

Figure 4-18
Alternative client worklist handler implementations (Workflow Management Coalition).

The functions necessary to interface workflow clients to enactment services include the commands described in Table 4-14.

TABLE 4-14: WORKFLOW CLIENT-TO-ENGINE INTEROPERABILITY FUNCTIONS

SET OF COMMANDS	DESCRIPTION
Session Establishment	These commands establish and disestablish communications sessions between client applications, worklist handlers, and the workflow enactment service.
Workflow Definition	These commands support query and retrieval of process-definition names, types, activities, and other attributes from a client application.
Worklist/Work-Item Handling	These commands support query and retrieval of worklist items, assignment of worklist item attributes, and notification of a work item's selection, reassignment, or completion.
Data Handling	These commands support retrieval of workflow relevant and application data, supporting viewing and manipulation of workflow application data organized into hierarchical or hyperlinked cases, folders, documents.
Process Status	These commands support queries of the status of a process or activity instance.
Process Control	These commands support creation, modification, suspension, resumption, and termination of process instances from a client application (for users with supervisory privileges).
Process Supervision	These commands support modification and termination of process and activity definitions and instances (for users with process supervisor privileges).

Invoked Applications

Invoked applications provide tools for users to work with cases, folders, documents, data, images, and other information routed to them by the enactment service.

Ideally, users should be able to launch the appropriate application and data files automatically when accepting or opening a routed work item. Invocation may be controlled by either the workflow enactment service or the client application's worklist handler. Application invocation by the enactment service may be the best approach if invocation is driven by transition rules maintained at the workflow engine, or if the applications in question (for example, document, database, and image management) reside on the server. The name, access path, and run-time parameters of the invoked application would have to be provided to the enactment service by the process definition or from within the routed work item. The enactment service might also invoke applications through an intermediary software module known as an *application agent*, which would translate the enactment service's APIs into whatever invocation calls are understood by the addressed application. Invocation by the worklist handler may be preferred if application selection is under user control or if the applications run on user workstations.

As a second-best approach, the user may be required to launch the application and data files using existing applications external to the workflow environment. Typically, the user would receive a routed work item that indicates what application should be used and where the workflow-relevant data resides. The user would then have to leave the workflow application in order to invoke the referenced application, which may reside on his or her workstation or a network server, and retrieve the data for manual processing.

An API for workflow enactment services to invoke external applications might support the functions described in Table 4-15.

TABLE 4-15: APPLICATION INVOCATION FUNCTIONS

SET OF COMMANDS	DESCRIPTION
Session Establishment	These commands establish and disestablish communications sessions between workflow engines, worklist handlers, application agents, and invoked applications.
Activity Management	These commands support engine-driven invocation, suspension, resumption, and termination of application activities, as well as application-driven synchronization and completion notification.
Data Handling	These commands support addressing and transfer of application data to and from workflow engines, application agents, and worklist handlers. Referenced data need not be physically routed with the work item. In fact, many production workflow systems leave documents and data in place at the server and simply transfer access paths, pointers, and read/write privileges to new users. This allows workflow application developers to minimize the amount of data piped over the network — a critical concern when an application manipulates large files such as scanned document images. On many production workflow products, the flow is logical rather than physical. Messaging-based workflow applications are entirely different, because they are engineered to route data physically as file attachments.

As noted previously, production workflow systems synthesize a growing range of technologies. Almost any application can (and eventually will) be invoked from within workflow management environments, either through standard computer script files, vendor-proprietary APIs, or industry-standard APIs exposed in vendor implementations. Consequently, it's useful to review the diverse technical standards, existing and emerging, in the principal workflow-related technologies. This is the subject of Chapter 6, which discusses image management, database management, document management, forms management, object management, product data management, project management, CASE, electronic messaging, directory services, Internet/intranet services, and electronic commerce technologies and standards.

Administration and Monitoring Tools

Administration and monitoring tools keep production workflow systems running smoothly. They enable process administrators to perform the following functions:

- Set up, configure, and optimize the many software components that make up a workflow application

- Activate process definitions or segments thereof

- Assign particular individuals to functional roles in accordance with the process definition

- Allocate run-time processes, activities, applications, and data to various workflow engines

- Initiate, suspend, resume, redirect, and terminate process instances

- Monitor executing processes and analyze historical data on completed and terminated processes

APIs to facilitate workflow administration and monitoring should support the functions described in Table 4-16.

TABLE 4-16: WORKFLOW ADMINISTRATION AND MONITORING FUNCTIONS

SET OF COMMANDS	DESCRIPTION
Resource Control	These commands support monitoring, analysis, allocation, balancing, and optimization of hardware, software, and network usage by workflow applications.
Role Management	These commands support definition, revision, and deletion of roles and privileges within the context of process definitions.
User Management	These commands support assignment of workflow roles to particular groups or individuals, per process definitions, as well as revision, suspension, and deletion of privileges within the context of those role assignments.
Process Supervision	These commands support activation, modification, and deactivation of process definitions; revision of the attributes or status of a run-time process instance or activity; or termination of a process instance.
Process Status	These commands support query of the current status of run-time process and activity instances.
Audit Management	These commands support definition, query, retrieval, printing, archiving, and deletion of logs and statistics associated with particular workflow processes, activities, and events.

Standards

Bringing order to the workflow marketplace are two complementary sets of technical standards that are gaining broad vendor support: WfMC's workflow APIs, grounded in the production workflow marketplace, and Microsoft's MAPI Workflow Framework, which define interoperability interfaces for messaging-based workflow. No standards have yet been defined specifically for the Web-based workflow market segment. Suite-based products are usually based on either messaging or production workflow architectures, so these products can be expected to draw on the WfMC and MAPI Workflow specifications as necessary.

WfMC's Workflow APIs

The foregoing in-depth discussion of workflow architecture and functions is strongly indebted to the Workflow Management Coalition's Reference Model. To enable interoperability between these functional subsystems in commercial workflow products, WfMC is defining the standard workflow APIs presented in Table 4-17.

TABLE 4-17: WORKFLOW MANAGEMENT COALITION STANDARD
APPLICATION PROGRAMMING INTERFACES

STANDARD	DEFINITION
Interface 1: Workflow Definition Interchange	This is the standard interface, published in February 1996, between process-definition tools and the workflow enactment service, providing industry-accepted formats for process-definition import and export. Workflow application developers will use these standard API commands to create, retrieve, modify, and delete process definitions or particular items (such as activities and transition conditions) within a process. Of course, nothing is stopping tool vendors from continuing to pursue their proprietary approaches to process definition, which in many cases may be richer, more sophisticated, and more nuanced than the WfMC's framework.
Interface 2: Workflow Client Application Interface	This is the standard interface, published in November 1995, between workflow client applications and the workflow enactment service. It interfaces client applications to worklist handlers, worklists, and workflow engines. These APIs have been designed to work without regard for the workflow client-server communication model used in a particular product. Industry support for these APIs would, in theory, allow one vendor's workflow client application to retrieve work items from many vendors' enactment services.
Interface 3: Invoked Applications Interface	This is the standard interface (not yet published) between invoked applications and workflow enactment services. The WfMC is attempting to standardize remote invocation of networked applications rather than local invocation of software pre-installed on user workstations. Local invocation is supported by a diverse range of command sets and shell scripting techniques specific to various computing environments. Candidates for remote-invocation standardization include Remote

(continued)

TABLE 4-17: WORKFLOW MANAGEMENT COALITION STANDARD
APPLICATION PROGRAMMING INTERFACES *(continued)*

STANDARD	DEFINITION
Interface 3: Invoked Applications Interface *(continued)*	Execution Call (e.g., Remote Procedure Calls and Open Systems Interconnection Remote Operations Service Element) for invoking a wide range of applications; Object-Request-Broker Call (e.g., Common Object Request Broker, Object Linking and Embedding and OpenDoc, ActiveX) for invoking object-oriented applications; Message Passing (e.g., Multipurpose Internet Messaging Extensions and X.400 Message Handling Services) for invoking messaging applications; and Database Transactions (e.g., Structured Query Language and Open Systems Interconnection Transaction Processing) for invoking database applications.
Interface 4: Workflow Application Programming Interoperability Functions	This is the standard interface, published in June 1996, between heterogeneous workflow management services. It will support sharing of process definitions and control data between different vendors' heterogeneous workflow enactment services. The WfMC is making no attempt to standardize how vendors implement sharing of process definition and control data within their own enactment services, referred to as *homogeneous environments*. Vendors have the flexibility to implement whatever technical architecture provides the best performance, utilizes system and network resources most efficiently, and minimizes overall cost of the workflow solution.
Interface 5: Administration and Monitoring Interface	This is the standard interface, published in August 1996, between administration/monitoring tools and the workflow enactment service. It will allow one vendor's tool to manage another's workflow enactment services.

As of this writing, the following WfMC members had indicated their intention to build products implementing the Coalition's Workflow Client Application Interface (Interface 2): Action Technologies, BancTec's Plexus Software Division, Computron Technologies Corp., CSE Systems, Fujitsu, IBM, ICL, Integrated Work, Lion GmbH, SAP AG, Siemens Nixdorf Informationssysteme, Staffware, Telstra Applied Technologies, and Xsoft.

Microsoft, a funding WfMC member, has agreed to make its MAPI Workflow Framework (discussed in the next section) one of the first commercial implementations of Interface 4, to support interoperability between workflow enactment services utilizing messaging transports and those running over distributed databases, intranet Web servers, and other run-time network platforms. In July 1996, Microsoft participated with five other WfMC members — including DEC, IBM, and Wang — in successful demonstration of Interface 4 interoperability for structured, interorganizational EDI transaction routing.

Microsoft's MAPI Workflow Framework

Microsoft has developed a set of workflow standards that is largely complementary to WfMC's specifications. Although WfMC's standards are primarily grounded in and addressed to the production workflow market, Microsoft's MAPI Workflow Framework defines interoperability standards for messaging-based workflow products based on Microsoft's Messaging Application Programming Interface (MAPI).

A first public draft of MAPI Workflow Framework was published around the same time that Exchange 1.0 (Microsoft's new groupware product) was released. Microsoft developed the document with assistance from Wang and other production and messaging-based workflow vendors and in consultation with the WfMC. The document defines APIs, message classes, and conversational dynamics needed for client applications to request and track workflow-engine services in the MAPI messaging environment. The focus of interoperability between the Microsoft and WfMC specifications is at the client-application interface, invoked applications interface, and enactment service interface (WfMC Interfaces 2, 3, and 4, respectively).

In its framework, Microsoft has adopted a workflow nomenclature consistent with that contained in the WfMC's Workflow Reference Model and has endeavored to make its specifications consistent with those being developed by the WfMC. At Microsoft's urging, the WfMC modified its Reference Model to make the cross-platform workflow interoperability specification independent of underlying communications transports, be they synchronous (such as remote procedure calls) or asynchronous (such as store-and-forward messaging systems).

Microsoft's specifications support sequential, parallel, and conditional routing of work items over MAPI-compliant e-mail systems. Workflow-enabled applications will be able to route formatted work items transparently through MAPI-compliant message transfer agents to workflow engines, which function as specialized inbox processors. The specification defines mechanisms for connecting multiple workflow engines through MAPI-compliant e-mail systems. It supports the tracking of message locations and status, as well as the consolidation of recipient responses into the original message or a public folder.

In placing its considerable clout behind workflow standardization, Microsoft is performing a great service to the industry. The MAPI Workflow Framework will contribute to the workflow-enabling of all desktop applications throughout the business world and to the establishment of basic interoperability between previously incompatible messaging-based and production workflow environments. The framework takes much of the routing logic away from the workflow client application and electronic forms, invests it in a background service process, and increases administrators' ability to monitor and control e-mail-enabled workflow in real time. In future upgrades to Exchange, the product will support quasi-production workflow capabilities such as leaving application data in place on public folders and simply routing access pointers and privileges that reference appropriate folders.

Summary

In summary, this chapter has provided a detailed primer on workflow process modeling techniques, workflow system architectures, and workflow technical standards. For business readers, the discussion provides an introduction to general issues and requirements associated with investments in workflow tools. For technical readers, it serves as a basis for evaluating different workflow products and designing and integrating workflow applications for their companies. For all readers, it's a foundation for understanding the discussions throughout the book. The next chapter uses this Workflow Reference Model as the basis for characterizing architectural differences between four broad categories of commercially available workflow products: production, messaging-based, Web-based, and suite-based workflow management systems.

CHAPTER FIVE

WORKFLOW SYSTEM SPECIES

Workflow technology is evolving faster than this book can fully capture. Nevertheless, as noted in Chapter 3, available technical solutions fall into four broad categories, distinguished principally by the transport mechanism used to route work items. Production workflow systems — more accurately referred to as *filestore-based systems* — revolve around shared filestores, which typically include server-based image, document, and database management systems. Messaging-based workflow systems route files over users' e-mail systems. Web-based workflow solutions route files over the World Wide Web. Suite-based solutions are tied to particular vendors' groupware or desktop application suites.

This chapter presents a detailed discussion of each segment, providing some historical perspective and showing that their differences go far beyond issues of networking platform. Production workflow is discussed first, because it is the oldest, most mature, most diverse, and, arguably, most feature-rich and robust segment of the industry. Then the discussion turns to messaging-based workflow, a well-established maturing market segment that, with the growing acceptance of the MAPI Workflow Framework, will challenge production solutions for market supremacy. Following this is an overview of Web-based workflow, a much younger but fast-rising niche. Finally, you explore the technology underlying suite-based workflow capabilities embedded in such applications environments as Lotus Notes and Microsoft Office.

Production Workflow

Production workflow products make up the traditional high-end of the market. They are designed primarily to route electronic folders consisting of one or more forms or documents. These products typically support more features and functions than messaging-based tools, allow greater customization, and run in a wider range of network and computing environments. However, they often come with a heftier price tag per user. And they frequently require expensive application development and integration services from a third-party workflow system integrator, value-added reseller, or consultant. Leading production workflow vendors and solutions are profiled in Chapter 7.

Many organizations have adopted production workflow applications for a wide range of mission-critical applications. The production workflow market was expected to reach over $1.3 billion in revenues in 1996, almost doubling over the previous two years, according to the Delphi Consulting Group (Boston, MA), and will continue to grow at a healthy clip through the remainder of this decade. At the time this book was published, there were more than 100 vendors of production workflow solutions, with new competitors entering the fray every month.

From the dawn of computing, people have envisioned paper-free, technology-enabled work environments.

Much of this growth has been fueled by traditional vertical-market workflow applications in finance, government, insurance, and manufacturing. According to Delphi, workflow market revenues in 1994 broke down as follows by sector:

- Finance/banking: 23 percent
- Insurance: 16 percent
- Manufacturing: 12 percent
- Government: 12 percent
- Medical/health care: 6 percent
- General business: 5 percent
- Transportation: 5 percent
- Aerospace/defense: 4 percent
- Utility: 4 percent
- Pharmaceutical: 2 percent
- Engineering/design: 2 percent
- Telecommunications: 2 percent
- Other: 7 percent

What these industries have in common is a strong need to reduce the volume of back-office paperwork in daily operations. Paper is costly to process, organize, store, search, and retrieve. It tends to create massive, self-perpetuating bureaucracies. It also slows an organization's response to customer inquiries and changing competitive conditions.

From the dawn of the computing age, people have envisioned paper-free, technology-enabled work environments. In the early 1980s, many companies built proprietary and commercial forms-routing applications — typically, in the pre-PC era, running in mainframe or minicomputer environments. However, *proto-workflow* applications seldom provided all the sophisticated routing, management, and tracking capabilities that would become standard in the workflow industry.

Pioneering vendors (such as FileNet and ViewStar) created the workflow market in the mid-'80s by combining such capabilities as image scanning, compound documents, structured routing, case tracking, keyword indexing, and support for optical storage devices. Large organizations quickly realized that paper need be touched only once, when it came in the front door, at which point it could be scanned into optical storage and be processed electronically from then on. Or better yet, route purely electronic documents from beginning to end, outputting them to paper only as needed. Clearly, here was a new tool well suited for carrying out downsizing, flattening, decentralization, reengineering, and many of the other critical business imperatives of the time.

Conceived as a value-added synthesis of several technologies, production workflow systems continue to evolve by integrating with more and more technologies. File management systems, databases, e-mail, mobile computing, Internet services — all of these and more are being drawn into workflow environments. "[W]orkflow is an operating environment that provides a context for working with other technologies," states Thomas Koulopoulos in *The Workflow Imperative*[1], and may ultimately evolve into a high-level *business operating system* layered over today's diverse desktop and network operating environments, such as Microsoft Windows and Novell NetWare.

The architecture of production workflow products aligns closely to the Workflow Management Coalition (WfMC's) Reference Model, presented in Chapter 4. This model defines a generalized target architecture driving the development of most production workflow solutions, whether or not their vendors plan to implement all the WfMC's standard technical interfaces. It also presents an enterprise-worthy workflow architecture and feature superset toward which vendors of messaging-based, Web-based, and suite-based solutions are also migrating. Evidence for this trend is the proposed addition of server-resident workflow engine functionality to two messaging-based solutions: JetForm's eponymous product and Microsoft Exchange 2.0 (the latter is expected in late 1997).

To better understand the production workflow market's origin and likely future development, you should review each of the core capabilities supported in most of today's production workflow solutions: image management, database management, document management, forms management, object management, product data management, project management, computer-aided software engineering, electronic messaging, directory services, Internet/intranet services, and electronic commerce services. A detailed presentation of these technologies and their role in workflow applications is presented in Chapter 6. The ability of production workflow tools to integrate this diverse third-party functionality supports Koulopolous' vision of workflow as a business operating system. In fact, you may find that workflow management products are also referred to as document-image processing systems, forms management systems, and the like, in marketing literature and the trade press, reflecting the multifunctional nature of this technology.

Messaging-based Workflow

Once you've looked at production workflow systems in all their sophistication and complexity (per Chapter 4's framework discussion), you are ready to visit a lower-end segment of the market: messaging-based workflow tools. The same framework, drawn from the WfMC Workflow Reference Model, can be used to understand messaging-based workflow applications, even though they differ significantly in architecture and functionality from production workflow systems. Leading messaging-based workflow vendors and products are profiled in Chapter 8.

Messaging-based workflow products are stand-alone tools that route documents over users' existing e-mail systems. They are designed primarily to route electronic forms and file attachments. Messaging-based tools support rapid definition and activation of simple business processes, usually of a sequential or parallel nature. They are designed to be used with minimal training and customization by nontechnical personnel.

What best distinguishes messaging-based workflow products is their support for the typical quick-and-dirty business process: a workflow with minimal preplanning, few participants, and simple routing rules that are being redefined from day-to-day depending on what works. These tools are sometimes called *administrative workflow systems*, because they are often used to automate routine office procedures that have traditionally relied on paper forms and transmittal slips. They often allow process models to be defined with a *routing list* screen similar to an e-mail addressing function.

The messaging-based workflow market is younger than its production workflow counterpart, dating more or less from Delrina Corp.'s initial product FormFlow, introduced in 1988. Currently, over a dozen companies, including most major e-mail vendors, provide messaging-based workflow solutions. Intelligent e-mail systems — such as Digital Equipment Corp.'s TeamLinks and Banyan Systems' BeyondMail — also fall into this category. These systems provide such capabilities as sequential routing, cycle back to originator, and rule-based message management. This latter capability is similar to worklist handling in production workflow systems, in that the mail client sorts incoming messages by sender, subject, priority, or some other user-specified criteria.

Messaging-based workflow is more of a horizontal-market technology than production workflow, which has traditionally been sold by value-added resellers targeting specific industries such as finance, government, and manufacturing. Messaging-based systems still require some integration, but, by providing simpler application development tools and working over users' existing e-mail systems, they are more likely to be used by smaller workgroups for informal pilots and limited applications.

A synthesis of technologies

Messaging-based workflow technology has traditionally been perceived as *workflow-lite*, integrating a narrower range of technologies than the more established production workflow products. Most notably, messaging-based workflow systems typically lack document-image processing and management capabilities. Messaging-based workflow products can best be understood as a synthesis of forms management, database management, and electronic messaging technologies.

FORMS MANAGEMENT

Electronic forms routing has long been a standard feature of imaging-based production workflow systems and it was an obvious focus for messaging-based tools. Forms are documents that imply a process, and they can easily be designed with standard application development tools. Forms are such a familiar, user-friendly interface that you can expect them to figure large in mass-market workflow applications involving mobile computing and electronic commerce.

DATABASE MANAGEMENT

In messaging-based workflow applications, electronic forms have always served primarily as application front ends to shared network databases. As noted previously, a filled-in electronic form often corresponds to one or more database records. When a form reaches the end of a review chain, its field contents can either be written to new records or update existing records in a database. Forms-oriented update may be the only feasible approach when users lack interactive access to the database or, for performance or security reasons, are forbidden from directly accessing the database. Users can employ electronic forms to query databases graphically, specifying the fields on which to query or sort. Forms may also be used to build databases from scratch by visually specifying fields and relationships among them. Expect future messaging-based workflow systems to integrate with a wider assortment of object-oriented databases, using electronic forms to display multimedia objects gathered from multiple databases. Java-compliant browsers will become the preferred platform for messaging-based workflow, because they provide a forms interface and connect to object-oriented, multimedia Web document databases.

ELECTRONIC MESSAGING

E-mail has always been the obvious transport medium for ad-hoc workflow or any other application built on *store and forward* communications. E-mail is ubiquitous and quite often the only data-communications service connecting all workflow participants. E-mail systems also provide a resource critical to workflow applications: network user directories that can be used to specify routing paths. E-mail-based workflow systems will have to surmount some serious technical obstacles if they're to scale up to supporting enterprise-wide, high-volume, multimedia applications. First, they will have to support document routing and tracking over heterogeneous e-mail environments, a capability not widely found in today's products. Second, they will have to allow documents or data sets over a certain size threshold to remain physically at the server rather than be transmitted as file attachments to each successive recipient. This would involve referencing the objects through network addresses or pointers in the routed e-mail. Third, they will have to allow a transmitted document's file format to be identified easily within the message, so that the appropriate application can be invoked at the receiving end, a capability that can be achieved by using MIME as the standard messaging protocol.

Messaging-based workflow components

The technical architecture of a messaging-based workflow system is not as complex as a production workflow system. See Figure 5-1 for the diagram of a typical messaging-based workflow system. The following discussion describes how the principal run-time architectural subsystems of production workflow solutions — presented under the Reference Model — correspond to components in messaging-based workflow systems.

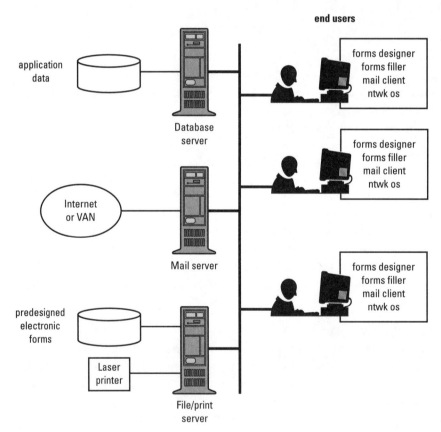

Figure 5-1
Configuration of typical messaging-based workflow system.

FORMS DESIGNER

In the forms designer, users are provided with graphical tools for designing their own electronic forms and defining routes and rules associated with forms. In a messaging-based solution, the primary process-modeling tools are the forms designer and the mail client, to be discussed shortly.

In their use of forms designers, messaging-based and production workflow systems are comparable: both technologies rely heavily on electronic forms as the user interface. However, production workflow solutions also support design of multidocument electronic folders, while messaging-based products rely almost entirely on a forms-oriented user interface.

Forms design tools support development of single- or multipage forms. Forms may be composed of any or all of the following elements, which you can often drag and drop into place from component libraries:

- **Graphic elements:** You are provided with a palette of graphics tools to replicate a paper form on-screen or to design eye-catching new layouts. Many packages allow you to display a scanned or faxed paper form on-screen and then *trace* the new electronic form over that template. You can also import layouts, bar codes, and graphics created in other packages.

- **Tables:** The quickest way to lay out a form's basic structure is often by creating an on-screen tabular row-column format. Cells in the table can then be linked to particular files, records, and fields in an existing or new database. The forms designer can import database structures directly from the target RDBMS and use these in building the table. Some cells can be mapped to a *parent* record in one relational data file (for example, customer name, address, phone number, and social security number) while others are mapped to several *child* records (for example, items ordered) in another file.

- **Data-entry fields:** Cells can be laid down in the tabular format just described or as noncontiguous form fields. Some cells may be mapped to database entry fields. Data values can be automatically entered into particular fields through automated database lookups or calculations based on values in other fields. Manual data entry can be mandatory for some fields and optional for others. Users can be allowed to enter only prespecified data types, such as alphanumeric or date/time. Limits can be placed on the data values that can be entered. Entries can be constrained to a predefined *pick list* of data values.

- **Viewers:** Some fields can be mapped to application-file viewers, which would allow users to read data in external files while still in the form. Users can be given the option of placing the viewed data in a special on-screen window or displaying it in the associated field. Users can also be allowed to write the data (or some segment thereof) to the field. Alternately, they can attach the external file to the form before routing.

■ **Formulas:** Formulas — sometimes known as *macros* — can be defined to implement business rules specifying how a form is to be processed and routed. Formulas can perform arithmetic or statistical operations on the value of single field, multiple fields in a single form, or in multiple forms. Database values can be looked up and inserted into form fields depending on manually entered values in other fields. It may be possible to merge data from multiple databases into a single form, which can then be written to another database altogether. Forms-routing paths can be redirected depending on values entered into particular fields, such as an approval field. Values of particular fields can be displayed for some users and not others.

Electronic forms are often placed in a shared, server-resident forms library to be downloaded by users as needed. In addition, some messaging-based workflow products allow external applications to automatically invoke, complete, and initiate routing of predefined electronic forms in response to database and network events.

FORMS FILLER

After a form has been designed, it is ready to be routed to and filled in by its target users. The forms filler is desktop software that allows users to open forms routed to them, view their contents, enter or change data values, query server-resident databases, and route forms (via the e-mail system) to their next recipient. Within the workflow Reference Model, forms fillers belong in the category of workflow client applications.

In a messaging-based workflow application, all business rules associated with a process are embedded in the forms filler or the form itself. All messaging-based process logic is maintained at a network client that currently has possession of a work item. In other words, workflow enactment services in messaging-based solutions are executed totally within user client software: forms filler, electronic form, and mail client.

Contrast this to production workflow systems, which maintain process definitions and control data within the network of servers that constitute the workflow enactment service. Messaging-based workflow is very much a client-centric technology, while production workflow is server-centric.

Filler software is usually pre-installed on the desktops of all users involved in messaging-based business processes. Only the forms and data are routed to users at process run time. The forms themselves may also be pre-installed, in which case only the data associated with particular workflow instances would be routed at process run time, taking a significant bit-load off the network. This may also be the best approach if users have a mix of graphical and text-based forms fillers running under various operating environments, in which case it might be difficult or impossible to get a routed form to display identically on different platforms.

The filler invokes application/file viewers linked to various form fields, using object and data linking services provided by the operating environment (for example, Microsoft Windows' Dynamic Data Exchange and Object Linking and Embedding). The filler might also interact with a server-resident security subsystem to authenticate users via digital signature technology, control access to particular form fields or server databases, or encrypt form contents before routing. The filler might also display a bit-mapped replica of the user's signature in an approval field after he or she has approved the form.

MAIL CLIENT

The forms filler must have access to another workflow client application — the locally installed e-mail client software — in order to define routing lists and send and receive messages. Consequently, the mail client, in a messaging-based workflow environment, is one part process-definition tool and one part workflow client application.

Most messaging-based workflow systems run on top of the same mail client used to send and receive the office's standard e-mail messages. Workflow items are usually listed with normal interpersonal messages in users' inboxes. To distinguish workflow items from run-of-the-mill e-mail messages in user inboxes, some messaging-based workflow products — typically, those provided by e-mail vendors — provide special icons, fonts, or other indicators. Another approach sometimes used is for an intelligent mail client to identify incoming workflow items and place them in a separate inbox. As noted previously, this feature sets messaging-based workflow tools apart from production workflow systems, which usually require users to check a workflow inbox that is entirely separate from their existing e-mail inbox.

The forms filler software can invoke the mail client using an industry-standard API set (such as MAPI or VIM) or vendor-proprietary mail commands supported by most e-mail systems. The filler program might invoke any or all of the following functions provided by the mail client (with the available mail-client functionality varying greatly by vendor and underlying mail protocol):

- Addressing new outbound messages
- Attaching files to new outbound messages
- Encrypting outbound messages and file attachments
- Including digital signatures with outbound messages and file attachments
- Requesting delivery, receipt, and forwarding notifications for outbound messages
- Submitting outbound messages to the mail server
- Retrieving new inbound messages from the mail server
- Sorting new inbound messages into various inboxes and folders as determined by sender, priority, subject, or other criteria
- Invoking different viewers and external applications to handle different types of inbound attachments
- Authenticating, decrypting, and checking the content integrity of inbound messages and file attachments
- Converting file attachments from one format to another
- Forwarding inbound messages to other local or remote users
- Generating receipt and forwarding notifications to senders of inbound messages

E-mail delivery reports, receipt notifications, and forwarding notifications are critical for messaging-based workflow tracking. They enable mail clients to report the current location and status of items that they receive. Depending on the capabilities of the mail client, these reports and notifications may be returned to the item's originator, sent to the previous person in the routing chain, posted to a shared e-mail bulletin board, or written to a special shared database accessible to workflow participants. E-mail systems have different notification and reporting capabilities, which makes effective workflow tracking across mail system boundaries a challenge, at best.

Messaging-based workflow systems may define their own special notification events and formats using mail clients to circulate these notifications among workflow participants. Some messaging-based workflow clients may return formatted notification messages when certain predefined events occur (for example, management approvals, rejections, or changes) or fail to occur (for example, failure to begin or complete work on a form within five days of receipt).

Many messaging-based workflow systems allow the forms filler to be launched from within the mail client by clicking on an icon representing the received form. This level of integration is made possible by object services such as OLE and CORBA.

MESSAGE TRANSFER AGENT

Message transfer agents (MTAs) — sometimes called *mail servers* or *post offices* — perform routing, delivery, forwarding, and communications functions on e-mail systems. MTAs route messaging-based workflow items much the same as any other e-mail, based on the recipient address and delivery options contained in the message header. These functions are supported by MTA access to an e-mail address directory and security database.

MTAs are not workflow engines — an architectural concept that has applied traditionally only to production workflow systems. MTAs have traditionally lacked the important ability to execute run-time process models (a capability, it should be noted, that is being provided in a growing number of messaging-based workflow products).

MTAs represent an invoked application essential to messaging-based workflow products. They simply route messages and process various delivery options (for example, requests for delivery/nondelivery reports and for deferred delivery). MTAs do not implement workflow process definitions, maintain workflow control data, administer user work lists (other than routing inbound e-mail and workflow items to user inboxes), or track workflow status. These functions are performed collectively by the electronic forms, forms filler software, and e-mail clients resident at user workstations.

Multiple MTAs are often implemented in a distributed message handling system that spans local- and wide-area networks. MTAs often use authentication schemes (such as passwords or digital signatures) to establish trusted connections before exchanging messages. An item is routed from one local user to another; the MTA simply moves messages from one person's outbox to another's inbox on the same server. If routing is between users on different MTAs provided by the same vendor, the MTAs sometimes use a vendor-proprietary communications protocol to transfer items over local- and wide-area network links.

On the Internet and many corporate intranets, it's becoming exceedingly rare for a message to be routed from end-to-end by a single vendor's MTAs. In today's increasingly heterogeneous e-mail world, intercommunicating MTAs will probably use an industry-standard protocol (such as SMTP or MIME) to exchange messages. When messages are routed between mail clients and MTAs utilizing different mail protocols, mail gateways will be installed to convert between various address and message formats.

MESSAGE STORE

On-line message stores receive inbound and outbound messages routed by MTAs and retain them pending subsequent delivery to their intended recipients. Message stores are an essential component in e-mail systems, because MTAs often communicate with each other over dial-up modem connections at 15-, 30-, 45-, or 60-minute intervals, requiring that outbound messages be deposited to temporary on-line storage pending transmission. Message stores also buffer inbound messages pending their retrieval by local users when they log into their e-mail accounts.

Message stores might be regarded either as a part of the workflow enactment service — in products that support rule-based process execution in conjunction with the message store — or as a type of invoked application, similar to document and database management systems that retain process-relevant and application data in a production workflow solution. Message stores may be set up to retain past messages in user folders, bulletin boards, or archives. They provide a potential audit trail for completed or in-process workflows, provided that all or most workflow activities occur in the domain of a particular MTA.

DIRECTORY SERVICE

Directories — a critical invoked application required by both production and messaging-based workflow environments — maintain information necessary for e-mail system operation and administration. Directory information includes the addresses, privileges, and environments of users, mail clients, MTAs, and other distributed system components. Increasingly, e-mail address directories are drawn from master network directories maintained by LAN, WAN, and computer system administrators. Many network directories are being designed to conform with hierarchical, object-oriented X.500 specifications. See Figure 5-2 for a typical X.500 *directory information tree*.

Directories are accessed by user mail clients to facilitate message addressing to local and remote recipients. They are also used by MTAs to determine appropriate routing paths, address-mapping formats, and mailing-list expansions. Mail directories may maintain any or all of the following information (depending on the implementation of the mail system in question):

- **User directories:** Name, ID, password, public-key certificate, local MTA, position, group or department, mail-client protocol support, mail-client operating environment
- **MTA directories:** Name, ID, password, public-key certificate, network address, administrator, public or private management domain

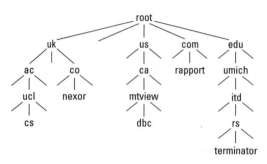

Figure 5-2
X.500 directory information tree, including domain
names for countries ("uk""us"), industries ("com""edu"),
organizations ("nexor""rapport"), organization units
("cs""itd"), localities ("mtview"), and individuals ("terminator").

As a messaging-based workflow forms designer, you access mail directories when defining a routing path. Typically, messaging-based workflows are designed by specifying sequential or parallel chains of user addresses in a *routing slip* screen similar to a standard e-mail addressing dialog box. Depending on the mail system, it may be possible to save a sequential routing list under a single name, which can be specified in future workflows and then expanded at run time to its constituent names.

Consequently, most messaging-based workflow applications can be regarded as supporting address-driven modeling, as discussed in Chapter 4.

SECURITY SERVICE

Security services are another type of invoked application. The mail client or MTA might invoke security services appropriate to the message recipient, priority, or topic. Security parameters would usually be retrieved from the directory service and used to call any or all of the following capabilities provided by the messaging system's security service:

- **Authentication:** Users are authenticated to the workflow and/or mail system using the familiar ID/password scheme or something fancier, such as digital signatures, smart cards, or biometrics. Application components (such as forms fillers, mail clients, and MTAs) can also be authenticated on a peer-to-peer basis to each other. Furthermore, digital signature technology, built on public-key cryptography, enables messages and file attachments to be authenticated as originating from their purported senders. Digital signatures are, to you and me, unintelligible strings of computer characters; however, some e-mail systems may represent them on-screen as a bit-mapped replica or facsimile of a user's actual handwritten signature.

- **Access control:** User access to directories, forms libraries, form fields, and databases may be controlled in keeping with privileges maintained by the security service.

- **Confidentiality:** Users may be allowed to encrypt and decrypt messages and file attachments using public-key certificates and algorithms maintained by the security service.

- **Content integrity:** In authenticating a message or file's digital signature, users are also verifying that the item was not modified in transit.

- **Nonrepudiation:** Nonrepudiation refers to several security features designed to verify that transactions cannot be denied after-the-fact by involved users:

  - Nonrepudiation of origin is the ability to verify that someone who claims to have sent an item in fact did so, usually accomplished by applying a digital signature to the message.

  - Nonrepudiation of delivery is the ability to verify that a message was delivered to the recipient's MTA, by applying the MTA's digital signature to a delivery report returned to the message originator.

  - Nonrepudiation of receipt is the ability to verify that the message was actually retrieved by the user to whom it was addressed, by applying the recipient's digital signature to a receipt notification returned by the recipient's mail client.

  - Nonrepudiation of content received is the ability to verify that the file attachment or body part sent to the user was retrieved intact by that user, by applying the recipient's digital signature to the attachment or body part and attaching the digital signature to a receipt notification.

  - Nonrepudiation of forwarding is the ability to verify that the message was actually forwarded by the recipient to a third party, by applying the recipient's digital signature to a forwarding notification returned by the recipient's mail client.

These services are used to sign, seal, deliver, and track work items that involve electronic commerce, legal matters, and other high-stakes transactions conducted over e-mail transports. The security service invokes public-key certificates, secret encryption keys, encryption algorithms, and other software- and hardware-based capabilities as necessary.

DATABASE AND DOCUMENT SERVERS

One or more servers may support and invoke database and document management systems shared by participants in messaging-based workflows. Users may access such information in addition to any databases and documents they maintain locally on their PCs.

As noted previously, you can design electronic forms by importing existing database structures and linking database fields to form fields. Links can be established between form fields and document viewers, so that relevant files can be invoked through mouse-clicks in an on-screen form. Data-import capabilities (for example, Microsoft Windows DDE/OLE facilities) may allow individual data elements from external files to be placed into form fields as necessary. It may also be possible to attach external application files to electronic forms, so that they may be routed down the review chain. The resultant web of document and database links to a particular form can become fairly intricate.

One critical workflow-relevant feature provided by shared network database and document management systems is *concurrency* or *version control*. Users may not be allowed to overwrite database records directly; instead, when a form has reached the end of a routing chain, its contents may be written to a new record that is tagged as a version of original record. Likewise, changes made by successive users to a document may not be allowed to overwrite the master; instead, they may be written to the server with different filename extensions.

Another important feature of network document management systems is the ability to support a shared library of business forms and instructions. A typical messaging-based workflow begins with a user searching for the appropriate form. He or she could search the server-resident library by forms titles, topics, or keywords. After the form is located, it can be downloaded and automatically populated, from the directory service, with data specific to that user (for example, name, title, address, office number, and phone number). On-line searches can be performed for other relevant documents, which may then be linked, attached, or referenced in the form.

On the leading edges of the workflow market are the Web-based solutions.

COMMUNICATIONS GATEWAYS

Many messaging-based workflow systems are not limited just to e-mail-based communications. A growing number invoke outbound facsimile gateways that can transmit documents to recipients that lack e-mail clients, require simple notifications of workflow events, need forms to be output immediately on paper, and/or are the last link in the routing chain. Support for outbound paging and voice-mail notifications, via specialized gateways, is also becoming more prevalent in the messaging-based workflow industry. Inbound fax, sometimes accompanied by optical character recognition, may also be employed to initiate workflows. Gateways to the Internet or corporate intranets are also becoming more prevalent in messaging-based workflow products. See Figure 5-3 for a diagram showing external communications options supported by some messaging-based workflow products.

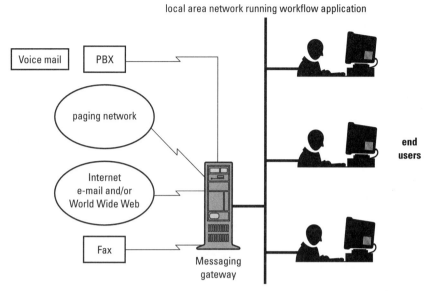

Figure 5-3
External communications options supported by some messaging-based work flow products.

Web-based Workflow

On the leading edges of the workflow market are the Web-based solutions. Commercial Web-based workflow products, targeted at the fast-growing intranet market, have been on the market since early 1996, so the following discussion can claim to capture only an embryonic snapshot of this dynamic new technology. Noteworthy early entrants to this market segment are profiled in Chapter 9.

Web-based solutions represent a potentially lucrative horizontal market for workflow products, driven by the explosive growth in Internet/intranet-based communications and the concomitant search for new applications to run on this infrastructure. Many of the Web-based products presented in Chapter 9 come from established vendors (such as Action Technologies, JetForm, Novell, Reach, and ViewStar) that have products in the production, messaging-based, and/or suite-based segments. Inevitably, a flurry of startup vendors (including Ultimus and WebFlow) has cropped up to pursue this opportunity.

Intranet/Web-based workflow will become a sizeable market segment — and it may increase the overall size of the workflow industry — but it probably won't make production, messaging-based, and suite-based workflow solutions obsolete. Workflow capabilities are becoming part of the fabric of every network-connected information system, and the other solutions (production, messaging-based, suite-based) provide those features for their respective platforms. It would be naive to believe that companies will move all their workflow applications to their HTTP-based intranets and not seek to provide these capabilities in conjunction with their existing database servers, document management systems, document-imaging systems, messaging systems, groupware, desktop application suites, and other legacy environments. The aggregate corporate investment in these other technologies far outstrips the outlays for intranet technologies, and probably will continue to do so for the forseeable future.

Intranet/Web-based workflow products combine features of production and messaging-based solutions with some features all their own. What principally distinguishes Web-based offerings from the rest of the workflow market is the narrowly circumscribed, industry-standard Internet/intranet platform on which they operate. Whereas production, messaging-based, and suite-based solutions operate over application infrastructures that incorporate a wide range of protocols and application services. Web-based workflow, however, requires the following standardized network environment (depicted in Figure 5-4):

- **Wide-area World Wide Web (Web) Internet or intranets:** Web-based workflow solutions operate only over networks implementing the following protocols: HyperText Transfer Protocol (HTTP), Transmission Control Protocol (TCP), Internetwork Protocol (IP), Serial Line Interface Protocol (SLIP), and/or Point-to-Point Protocol (PPP). This sets Web-based products apart from production, messaging-based, and suite-based workflow solutions in three ways. First, Web-based products are geared primarily to supporting enterprise, wide-area Internet/intranet applications, while other workflow solutions usually support a mix of wide- and local-area applications for large and small workgroups. Second, Web-based solutions will not run over other backbone network protocols (such as IBM's Systems Network Architecture, DEC's DECnet, and Novell's IPX/SPX) that your corporation may have implemented. Third, Web-based solutions may not integrate as closely with your company's existing application infrastructure (messaging, databases, document management, directories, groupware, and so on) as do the other products, due to the need to translate or convert between Web protocols/services and legacy technologies.

- **Web servers serving HyperText Markup Language (HTML) forms and/or Java applets:** Web-based workflow applications rely heavily on electronic forms delivered to the user as HTML pages and/or sets of Java applets. This reliance on HTML/Java-standard forms is one of the great advantages of Web-based workflow products, because it enables electronic forms to be defined once and display uniformly across many vendors' browsers. The industry trend toward standardization on HTML forms puts vendor-proprietary forms formats (such as those found in other workflow technologies) on the defensive. One traditional limitation of the HTML standard has been its inability to support forms processing in the client browser; instead, data validation and other processing functions have had to be performed at the Web server, which then communicates to the browser/user whether a particular form/field input has been accepted as valid. The industry is addressing this limitation through implementation of JavaScript-enabled HTML forms, which contain applets — small programs — that can perform some processing functions locally.

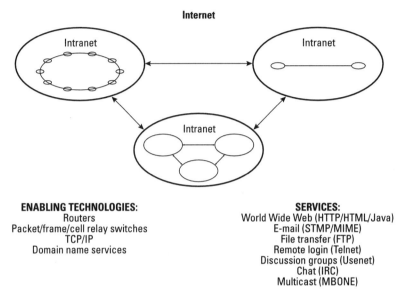

Figure 5-4
Intranets, the Internet, and enabling technologies and services.

- **Web browsers on desktops:** Web-based workflow applications work with a universal client — any browser (although some types of browsers work better with some products). The browser, therefore, replaces the forms fillers and worklist handlers used in production workflow, as well as the fillers and mail clients used in messaging-based and suite-based offerings. One open question is whether browsers are an inherently better or worse desktop environment for everyday workflow applications than the run-of-the-mill e-mail inbox. Some could argue convincingly that e-mail is superior, because it is the predominant communications tool for knowledge workers and, under today's desktop application suites, can present inbound workflow items in a unified list with messages, appointment reminders, and file transmissions. Others might argue that this e-mail advantage is on its way to becoming moot as the distinction between mail clients and browsers disappears — very soon we might all use one integrated communications tool for global messaging and information access.

Web-based workflow is similar to its messaging-based cousin in its orientation to electronic forms, which makes it best suited to handling routine administrative functions, as opposed to the document-imaging applications that have long been the bread and butter of production workflow. Forms-based workflow is a logical upgrade capability for corporate intranets, many of which utilize HTML forms for database query, retrieval, and updates. Almost half of all Web pages use forms to gather information, according to a November 6, 1995 *Computerworld* article.

However, Web-based products are similar to production workflow products in the skill level required to develop and deploy the applications — you don't expect end users to develop corporate Web pages for electronic-commerce applications, and you probably won't ask them to develop your Web-based workflow applications either. Web-based offerings allow your developers to define processes ranging from simple to complex, with the sophisticated routing capabilities they've come to expect from production workflow toolkits.

Web-based workflow can be understood as a fresh new synthesis of forms management, database management, document management, and Internet/intranet services, with a smattering of security thrown in. The architecture of Web-based solutions typically consists of the following components:

- **Workflow process-modeling tools:** Web-based workflow process-definition tools are graphical and flowchart-oriented. They are very similar, if not identical, to those used with production solutions. They model the same types of workflows — sequential, parallel, concurrent, and conditional — to varying degrees of complexity. Where Web-based tools differ is not so much in the type of workflow supported as in how workflows are executed — across the Web versus over distributed document/databases.

- **Web authoring and forms design tools:** Any Web-authoring tool can be used to build HTML forms for workflow and various data query, display, and collection applications. Most of the industry is moving quickly to HTML Version 3.2, which provides enhanced support for forms tables and applets.

- **Web browsers and form fillers:** Browsers are the universal workflow client application in this market segment, and can usually interface to most vendors' Web-based workflow products, though vendors may have optimized their products to interoperate with one of the leading browsers (that is, Netscape Navigator and Microsoft Internet Explorer). Browsers are usually acquired for general Web-surfing applications, but can be seamlessly redeployed for workflow applications, as long as they support requisite security standards, such as Secure Sockets Layer (SSL), which authenticates and encrypts transactions between browsers and servers. In the context of workflow applications, browsers download HTML-formatted worklists, inboxes, documents, and forms from Web servers, enabling users to initiate, process, and monitor work items. They provide a user interface for completing forms and querying document locations and status. Some Web-based workflow vendors may have built *plug-in* software modules for specific browsers to support client-based forms display, filling, validation, and processing. Some vendors allow the browser to download Java applets as needed to support client-side forms filling and processing.

- **Web servers:** Web servers may be regarded as a component of the enactment service as well as the primary interface for invoking external applications. Web servers (such as Netscape Commerce Server and Microsoft Internet Information Server) perform several functions in workflow applications. First, they provide user/browsers with access to workflow-relevant data, usually formatted as HTML forms or pages, and download applets that browsers require to complete forms properly. Second, they interface with workflow engines, discussed in the following paragraph. Third, they interface to legacy corporate database and document management systems to extract information requested by browser/users and update data records/fields submitted from browsers. Fourth, they maintain gateways to other communications services (such as e-mail, faxing, and paging) that may be used by Web-based users to transmit or receive work items.

- **Workflow engines:** Workflow engines, which may or may not be installed on the same computer as the Web server, determine the appropriate routing and processing of work items originated from or transmitted to user/browsers. For intranet applications, the workflow engine and most user/browsers will be installed inside the corporate *firewall*, which is a security gateway that enforces access controls and attempts to prevent malicious or inadvertent damage to corporate systems from hackers on the Internet. (For a description of the functions of workflow engines, refer to Chapter 4.) Suffice it to say that Web-based workflow is similar to production workflow in its reliance on server-based rules processing, execution, and monitoring. Contrast this to most messaging-based and suite-based products, which install the routing intelligence in the client-resident forms filler, form, and/or mail client. In Web-based intranets, the browser is very much a *thin client* with minimal application intelligence, which it may download as needed in the form of Java applets.

Suite-based Workflow

Suite-based products are bringing workflow functionality to the mass market by embedding it in the applications installed on the desktops of business users worldwide — typically, through simple commands, such as *add routing slip* and *send,* implemented in on-screen menu entries and buttons. Suite-based workflow products support document routing from within users' familiar groupware environments (such as Lotus Notes, Novell GroupWise, and Microsoft Exchange) or desktop application suites (such as Microsoft Office and Lotus SmartSuite). These and other suite-based workflow vendors and products are profiled in Chapter 10.

Suite-based workflow solutions are designed to allow users to route individual desktop application files (such as word-processing documents or spreadsheets) rather than folders, forms, or any other data structure that smacks of a formal process (though many workflow-enabled applications support electronic forms as another routable data type). Routed application files may be reviewed, annotated, or revised by recipients, depending on privileges bestowed by a document's originator. These applications are usually employed to facilitate and track the flow of a single document on a single occasion.

What best distinguishes suite-based workflow applications is their support for unplanned, one-time, sequential or parallel processes in which an author unilaterally distributes a document to peers for review, annotation, and revision. These applications facilitate structured interpersonal transactions rather than formal or semiformal business processes. Document originators use workflow-enabled applications in a very concrete, task-oriented manner and seldom intend to define a reusable process model. You can think of suite-based workflow tools, per the collaborative framework presented in Chapter 3, as *high media* tools, meaning they focus more on interpersonal data sharing than developing complex, repeatable process definitions.

Production workflow systems, by contrast, could be regarded as *high structure* environments, in that they emphasize complex process modeling and enactment capabilities. Consequently, production workflow is usually the preferred solution for companies seriously interested in reengineering business processes to a fine level of detail.

Messaging-based and Web-based workflow tools are intermediate solutions that emphasize a particular application data type — electronic forms — and support moderately sophisticated routing features. They stand poised to become a serious platform for business-process reengineering, if for no other reason than they can be deployed transparently within familiar desktop environments — in other words, e-mail clients and Web browsers — available to most business users.

Suite-based applications have been around since the late 1980s and have been recognized as a building block of any well-designed collaborative computing environment. These applications fall into two principal categories: office application suites and groupware application environments.

Office application suites are specially priced, bundled groups of networked desktop applications (for example, word processors, spreadsheets, presentation, and mail) that share a common user interface, functions, menus, icons, wizards, macros, and scripting languages. Applications route documents through transparent access to back-end mail services. Applications on a given platform route data among themselves using macro/scripting languages, dynamic data exchange, object linking and embedding, or similar capabilities.

Groupware application environments are collaborative application environments that integrate media-oriented collaboration capabilities (such as electronic messaging, computer conferencing, and document, database, image, and object management) and structure-oriented collaboration capabilities (such as workflow, time, and project/task management). Groupware products often look similar to application suites — the one major difference being that application suites can also be sold as separate, nonnetworked desktop applications. Groupware products, by contrast, usually integrate the constituent applications so tightly that they can scarcely be decomposed.

It is difficult to estimate the number of commercial groupware and desktop application suites that provide some workflow capabilities. However, many of the major products (for example, application suites such as Microsoft Office, Novell PerfectOffice, and Lotus SmartSuite, and groupware products such as Lotus Notes, Microsoft Exchange, and Novell GroupWise) provide routing capabilities.

Suite-based workflow applications may be acquired and implemented off the shelf or through value-added resellers. Users frequently use vendor-provided cross-application macros to provide routing capabilities that integrate existing desktop applications. The market is very horizontal, in the sense that these products are applicable to a wide range of industries and applications.

Suite-based workflow applications are very similar to messaging-based workflow solutions in architecture and capabilities — both categories rely almost exclusively on electronic messaging as a routing vehicle. However, some groupware products may provide some capabilities from all four categories: suite applications that use e-mail as a transport; messaging-based workflow tools that use structured electronic forms; Web-based workflow that publishes shared groupware databases and documents as HTML files; and production workflow that provides graphical process-design tools, shared document/database libraries, and workflow engines.

As workflow technologies gain popular acceptance, we might begin to see the different technologies coexist within any given enterprise, supporting different business processes and requirements. Suite-based applications would support unplanned, spur-of-the-moment requirements for document routing and review. Messaging-based workflow systems would support routine, forms-oriented administrative processes. Web-based workflow would support more unplanned EDI and electronic commerce applications. Production workflow systems would support heavy-duty business processes that draw on a range of networked enterprise-wide image, document, database, and other information systems.

Workflow capabilities may be embedded in larger, more complex application suites and groupware offerings. However, the workflow piece of such environments is usually simple, consisting of the following core components (see Figure 5-5 for a diagram of the typical suite-based application architecture):

- **Applications:** Almost any existing desktop application can be workflow-enabled, and almost any user can initiate a document routing procedure. E-mail systems can be given sequential-routing capabilities by modifying mail clients to automatically forward messages in accordance with a prespecified review chain. Applications can be upgraded to support version control and consolidation by modifying their file formats to embed links to alternate versions and ancillary information. In many suites, scripts and macros can be written to automatically generate documents in response to various events, pull information from various applications, encrypt and digitally sign the final document, wrap it in an e-mail envelope, address it, and submit it to the workflow environment. Object and data passing protocols such as DDE, OLE, and OpenDoc can be used to share information among applications.

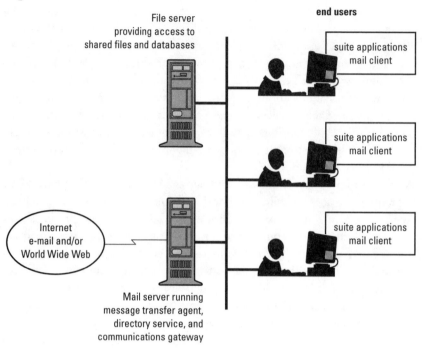

Figure 5-5
Configuration of typical suite-based workflow system.

- **Mail clients:** E-mail is the universal routing mechanism for workflow-enabled applications. As long as an application can speak MAPI, VIM, or some similar mail-enabling protocol, it can participate in automated workflows. After the application is implemented widely, the MAPI Workflow standard makes that MAPI-compliant mail system a preferred platform for deploying messaging-based workflow applications. Mail client conforming to the standard would be able to do double as work list handlers, with the ability to distinguish inbound workflow items and place them in appropriate folders. Users will be able to both send and receive mailed documents without exiting their applications. A less well-integrated mail client might require users to endure a clumsier procedure for receiving mailed documents: go into their e-mail application, save a message's file attachment to disk, and then return to the application appropriate to that file format to work on it. All workflow tracking would be performed through notifications generated by recipients' mail clients, as with messaging-based workflow applications.

- **Message transfer agents:** MTAs simply route messages and their file attachments, regardless of whether the originating applications are e-mail clients, word processors, spreadsheets, or something else. To the MTA, it's all just routable cargo, provided that it comes wrapped in an e-mail envelope with a valid recipient address. As with messaging-based workflow applications, the MTA has no knowledge whatsoever of the end-to-end process into which a particular message figures.

- **Message stores:** Message stores maintain copies of inbound and outbound messages before delivery. This is an important feature for workflow-enabled applications, which may be installed on mobile computers that connect infrequently to the MTA.

- **Directory services:** Directory services support message addressing by the mail client, as well as address mapping and routing by MTAs. Most workflow-enabled applications support addressing through a *routing slip* dialog box, similar to messaging-based workflow systems. Some applications might provide visual flowcharting tools for users to define complex routing procedures.

Summary

In summary, this chapter presented a detailed discussion of the four principal workflow technologies: production (or *filestore-based*), messaging-based, Web-based, and suite-based. The historical development of the workflow market and technology was presented, looking back at its origins in production workflow technology and highlighting the growing importance of messaging-based, Web-based, and suite-based products. The development of production workflow solutions into *business operating systems* capable of integrating diverse enterprise technologies was also discussed. Messaging-based, Web-based, and suite-based products were distinguished from production workflow solutions — the industry's historical mainstream — in terms of architecture, functionality, and applications.

Business readers should use this discussion to understand the fundamental architectural differences between commercial workflow solutions, in order to select the commercial solution that makes best use of their existing network platform, be it an e-mail system, Web-based intranet, or something else. Technical readers should use it as a basis for developing sophisticated applications that integrate tightly with existing databases, messaging systems, directories, security software, and other components of their enterprise network infrastructure.

The next chapter provides a detailed discussion of the application infrastructure essential to the successful deployment of any full-featured workflow solution, no matter which category it falls into. Workflow solutions depend on third-party application services (such as databases and messaging) in the same way that carbon-based organisms depend on food and water. These application services provide information that is necessary to sustain a living, breathing, workflow-enabled business process.

Having covered all three major segments of the workflow market, we're ready to look at some example software in Part III.

CHAPTER SIX

WORKFLOW APPLICATION INFRASTRUCTURE

W orkflow applications integrate a wide range of applications and systems in the user's local- and/or wide-area network. The difficulty is in the technical details of workflow application development. Your information systems and telecommunications staff will need to assist you in defining your requirements for interfacing workflow solutions with your current network infrastructure. This staff will shoulder the ultimate burden of integrating workflow applications into your environment.

This chapter helps you think through these workflow design, development, and implementation issues, by describing the principal systems with which you will need to integrate. The application systems and services required to support workflow applications include (in rough order of importance for most real-world applications):

- Image management
- Database management
- Document management
- Forms management
- Object management
- Product data management
- Project management

- Computer-aided software engineering
- Electronic messaging
- Directory services
- Internet and intranet services
- Electronic commerce services

Obviously, your specific interoperability requirements depend on your network and systems configuration, as well as on the intended functional scope of your workflow applications.

Image Management

Paper glut is the curse of modern bureaucracies and was the impetus for the development of modern workflow technology.

Workflow and image management technologies have been intertwined in the industry's consciousness since 1984, when the first commercial LAN-based document-image processing system was introduced by FileNet Corp. Most of today's market-leading production workflow vendors provide image processing products that route bitmapped representations of the original paper documents, entered through an optical scanner. Document-image processing systems are used principally to automate high-volume, back-office records-management functions, such as processing medical records, insurance claims, and tax returns.

Many companies in the document imaging market are systems integrators that provide complete LAN-based document-image processing solutions. These solutions generally include document scanners, image servers, optical storage devices, high-resolution viewing and editing terminals, laser printers, optical character recognition (OCR) workstations, and gateways to host data-processing systems, as well as customized software to tie it all together. The network configuration of a typical image management application is shown in Figure 6-1.

Based on the figure, the typical flow of a document image in a network environment is as follows:

- Scanned into a bitmapped format (for example, TIFF and GIF) with a document scanner
- Converted to ASCII computer-text using optical character recognition software
- Saved to optical storage (such as a Write Once Read Many (WORM) drive) on an image server
- Integrated or linked to database records or other files extracted from a file server or mainframe host processing system, perhaps through a gateway system that performs protocol or data conversions
- Retrieved, viewed, modified, and/or edited by users at terminals or workstations
- Printed to laser or inkjet printers attached to a print server

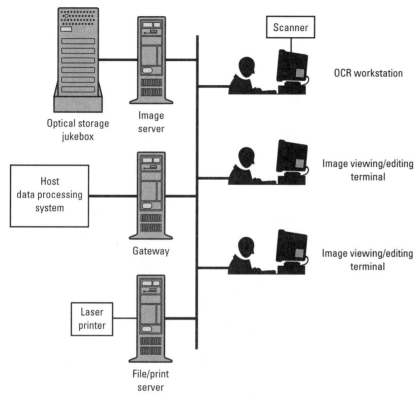

Figure 6-1
Typical image management system configuration.

Most document imaging products support these core capabilities. Commercial image management products differ in the following principal areas:

- Support for various server and client hardware platforms, operating systems, applications, and storage devices
- Image-file formats that can be captured, compressed, and manipulated
- Workflow process modeling and execution capabilities
- Document management capabilities
- Level of integration with host data-processing systems

Document-image processing systems are rapidly dropping in price but may still be a bit too pricey for many mainstream LAN/WAN applications. Imaging systems are bandwidth hogs, so any decision to invest in such products should be accompanied by a full-blown network traffic and design analysis, as well as a stringent cost-benefit analysis. Wherever possible, network managers should store document text and images on local servers to control traffic volumes over the WAN. Indexes and catalogs may be kept on central host processors separate from the documents to which they reference.

Support for high-capacity optical storage devices is essential to document-image processing, due to the very large sizes — in the megabyte range, especially where high-resolution color photographs are concerned — of a typical scanned-in document. Products typically work with optical disk jukeboxes, tape drives, and other removable, high-capacity storage media on the LAN. One very important feature is hierarchical storage management, which enables flexible migration of document image files among backup subsystems. Hard drives, for example, would store active files used regularly. Optical disk jukeboxes could be used for read-only access files, while off-line systems (such as tape drives) would be used for file archival.

Most document-imaging products support a variety of image manipulation capabilities, including enhancement, reduction, enlargement, cropping, compression, conversion, and OCR. The latter capability makes it possible to convert text in TIFF and other scanned images to ASCII format.

Image management standards

There are no industry-standard APIs for interfacing third-party applications to imaging servers. Today's imaging products generally provide vendor-specific APIs and development tools for various procedural (for example, C) and fourth-generation (for example, Visual Basic) languages. Vendor-proprietary APIs allow workflow applications to invoke manipulation capabilities on only one vendor's imaging servers. Workflow applications that invoke vendor-proprietary imaging APIs cannot interoperate with another vendor's imaging products without some reprogramming.

Some operating system and groupware products come bundled with image management capabilities that can be accessed by workflow and other third-party applications through published APIs, facilitating in-house development of image-based workflow applications. Novell has partnered with Kodak to provide Image-Enabled NetWare, a set of client software, server routines, and APIs that implement server-based imaging, document management, and storage management on top of Novell's market-leading network operating system. IBM/Lotus provides Lotus Notes: Document Imaging (LN:DI), a set of imaging APIs and client/server tools for that groupware environment. Microsoft has announced plans to bundle image viewing and manipulation capabilities in future versions of Windows 95 and Windows NT, making these features accessible through published APIs.

Many workflow applications can read, write, and manipulate image files in any or all of the following imaging-industry-standard formats for scanning, formatting, encoding, compressing, transmitting, decompressing, and outputting document images (see Table 6-1).

TABLE 6-1: IMAGE FORMAT STANDARDS

STANDARD	DESCRIPTION
ITU TSS Raster Groups III and IV	These are worldwide standards for encoding, compressing, decompressing, and transmitting black-and-white document images over analog and digital telecommunications circuits, respectively. They use lossless compression algorithms, which ensure that no document details are lost in transmission. Raster Group III is supported in the vast majority of fax devices worldwide.
TIFF (Tagged Image File Format)	This is a standard file format for describing, encoding, and storing bit-mapped, gray-scale still images. It is supported by most optical scanners and graphics manipulation programs.
GIF (Graphics Interchange Format)	This is a raster image format standard that is often used for in-line graphics embedded in and downloaded with HyperText Markup Language (HTML) pages on the World Wide Web.
JPEG (Joint Photographic Experts Group)	This is an ISO standard for describing, encoding, compressing, and decompressing continuous-tone, color still images. It uses a lossy algorithm that achieves superior compression to Raster Groups III and IV by eliminating some redundant pixels from the original image. JPEG is designed for compressing 24-bit full-color or gray-scale digital images of real-world scenes, rather than black-and-white sketches or motion pictures. It is a general-purpose technique for applications as diverse as photo videotex, desktop publishing, graphic arts, color facsimile, newspaper-wire photo transmission, and medical systems.
MPEG (Motion Picture Experts Group)	This is an ISO standard for describing, encoding, compressing, and decompressing continuous-tone, color moving images. MPEG defines a bit-stream representation for synchronized video and audio compression to fit a basic 1.5 Mbps bandwidth; a fellow standard, MPEG II, is designed to operate bandwidths between 4 and 10 Mbps. MPEG is supported in many multimedia application software products and in computerized video recording, storage, and playback devices, including CD-ROMs.
JBIG (Joint Bi-Level Imaging Group)	This is a standard for describing, encoding, compressing, and decompressing black-and-white still images. It supports progressive image buildup on the receiving display, which allows an image to be decompressed incrementally, starting with a low-resolution rendition, which then builds up to a higher quality image as more data is decoded. JBIG is applicable to fax devices and offers superior image compression to the ITU TSS Group III and Group IV Raster standards. It supports lossless compression.
EPS (Encapsulated Postscript)	This is an image description format that translates graphics and text into descriptions that instruct a printer or typesetter on how to draw them.

This list just scratches the surface of document-image formatting standards on the market today. Compression algorithms are a near-universal component of these standards, because scanned document images are huge and, left uncompressed, can easily swamp networks and storage devices. Many production workflow applications are designed to keep scanned images on the same storage device and simply route access paths and privileges to new users.

Document Management

Networks have made it next to impossible to find the document you want when you want it. Files are often scattered across myriad computers (that is, hosts, servers, workstations), storage devices, applications, directories, and file formats on the corporate LAN and WAN.

The rapid development of the World Wide Web has exacerbated the problem of maintaining, managing, indexing, and finding important business documents — under the guise of *home pages* — by allowing users to publish and distribute HTML-formatted files far and wide across the Internet and corporate intranets. The development of powerful *search engine* software (such as Digital Equipment Corp.'s Alta Vista) was an inevitable consequence of this trend, enabling users to tap into basic document-management functions — text indexing, search, and retrieval — in order to harness the unruly but infinitely rich information resources of this new world order.

Many commercial workflow tools integrate with third-party LAN/WAN document management software. LAN/WAN document management systems are hardware and software environments that provide services to create, retrieve, view, edit, organize, and route files across multiple systems and applications on the network. Document management systems usually manage text-based files, such as those produced by word processing, database, spreadsheet, and e-mail applications, which distinguishes them from document-imaging products (though, in fact, the two technologies have been merged to varying degrees in a growing number of products). See Figure 6-2 for the configuration of a typical network-based document management system.

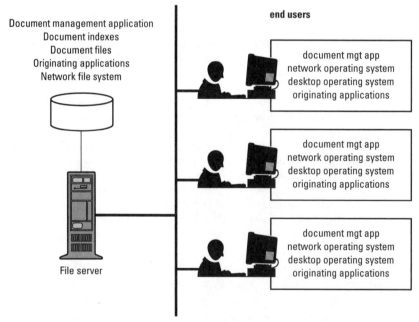

Figure 6-2
Configuration of typical network-based document management system.

Basic requirements

In recent years, the number, variety, and sophistication of network document management products have grown steadily. Users have come to expect the following document search, retrieval, and manipulation capabilities from most application environments:

- Load and run third-party or custom applications
- Automatically launch into a file and its associated application from a directory screen
- Automatically index the full text of documents
- Allow users to define document keywords, subjects, and extended profiles
- Search for files by full text, keywords, subjects, and profiles
- View the contents of files — through queries of full-text indexes, keywords, or profile screens — without loading the applications that created them
- Edit a file and save it in its original format
- Enforce document version controls by automatically saving revised files to new filenames
- Enable users to merge or consolidate multiple versions to a new master document
- Store commentary and graphical annotations about the file within the file itself
- Build hypertext cross-references between files (such as through HTML links)
- Provide flexible file import and export vis-à-vis third-party applications

Such document management capabilities are at the heart of groupware environments such as IBM/Lotus Development Corp.'s Notes and Digital Equipment Corp.'s TeamLinks products. Likewise, improved document search, indexing, and retrieval capabilities are supported in newer object-oriented generations of operating systems such as Microsoft Windows 95, UNIX, and Apple Macintosh.

Workflow capabilities are a natural extension of document management systems and are supported in many of today's commercial products. Users can check out files from server-based *virtual libraries,* route them to others for review and revision, track who has the file at any time, reconcile and merge multiple comments and versions into a final draft, and then check the resultant files back into the *library,* either overwriting the original or saving the final version to a different filename. Figure 6-3 graphically depicts the flow of such a document.

The core and historical root of the document management market is in text indexing and retrieval. Text indexing and retrieval systems were developed in the mid-1960s to support bibliographic research by legal assistants. The systems ran on mainframes and used complicated, cryptic query languages that baffled all but the patient, educated few.

Text indexing and retrieval technology migrated to PC and LAN platforms in the 1980s, making the technology easier to use. Full-text indexing, keyword searching, profile queries, and other capabilities became standard features of commercial word processors and other applications that allow users to originate and manage predominantly textual information. Indexes may be kept on the same storage volume with the documents referenced or, as indexes grow in size and begin to reference documents on many servers, may be kept on processors separate from the documents.

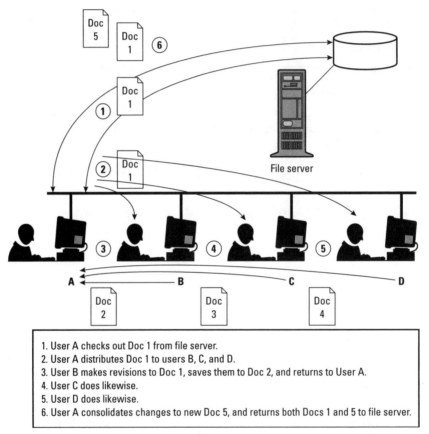

1. User A checks out Doc 1 from file server.
2. User A distributes Doc 1 to users B, C, and D.
3. User B makes revisions to Doc 1, saves them to Doc 2, and returns to User A.
4. User C does likewise.
5. User D does likewise.
6. User A consolidates changes to new Doc 5, and returns both Docs 1 and 5 to file server.

Figure 6-3: Typical flow of document checked out of virtual network library.

Today's vendors of network-based document management systems address two fundamental limitations of application-bound text-retrieval systems. First, vendors of word processing and other applications generally limit their products' text management functions to native file formats and ASCII text. In contrast, text retrieval system vendors pride themselves on their products' ability to read, index, and import more file formats than the next vendor's offering. Second, native text-retrieval capabilities are often rudimentary, limited to simple word searches. Full-blown text-retrieval systems usually provide sophisticated indexing and query capabilities — for example, the ability to determine which files contain the words *vehicle* and *accident* but not *truck*, referred to in the industry as a *Boolean search*.

Searching for the next generation of distributed document management systems? Look no further than the nearest Web server.

Design concepts

Developing document management systems to run over distributed networks poses many design and technical challenges. Users demand the ability to search for documents across a LAN/WAN without having to know where those documents reside physically or in what applications they were created. Users should be able to search for documents by such *attributes* as title, author, and keywords. The system should retrieve the document and *launch* into the associated application. A distributed document management system should be based on the following architectural concepts:

- **Multiplatform transparency:** The system creates a single virtual *library* of documents across the LAN/WAN or intranet through integration with native file management, security management, and other capabilities of the network operating system, such as Novell NetWare, Banyan Vines, or Microsoft Windows NT Advanced Server. Users search for and retrieve documents from within familiar applications (such as WordPerfect or Microsoft Excel) without having to know whether the files reside on a local server or one overseas. Distributed servers route all searches to the target storage device, wherever it may be on the LAN/WAN. System administrators establish user accounts, define access controls, set passwords, backup directories, and perform other chores transparently across all platforms.

- **Distributed *card catalog* utilizing extended file attributes:** The system should maintain a distributed database — basically a *search engine* — that contains detailed profiles of all documents on the LAN/WAN or intranet. The profiles should hold dozens of attributes for each document, including user-defined descriptors and system-generated information (for example, name, creation date, and size) culled from native file systems. Finding the right document across a vast network could be as simple as querying this distributed *card catalog*.

- **Flexible search tools:** The system should support document searches by various file attributes, as well as profile queries, full-text searches, simple and complex Boolean searches, wildcard searches, and proximity searches. Users should be able to store customized, reusable text query profiles in the system. In response to queries, document *hits* should be ranked by relevance to user requirements. Keywords should be highlighted within documents when displayed.

- **Security management:** The system should provide consistent access controls across the LAN/WAN. Access rights should have to be defined only once for each user and each document. The same set of access controls should follow users to any workstation and documents to any other volume on the network.

- **Concurrency and version management:** The system should allow multiple versions of a document to be present on the network while clearly identifying the latest version. When several people edit the same document concurrently, their changes should be saved to different versions, each with its own queriable profile and attributes. Administrators should be able to set limits on the number of versions the system maintains of any document and specify the disposition (for example, deletion and archiving) of older versions.

- **Storage management:** System administrators should be able to transfer documents between LAN/WAN storage devices without having to inform users, who only see a single virtual distributed-storage system. New files should be automatically stored on disk volumes prespecified by system administrators, based on file types and other attributes contained in document profiles. File replication, backup, and archiving could also be controlled by parameters specified in document profiles.

- **Application development support:** Client front-end applications could be linked to document management servers through fourth-generation-language (4GL) application programming interfaces (APIs), data-sharing protocols such as Dynamic Data Exchange (DDE), object-invocation protocols such as Object Linking and Embedding (OLE), and macro programming languages built into commercial applications.

The Web is the future

Anybody searching for the next generation of distributed document management systems should look no further than their nearest World Wide Web (also referred to as Web) server. The Web is quickly becoming the preferred filestore for Internet electronic commerce, superseding vendor-specific environments such as IBM/Lotus Development Corp.'s Notes, which are typically devoted to intraorganizational applications. Figure 6-4 presents an architectural overview of distributed, hyperlinked Web-site *home pages*. As illustrated in detail in Chapter 9, workflow vendors are starting to port their products to run over the Web, supporting both intra- and interorganizational document routing applications. Vendors in the burgeoning Web-based workflow market include Action Technologies, Banyan Systems, JetForm, Novell, Reach Software, Ultimus, and WebFlow.

Multiplatform transparency, distributed search tools, and standard application programming interfaces are inherent to the Web. Unlike the hierarchically organized file management systems bundled with most operating systems, the Web is a purely decentralized *virtual library*. Embedded cross-references can be established from any Web *page* to any other local or remote Internet resource. Services such as Yahoo! and Excite allow users to search the world for Web-resident information with as little as a single query. Authoring new Web applications is facilitated by near-ubiquitous implementation of the HyperText Markup Language (HTML) document formatting/hyperlinking and Java application-development standards.

Look for future generations of document management systems to support Web searches as easily as they can locate documents on a multiserver corporate LAN/WAN.

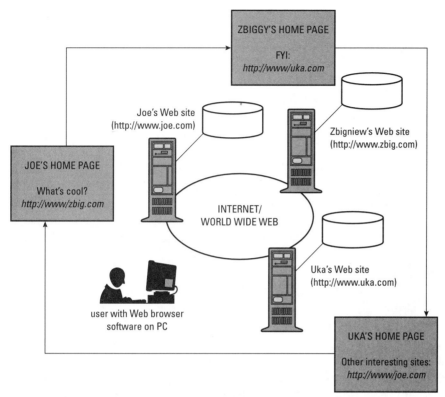

Figure 6-4
Architectural overview of distributed, hyperlinked World Wide Web home pages.

Document management standards

The document management industry is currently a hotbed of standardization activity, reflecting the increasingly document-centric, network-computing world of the late 1990s. Document management and retrieval systems are being groomed as the preeminent workhorse application on enterprise networks, edging out database management systems (DBMSs) as the primary medium for collaborative computing. At least 80 percent of corporate electronic information is kept in document form, rather than in databases, according to Frank Gilbane, editor of *The Gilbane Report on Open Information and Document Systems* (Cambridge, MA), and the proportion is likely to grow. The Web, with its ubiquitous *home pages,* is the prime example of the new generation of document-oriented enterprise computing.

Workflow applications often revolve around server-based document stores and, increasingly, Web-based *virtual libraries.* Consequently, workflow systems will increasingly invoke standard APIs to index, search, retrieve, and manage distributed document libraries. Standard APIs are being developed to support transparent access to document stores across multiple file formats, applications, and network locations. In addition, standard file formats have been developed to support cross-platform interchange of structured, multimedia, manipulatable, high-fidelity electronic documents.

The leading document management APIs are ODMA (Open Document Management) and DMA (Document Management Alliance).

ODMA, developed by the Association for Information and Image Management (AIIM) and introduced in mid-1994, has been incorporated in document management, workflow, and other applications from Novell, Saros, Action Technologies, Xerox, Kodak, PC DOCS, and other vendors. It consists of platform-independent APIs that enable document management systems to be integrated with word-processing, spreadsheet, desktop publishing, and other applications. ODMA provides document management systems with a unified command set for opening files, generating full-text indexes, performing profile and keyword searches, and tracking document versions across many formats, applications, and servers. It also supplies desktop applications with a standard interface for accessing document management systems to search for and open files across the network. The standard spares document management and retrieval system vendors from having to revise their products to integrate with each new release of desktop applications such as Novell, WordPerfect, and Microsoft Word.

The Document Management Alliance was established in April 1995 under AIIM auspices, absorbing two competing standardization efforts: Document-Enabled Networking (spearheaded by Novell and Xerox) and Shamrock Document Management Coalition (sponsored by Saros, IBM, and others). DMA is developing uniform APIs for execution of file searches across multiple, heterogeneous document management systems, flat-file databases, file servers, network operating systems, and potentially any other data store. DMA will allow many document management applications to share a common document repository. The standard will support all ODMA function calls and provide additional data-access, security, administration, conversion, and printing capabilities.

One of the core functions of document management systems is to locate and open files in multiple formats. Almost every application on the market has its own vendor-proprietary file format, but many can read from and write to a range of other vendors' formats, as well as a growing assortment of open industry-standard formats. The most familiar industry standards are the American Standard Code for Information Interchange (ASCII) flat, tab-delimited, and comma-delimited file formats, which comprise a common denominator for exchange of purely textual documents. ASCII's primary limitations are its inability to embed graphics and convey information on a document's originating application, internal structure, formatting, appearance, or links to other documents. To remedy these limitations, a growing assortment of industry-standard file formats have been introduced in the past several years — sometimes by standards bodies or vendor consortia, in other cases by single vendors trying to leverage their market influence. Table 6-2 presents leading document-formatting standards, which will increasingly be routed and managed by workflow applications.

TABLE 6-2: DOCUMENT FORMAT STANDARDS

STANDARD	DESCRIPTION
SGML (Standard Generalized Markup Language)	SGML is a longtime ISO and ANSI standard language used to tag the structural elements in a document, such as titles, headers, sections, paragraphs, and footnotes. These tags — essentially structured character strings within ASCII files — are used by desktop publishing, layout, and other applications to interpret how a document originated in another application should be formatted and organized. SGML does not describe a document's originating application, author, typeface, type size, or graphics layout.
ODA (Open Document Architecture)	ODA, another longtime ISO standard, is similar to SGML in many respects. However, ODA supports structural tagging of a wider range of documents, ranging from simple text-only files to complex documents containing text, raster graphics, and computer graphics with complex layout specifications.
HTML (Hypertext Markup Language)	HTML, administered by the World Wide Web Consortium, is an extension to SGML that has become the standard format for Web home pages. HTML tags describe a document's internal structure and links to external files, servers, and Internet sites, which may support Web, File Transfer Protocol (FTP), Wide-Area Information Services (WAIS), Usenet/Network News Transfer Protocol (NNTP), Gopher, or other Internet application services. HTML tags indicate where the interpreting browser software should embed icons, highlighted text, or other graphical elements that represent hyperlinks. When mouse-clicked by the user, hyperlinks invoke the referenced section, page, service, or Web site, causing the resource to be downloaded automatically for display in the user's browser.
PDF (Portable Document Format)	PDF, developed and promoted by Adobe Systems, Inc., supports cross-platform high-fidelity document distribution between dissimilar operating environments and applications. PDF documents retain their original layout, with the text, graphics, and photographs appearing at the highest resolution available on the recipient's monitor, printer, or other output device. Design parameters of the original typeface — the size, width, and style of characters, for instance — are transmitted with the PDF file so they can be replicated on computers that do not have the original typeface. Other PDF advantages are the ability to bundle document outlines and graphic thumbnail representations with documents and the standard's inherent support for alternate file-compression schemes. PDF allows document originators to embed textual links among documents on a given volume, but, unlike HTML, lacks support for cross-network hyperlinking. PDF is based on 7-bit ASCII code and Adobe's PostScript page-description language, a near-universal technology for interfacing disparate operating systems and applications to printers. Adobe Acrobat software is required to produce and read PDF files; to establish the standard, Adobe has basically given the readers away for free, and they are often bundled with commercial CD-ROMs or are freely downloadable from many Web sites. Several comparable standards have been promoted by other vendors (e.g., Novell Inc.'s Envoy; Farallon Computing, Inc.'s Replica; and No Hands Software, Inc.'s Common Ground), but none has gained the significant industry support enjoyed by PDF.
Postscript	As previously noted, PostScript is a page-description language, developed by Adobe, that is supported by the vast majority of desktop publishing applications and laser printers. PostScript files consist of the textual content swaddled in extensive control code, which tell the printer or other output device how to layout the document precisely in terms of type face, size, graphics, and other elements.

You can easily spot today's standard file formats if you've spent any time on the Web. Many organizations publish documents on their Web sites and typically make the files available in ASCII, SGML, ODA, HTML, PDF, and/or PS, recognizing that most users' applications will be able to read at least one of these formats.

Database Management

Database management systems have long been the principal platform for development of mission-critical corporate applications. Databases are at the heart of most production workflow applications. One database contains the process model, which specifies the routes, roles, and rules for document routing. Another database may contain information on the current location and status of documents in process. Others may contain the information input by users in on-screen electronic forms. Figure 6-5 illustrates the central role of databases in production workflow environments.

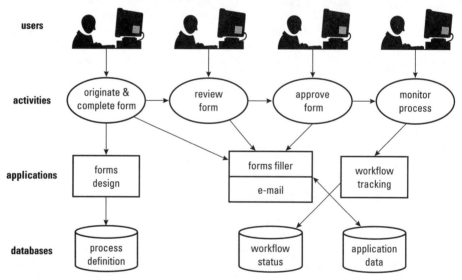

Figure 6-5
Role of databases in production workflow environments.

What chiefly distinguishes database management from document management systems is the format of the information they manage. Document management systems can handle the vast majority of information used in any organization, whether it's semistructured and unstructured information, such as the running text in a word-processing file, or e-mail message. Database management systems, by contrast, work principally with alphanumeric character text that can be organized into a highly structured set of files, records, and fields. This information can be linked, indexed, sorted, and filtered in countless ways, which makes databases well suited to supporting complex, custom-built, function-specific applications. Many databases provide a common pool of information accessible to multiple applications.

Over the past 30 years, database technology has evolved through successive waves of technical innovation, none of which has completely replaced the previous generation. Database architectural options continue to proliferate, absorbing, enhancing, and enriching previous generations. One can identify the following evolutionary tracks in database technology: data modeling, network platform, and application development.

Data modeling

Data modeling refers to alternate conceptual models used to organize relationships among data. Different database technologies are based on divergent data-modeling paradigms: hierarchical, network, relational, and object[1] (see Table 6-3).

TABLE 6-3: DATA-MODELING PARADIGMS

DATA-MODELING PARADIGM	DISCUSSION
Hierarchical	The first generation of database management systems in the 1960s organized data records as a hierarchical set of separate files. Hierarchical databases can be designed to handle rigidly structured, high-volume, batch-processing applications very efficiently, such as payroll and inventory processing (in other words, the mundane but essential back-office functions for which computers have been used since the 1950s). However, they make it difficult for users to query, sort, or reorganize data according to any hierarchy other than that which has been hard-coded into the application. Consequently, they are ill suited to flexible data reporting. For example, if a sales database is organized by quarters, regions, salespeople, invoices, and products — in that descending order — the user cannot easily produce per-customer sales reports, because this would require scanning records throughout the entire database. This could eat up considerable computing time, especially if the database is very large.
Network	To bring greater flexibility into data modeling while maintaining superior performance for high-volume transaction processing, network database management systems were introduced in the 1970s. Network databases allow a single record to be linked to — hence, sorted and queried through — multiple hierarchies. In the example just presented, a network database could be set up to facilitate reporting by customers, products, quarters, or any other attribute that its programmers considered important. These relationships are established through permanently programmed links between data files. However, generating reports based on attributes other than those specified in the original data schema requires some reprogramming. Network databases are a bit too complicated for most users to manage or query directly.
Relational	Around the same time that network databases were being introduced, the concept of relational databases — which allow greater flexibility in data query and retrieval — was being proposed by Edgar Codd, a researcher at IBM. Relational databases consist of one or more tables, each of which contains multiple rows (records) and columns (fields). Figure 6-6 shows the structure of a typical multitable relational database. Unlike preceding database technologies, relational databases require no predefined hard-coded links between data files. Instead, users can retrieve information from multiple tables

(continued)

TABLE 6-3: DATA-MODELING PARADIGMS *(continued)*

DATA-MODELING PARADIGM	DISCUSSION
Relational *(continued)*	simultaneously using a query language, as long as the tables contained some common data fields or keys (e.g., customer social security number). The relational database industry has standardized on the Structured Query Language (SQL), which is still a bit too complex for most users. Many mass-market database products provide a user-friendly graphical interface that translates queries into SQL (pronounced sequel) so that they can be processed by relational databases. Even with user-friendly query screens, navigating a relational database can be a chore, especially if the database has, as many do, dozens or hundreds of distinct tables. In addition, relational databases are usually designed for ad-hoc queries and reporting. Consequently, they may perform poorly on high-volume transaction processing, for which large companies, even to this day, may turn to hierarchical or network databases.
Object	In the 1980s, object databases were introduced as an extension and enhancement to relational technology. Object databases support complex record structures that include data plus compact representations of repeating data, pointers to other records and files, and links to executable software associated with the record. Object design allows programmers to eke greater performance out of database applications by explicitly linking related files and records. It also facilitates development of hypertext and multimedia applications by enabling complex relationships between information and software modules to be embedded in the data structure.

Network platform

The term *network platform* refers to alternate architectures for distributing database application components among such network nodes as mainframe computers, servers, and user workstations. In a network environment, a database application can be implemented on any or all of the following platforms: terminal-to-host, file server, and database server (Table 6-4 discusses these alternatives and Figure 6-7 presents them graphically.)

CUSTOMER DATA

CUSTOMER ID#	NAME	STREET ADDRESS	CITY	STATE	ZIP
00001	Wilfred Wolfe	3 Oak	Cary	IL	31060
00002	Henna Harlow	12 Elm	Cary	IL	31060
00003	Barbara Bunning	256 Ash	Gary	IN	53105
....	....	....	....	....	....
....	....	....	....	....	....
....	....	....	....	....	....
nnnnn	....	....	....	....	....

key field

PRODUCT DATA

PRODUCT SKU#	MANUFACTURER	DESCRIPTION
621126	Bilbo & Associates	Picnic basket
538142	Moxham Brothers	Marble statuette
976543	Alphasoup Inc.	Flexible straws
....	....	....
....	....	....
nnnnn	....	....

key field

ORDER DATA

CUSTOMER ID#	PRODUCT SKU#	QUANTITY ORDERED	UNIT PRICE
12351	555193	6	10.00
35212	789345	25	5.95
68715	311112	30	25.50
....	....	....	....
....	....	....	....
nnnnn	....	....	....

Figure 6-6
Structure of typical multitable relational database.

TABLE 6-4: DATABASE NETWORK PLATFORM ALTERNATIVES

DATABASE NETWORK ARCHITECTURE	DISCUSSION
Terminal-To-Host	This — the oldest approach — involves installing the database and application logic on a single mainframe, minicomputer, or other host computer. The user can update or query the database by logging into the host from a dumb terminal or a PC emulating such a terminal. For example, consumers use automated teller machines as dumb terminals to access account information contained in a bank's mainframe database. Terminal-to-host applications enable a centralized administrative staff to maintain tight controls on data security, integrity, and updates. This architecture allows many low-cost terminals to be deployed to the field, but precludes the ability of users to perform specific data manipulation or display off-line from the host.
FIle Server	This approach — which grew in popularity with the spread of PCs and LANs in the 1980s — involves placing the database on a central server computer and application software on networked PCs. When users want to retrieve information from the database, they download all database files to their PC and execute the query locally. This approach takes advantage of the network, processing, and storage capacity available to PCs. However, application performance can degrade as the size of the database grows and the network reaches capacity.
Database Server	This approach uses the server to perform all database functions that require significant computing horsepower, such as database retrieval, indexing, updating, sorting, joining, and query execution. Users enter queries from their PCs and receive only the data records, fields, and values they requested — not a copy of the entire database. The PC — typically a less powerful machine than the server — provides a graphical user interface for data entry, display, and manipulation. This approach allows system administrators to maintain tight database controls, minimize network traffic, and balance processing workloads across the network. Some products support execution of queries, updates, and other real-time database operations across multiple network servers. When distributed servers are used, specialized transaction monitor software is required to ensure the security and integrity of end-to-end database operations.

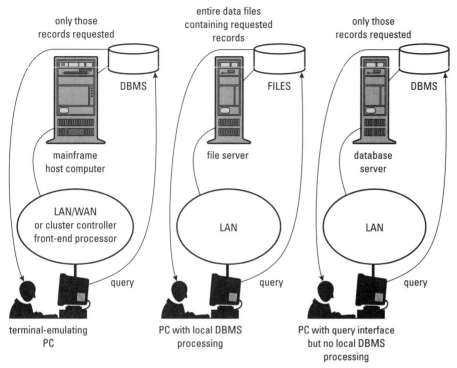

Figure 6-7
Architectural alternatives for implementation of networked database.

Application development

Application development refers to alternate approaches for writing database applications, including procedural programming languages, fourth-generation languages, and object-oriented programming (see the discussion in Table 6-5).

TABLE 6-5: DATABASE APPLICATION PROGRAMMING TECHNIQUES

PROGRAMMING APPROACH	DISCUSSION
Procedural Programming Languages	Since the 1950s, procedural programming languages (such as COBOL, FORTRAN, BASIC, and C) have been used to write computer software. These languages require software developers to specify the precise procedural logic, user interface design, and environmental variables governing program operations. To interface a program to a database management system, a programmer must embed calls to the appropriate query language (such as SQL) in their source code. Source code must then be translated, or compiled, into low-level machine code executable by the computer.

(continued)

**TABLE 6-5: DATABASE APPLICATION PROGRAMMING
TECHNIQUES** *(continued)*

PROGRAMMING APPROACH	DISCUSSION
Fourth-Generation Languages	The 1970s saw the introduction of fourth-generation languages (4GLs) as a means for improving programmer productivity by partially automating the production of source code. 4GLs hide the details of the previous three language generations — referring to procedural, assembly, and machine code, respectively — from programmers. This feature frees programmers to focus on application design rather than low-level machine operations such as memory and task management. One critical feature of 4GLs is code generation, whereby procedural code is created automatically once the programmer defines a high-level application functional specification. Often, applications can be prototyped rapidly with 4GL tools that support graphical definition of input screens, database structures, and report formats. One caveat about 4GLs is that the resulting source code may be inefficient, requiring programmers to make modifications at the procedural level. Vendor-specific 4GLs are usually included with relational database management systems.
Object-Oriented Programming	The 1980s marked the emergence of the new school of object-oriented programming. This paradigm is grounded on the notion that programming work can be accelerated by reusing existing software modules — referred to as objects — when developing new applications. Objects, each of which performs a well-defined set of functions, contain executable program code plus the data that may be manipulated by this code. An application may consist of a single object or multiple objects, which interact by passing requests and data in structured messages. New objects can easily be spun off from existing objects, inheriting most capabilities from their forebears while taking on additional functions and privileges. Most practitioners of object-oriented programming utilize graphical development tools and specialized languages such as C++ and Smalltalk. Object-oriented programs may work with standard relational databases or tap into multimedia object databases.

Who uses what

Every one of these database management and programming technologies is supported somewhere in today's workflow market. Increasing numbers of users will adopt object-oriented programming and databases to support high-performance, distributed, multi-media workflow applications. In the future, expect more and more database management system vendors to include workflow capabilities with their products. It's not much of a stretch for database vendors to add document-routing capabilities to their report-writing modules.

Most or all of these programming techniques will be used by workflow application developers and integrators to design and code client applications and integrate the enactment service with third-party applications and databases. When selecting workflow products, make sure that your MIS staff is experienced with the programming tools bundled with that environment.

Database management standards

The dominant data query, retrieval, update, and administration language for relational database management systems (RDBMSs) is Structured Query Language (SQL), which has been in use since the 1970s. Most production workflow products provide interfaces to SQL-based RDBMSs residing on network database servers.

SQL provides an English-like language for formulating queries, but it is a bit too arcane for the average end user, who rarely is required to learn it. Instead, RDBMS products let users specify query parameters (that is, files, fields, filters, and sort criteria) through dialogue and check boxes. Alternately, SQL statements may be embedded within a full-featured programming language (such as C or COBOL) prior to compilation and invoked transparently from within the end application.

SQL is an ANSI- and ISO-certified standard. However, many RDBMS vendors have developed proprietary extensions to it. SQL extensions usually serve a worthy purpose — namely, to enhance performance, functionality, and database integrity. However, they have the unpleasant side effect of inhibiting application portability and interoperability among DBMS systems.

Several leading RDBMS vendors have developed SQL extensions that have won considerable support throughout the industry. These SQL extensions are supersets of the standard language, supporting a wider range of data access, retrieval, and administration capabilities. They are implemented through software *drivers* that translate client database calls into formats that can be interpreted by RDBMS servers. The most popular SQL variants are ODBC (Open Database Connectivity) and IDAPI (Independent Database Application Programming Interface). Championed by Microsoft and included in its Windows Open Services Architecture (WOSA), ODBC is by far the most popular SQL implementation. It defines APIs used by applications to call local or networked RDBMSs. It was based on the Call-Level Interface specification developed by the SQL Access Group (a multivendor consortium that is now part of X/Open). ODBC is now supported in all major operating environments. Promoted by dBASE vendor Borland, IDAPI has been eclipsed in the RDBMS API wars by Microsoft's ODBC. Still, it's not uncommon to find both IDAPI and ODBC APIs supported by many commercial RDBMS products, because they provide similar extensions to the underlying SQL command set.

Standards bodies are still wrangling with the problem of how to bridge among different SQL implementations. Efforts are also underway to extend SQL into a language that can access and manage complex, specialized, user-defined data objects.

Forms Management

Business forms are documents designed with processes in mind. A form gets completed, routed appropriately, and, once approved, used as the basis for authorizing some action.

Forms automation

Commercial electronic forms management and routing products have been around since the late 1980s, pioneered by companies such as JetForm. Forms routing has also become a standard feature of many image-based workflow products. Anybody who submits the same form regularly (for example, timesheets, expense forms, and purchase requests) to a sluggish bureaucracy has probably wondered whether the process could be automated.

Electronic forms applications are usually implemented in conjunction with corporate database management, document management, and e-mail systems. Figure 6-8 presents an architectural diagram of the typical forms management application. Typically, a filled-in form corresponds to one or more database records. Forms are routed as attachments to e-mail messages. When a form reaches the end of a review chain, its field contents are either written to new records or they update existing records in a database. Further detail on the architecture of these applications is provided in Chapter 5, under "Messaging-based workflow components." Messaging-based workflow systems primarily utilize electronic forms interfaces. Keep in mind, however, that electronic forms are used across all segments of the workflow market (though the characteristic user interfaces of production, Web-based, and suite-based workflow products are folders, HTML pages, and desktop application files, respectively).

HTML, discussed earlier, is in many ways a forms standard — indeed, it has become the world's first widely cross-platform forms formatting standard. HTML pages can be structured and displayed as on-screen forms, which seem to be the preferred format for many Web-based electronic commerce applications.

One little-recognized cousin of forms management is the long-established discipline known as *electronic data interchange (EDI)*. In use since the early 1970s, EDI is the electronic exchange of standardized business documents — such as specifications, purchase orders, invoices, and bills of lading — between companies and their suppliers, distributors, customers, and other trading partners. EDI documents may be exchanged through batch or store-and-forward network connections, or through courier delivery of documents on magnetic tape or disk. EDI is standard practice worldwide for many large companies and has been mandated for all the U.S. government's small purchases by 1997.

In EDI parlance, a standard form is known as a *transaction set*, which may be bundled for transmission into larger aggregations known as *functional groups* and *interchanges*. Collectively, transaction sets define a sort of universal data dictionary for electronic commerce, specifying the syntactics and semantics for business forms down to the field level. Transaction-set standards are defined for the U.S. by the American National Standards Institute's X12 working group and for the rest of the world by the United Nations' Electronic Data Interchange for Administration, Commerce, and Transport (EDIFACT) group.

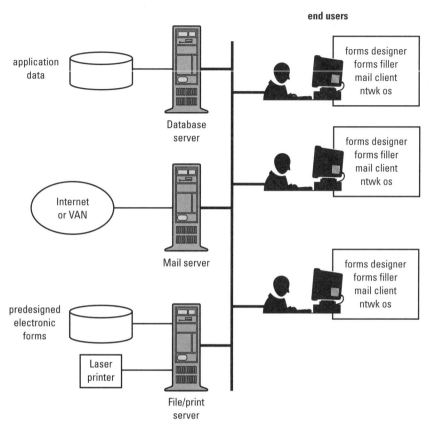

Figure 6-8
Architecture of typical networked forms management application.

Typically, an EDI transaction set is filled with information either extracted automatically from corporate information systems or translated from an internal format. The filled-in transaction set is then transmitted to the trading partner via dial-up connections or packet-based, value-added networks. Increasingly, companies are sending EDI documents over existing e-mail networks using such protocols as X.400, X.435, Simple Mail Transfer Protocol (SMTP), and Secure MIME (S/MIME). Upon receiving an EDI transaction set, the trading partner translates it into a format comprehensible to its internal information systems. Figure 6-9 depicts the inter- and intra-organizational flow of typical EDI document.

One weakness of EDI — compared to traditional intra-organizational forms management — is the lack of automated means for one trading partner to track the location and status of an electronic document after it has entered another's internal network and system. This situation is remedied partly by the X.435 messaging-based protocol, which allows trading partners to request delivery, receipt, and forwarding notifications for EDI documents upon their arrival at third-party mail-systems. In addition, ANSI and EDIFACT have defined transaction-set standards that allow trading partners to send each other functional acknowledgments indicating that a document has been processed or approved.

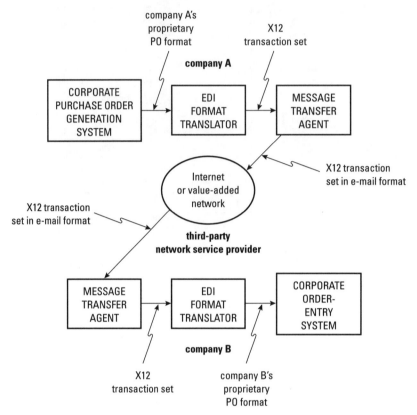

Figure 6-9
Inter- and intra-organizational flow of a typical EDI document (in this case, a purchase order).

Expect EDI and traditional forms management to merge on the Web and Internet. Universal forms routing requires a shared database or filestore — such as the Web — from which documents can originate and to which their contents will be written at the process' end.

Object Management

Object management standards are proliferating with no clear pull-ahead winners, reflecting the dynamic, innovative, unsettled state of object-oriented computing in the mid to late 1990s. Workflow systems are becoming increasingly object-oriented and will depend intimately on the object services provided by invoked applications.

Object-oriented computing supports flexible integration of images, documents, databases, executable software, and other digital items into compact, reusable application structures. Objects are paving the way for truly *componentized* computing environments, such as Microsoft's long-awaited *Cairo* upgrade to Windows NT. The day is soon coming when applications will completely merge and decompose into a spectral palette of capabilities applicable to any object (for example, text, graphics, images, video, and audio) on the user's computerized work surface. This will be truly document-oriented computing — specifically, compound multimedia documents — as opposed to the traditional application-oriented paradigm with which most of us are familiar.

Fully distributed object-oriented computing requires that identifiers and attributes of all executables and files be registered in a master network directory and maintained in repositories, ensuring that these items can be easily located and invoked when needed. A functional entity known as an *object request broker* (*ORB*) performs the registry, directory, and locator functions in a network environment. Several competing, overlapping object-computing standards have been proposed, each of which defines APIs, ORB mechanisms, and repositories:

TABLE 6-6: OBJECT MANAGEMENT STANDARDS

STANDARD	DESCRIPTION
COM (Component Object Model)	Microsoft's COM framework is based on Object Linking and Embedding (OLE), the company's established file-sharing technology allowing any file created in an OLE-compliant Windows application to be placed into an open document in another OLE-compliant application. COM will serve as the basis for the object-oriented Windows NT file system (i.e., Cairo), supporting a wider range of attributes than the native file systems provided with MS-DOS or Windows NT. COM will, as necessary, redirect file operations to other object-oriented environments (discussed momentarily) or to legacy file, document, database, and image environments. COM's limitations include the inability to run in environments other than Microsoft Windows, lack of support for distributed objects, and lack of support for object-oriented concepts such as attribute inheritance.
CORBA (Common Object Request Broker Architecture)	The Object Management Group (OMG) vendor consortium released the first CORBA specification in 1990, and it has since achieved wider industry support than any other object architecture (though OLE/COM have achieved greater installed base due to Windows' desktop ubiquity). CORBA provides high-level object wrappers that allow one application to locate and invoke data and functions internal to another application. CORBA 2.0 supports distributed objects, supports TCP/IP (the fundamental Internet/intranet protocol) as a standard telecommunications protocol for linking diverse applications objects, and uses OLE 2.0 to interoperate with COM object stores. The Internet Inter-ORB Protocol (IIOP) is a subset of CORBA that allows distributed applications to interoperate over the Internet and intranets. IIOP is central to Netscape's Open Network Environment for Web-based distributed computing; consequently, IIOP is likely to form the basis for many intranet-based workflow applications.

(continued)

TABLE 6-6: OBJECT MANAGEMENT STANDARDS *(continued)*

STANDARD	DESCRIPTION
DSOM (Distributed System Object Model) OpenDoc	DSOM, developed and promoted by IBM, supports distributed objects and full-featured object-oriented programming functionality. It is based on CORBA and, like that specification, supports location transparency, which allows client applications to invoke objects without knowing their physical location. Apple and Novell have spearheaded the OpenDoc standard, which allows many application modules — known as *applets* — and externally originated information objects to be invoked within a single electronic document. The OpenDoc specification supports COM/OLE, CORBA, and DSOM function calls.

Product Data Management

Production workflow systems designed to track the flow of computer-aided design (CAD), computer-aided manufacturing (CAM), and other engineering documents are referred to as product data management (PDM) solutions. PDM solutions increasingly handle CAD/CAM drawings, graphics, and other digital objects output from multi-vendor application packages, which requires a common product-data interchange format. The dominant PDM interchange formats are IGES (Initial Graphics Exchange Specification) and CGM (Computer Graphics Metafile).

IGES is an ANSI standard that has been adopted by the U.S. government for exchange of computerized graphical design models capable of modification and revision by the recipient. IGES specifies a standard file structure and attributes for characterizing digital, vector-based product design and manufacturing models. The IGES format can be used to describe geometric, topological, and nongeometric product attributes. It accommodates both two- and three-dimensional product models, including edge-vertex, surface, and solid models.

CGM, like IGES, defines a standard file format for exchanging graphical product depictions, and has also been adopted as a standard by ANSI and the U.S. government. However, unlike IGES, CGM files are simply pictures — they are not analytical models that can be revised directly by the recipient. A graphics metafile is intended for information interchange between a source system and a target system that are not necessarily compatible.

Project Management

Project-management applications allow managers to define a package of work to be performed by a group of people, including such details as participants, responsibilities, tasks, dependencies, resources, deliverables, outputs, hours, costs, and budgets. Typically, these software tools allow projects to be defined through textual inputs and displayed in such graphical formats as PERT flowcharts and Gantt charts.

The spread of PC LANs and departmental e-mail in the 1980s created a growing niche for network-enabled project management systems built around a generalized workflow process model. Typically, these tools use e-mail to support team coordination in any or all of the following ways:

- Managers e-mail task assignments and supporting documentation to project participants.

- Staff returns e-mail replies indicating their acceptance, rejection, postponement, or delegation of tasks.

- Staff reviews a list of outstanding to-do items posted to their e-mail inboxes or a bulletin board.

- Staff automatically launches desktop applications needed to work on documents attached to e-mail messages.

- Staff receives automatic e-mail reminders of upcoming project milestones or due dates.

- Staff sends periodic messages reporting on task status.

- Staff sends messages reporting task completion.

Today's workflow tools may be regarded as a species of project management software. Production workflows may be modeled as recurring, replicable projects, while ad-hoc workflows can be regarded as one-time or loosely structured projects. Document routing to a prespecified list of people is equivalent to formal task assignment. E-mail-based reminder, notification, and completion-reporting procedures are almost identical between production workflow and network-enabled project management environments.

Computer-aided Software Engineering

Computer-aided software engineering (CASE) tools support development of database applications by enabling systems analysts to depict pertinent organizational interrelationships graphically. CASE tools — which grew in popularity in the 1980s and have long been associated with the UNIX operating system — support business-process reengineering by allowing analysts to model and redefine processes, roles, and relationships. Indeed, the process-modeling tools included with production workflow systems bear a strong resemblance to CASE tools.

Many CASE tools support the popular *entity-relationship (E-R) modeling* approach, which, though geared to database design, is also a handy framework for building workflow process models. (See Figure 6-10 for a typical E-R diagram.) E-R modeling is grounded in three basic concepts: entity, relationship, and attribute[2], presented in Table 6-7.

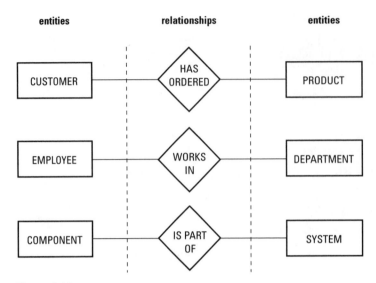

Figure 6-10
Typical entity-relationship diagrams.

TABLE 6-7: ENTITY RELATIONSHIP DIAGRAM TERMINOLOGY

TERM	DEFINITION
Entity	A person, place, or thing that can be defined clearly and described in a database; some common entities described in corporate databases include tasks, customers, distributors, products, employees, facilities, and accounts.
Relationship	A role or association among entities that can be defined clearly and described in a database; some common relationships include customer *orders product* and employee *contacts customer.*
Attribute	A property or characteristic of an entity or relationship that can be represented in a database; some attributes of customer include name, address, phone number, social security number, and current account balance.

Clearly, workflow participants, documents, databases, and other media can all be modeled as entities, while routes, roles, and rules may be regarded as relationships among these entities. Attributes correspond to fields in process-model data files associated with entities or relationships.

One dimension of user-friendliness in a workflow product is the ease of developing a graphical process map — for example, being able to use familiar paradigms such as E-R modeling, organizational charts, or plain-English task specification — to define the workflow. A user-friendly process map would facilitate quick process definition and revision by the average manager. It could also be used by the average staffer to view the current location and status of documents in process.

Electronic Messaging

Electronic mail, since its introduction in the late 1960s, has been designed primarily to support the free-form nature of interpersonal communications. E-mail systems have been used to facilitate unplanned, unstructured, or semistructured workflows. Figure 6-11 presents the architecture of a typical e-mail system.

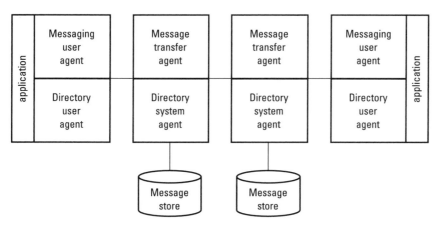

Figure 6-11: Configuration of electronic messaging system.

The typical interpersonal e-mail-based workflow might involve mailing a note and attaching a file to several recipients. Some of the recipients may choose to reply to the originator, who might reply to only one of the replies but send a carbon copy of that *second-order* reply to all the original recipients. Meanwhile, a couple of original recipients may have independently forwarded the original note and file attachment to several other people, who could *redline* (revise) the document and e-mail it directly back to the originator or indirectly through the people who forwarded it. The originator may end up with several marked-up or revised copies of the original document. All the while, the original note may have generated a volley of replies-on-replies with new file attachments between the original correspondents.

However, e-mail systems increasingly have begun to support more structured workflow processes, such as sequential routing, conditional routing rules, and version tracking. In addition, e-mail address directories are being enhanced — via technologies such as X.500 Directory Services and NetWare Directory Services — to include workflow-relevant information, such as a person's job title, organizational role, and approval authority.

One can expect e-mail and production workflow products to become ever more tightly intertwined. Already, e-mail has become an integral component in most production workflow products, providing a mechanism for circulating automatic reminders, prompts, notifications, and warnings in response to process events. E-mail systems provide ubiquitous infrastructural capabilities (such as directory services, user in-boxes, routing rules, and message transfer agents) that could be adapted to support high-volume structured processes. For example, workflow items and standard e-mail messages could be displayed in a single in-box (rather than separate in-boxes, as required by most current workflow systems), distinguished by different icons, type-faces, or some other convention.

Electronic messaging standards

Electronic messaging systems have become a ubiquitous adjunct to production workflow applications, which usually employ e-mail to generate user notifications. By contrast, messaging- and suite-based workflow systems use electronic messaging systems as their basic transport vehicle for routed documents. Today's workflow enactment services can invoke any or all of the popular messaging protocols discussed in Table 6-8 (not to mention the myriad vendor-proprietary e-mail technologies).

TABLE 6-8: ELECTRONIC MESSAGING STANDARDS

STANDARD	DEFINITION
MAPI (Messaging Application Programming Interface)	This standard, developed by Microsoft and primarily geared to Windows environments, defines APIs that can be used by client applications to connect with MAPI-compliant mail servers to address, submit, and retrieve messages. Service provider interface (SPI) software must be installed on the mail server to support connections with MAPI clients.
VIM (Vendor Independent Messaging)	VIM, championed by Lotus and other e-mail vendors, provides APIs functionally equivalent to MAPI. VIM was developed from the outset to run in many vendors' desktop and network operating environments.
MHS (Message Handling Service)	MHS, developed by Action Technologies and Novell, provides standard procedures for client software to send and receive messages. MHS will send as a message any ASCII file that is placed in the proper directory and conforms to Novell's Standard Message Format (SMF). An MHS mail server periodically looks in specified directories for outgoing mail and automatically routes them to recipient addresses.
X.400	X.400 Message Handling Service, developed by the International Standards Organization (ISO) under the Open Systems Interconnection (OSI) umbrella, defines a set of protocols to connect mail user agents (UAs), message transfer agents (MTAs), and message stores (MSs). X.400 e-mail addresses are long, unwieldy character strings.
SMTP (Simple Mail Transfer Protocol)	SMTP — also known as RFC821 — is the e-mail *lingua franca* of the Internet. SMTP e-mail addresses use the concise naming format (e.g., jkobielus@juno.com) that have become familiar worldwide. SMTP's basic message-format standard — RFC822 — only supports plain ASCII-text messages. The most common way of supporting nontext information in an SMTP message is encoding and decoding it with the UUENCODE and UUDECODE protocols, respectively, a technique that does not indicate the nature of the contents so encoded.

STANDARD	DEFINITION
MIME (Multipurpose Internet Messaging Extensions)	MIME — also known as RFC1521 — is an extension to SMTP that supports descriptive tagging of binary file attachments and identifies the originating applications. MIME also supports several types of nontextual message contents, including JPEG images, Graphics Interchange Format (GIF) raster images, PostScript files, and digital audio.
CMC (Common Messaging Calls)	CMC, defined by the X.400 Application Program Interface Association (XAPIA), provides a master set of APIs that can be used by desktop applications to connect to MAPI, VIM, SMTP, MHS, or X.400 mail systems.
IMAP4 (Interactive Mail Access Protocol 4)	IMAP4 is an Internet standard protocol that supports a uniform, operating system-independent means for messaging user agents to manipulate and retrieve message data (e-mail or bulletin board) on remote message stores, on which the messages may be retained for future reference.
POP3 (Post Office Protocol 3)	POP3 is an Internet standard protocol (RFC 1225) that supports a uniform, operating system-independent means for messaging user agents to retrieve message data (e-mail or bulletin board) on remote message stores, from which the messages are automatically deleted. It requires that the messaging user agent have an IP address.

In addition, production workflow systems can be set up to send and receive fax documents, communicate with pagers, and even send synthesized voice messages to voice mail systems. Any messaging medium can be plugged into a production workflow system, thanks to advances in computer telephony.

Directory Services

Directory services are an essential component of workflow environments. Directories are application tools that workflow process designers and users invoke to look up and specify recipient addresses.

The dominant directory services standard is X.500, a worldwide ISO standard. X.500 describes an architecture for integrated query, viewing, updating, and management of dissimilar directories across the network. X.500 applications incorporate directory system agents (DSAs), which manage the entirety or a well-defined branch of a distributed directory, and directory user agents (DUAs), which support user query of DSAs. (See Figure 6-12.)

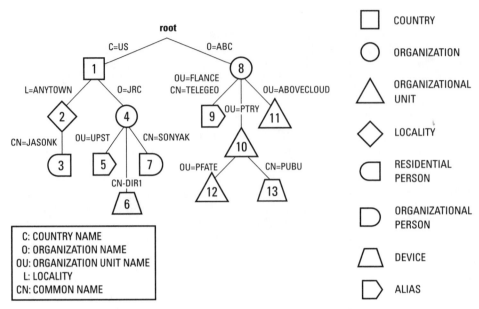

Figure 6-12: A typical (but fictitious) X.500 directory information tree.

One of the initial applications of X.500 has been for synchronizing dissimilar e-mail directories to support transparent message addressing and transport. However, X.500 is a high-level capability that may be adapted for use in workflow, electric data interchange (EDI), electronic software distribution, and other network applications. X.500 defines directories as hierarchical, object-oriented information *trees*, in which every network user and resource may be designated by a unique identifier, called a *relative distinguished name.*

One emerging standard that appears to be taking hold in the Internet/intranet arena is the Lightweight Directory Access Protocol (LDAP), a streamlined version of the X.500 Directory Access Protocol. LDAP supports anonymous browsing of directories, authenticated communications between a client and server directory, and referencing and replication between directory servers. Microsoft and Netscape have announced that LDAP will be supported in future versions of their operating environments and browsers.

Two vendor-proprietary directory services worth mentioning are Novell NetWare Directory Services (NDS) and Banyan StreetTalk, both of which are being developed into Web-based directories to support these vendors' moves into Internet/intranet services. Novell NDS provides an X.500-like directory service for the NetWare 4.X LAN/WAN environment. NDS provides a rich hierarchical, store of user, device, and resource information that can be used in workflow, e-mail, and other applications. NetWare's predominant share of the network operating system (NOS) make NDS and its predecessor, the NetWare Bindery, a ubiquitous resource for application developers.

A great advantage of creating intranet applications for browser-based desktops is that the application need only be developed once.

Banyan's X.500-like StreetTalk directory service, initially provided only with the vendor's VINES NOS, has been on the market much longer and achieved a more enthusiastic core clientele than NDS. The company has in recent years ported StreetTalk to run on NetWare and other NOSs.

Internet and Intranet Services

Workflow applications are increasingly running over the Internet or intranets, which are company-specific segments of that global, packet-based, distributed data network. Consequently, Internet/intranet applications, services, and protocols — especially those associated with the World Wide Web — will increasingly be invoked by workflow client applications and enactment services.

One hallmark of the Internet/intranet trend is the ubiquity of Web browsers on corporate desktops everywhere. Browsers are nudging out desktop operating systems (such as Microsoft Windows and Apple Macintosh) as the preferred client operating environments for the new generation of *network-centric* applications (such as workflow and groupware). Browsers are being developed with a dizzying array of sophisticated features — supporting capabilities such as object management, streaming video/audio, 3-D real-time modeling, transaction security, and smart forms — to prepare them for mainstream corporate applications. Ironically, operating environments (such as Microsoft's upcoming Windows 95 upgrade, code-named *Cairo*) are being made more browser-like, by incorporating more network-oriented hyperlinks in all components and providing stronger, integrated network access tools for applications.

One great advantage of developing intranet applications for browser-based desktops is that the application need only be developed once, and, if properly implemented, will execute and display the same across all operating systems, including Microsoft Windows, Macintosh, UNIX, and OS/2. Browsers such as Netscape Navigator and Microsoft Internet Explorer operate consistently across all these environments. This cross-platform advantage has not escaped the notice of short-staffed MIS departments everywhere, which partly explains why we're seeing an explosion of Web-based intranet applications.

One sign of the dramatic growth of intranet applications is Netscape Communications' recent announcement that it ships several times as many copies of its Web server software package for internal corporate applications as for publishing over the public Internet.

Open industry standards define the network *plumbing* underlying intranets, resulting in a fiercely competitive market in which no one network vendor dominates, commercial offerings are diverse, and the pace of technical innovation is breathtaking. The fundamentals of intranetting are now common knowledge throughout information systems and network staffs everywhere. Any system that communicates over the Internet must speak the ubiquitous Transmission Control Protocol/Internetwork Protocol (TCP/IP) and specify network, host, and service addresses defined in the Domain Name Service (DNS). At a higher level in the protocol stack, applications may use any of the service protocols listed in Table 6-9.

TABLE 6-9: INTERNET AND INTRANET STANDARDS

STANDARD	DEFINITION
HTTP (Hypertext Transfer Protocol)	HTTP is the basic network protocol of the Web. It supports communications between browsers and Web sites, using addresses referred to as *Uniform Resource Locators* (URLs). It allows a browser to specify whether it wants to communicate with a site supporting Web HTML filestores or some other Internet service, such as File Transfer Protocol, Simple Mail Transfer Protocol, Network News Transport Protocol, Wide-Area Information Services, and Gopher.
FTP (File Transfer Protocol)	FTP supports remote downloading and uploading of files across the Internet.
SMTP (Simple Mail Transfer Protocol)	SMTP, discussed previously in Table 6-8, is the Internet's primary e-mail transport protocol.
NNTP (Network News Transport Protocol)	This is the standard Internet protocol for connecting distributed, asynchronous, text-based discussion groups, referred to as *Usenet groups*.
Java	This is the dominant programming language for World Wide Web applications. Java, developed by Sun Microsystems, is a platform-independent, object-oriented language based on a simplified subset of C++. Java application components, called *applets*, are invoked from within HTML pages, either automatically upon page retrieval or manually through user commands and/or mouse-clicks. Upon invocation, applets are transmitted from Web servers to the user's browser, where they are security-checked, interpreted, and executed on the fly, with results displayed within the current HTML page displayed.
Javascript	This script language allows programmers to control invocation, execution, and display of Java applets from within the Web browser or server, supporting a greater degree of application partitioning than is possible with the Java language alone.

Electronic Commerce Services

Electronic commerce standards provide specifications for exchanging and securing commercial transactions over networks. These standards describe value-added functionality that works in conjunction with database, document, messaging, directory, and other network services. Workflow management systems are increasingly being developed for electronic commerce applications, based on incorporation of EDI and transaction security technologies.

As noted previously, EDI standards describe the formats and protocols used to exchange structured electronic business documents between organizations and their trading partners, such as customers, distributors, and suppliers. The principal standards — ANSI X12 and UN EDIFACT — in this arena describe the structure and contents of *transaction sets* for conveying electronic business documents such as purchase orders and invoices. Typically, corporate information systems invoke EDI translation software to create X12 or EDIFACT transaction sets or map received transaction sets into proprietary corporate formats.

To exchange EDI transaction sets over networks, companies might use dial-up modem connections or convey transaction sets as file attachments to e-mail messages. Companies that go the latter route might use the X.435 protocol — which interoperates with X.400 e-mail backbones — thereby taking advantage of sophisticated content-handling, delivery, notification, and security options not available on normal X.400 communications. The S/MIME protocol is designed to provide similar value-added functions to support message-oriented electronic commerce over the Internet's MIME/SMTP mail backbone.

Strong transaction security is the *sine qua non* of high-volume electronic commerce. Transactions typically involve exchange of money, intellectual property, and other items of commercial value. Consequently, they must be electronically signed, sealed, delivered, and tracked in a manner that can stand up in a court of law. Workflow applications provide a natural environment for electronic commerce transactions and may invoke firmware or software modules incorporating any or all of the security standards listed in Table 6-10.

TABLE 6-10: ELECTRONIC COMMERCE STANDARDS

TYPE OF STANDARD	DISCUSSION
Public-Key Cryptography	Developed in the 1970s, public-key technology has made it possible to deploy mass-market cryptographic applications on a global basis. Every user on a public-key system has two different asymmetrical keys for encrypting and decrypting information; one key is published to the world and the other is held in private. User A's public key may be used by others to encrypt items that may be read only by User A, who uses his private key to decrypt them. Likewise, User A may encrypt an item with his private key and make it generally available; others may decrypt it by using his public key, in the process certifying that he was the one who encrypted it. This scheme spares users from the logistical difficulties inherent in

(continued)

TABLE 6-10: ELECTRONIC COMMERCE STANDARDS *(continued)*

TYPE OF STANDARD	DISCUSSION
Public-Key Cryptography *(continued)*	exchanging and securing secret keys prior to exchanging encrypted items. Most commercial implementations of public-key technology license basic mathematical algorithms from RSA Data Security, a firm founded by cryptography pioneers Rivest, Shamir, and Adelman. The world's dominant public-key standard is RSA's Public Key Cryptographic Services-7 (PKCS-7). The Internet community has developed a PKCS-based secure messaging standard, Secure MIME (S/MIME), that integrates with MIME mail backbones and supports user authentication, message encryption, and content tamperproofing. A shareware public-key algorithm called *Pretty Good Privacy (PGP)*, developed by Phillip Zimmermann, has achieved significant presence in spite of its questionable legal status (RSA claims that PGP infringes on some of its key PKCS patents).
Digital Signatures	A digital signature is a string of data bits that the computer uses to mathematically certify that a document was originated by a particular user and has not been altered or tampered with during transmission. To produce a digital signature, a user's application reduces the document's bit sequence to a condensed string known as a *hash*, and then encrypts the hash with the user's private key. The digital signature is typically attached to the document for transmission. At the receiving end, the digital signature is decrypted with the user's public key and compared to the document hash; if the two match, the document is authentic and was not tampered with. The main digital signature standards are PKCS-6 from RSA Data Security and the U.S. government's Digital Signature Algorithm (DSA).
Encryption	Symmetrical cryptography (i.e., same key to encrypt and decrypt) predates public-key cryptography by generations — some might say it's been around since the dawn of civilization. As noted previously, symmetrical schemes require that secret keys be conveyed or transmitted to the recipient prior to exchange of encrypted materials, which makes them vulnerable to theft or misappropriation of keys. Nevertheless, symmetrical schemes have proven to be more efficient for fast, high-volume encryption and decryption. In many commercial applications, a symmetrical scheme — such as the U.S. government Data Encryption Standard (DES) — will be used to encrypt the body of a message, while public-key cryptography will be used to encrypt the DES key so that it may be transmitted along with the DES-encrypted message.
Certification Authorities	In public-key systems supporting mass-market applications, it may be necessary to post public keys to a bulletin board or other shared network device. To obtain the public key that authentically belongs to a particular user, someone would retrieve that user's public-key certificate from a bulletin board maintained by a recognized certification authority (CA), such as a government agency. The certificate would contain the person's name, public key, other descriptive information, and the CA's authenticating digital signature. The dominant standards for public-key certificates are X.509, an ITU TSS specification, and PKCS-6, developed by RSA Data Security. These standards define formats for certificates that bind user identifiers to public keys.

TYPE OF STANDARD	DISCUSSION
Internet Transaction Security	Growth of Internet-based electronic commerce depends on widespread implementation of security services integrated with Internet application protocols. One set of protocols would support secure connections between Web browsers and servers, addressing such concerns as user authentication, content confidentiality and integrity, and origin and delivery nonrepudiation. Contenders include Secure Sockets Layer (SSL), proposed by Netscape Communications, and the Secure HyperText Transfer Protocol (SHTTP), championed by Enterprise Integration Technologies. Another standard — called *Secure Electronic Transactions (SET)* — will support secure payments involving consumers, merchants, banks, and credit card processors. SET is the product of MasterCard International Inc. and Visa USA's agreement to merge separate standardization efforts to produce a universal secure payment protocol. The protocol enables consumers to pay for goods on the Internet using authenticated X.509-based *electronic certificates* in lieu of credit-card or debit-card numbers.

Summary

In summary, this chapter has presented a wide-ranging tour of technologies that make up the application infrastructure for a workflow management system, including image management, database management, document management, forms management, object management, product data management, project management, computer-aided software engineering, electronic messaging, directory services, Internet/intranet services, and electronic commerce services. The roles or functions of each technology in workflow applications have been discussed, and the dominant and emerging standards for each technology have been presented.

Now that you have a broad grasp of workflow system architectures, functionality, application design principles, and standards, you can move on to Part III, which presents a market survey of leading vendors of production, messaging-based, Web-based, and suite-based workflow products. The basic business and technical issues discussed in Parts I and II are reinforced through examinations of workflow vendors' product families and strategic directions. After the market survey, the book closes with Part IV, which lays out evaluation and implementation guidelines for ensuring successful implementation of workflow-enabled business-process reengineering.

PART III
Market Survey
*Workflow Solutions for Serious and
Casual Business Users*

This part provides a survey of workflow management products available at the time of publication in each of the categories discussed in Chapter 5. Brief vendor profiles and product overviews are presented for the most noteworthy solutions. Workflow product development strategies are presented for the largest, most influential software vendors, including Action Technologies, FileNet, IBM/Lotus, JetForm, Novell, Microsoft, and Wang Laboratories.

CHAPTER SEVEN

PRODUCTION WORKFLOW MARKET

Today's production workflow vendors have converged on this market from various starting points. Most come from a document-image processing background, having added structured routing, real-time tracking, version control, and other workflow capabilities to their products. Some are document management system vendors that have added workflow functionality to support complex editorial processes. Some computer-aided design (CAD) system vendors are providing workflow functionality to support concurrent workgroup engineering. Other production workflow vendors come from a business-process-reengineering background, emphasizing visual-process definition and flowcharting tools.

Market Trends

This chapter provides an overview of leading vendors and solutions in the production workflow market. The vendors profiled are among the most dynamic companies in the production workflow market and they set the pace and direction of the industry in general. Before delving into vendor profiles, however, consider some of the trends presented in Table 7-1. You might conceivably use this as a checklist to determine whether a production workflow vendor is keeping up with the state of the art.

TABLE 7-1: PRODUCTION WORKFLOW MARKET TRENDS

CATEGORY	TREND	EXPLANATION
Operating Platforms	Continuing maintenance of multiplatform workflow environments with increased product development emphasis on Microsoft's Windows NT, Windows 95, Exchange, and BackOffice platforms	You'll be able to run most production workflow products on your legacy desktop and server operating systems, especially the various flavors of Microsoft Windows and UNIX. However, workflow vendors will be nudging you in the direction of a more complete embrace of Windows and the various database, electronic messaging, groupware, Internet/intranet, imaging, security, and other products developed for that environment. Microsoft is the technological thread underlying much of modern distributed computing, and it would be nearly impossible to develop a production workflow application that does not rely on one or more interfaces to the infrastructure laid down by Mr. Bill Gates. Over time, you'll find it increasingly difficult to obtain workflow products that run on other operating systems — especially the Macintosh and OS/2 — at either the desktop or server.
Architectures	Increasing re-architecting of production workflow environments to interface or interoperate with e-mail-based, Internet/intranet, and groupware environments	Some production workflow vendors — most notably, Action, FileNet, Keyfile, and ViewStar — also provide messaging-, Web-, and/or suite-based solutions, with increasing linkages between these environments. The line between production and messaging-based workflow is blurring, especially as production workflow vendors build interfaces to Microsoft's MAPI Workflow Framework, which supports mail-server-based workflow-engine functionality (more on messaging-based products in Chapter 8). Likewise, you may have increasing trouble distinguishing production and Web-based workflow tools (featured in Chapter 9), because the distinction has been fuzzy at best from the start. This green and growing niche began as an extension of production workflow tools to work over the Internet and corporate intranets. Similarly, your production workflow application may be able to access distributed document and database management systems maintained under groupware environments (such as Lotus Notes and Microsoft Exchange), blurring the line between production and suite-based workflow.
Application Development Tools	Increasing reliance on graphical, industry-standard, object-oriented form, folder, application, and process design tools	Production workflow vendors — including all market leaders featured in this chapter — boast of their graphically oriented tools for laying out electronic forms and folders, embedding application functions in those objects, and specifying workflow routing and handling procedures associated with the objects. Any serious production workflow vendor should allow you to embed ActiveX controls in workflow objects, using Microsoft's popular object-oriented application development tool; it should also support CORBA interfaces to heterogeneous network and computing resources.

CATEGORY	TREND	EXPLANATION
Third-Party Business Process Reengineering (BPR) Tools	Increasing integration with third-party business-process reengineering tools for process design and tracking	Production workflow vendors are realizing they may not always be able to provide *best of breed* process-modeling tools, so they increasingly support interfaces to popular, third-party BPR tools. In this regard, BancTec, FileNet, and Wang are the most proactive production workflow vendors, providing interfaces for third-party BPR tools to export their process models so that they can be executed on the vendors' workflow enactment services. Your business analysts may already be using one or more BPR tools and may prefer that the company select a compatible workflow enactment service.
Dynamic Rerouting	Increasing emphasis on dynamic workflow rerouting to support fast-changing business processes, on-the-fly delegation, and exception handling	Relaxing their traditionally rigid routing procedures, production workflow products increasingly allow end users to reroute work items as needed, within boundaries defined by process modelers and workflow administrators. Of the vendors featured in this chapter, BancTec, FileNet, InConcert, and Keyfile boast dynamic rerouting capabilities. This feature enables production workflow systems to support some of the ad-hoc processes that have traditionally relied on messaging- and suite-based tools.
Object-Oriented Databases	Increasing utilization of distributed, object-oriented database and filing systems	Production workflow systems increasingly store and manage workflow process definitions, control data, workflow-relevant data, and application files in object-oriented databases, which provide a flexible, reusable repository for data and associated software routines. Object-oriented data repositories, found in most market-leading solutions, are designed to streamline and speed workflow application development and maintenance while maximizing code reuse. Your technical staff won't be able to manage production workflow applications without a strong grasp of object-oriented technology.
Workflow Management Standards	Increasing vendor compliance with emerging workflow industry standards	The WfMC's Workflow Reference Model (discussed extensively in Chapter 4) has defined the standard architecture and nomenclature for production workflow products and components. You should familiarize yourself with the Reference Model as a way of comparing rival production workflow solutions. You should also ask production workflow vendors to describe their level of support for the five technical interfaces specified in the WfMC Reference Model, especially Interface 4 (Workflow Application Programming Interoperability Functions). Support for Interface 4 would allow you to interface two or more vendors' enactment services, so that process definitions and control data can be shared and work items transferred between divergent workflow environments. This would allow your company to deploy different production workflow products across various regions or divisions with some assurance of cross-enterprise

(continued)

TABLE 7-1: PRODUCTION WORKFLOW MARKET TRENDS *(continued)*

CATEGORY	TREND	EXPLANATION
Workflow Management Standards *(continued)*		interoperability. Check out the WfMC's Web site for a current list of vendors that have commercial products complying with this and other interface standards, and to download copies of the standards documents. Of the production workflow market leaders, Action, BancTec, IBM, and InConcert have so far shown the greatest commitment to implementing WfMC standards in their products.
Database Management System Interface Standards	Increasing integration with third-party RDBMSs through ODBC-standard drivers	Production workflow products excel in their ability to pull information from all manner-of-legacy corporate databases, including those based on hierarchical, network, relational, and object-oriented database management technologies (discussed at length in Chapter 6). However, relational database management systems (RDBMSs) increasingly prevail and, with them, the Structured Query Language (SQL) for data retrieval and manipulation. In the past few years, Microsoft's Open Database Connectivity (ODBC) specification has achieved near-universal industry support as a standard software interface that allows one vendor's client or server application to retrieve information from another's SQL RDBMS. You'll find ODBC support mentioned in almost every workflow vendor's product literature.
Document Management System Interface Standards	Increasing integration with third-party document management and retrieval applications through ODMA and DMA standards	Similarly, the Open Document Management API (ODMA) and Document Management Alliance (DMA) specifications have been adopted as industry standards for interfacing applications to third-party document management systems. You'll increasingly find these standards supported by production workflow vendors, whose solutions rely on the ability to access, search, retrieve, view, and manipulate documents scattered across local and wide-area networks. Of the vendors profiled here, Action, AutoDesk, and FileNet report document-management system interoperability through ODMA and/or DMA.
Messaging Integration Standards	Increasing integration with third-party e-mail systems through MAPI and VIM standards	Traditionally, most production workflow products have interfaced with e-mail systems to transmit notifications, reminders, and status updates to users (using distributed database and document management systems to transport work items). This requires the ability of the workflow enactment service to invoke mail-client features and access mail servers through standard programmatic function calls. Most production workflow products interface to enterprise e-mail systems through either or both of two industry standards: Messaging Application Programming Interface (MAPI) and Vendor-Independent Messaging (VIM).

CATEGORY	TREND	EXPLANATION
Security Standards	Increasing emphasis on application security	Production workflow tools need strong security features to support electronic commerce and other mission-critical corporate applications. You'll increasingly find production workflow products incorporating various public- and secret-key cryptographic technologies to support authentication, access control, confidentiality, and tamperproofing services.
Vertical Market Workflow Application Templates	Increasing development of vertical-market workflow application templates	Production workflow vendors realize the importance of providing prepackaged application templates, which consist of electronic forms, process models, and other features geared to the needs of particular vertical industry applications. Vertical-market templates enable customers in those industries to minimize the amount of custom application development needed to implement production workflow systems. Templates also provide a convenient launching point for value-added workflow resellers to craft applications for the special needs of individual customers.

You'll find it increasingly difficult to obtain workflow products that run in non-Microsoft operating environments — especially the Macintosh and OS/2.

With these trends in mind, you should first review product offerings from the production workflow market's leading vendors, to be discussed shortly. This chapter's market survey provides an overview of each company, discusses the general architecture and functionality of its production workflow products, and outlines its workflow product development strategy. Contact each vendor directly (or, easier still, check their Web sites) for detailed information on specific products.

Pricing and Purchasing Notes

Pricing has been omitted from this survey because product prices change rapidly; often depend on the number of clients, servers, sites, nodes, and functional software modules supported; and may significantly understate the final cost of developing and deploying workflow applications. For up-to-date pricing comparisons, review the latest workflow market surveys in *Network World* and other trade papers. For a closer approximation of your final workflow implementation cost, create a detailed specification of your feature, configuration, and development/support requirements and then send it out for bids to multiple vendors, value-added resellers, and systems integrators. Make sure the project cost they quote you encompasses all necessary software, hardware, and technical development and integration services.

For a comprehensive listing of production workflow vendors and contact information, see Appendix A. Call these vendors to find the value-added resellers nearest to you. Most likely, vendors will refer you to resellers to support application development and integration needs.

The next few sections review the production workflow market leaders.

Action Technologies Inc.

Action Technologies, headquartered in Alameda, CA, is one of the most eclectic and innovative production workflow vendors. The company takes pride in holding the first workflow patents granted by the U.S. Patent Office. As discussed in Chapter 9, Action is also a pioneer in the Web-based workflow market.

Action specializes in developing and evangelizing new paradigms for process design and coordination, primarily through its workflow, e-mail, and business-process-reengineering (BPR) tools. What distinguishes Action from many BPR solution vendors is that it provides its own run-time workflow enactment service to implement process models composed with its flowcharting tools. This allows Action to offer a complete workflow management solution including all of the architectural components contained in the WfMC's Workflow Reference Model (see Chapter 4). Other BPR tool vendors on the market today (none of which yet provides its own run-time enactment service) are listed in Appendix A.

Action bases its workflow products on a language-oriented model of management and organizational effectiveness, formulated by company founders Terry Winograd and Fernando Flores. This model categorizes all utterances as *linguistic acts* of one sort or another, such as requests, promises, commitments, suggestions, and reports. Released in 1985, the company's initial product, The Coordinator (later sold to Da Vinci Systems, which was itself acquired by ON Technology Corp.), was a LAN-based e-mail system that provided the following groupware-style capabilities:

- Allowed users to assign topic categories, linguistic acts (for example, requests, promises, and commitments), and time-based response requirements to outbound messages
- Maintained topic-oriented linkages across multiple messages
- Presented users with lists of active promises and commitments
- Flashed reminders of pending or delinquent promises and commitments

ActionWorkflow System

Action introduced its current workflow product line, ActionWorkflow System, in 1992, a year after it sold The Coordinator product to Da Vinci. Common parentage notwithstanding, the two products are completely separate and distinct in design, functionality, and technology.

ActionWorkflow System consists of a process-modeling tool (ActionWorkflow Analyst), application development tool (ActionWorkflow Builder), and run-time workflow enactment service (ActionWorkflow Manager). ActionWorkflow Analyst incorporates a transaction-oriented process-modeling paradigm that is distinct from that which underlay The Coordinator. Per the ActionWorkflow framework, users define customers, performers, and conditions of satisfaction (including scheduling constraints) for the process as a whole, as well as for each milestone activity within the process. Each segment of the process is then broken down into the following four phases, each of which may be identified with a specific type of linguistic or conversational act:

- **Preparation:** The customer or performer proposes work to be done by the performer.

- **Negotiation:** The customer or performer enters into a cycle of offers and counteroffers, eventually agreeing on the work to be performed.

- **Performance:** The performer performs the work, reporting progress and, eventually, completion.

- **Acceptance:** The customer evaluates the work performed, declaring satisfaction or dissatisfaction, and possibly returning the work to the performer to be done over.

Action's modeling framework is sophisticated and definitely requires a significant learning curve for most corporate workflow implementers. It is well-suited to business-process-reengineering efforts driven by Total Quality Management concerns, such as increasing customer satisfaction and decreasing cycle time. ActionWorkflow Analyst supports development and optimization of graphical process maps incorporating the aforementioned concepts.

The next upgrade to the ActionWorkflow product line will incorporate an *open process modeling* paradigm, according to Rodrigo Flores, the company's vice president for product management. Users developing applications will be able to design processes via Action's current modeling approach or any other methodology they prefer. "We're going to let users elaborate whatever process-modeling methodology they're used to," said Flores. In addition, workflow application development will be simplified through the use of standard process templates, dialog-based process definition, Network OLE object orientation, and utilization of a scripting language in Visual Basic.

Developing actual workflow applications based on Action's process maps requires the ActionWorkflow Builder (see Figures 7-1 and 7-2), which associates activities with specific participants, routing rules, execution conditions, and databases. Running, administering, and monitoring the applications requires the ActionWorkflow Manager run-time workflow enactment service.

Action's products run over Microsoft Windows 3.1, Windows 95, Windows NT, and OS/2, with support for UNIX promised for the near future. ActionWorkflow System products are Microsoft BackOffice compatible, which means they integrate with Windows NT Advanced Server, the SQL Server RDBMS, Visual Basic development tool, and MAPI-compatible e-mail systems. (Action's workflow environment also interfaces with MHS- and VIM-compatible e-mail systems.) Action provides alternate versions of ActionWorkflow Manager that utilize Lotus Notes and SQL Server data stores to store workflow definitions and application data.

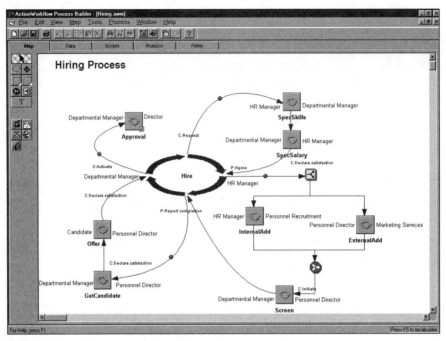

Figure 7-1
Model from ActionWorkflow Builder depicts a hiring process.

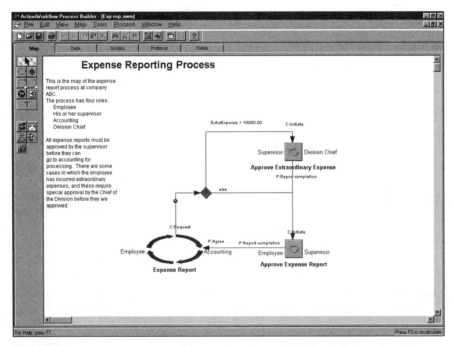

Figure 7-2
Model from ActionWorkflow Builder maps an expense reporting process.

Partnerships and plans

The company continues to develop add-on products that integrate third-party software with its workflow environment. It also provides third-party software developers with APIs and function libraries that allow desktop applications to access, filter, and manage worklists.

Action is actively introducing workflow management capabilities throughout the world of computing. Action is actively engaged in workflow product co-development efforts with a wide array of strategic partners, which, past and present, include the likes of IBM/Lotus Development, LaserData, Microsoft, Novell/SoftSolutions, ON Technology, Platinum, and Verity.

One of the company's more noteworthy efforts was co-developing the Message Handling System (MHS) e-mail specification with Novell, which is now supported by many LAN/WAN e-mail products. Since 1994, it has been working with document management vendors to integrate workflow capabilities with their products, primarily through ODMA and Shamrock API libraries. The ActionWorkflow DocRoute product provides intelligent routing, version control, notification, and other workflow functions for PC DOCS' DOCS OPEN, FileNet/Saros' Document Manager, and Novell's SoftSolutions. Through its Team Action initiative, Action is also developing vertical-market workflow applications with firms such as PeopleSoft Inc., which produces human resources and financial application software packages.

Action is committed to supporting open, standards-based workflow. At the time of publication, it had already demonstrated interoperability support for the WfMC's Client API in its product line. Action has withheld unconditional endorsement for future WfMC APIs, preferring to evaluate which ones to support and in what order. The company's own proprietary workflow APIs support a wider range of functions than the WfMC specification.

Autodesk Inc.

Autodesk, headquartered in San Rafael CA, has added workflow features to its market-leading computer-aided design (CAD) software products, transforming its network-based CAD tools into environments for concurrent engineering.

Though not a leader in the broader workflow marketplace, Autodesk has been included in this survey due to its predominant position in a production workflow niche known as *product data management (PDM)*. PDM products (such as Autodesk WorkCenter) are workflow-enabled CAD tools that help companies control the flow of product-related information from conception through specification, design, engineering, and manufacturing. Other PDM products include Hewlett-Packard's Work Manager and Adra Systems' Cadra.

Autodesk WorkCenter, introduced in December 1994, serves as a workflow and document management add-on to the company's Windows-based AutoCAD and

AutoCAD LT products, when installed in client-server configurations on Novell NetWare or Windows NT. It supports such PDM features as access control, document check-in/check-out, integrated worklist display, forms and file routing with checkoff responses and due dates, configuration management, compound document management, multidocument, hierarchical project folders, multiformat viewing and redlining, concurrency control, version control, event-triggered notifications, signoff, task tracking, and profile-based searches. These features can control information transfers between development and manufacturing team members such as design engineers, electromechanical engineers, software developers, moldmakers, and numerical-control system programmers. Product managers can track work and secure necessary approvals before allowing product designs to pass to the next phase.

WorkCenter features are available from AutoCAD pull-down menus, so the user sees them as fully integrated with their familiar CAD tools. The product includes *personality templates* that utilize on-screen terminology and workflow models specific to two of AutoCAD's key markets:

- Architects, engineers, and construction users
- Mechanical designers and engineers

Users may access Autodesk WorkCenter from a stand-alone application separate from AutoCAD. Almost any file format — CAD or otherwise — on the user's system can be routed, accessed, viewed, redlined, and queried from within Autodesk WorkCenter. Autodesk recognizes that the majority of personnel on design teams are usually non-CAD users. "[I]n many companies, people that use or add value to project documents outnumber the AutoCAD designers ten to one," says James D'Arezzo, vice president of marketing for AutoCAD. "With Autodesk WorkCenter, it is easier for everyone, including managers, administrators, and other users, to become part of the automated design process."

Autodesk WorkCenter is an extensible engineering environment. Autodesk has published APIs — including ODMA document-management functions — for use by third-party software developers in crafting add-on utilities. Already, more than 50 developers are using the APIs to build add-ons for file viewing, plotting, and other functions. Third-parties can also use C, C++, and Visual Basic to build add-on functionality or integrate Autodesk WorkCenter with other corporate information systems.

One important recent extension to WorkCenter is providing Web-based access. WorkCenter for the Web allows authorized Internet/intranet users to access, search, review, check out, and route AutoCAD drawings and other files stored in the WorkCenter document repository. The Web-site-based software runs on a Windows NT-based Pentium machine with a minimum of 32MB RAM, a 20MB hard drive, and Microsoft Information Explorer or Netscape Enterprise server software. Client PCs require either a Netscape Navigator or Microsoft Internet Explorer browser running under Windows NT Workstation or Windows 3.11.

BancTec Inc.

BancTec, headquartered in Dallas, TX, entered the workflow market in 1995 when it acquired Recognition International Inc., maker of Plexus FloWare. The product is now managed by BancTec's new Plexus Division.

BancTec has long been a leading provider of image-based solutions for banking, financial services, insurance, government, and other industries. Introduced in June 1992 and now in its third generation, Plexus FloWare is one of the top brand names in the production workflow market, based on revenues (according to the Delphi Consulting Group). Other leading production workflow products include FileNet WorkFlo Business System, ViewStar's flagship product of the same name, and IBM ImagePlus and FlowMark. Being in this elite group has its benefits: The Plexus FloWare workflow engine technology has been licensed to AT&T Global Information Systems for use in its ProcessIT workflow product.

Plexus FloWare 3.0, the latest version, runs across a broad range of computing environments, as befits any production workflow solution that aims at a horizontal market. It runs on Windows NT and various flavors of UNIX at the server and integrates with Informix, Oracle, Sybase, Plexus XDF DataManager, and Lotus Notes data stores. It supports almost any client operating environment on the market, including MS-DOS; Microsoft Windows 3.1, 95, and NT; OS/2; Macintosh; and many UNIX variants. Clients interoperate with servers via TCP/IP, the lingua franca protocol of corporate internetworking, and use FileNet/Watermark's popular document-imaging libraries to access, view, and manipulate scanned images.

> *Processes can be redefined on the fly and resituated on new servers without interrupting work in progress.*

Under FloWare, workflow processes may be distributed across many servers, which allows applications to scale up to enterprise-wide proportions. The physical location of workflow definitions, workflow-relevant data, and control data is transparent to user client applications. Processes can be redefined on the fly and resituated on new servers without interrupting work in progress. Administrators can manage distributed workflow applications from a single location, and users are provided with a unified view of workflow status.

FloWare's Microsoft Windows-based MapBuilder tool enables process models to be defined through graphical flowcharts, with no scripting or programming required. Defining a process model automatically creates the data structures needed to implement the workflow. Corporate application developers can define deadlines and e-mail-notification procedures tagged to events in the process map. External programs can be linked into FloWare applications through Visual Basic function calls. Third-party BPR, process-definition, and analysis tools can access MapBuilder functionality through open APIs.

FloWare's Exerciser utility allows application developers to simulate and optimize workflow applications that were defined with MapBuilder. Simulations can be run under various performance scenarios by modeling different work volumes, activity sequences, and routing decisions. Each unit of information routed through a FloWare application is represented on-screen by a *courier* icon. Multiple workflow simulations can be run concurrently.

Plexus FloWare provides sophisticated status tracking and reporting capabilities. Users can always call up an up-to-the-second display on each workflow in which they are an authorized participant or observer. Administrators can produce detailed status reports from Plexus FloWare's application log, using fourth-generation-language report-writing tools to identify bottlenecks and inefficiencies that can be addressed through dynamic process redesign and rerouting. Roles and privileges of individuals and groups can be real-located on the fly to respond to changing business conditions.

FileNet Corp.

FileNet, headquartered in Costa Mesa, CA, is the undisputed pioneer in the production workflow industry, having introduced its imaging-oriented product family, WorkFlo Business System, in 1984. FileNet remains the market leader and one of the most dynamic vendors in the workflow industry. Thanks to superior technology, innovation, and distribution, it enjoys more than twice the market share of its nearest competitor, ViewStar, according to Delphi Group figures.

FileNet has grown rapidly in recent years, due to skyrocketing sales and strategic acquisitions and alliances. In 1995-96, it acquired Watermark Software Inc., a fast-growing vendor of low-end workflow/imaging solutions; Saros Corp., a leading supplier of enterprise document management and Web server software; and International Financial Systems Ltd., a vendor of computer output to laser disk (COLD) software for document indexing, archiving, and retrieval. A recent strategic alliance with Novell has produced Ensemble, which is FileNet's first offering in the messaging-based workflow market (profiled in Chapter 8).

FileNet's strategic directions are diverse and position it to hold onto its workflow market share and branch off into associated markets. First, it aims to provide workflow, document imaging, document management, and COLD technologies in one integrated product suite. Second, it is attempting to leverage its lead in the high-end production workflow market into significant market share in low-end, departmental document-image processing. Third, it is moving rapidly into messaging- and suite-based workflow through new e-mail-enabled products developed with its Watermark subsidiary and a strategic alliance with Novell Inc. Fourth, it will incorporate support for remote users and Internet connectivity in its products. Fifth, it has synchronized its workflow/imaging product development with Microsoft's Enterprise Computing Standards, which include Microsoft Office, BackOffice, OLE Automation, MAPI Workflow Framework, and the Microsoft Internet strategy. Sixth, it will link third-party business-process-reengineering

(BPR) tools to its run-time workflow environment, so that process flowcharts can be translated automatically into application control code.

WorkFlo Business System

Through its acquisitions, FileNet has acquired imaging, document management, and other technologies that it will use to strengthen its flagship product family: the WorkFlo Business System. WorkFlo Business System is a scaleable, function-rich, imaging-oriented workflow system for high-performance distributed applications. The suite consists of almost two dozen separate component software packages supporting access, development, and management of high-end, document-image-oriented workflow applications. It runs under various high-performance server operating systems (Windows NT, Solaris, AIX, HP-UX, MPE/iX, DPX/20), SQL RDBMSs (for example, Oracle 7, Sybase System 10, and HP Allbase), and network operating systems (Novell NetWare, IBM LAN Server, Banyan Vines, Microsoft LAN Manager, and DEC Pathworks). The following discussion is targeted at system integrators and software programmers; applications running on FileNet WorkFlo Business System are too complex, sophisticated, and demanding to be built or managed by end users themselves.

At the core of WorkFlo Business System is a group of functional modules called *Image Management Services (IMS)*. IMS provides document-image routing, indexing, storage, retrieval, and management services. IMS contains the following software modules, which may be installed in various mix-and-match configurations across multiple distributed servers:

- **WorkFlo Queue Services:** Supports creation and management of work queues. A WorkFlo script examines queue contents and then initiates the prefetching of documents requiring processing. All information is readily available in a cache and can be displayed at the user's workstation within seconds. The system automatically tracks and reports on the number of work items in each queue, how long they have been in queue, and their current processing status. Notifications can be generated automatically to administrators if a particular document is not processed within a prespecified timeframe.

- **Object Entry Services:** Supports individual or batch entry of documents from scanners, facsimile machines, mainframe COLD data, intelligent character recognition (ICR) data, and microfiche.

- **Index and Object Management Services:** Supports indexing and hierarchical organization of documents into folders and classes. Indexes are kept in any of several third-party RDBMSs and may be migrated between magnetic and optical storage, depending on access and performance requirements.

- **Optical Library Management Services:** Manages real-time access to optical storage subsystems from FileNet, Hewlett-Packard, and IBM. A resource scheduler maintains a list of outstanding object requests and prioritizes requests by type, such as retrieval, write, and print jobs.

- **Cache Management Services:** Ensures high-performance retrieval operations by caching frequently requested objects to magnetic-storage devices and archiving seldom-requested items to optical disk.

- **Object Locator Services:** Optimizes system performance by clustering related documents or folders on the same storage device and, if redundant copies of a particular object exist on several storage devices, by automatically routing a retrieval request to the one that will provide the fastest response.

- **Object Output Services:** Spools and prioritizes print and outward-bound fax requests among available devices.

- **System Management Services:** Supports system administration functions such as system configuration, monitoring, status reporting, storage management, queue management, transaction logging, disk mirroring, backup and restore, and capacity planning.

- **Object Security Services:** Allows access privileges to be defined for individual users or groups of users. Access privileges can be associated with individual documents, document classes, folders, notes, annotations, functions, menu items, and WorkFlo scripts.

- **Network Directory Services:** Enables client applications to find all necessary image management services on a distributed network. Each server and client has a copy of the directory, enabling requests to be routed to the appropriate servers.

- **Intersystem Communication Services:** Enables sharing of optical libraries, printers, and other resources across multiple distributed systems, with security and access rights maintained consistently across all systems.

Custom workflow applications can be developed for WorkFlo Business System through FileNet's WorkFlo Application Libraries (WAL) software development kit. WAL consists of more than 300 APIs that can be used to invoke all IMS functions. WAL provides a powerful scripting language that can be integrated with development tools such as C, C++, Microsoft Visual Basic, PowerBuilder, and Uniface. WAL is available for Microsoft Windows, OS/2, SunOS, HP-UX, AIX, and Macintosh. FileNet also provides a forms-development tool, AutoForm for Windows, that allows on-screen forms to be defined and linked with external C-language application programs.

FileNet also provides WorkForce Desktop, a suite of off-the-shelf Microsoft Windows and OS/2 imaging/workflow products that integrate tightly with the WorkFlo Business System/IMS. One of these products, FileNet's FolderView software, enables users to organize, navigate, retrieve, view, and annotate large, complex folders of document images and other electronic documents.

FileNet:WorkGroup

FileNet is aggressively diversifying beyond the enterprise-wide, imaging-oriented workflow market, while maintaining tight links to its flagship WorkFlo Business System platform. In 1994, the company introduced two new workflow product platforms: the lower-end *FileNet:WorkGroup* and the higher-end multimedia-oriented *Visual WorkFlo*.

FileNet:WorkGroup is a downsized version of WorkFlo Business System that the company markets exclusively through resellers. FileNet:WorkGroup provides a subset of the same document-image management and workflow features as the higher-end product line but is priced and packaged for smaller workgroups. The product supports high-speed document scanning, indexing, and optical storage, as well as imaging application integration with legacy information systems. It runs on UNIX platforms such as RISC System/6000, HP 9000/800, and HP 3000.

FileNet Visual WorkFlo

Visual WorkFlo is a Windows-based client-server product family that supports workflows involving structured data, unstructured text documents, and other information in addition to document images (document images are primary object types handled by WorkFlo Business System and FileNet:WorkGroup). The product can integrate with WorkFlo Business System/IMS or with Visual WorkFlo/Services, a server-based module for nonimage applications. Visual WorkFlo's object-oriented graphical authoring tool (Composer) allows users at any level to quickly define and implement automated business processes, as well as to redefine workflows in process.

Within Visual WorkFlo, business processes can be defined as sets of reusable *work performer* objects that encapsulate all process definitions, role privileges, workflow-relevant data, control data, and input/output functions associated with a process, subprocess, or activity. Visual WorkFlo applications can be linked with WAL programs as well as external software modules written in C++, Visual Basic, and PowerBuilder. Integration with other Windows applications is enabled through support for DDE and OLE 2.0. Desktop inboxes and run-time workflow execution are managed by the Visual WorkFlo/Performer module. System administration, monitoring, and reporting are supported by the Visual WorkFlo/Conductor module.

The Watermark Software acquisition

The company's 1995 acquisition of Watermark Software gave FileNet a foothold in the market for low-end image-viewing and management solutions as well. Watermark, now a wholly owned subsidiary of FileNet, develops popular departmental document-imaging solutions that will be integrated into the FileNet WorkFlo product families while also continuing to be developed and sold under the Watermark name. Watermark's products, which run on Windows NT and NetWare servers, lack workflow capabilities, though Watermark has been able to connect with several third-party workflow solutions.

FileNet is positioning the Watermark offerings as its entry-level and departmental workflow/imaging solutions. FileNet has announced the following plans to integrate Watermark's technology into its workflow products within the coming year:

- Provide a low-cost FileNet imaging/workflow client incorporating Watermark's technology but able to talk to both FileNet and Watermark image servers; client will be invokable from users' existing applications and enables desktop integration of document images, COLD reports, and other information from FileNet and Watermark servers

- Enable FileNet workflow servers to manage Watermark clients

- Add FileNet WorkFlo capabilities to the Watermark document management system

- Implement distributed document caching, storage, and retrieval among FileNet and Watermark servers

Acquisitions and alliances

Another strategic FileNet acquisition was International Financial Systems Ltd., provider of Greenbar Software, a Windows NT-based COLD product providing electronic access to large volumes of archived computer data. FileNet has integrated Greenbar's COLD technology fully with WorkFlo Business System and FileNet:WorkGroup. The product provides a richer set of data indexing, analysis, viewing, annotation, compression, and manipulation capabilities than FileNet's long-established COLD software. Nevertheless, FileNet also plans to continue marketing its own COLD offering and the stand-alone Greenbar Software package as separate products under their existing names.

FileNet also moved into the nonimaging document management market through its late 1995 acquisition of Saros Corp., one of the market leaders in that segment. Saros is best known for Mezzanine, its middleware product that supports indexing, search, retrieval, control, and administration of distributed, multiformat electronic libraries. Mezzanine manages documents created in most commercial applications, such as word processors, spreadsheets, databases, and desktop publishing packages. It provides scaleable, high-performance *library* servers that can be called from desktop applications through Saros-proprietary APIs as well as through published industry standards such as ODMA and DMA. The product runs on a wide array of server operating environments (Novell NetWare, Banyan Vines, Microsoft LAN Manager, IBM LAN Server, Microsoft Windows NT Server, AIX, SunOS, Solaris, DG/UX, DEC OSF/1, and OS/2) and clients (Windows NT Workstation, Windows 95, Windows 3.1, Windows for Workgroups, Macintosh, OS/2 Warp, MS-DOS, and UNIX).

Saros has recruited an impressive range of third-party document management vendors to build products on top of Mezzanine. Saros itself offers a stand-alone, Windows-based document management product (Document Manager) that gives access to Mezzanine's distributed library services. Document Manager has been provided with workflow capabilities through Saros's co-development pact with Action Technologies. Saros has developed a package (dubbed Mezzanine) that supports organization, updating, protection, and maintenance of documents published on the Web. Saros also provides document-management client software that *plugs into* a Netscape Navigator Web browser.

FileNet plans to use Saros' expertise in cross-network document indexing, search, retrieval, and replication tools to develop a "single cataloguing engine for all FileNet products," according to Jordan Libit, FileNet vice-president of marketing.

FileNet is active in strategic alliances that will open up its workflow products to interoperate with third-party process-modeling and BPR tools. It has teamed with Meta Software Corp. to provide software that interfaces between Meta's BPR tool, WorkFlow Analyzer, and Visual WorkFlo. This product allows users to document, simulate, and optimize business processes and export the corresponding process definition to be executed within Visual WorkFlo. Similar interfaces are being developed for other third-party BPR tools.

IA Corp.

IA, headquartered in Emeryville, CA, is a leading vendor of enterprise-wide multimedia workflow solutions and specializes in developing very large-scale, high-performance, customized, production-oriented applications for customers in services industries. The company comes from a system integration background but is evolving rapidly into a product-oriented company, focusing, like most prominent workflow vendors, on selling licenses for its workflow, image, and document management software.

> *Unlimited numbers of workflow engines can be distributed across LANs and WANs to support growing workloads.*

Object-oriented workflow

IA's WorkVision is one of the most thorough object-oriented production workflow solutions on the market, which translates into advantages in the ability to scale application, performance, and flexibility. Unlimited numbers of workflow engines can be distributed across LANs and WANs to support growing workloads. Workflow engine software or individual software objects can be replicated and run in parallel on a single multiprocessing server. Workloads can be balanced dynamically across multiple servers or software modules. Software objects can be mixed and matched in various configurations on various servers, depending on the functions (such as document scanning, indexing, routing, queue management, file management, mass storage, archiving, printing, and so on) to be performed at those sites.

WorkVision is built around an object-oriented UNIX file system, which associates or *encapsulates* every information type (such as images, graphics, text, video, voice, and so on) with the software routines needed to process it. Electronic documents can be organized into hierarchical *folders* and *subfolders*, which contain pointers to associated software. One or more folders can be associated with a routable *work item*, to which is attached a form-like *transmittal sheet*. The transmittal sheet contains attributes that describe folder contents and contain workflow-relevant data used to compute routing decisions. A workflow may be changed at any time — even at run time — by adding, deleting, or modifying attributes in its transmittal sheet.

To enhance workflow application performance, only the transmittal sheet is routed and queued between WorkVision users. A folder or document is retrieved from WorkVision's file system when the user clicks on its reference in a transmittal sheet. Retrieving a data object automatically invokes the appropriate third-party file viewer. The file system also manages multiple versions of documents and supports partitioning, distribution, and replication of the object database and indexes in a distributed environment.

WorkVision runs across a distributed infrastructure of high-performance UNIX servers connected through TCP/IP connections. Currently, the product runs on Solaris, SunOS, and AT&T System V servers, and soon AIX and HP-UX machines as well. Client software runs on any of these operating environments, plus Windows 3.1 and OS/2. Workflow data objects may be stored in Oracle, Sybase, or Informix RDBMSs and accessed through SQL calls. WorkVision works with a wide range of document-image formats and printer definition languages and supports many high-performance imaging peripherals, including scanners, optical character recognition devices, optical storage devices, printers, and fax machines.

Published APIs provide access to all data objects stored in WorkVision's UNIX file system, as well as to encapsulated methods, supporting application development in C, C++, OLE, Visual Basic, PowerBuilder, and other object-oriented development tools. IA is using Sun's Open Network Computing/Remote Procedure Call specification for interobject communications and has laid out a migration path to OMG CORBA compliance.

Workflow process definitions

Workflow processes are defined in WorkVision with a graphical flowcharting tool and various on-screen dialog boxes. A process is built by defining paths between separate activities. Each activity is associated with one or more inbound or outbound work queues. Work items — represented by transmittal sheets and associated folders — flow into and out of queues in accordance with routing rules. Users are associated with one or more activities and granted various access, viewing, and processing privileges.

WorkVision centralizes administration, monitoring, and control of distributed workflow applications. Administrators and users can view real-time statistical reports and graphics showing trends in queue lengths, processing times, and the rate of work entering and existing queues. The product also includes a map-based simulation tool to determine the impact of various process designs on overall workflow performance, throughput, and capacity utilization.

Sophistication notwithstanding, WorkVision's process-definition tools are not terribly user-friendly. IA has geared its products to support the serious production-workflow professional, someone who needs power tools to craft complex, highly structured, multimedia applications.

IBM/Lotus Development Corp.

IBM, headquartered in Armonk, NY, has made a strong showing in the client-server oriented document-imaging and workflow markets. IBM has been providing production workflow solutions for high-volume document-imaging applications since 1988. Its products address desktop, LAN server, and Big Blue's traditional host-computing environments. The company also provides solutions for messaging-based workflow and document management. Its 1995 acquisition of Lotus Development Corporation adds that company's groupware, imaging, workflow, and application-suite products to IBM's portfolio. IBM's production workflow strategies focus on three product platforms: ImagePlus, FlowMark, and Lotus Notes: Document Imaging.

ImagePlus

The ImagePlus family of products is IBM's principal platform for high-volume document-image processing. ImagePlus allows paper documents, photos, or drawings to be scanned or captured as electronic images, organized as folders, linked to business applications, routed through the workflow, and launched or displayed from users' desktop worklists. ImagePlus runs on all of IBM's operating environments — OS/2, AIX, OS/400, and MVS — and on computers ranging from Intel-based PCs and PowerPC machines to AS/400 minicomputers and ES/900 mainframes. Support for Windows clients is planned.

The product family is scaleable from single-workgroup imaging applications to enterprise-wide image and document management solutions. It includes ImagePlus for MVS/ESA (for high-volume transaction environments in organizations of all sizes), ImagePlus for OS/400 (a midrange platform for OS/400-based applications supporting single to multiple departments), and ImagePlus VisualInfo (a client/server solution that, similar to FileNet's Visual WorkFlo, manages documents in various forms, including images, graphics, audio, video, spreadsheets, and word-processing text).

IBM is evolving ImagePlus into an enterprise document and workflow management solution addressing much more than just scanned document images. ImagePlus VisualInfo — the latest addition to the product line — can capture, store, index, locate, retrieve, integrate, and manage scanned images, word-processing files, spreadsheets, slide-show presentations, audio files, and other digital objects. VisualInfo includes a suite of IBM products that support document capture, fax management, intelligent forms processing, and workflow control, as well as complementary products developed by IBM business partners. VisualInfo functions can be accessed from the product's own client software or from existing desktop applications integrated through IBM's APIs.

At the heart of VisualInfo is a highly scaleable, distributed image and document repository. Its architecture includes one or more *object servers* (which store image, document, and other files) and one or more *library servers* (which track file locations and facilitate document search and retrieval by client applications). This distributed architecture enables VisualInfo to service a growing volume of document and workflow transactions without experiencing serious performance bottlenecks on LANs and WANs.

VisualInfo provides process-definition and application-development tools for workflow applications. It maintains workflow control and status data and provides administrative tools for controlling or modifying business processes from anywhere on the network. Alternately, a VisualInfo application may operate over the run-time enactment service provided by FlowMark, which is IBM's workflow management offering for enterprise-wide business processes.

FlowMark

FlowMark is IBM's production workflow offering (the company's messaging-based workflow products, IBM FormTalk and Lotus Forms, are discussed in the next chapter). Like ImagePlus/VisualInfo, FlowMark runs on a pure-IBM network consisting of OS/2, AIX, and MVS machines, although IBM is developing FlowMark servers for HP-UX and Windows NT and run-time clients for Windows NT and 95.

FlowMark process models are defined with IBM's OS/2-based *buildtime client* feature, which not only prepares a visual flowchart but also simulates the run-time process with an on-screen animated display. Process models can be defined by importing existing databases of staff, programs, and data structures from external applications. The models can be linked with custom applications via IBM-provided APIs; then they are output in IBM's proprietary FlowMark Definition Language to be executed on FlowMark Servers, which store the models in the FlowMark ObjectStore database. IBM will soon include a worklist API in FlowMark that is based in part on the WfMC's draft standard.

External applications may be invoked in run time through FlowMark's Service Broker Manager. IBM is developing run-time interfaces that will allow FlowMark, ImagePlus, and Lotus Notes to start and stop workflow processes, exchange work items, invoke applications, and track process status within each other's domain. See Figure 7-3 for an example of FlowMark.

Lotus Notes: Document Imaging

IBM's new Lotus subsidiary has been providing document-imaging workflow capabilities for several years in its Notes groupware environment. Lotus Notes: Document Imaging (LN:DI) is a set of companion software products to Notes that includes an image-viewing and manipulation client, image-processing server, mass-storage subsystem, optical character reader, and incoming and outgoing fax gateways. The server software enables images to be stored on separate image servers, typically an optical mass-storage jukebox. Document images stored in an image server separate from the main Notes database are not replicated to other Notes servers; instead, a *pointer* to the image is replicated, alerting remote users that they will need to address the originating server if they want to retrieve an image.

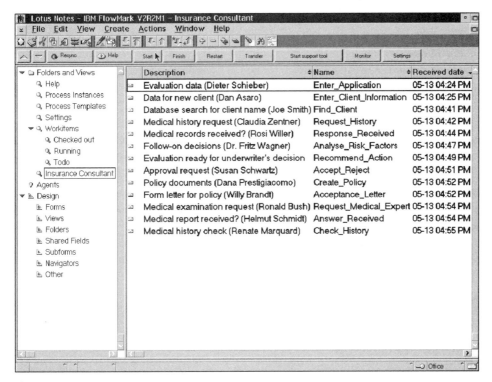

Figure 7-3
IBM's FlowMark workflow in-box.

IBM has integrated ImagePlus with Notes. Notes clients can retrieve files directly from ImagePlus servers over LAN/WAN connections. A gateway is provided for remote Notes users to access ImagePlus filestores. Users will soon be able to migrate any Notes data, documents, or images to ImagePlus VisualInfo servers, eliminating storage constraints associated with the Notes environment. Currently, LN:DI supports storage of up to four gigabytes of data on an image server. LN:DI users can define storage profiles for images that define where and when the files should be archived to optical jukeboxes, tape drives, and other devices. Soon you will be able to define ImagePlus servers as just another archiving target device in a Notes image's storage profile.

InConcert, Inc.

InConcert, Inc., a Xerox New Enterprise Company headquartered in Cambridge, MA, develops and markets a broad range of network-enabled, document-centric software applications, including workflow, document management, and electronic publishing solutions. The company was formerly known as XSoft.

InConcert

The company's workflow product, also named InConcert, was released in 1993. Now in its third generation, the InConcert product provides workflow capabilities in conjunction with customers' existing third-party desktop applications. External applications are invoked when associated files are mouse-clicked from task entries in a user's workflow inbox. The product supports routing and tracking of any type of data — text, graphics, images, and video — and includes basic document management features, such as file check in/out, version control, and keyword search. Unlike many production workflow solutions, InConcert does not include its own document-imaging subsystem.

InConcert supports structured workflows as well as those requiring dynamic rerouting/delegation and one-time, nonrepeating process runs. This flexibility, coupled with InConcert's support for third-party desktop applications, makes the product well suited to entry-level workflow solutions. With InConcert, you need not risk *hard-coding* a young, ill-defined workflow; instead, you can continually modify and elaborate the process definition as the underlying business process evolves through trial and error. The product is scaleable from as few as ten users to thousands, allowing increasing numbers of servers to be installed over WAN.

The InConcert client software runs on Microsoft Windows desktops and various UNIX operating systems. The run-time enactment service, called *Process Manager*, runs under NetWare 4.1 and UNIX. File sharing between servers and clients is supported by NFS interfaces, and workflow-relevant data is maintained in such SQL-compliant RDBMSs as Oracle, Sybase, and Informix. Users can create custom, hierarchical desktop folders for specific projects and custom task interfaces, such as those required for image-based and forms-driven processes.

The product's graphical object-oriented development environment, called *Process Designer*, provides C and C++ APIs and works with Windows-based development tools such as Visual Basic and PowerBuilder. All InConcert workflow processes are defined through on-screen flowcharts under Process Designer, eschewing the need to write scripts. The development environment is thoroughly object-oriented, allowing new applications to be built from reusable process and subprocess templates, which may contain standard or default values for due dates, task durations, priority handling, event-notification triggers, and other process attributes. Synchronization points can be defined between separate branches of a workflow, allowing, for example, initiation of one task to depend on completion of several other tasks.

Users and process administrators use the on-screen workflow map to monitor the current status of any job. Tasks are represented by icons, which provide real-time visual indicators of due dates and task completion. In addition, all information about jobs, tasks, documents, users, and workflow status is accessible through InConcert customized database reports.

The vendor's directions for its InConcert product include expanded support for object-oriented application development, integration of a wider range of in-house and third-party applications, greater emphasis on off-the-shelf, vertical-market applications, and support for Internet connectivity, according to Edward Chick, the company's director for strategic marketing. "We see InConcert as a systems integration platform for other products," he says, and as a strategic environment for interfacing to third-party applications.

The vendor plans to expose InConcert's component functions to a greater degree through support for ActiveX, according to Chick. He further says that this exposure will allow for more rapid application development through industry-standard tools such as Visual Basic and PowerBuilder.

Strategic alliances and vertical markets

The company is also pursuing strategic alliances with vendors of electronic forms, image processing, document management, project management, process modeling, and decision support tools. InConcert and third-party applications will integrate with the workflow product through WfMC specifications, as they are developed, and through proprietary interfaces, says Chick. InConcert has already integrated two project management tools — Microsoft Project and Digital Tools's AutoPlan — and it is used in process definition and tracking. InConcert will be able to import file attributes from InConcert company's document management solutions into workflow process definitions, providing a basis for triggering routing rules.

Vertical-market versions of InConcert are being developed for engineering product data management (PDM), telecommunications operators, publishers, and print shops. These specialized versions of the product will support InConcert's aggressive pursuit of workflow systems integration business with public and private sector clients.

Keyfile Corp.

Keyfile, headquartered in Nashua, NH, provides a versatile workflow solution — Keyfile Enterprise Edition Version 3.1 — that spans distinct product categories. On one hand, it competes with FileNet, IBM, ViewStar, and Wang's products as a production document-imaging system. On the other, it provides strong multiformat document indexing and retrieval capabilities similar to such products as PC DOCS' DOCS OPEN, FileNet/Saros' Document Manager, and Novell's SoftSolutions. Keyfile also has a new messaging/suite-based workflow product, KeyFlow (discussed in Chapter 8), that operates over Microsoft Exchange's groupware environment.

Keyfile Enterprise Edition

One of the distinguishing features of the Keyfile Enterprise Edition is its ability to support workflows that change rapidly. Users are able to develop graphical workflows quickly on-screen, implement them, and change them in-process without disrupting ongoing work. Routing lists can be built through on-line access to LAN and e-mail directories. Keyfile's product strategy is based on its recognition that *dynamic* workflows such as these constitute approximately 20 percent of a company's volume of documents but typically account for 80 percent of the cost associated with accomplishing the corporate mission.

Keyfile's graphical, Windows-based process-design tool, JobMaker, allows any user to create workflows by combining icon-based *step* modules that handle various activities and tasks (see Figure 7-4).

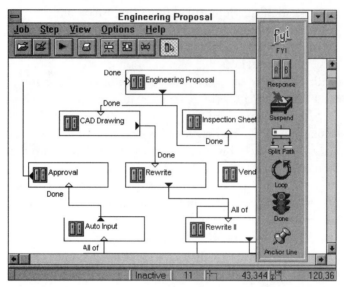

Figure 7-4
A production workflow process model created with KeyFile's JobMaker tool.

Users create process flowcharts by dragging and dropping the following six icons into place as needed:

- **FYI:** A work item that requires no activity from the recipient
- **Response:** A work item that requires some active response from the recipient to continue to the next step
- **Suspend:** An activity that cannot be started or completed until all required documents are collected from other workflow participants
- **Split Path:** An activity that sends its output over parallel routing paths
- **Loop:** A work item that will be routed back to a previous step
- **Done:** The activity that completes the workflow

Users can view a workflow's status in real time through automatic color-coding of these iconic steps, indicating whether they are in process or completed. Various business rules can be attached to these steps, including conditional out-routing, due dates, and delinquency notifications. Keyfile includes a scripting language allowing developers to build document routing and handling rules of moderate complexity. Prerequisites may be defined to suspend an activity until any number of prior conditions are realized, such as obtaining a vote from any number of users on the acceptability of a particular document in process. Workflow status records can be automatically logged and downloaded to other applications, such as Microsoft Excel and Access.

Keyfile Enterprise Edition is not truly enterprise-oriented yet; it runs on a single document server, although support for distributed, multiserver environments is in the works. Nevertheless, it runs in one of the widest range of operating environments in the workflow marketplace, supporting Windows clients; Windows NT, HP-UX, Solaris, and OS/2 servers; NetWare, LAN Manager, Windows for Workgroups, LAN Server, Digital PATHWORKS, and Banyan Vines LANs; any network supporting the TCP/IP, NetBIOS, or NetBEUI protocols; any RDBMS supporting SQL queries; and any mail system supporting the MHS or VIM specifications. Developers can write applications for Keyfile using commercial tools such as Visual Basic and Powerbuilder, linking through Keyfile's API set as well as such industry-standard interfaces as C, DDE, and OLE.

Keyfile manages almost any kind of document file format, including most commercial word-processing, spreadsheet, graphic, image, fax, and CAD formats — even voice and video files. These multimedia objects may be integrated into compound documents or arranged in hierarchical electronic *folders* and *file cabinets* under Keyfile. Converter tools allow application developers to easily import, integrate, and index other file formats into Keyfile's environment.

The product is distributed in architecture, consisting of desktop client software and any number of specialized LAN servers. A typical Keyfile installation often includes a document server, fax server, mail server, print server, scan server, and optical character recognition (OCR) server.

Keyfile's document server

The document server is the core component of a Keyfile document/workflow management application. All documents managed by Keyfile are kept in compressed format in a central *object store* on a document server and are decompressed when called up for reading or editing on an individual's desktop. Files are not physically routed within workflow applications; instead, master copies are kept on the document server and one or more simultaneous *pointers* to those files are placed in work folders, in and out baskets, and file cabinets displayed on users' desktops. These pointers — plus document profiles, indexes, version controls, access controls, and file attributes — are maintained in a network database that provides high-performance object management.

Keyfile provides a Windows-based desktop interface to manage various documents, folders, and file cabinets. Icons are presented for various applications (for example, image viewers, word processors, and spreadsheets), workflow resources (for example, File Room, In Basket, Out Basket, BasketMaker, JobMaker, FolderMaker, DocMaker, and Alert List), and document-processing resources (for example, scanners, facsimile machines, OCR devices, and electronic wastebaskets and shredders). Any of these tools can be dragged to the desktop and activated by dropping a document icon onto it. Routing a workflow folder or document is as simple as dragging it to your desktop out basket and selecting the appropriate recipient or routing list from the Keyfile directory. (See Figure 7-5.)

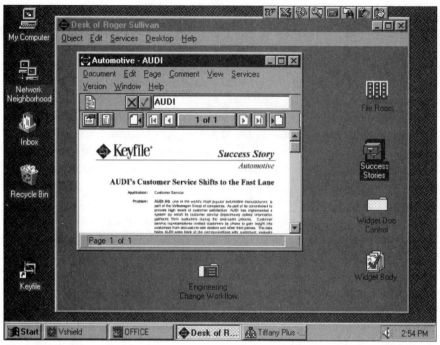

Figure 7-5
The Keyfile production workflow application running under Windows 95.

Almost any Windows- or DOS-based application can be set up as an application within the Keyfile environment, which automatically registers documents created with them as Keyfile-managed objects. Keyfile has viewers for more than 80 commercial application file formats. Its desktop imaging tool can display many formats and perform such functions as object import, page rotation, magnification, scaling, annotation, and highlighting. Advanced file locking supports simultaneous markup, viewing, and access to shared documents across a workgroup. E-mail integration allows any document to be e-mailed from a Keyfile desktop to external users through MHS- or VIM-compatible messaging systems.

Keyfile lacks a forms-design tool such as those included with other workflow products on the market. However, it can import forms created in packages from JetForm, and other vendors. Keyfile also offers the ability to create quasi-electronic forms by scanning or importing text forms, drawing what it calls TypeMatic fields over the existing text fields, and reading the filled-in information through OCR. Users can also add on-screen *sticky note* comment fields and mouse-input graphic elements to scanned forms.

ViewStar Corp.

ViewStar's flagship workflow product, called ViewStar, has been a workflow market leader since its introduction in 1988. Now in its fourth generation, the ViewStar product's Business Process Automation Server component runs on an impressive range of operating environments — from MS-DOS to Microsoft Windows NT, UNIX, and MVS — and integrates with such data stores as Gupta SQLBase, Microsoft SQL Server, Sybase SQL Server, Lotus Notes, and IBM DB2. It runs on all leading network operating systems, including Novell NetWare, Windows NT Advanced Server, and Banyan VINES.

The company provides a wide range of sophisticated tools to support application design, debugging, configuration, implementation, usage, monitoring, and operations. Its strategic directions include making its development tools faster and easier to use, supporting workflow applications over e-mail and Internet transports, and integrating its products with Microsoft's BackOffice suite, especially with the Microsoft Exchange e-mail/groupware product and MAPI Workflow Framework.

ViewStar's Process Architect is a visual process-modeling tool that supports animated workflow simulation and optimization. To speed development of workflow applications with minimal programming, Process Architect includes *task portfolios* that include standard object-module icons to define review routing, decision branching, and other workflow tasks. Tasks, maps, and portions of maps created in Process Architect are reusable in any number of processes.

ViewStar Application Designer allows process maps to be translated into application designs. The tool lets users design and edit their user interface display windows, menus, action bars, and buttons. You can speed the development process by invoking Process Script Assistants, which are object modules based on ViewStar's macro language. A forms-outliner tool is also available to build on-screen business forms linked to workflow rules. Powerful scanning and OCR capabilities are provided to facilitate high-volume, high-accuracy scanned-document input, including documents received via fax.

Complex, multidocument, multiformat folders can be developed under ViewStar. A folder is an object that can be linked with business rules describing how it and its constituents are to be routed, processed, and displayed. In addition to document images, ViewStar manages almost any binary or text file format available on your system. The Repository Manager supports flexible partitioning and distribution of the multimedia information base (for example, chronological, geographic, application-based, and volumetric). The Cataloger utility supports development of complex document indexes and cross-references in support of powerful search and retrieval capabilities.

ViewStar recently introduced its Business Process Interface (BPI) development tool, which supports rapid application development with ActiveX and Visual Basic Controls (VBX), which are object-oriented extensions to Microsoft's core client/server development tools. ViewStar developers are using BPI to create *application templates* for vertical-market workflow solutions. ViewStar markets the application templates to value-added resellers and systems integrators, who, in turn, use them as platforms for crafting custom workflow applications for particular customers.

ViewStar is embedded in Microsoft's workflow camp. It plans to integrate its workflow products with all components of Microsoft BackOffice. Already, ViewStar runs with two central components of BackOffice, Microsoft Windows NT and SQL Server, on the workflow engine. In addition, ViewStar will be upgraded to support Microsoft Systems Management Server (to streamline user administration, software distribution, and remote support), Exchange Server (to support standards-based e-mail interoperability), and Windows NT and Windows 95 on client workstations.

ViewStar's commitment to adapt its product to operate over Exchange Server — in conjunction with similar announcements from Action, FileNet, Keyfile, and Wang — is further evidence for the convergence of production, messaging-based, and suite-based workflow technologies. ViewStar will integrate its products with the MAPI Workflow extensions when Microsoft supports them in its second major release of the Exchange e-mail product, slated for late 1997.

To further blur the tidy market distinctions presented in this book, ViewStar in 1996 released three server-resident software products to connect Internet/intranet users with its workflow/document servers. InfoStore@Work allows users to access ViewStar document libraries from browsers, automatically transforming documents to HTML format so they can be displayed properly on Web browsers. (See Figure 7-6.) Process@Work enables users to initiate, modify, and track automated workflows from their browsers. Internet Transport Task transports EDI documents over the Internet between ViewStar systems maintained by separate companies. (For profiles of other Web-based workflow products, see Chapter 9.)

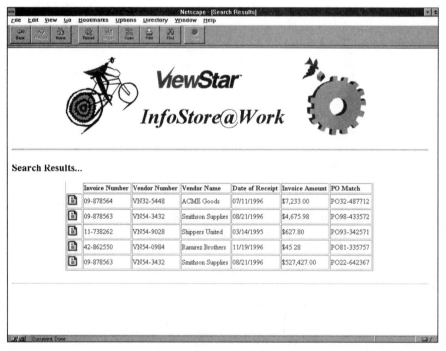

Figure 7-6
Database query results displayed in ViewStar's InfoStore@Work Web-based workflow product.

Wang Laboratories Inc.

Wang Laboratories, headquartered in Billerica, MA, has transformed itself into a powerhouse workflow, imaging, and COLD software provider over the past several years, leveraging its long experience in office automation and management information systems.

Wang is aggressively building its core workflow and imaging product lines through research and development, strategic acquisitions, and high-profile business alliances. Wang's OPEN/workflow and OPEN/image products have achieved significant market penetration in only a few short years on the market. In 1994 and '95, the company boosted its market share through acquisition of Sigma Imaging Systems and Groupe Bull's imaging/workflow software products, respectively. In 1995, it began a strategic alliance with Microsoft to embed Wang-developed imaging and workflow technologies in the Windows NT and 95 operating environments, as well as the Microsoft BackOffice and Exchange product suites. Wang is also providing its imaging, workflow, and COLD technology to Kodak to be incorporated in the latter's Imagelink document management products.

Wang's core product families are solid, high-performance, client-server imaging-based environments. It also markets an internally developed COLD product and several third-party document management products, including PC DOCs.

OPEN/image

Wang's flagship document-imaging product, OPEN/image, was introduced in the early 1990s. It provides a platform for developing and deploying distributed document-imaging applications across LAN and WAN environments. It runs under many client and server operating environments, including Microsoft Windows NT, 95, and 3.1, various UNIX flavors (AIX, HP-UX, Solaris), host operating systems (IBM CICS, OS/400, VMS, IMS/DC, HP MPE/iX), and the NetWare LAN operating system. OPEN/image features can be built into new applications built with most of the leading third-party development tools, including Microsoft Visual Basic, Microsoft C++, Gupta SQL Windows, Powersoft PowerBuilder, and any languages accessing DDE or C-level APIs. It supports remote dial-up access to production imaging stores over high-speed ISDN telephone lines.

OPEN/image includes an enterprise-wide *catalog* that lets users search for documents across multiple local or distributed servers without having to be concerned about a document's location or on what kind of server it resides. The Windows NT Advanced Server-based version of OPEN/image integrates with Microsoft BackOffice and includes Sigma's RouteBuilder, a graphical development tool for both imaging and workflow. RouteBuilder supports drag-and-drop creation of workflow maps, as well as graphical definition of routing rules and worksets, parallel routing, and automatching of documents upon rendezvous.

OPEN/workflow

OPEN/workflow, introduced in early 1994, is a development and run-time environment for imaging-based production-workflow applications. OPEN/workflow comes with the graphical RouteBuilder process-definition tool and maintains a workflow enactment service, control data, and directories on one or more dedicated workflow engines. It runs in the same server, client, and network operating environments as OPEN/image and uses that product as its back-end image server. Administrators can review workflow status metrics in real time or through regular reports. OPEN/workflow capabilities can be accessed from desktop applications through Wang-provided APIs.

Wang plans to integrate and merge its newly acquired products — Sigma's RouteBuilder and Omnidesk, plus Bull's FLOWpath and IMAGEworks — into the OPEN/image and OPEN/workflow product lines. New Windows NT-based versions of both Wang products have been available since 1995, primarily incorporating RouteBuilder and other Sigma technology. New UNIX and OS/2-based versions of both Wang products — incorporating technologies and features from the former Sigma and Bull units — are expected by the third quarter of 1996. The former Bull is building migration tools for moving ImageWORKS and FLOWpath customers to the existing OPEN/image for UNIX and to Wang's forthcoming, merged UNIX-based workflow environment.

Wang has indicated that it intends to keep selling its current product lines and those of the companies it acquired as independent solutions. Cross-platform interoperability between the products will be strengthened, feature sets will be harmonized, and user interfaces made more consistent. Eventually, a client on any of the current Wang imaging and workflow products will be able to interface to a server on any of the others, and servers will be able to migrate documents and transfer workflow items transparently across separate product domains. All products will be able to access a unified catalog for locating any document anywhere in the enterprise. A consistent set of administration, backup, security, and software-distribution capabilities will be implemented across all products. Wang will make the work management functionality of all its products available through a common set of 32-bit COM OLE controls.

Wang, Microsoft, and the future

Wang is doing its part to bring workflow and imaging applications to the business mass market, principally through its strategic alliance with Microsoft. Wang co-developed Microsoft's MAPI Workflow Framework, which provides an API set for linking workflow clients, servers, and applications over enterprise e-mail systems, including Microsoft Exchange.

Wang is also providing document-image client software that has been bundled with Windows 95 and NT since early 1996. The software allows users to scan, view, annotate, manage, store, and share faxes, paper documents, and electronic images from the desktop. With Microsoft's ubiquitous software products and marketing clout behind it, the document-image client could very well become the industry's de facto standard imaging desktop solution. The imaging client can be called through published ActiveX

APIs from other applications. Wang and Microsoft will publish their method of supporting desktop annotations on image files, providing a much-needed standard for users to be certain that the annotations they make on documents can be read by others.

Expect to see greater integration between Wang and Microsoft's workflow and imaging products. Microsoft has designated Wang as its only preferred workflow/imaging vendor and acquired a 10 percent equity stake in Wang plus the rights to some of Wang's imaging technology. Moreover, the Redmond WA-based software giant has committed to incorporating Wang-developed imaging and object controls into future versions of Windows. By the same token, Wang has committed to building the image and object controls into all of its own Windows-based products.

Wang plans to upgrade OPEN/workflow to support routing of workflow items via Microsoft Exchange and other messaging systems compliant with the MAPI Workflow Framework, according to Mordechai Beizer, Wang vice president for architecture and design. However, OPEN/workflow will remain a database-centric workflow environment, he says, because Wang has no plans to port it to run in an exclusively store-and-forward messaging-centric environment. "It is appropriate for a production workflow system to link to messaging-based workflow systems to support exception processing," he states.

Wang will provide its RouteBuilder tool with hooks into Exchange's enterprise directory service, promises Beizer. "It makes sense to define users in one place by piggybacking on directory services defined in the messaging system. This will facilitate workflow route and role definition and reduce the complexity of workflow administration."

According to Beizer, Wang is also discussing with third-party BPR tool vendors the possibility of integrating their software to support definition of processes that could run in the OPEN/workflow environment.

Summary

This chapter has presented an overview of major trends and vendors in the production workflow market. These companies are by no means the only production workflow vendors; indeed, there are dozens of suppliers in this market. You should by all means attempt to survey a broad cross-section of the industry when looking for a commercial solution to host your workflow applications. A more complete vendor list is provided in Appendix A.

When evaluating these vendors' products, you should be careful not to pigeonhole them as inherently production versus messaging-, Web-, or suite-based. This platform-oriented market distinction, which forms the superstructure of this book, is useful for sizing up and sorting solutions in the current workflow market. However, as stressed several times in the preceding profiles, production workflow vendors are eagerly integrating other collaborative platforms into their product architectures.

The platform distinctions between workflow products may become irrelevant by the year 2000. The production workflow market's rush to embrace Microsoft's MAPI Workflow Framework, Exchange groupware environment, Internet/intranet software products, and other BackOffice technologies shows that the day may soon be coming when all major workflow products interoperate transparently across standards-compliant distributed file systems, messaging systems, intranets, and groupware/application suites. At that point, you may be able to tap into any workflow enactment service with any user interface tool you prefer, including GUI-oriented desktop and mobile client operating systems, browsers, messaging clients, or, indeed, any application software package. Workflow-relevant and application data will be served to these client environments from any combination of back-end imaging, document, database, messaging, directory, and object information bases. Client environments will become more multimedia-ready to display and manipulate this rich assemblage of workflow data.

When platform distinctions disappear between today's market segments, we may begin to categorize workflow products differently. The meaning of *production* workflow may evolve from today's focus on filestore-based technologies to a concern with heavy-duty process reengineering and electronic commerce. The essential features that distinguish production workflow applications — regardless of what platforms they run on — are support for custom application software, intricate process models, complex routable objects, stringent application and transaction security, and high-volume, scaleable, multisite, multiserver enactment services. You may be able to develop messaging-, Web-, or suite-based products to satisfy these criteria and thereby qualify to support production workflow applications.

In contrast to this new sense of production workflow, you may refer to *ad hoc* workflow solutions that allow people to easily define, initiate, reroute, and track simple, limited-run workflows that route everyday documents from within familiar computing and communications environments. This is the low-end niche addressed by current messaging- and suite-based workflow products, and you're likely to see more downsized filestore- and Web-based workflow products to tap this potentially huge *ad hoc* market. Marketers might refer to this as *workflow for the rest of us* who haven't the time, need, or inclination to muck around with complex process models.

The next three chapters focus on leaders in each of these market segments. Some companies — Action, FileNet, IBM/Lotus, Novell, and Microsoft — appear in two or more segments, which testifies to the convergence just spoken of. Each segment also has its *pure players* — companies that focus only on that particular twist on workflow technology. Whether you select products from *switch-hitters* or pure segment-specific vendors should depend on the technical merits of their respective solutions, as well as such matters as cost, vertical-market applications, and vendor support (product-evaluation issues that will be discussed in greater depth in Chapter 13).

CHAPTER EIGHT

MESSAGING-BASED WORKFLOW MARKET

Today's messaging-based workflow vendors generally approach the market from any of three angles. Some (such as Banyan, Lotus, and Microsoft) provide forms-based workflow as an add-on to their established e-mail products. Others (such as JetForm) provide forms-design and filler tools that can interoperate with third-party e-mail products and groupware suites, lacking messaging and groupware products of their own. Still others (such as FileNet and ViewStar) have developed messaging-based products as an extension or offshoot of their production workflow solutions.

This chapter provides an overview of leading vendors and solutions in the messaging-based workflow market. For guidelines on when to choose a messaging-based solution over other workflow technologies, refer to Chapters 3 and 12. Table 8-1 summarizes the general trends in messaging-based workflow.

TABLE 8-1: MESSAGING-BASED WORKFLOW MARKET TRENDS

CATEGORY	TREND	EXPLANATION
Operating Platforms	Continuing maintenance of multiplatform workflow environments with increased product development emphasis on Microsoft's Windows NT, Windows 95, Exchange, and BackOffice platforms	This trend, discussed in Table 7-1, cuts across the entire workflow market. Microsoft is strengthening its de facto hegemony over the entire distributed-computing world, and its MAPI Workflow Framework and Exchange messaging/groupware product give it the upper hand in defining the future of messaging-based workflow.
Workflow Management Standards	Increasing vendor compliance with emerging workflow industry standards	The dominant messaging-based workflow standard is Microsoft's MAPI Workflow Framework (MWF). As of late 1996, no Microsoft or third-party products had yet implemented MWF, though statements of support and near-future compliance emanated from all throughout the workflow industry. Microsoft has stated that its first MWF implementation will be in Microsoft Exchange 2.0, slated for release in late 1997. MWF — which conforms with a subset of the Workflow Management Coalition's Reference Model — supports transparent forms routing and tracking across multivendor workflow and e-mail environments.
Architectures	Increasing re-architecting of messaging-based workflow products to adopt some features typically associated with production workflow	As noted in Table 7-1, the line between production and messaging-based workflow is blurring, especially as production workflow vendors port their products to messaging-based environment through incorporation of MWF interfaces and functionality. By the same token, messaging-based workflow vendors are evolving their traditionally client-centric products to more closely resemble production workflow, even without MWF, by increasingly relying on servers to manage workflow enactment, tracking, and database functions. In addition, messaging-based products, which have traditionally routed items physically as file attachments to e-mail messages, are increasingly supporting in-place *logical* routing of large image and multimedia objects through transfer of access pointers. This latter feature could enable messaging-based workflow systems to scale up to large transaction workloads while moderating utilization on scarce network bandwidth. As an additional note on workflow market convergence, we are already seeing messaging-based products that operate over groupware suites and the Web.
Application Development Tools	Increasing reliance on graphical, industry-standard, object-oriented form, application, and process design tools	The discussion in Table 7-1 applies equally to the messaging-based market. Most messaging-based workflow vendors allow you to embed Microsoft's object-oriented ActiveX and Visual Basic Controls in electronic forms, not to mention other sophisticated formatting, display, calculation, and other capabilities included in the vendors' own forms-design toolkits.

CATEGORY	TREND	EXPLANATION
Dynamic Rerouting	Increasing emphasis on dynamic workflow rerouting to support fast-changing business processes, on-the-fly delegation, and exception handling	As in production workflow solutions, dynamic rerouting is becoming a standard feature of messaging-based products, as users demand the ability to redefine workflows on an ad-hoc basis, as befits the ever-evolving nature of processes in the modern workplace.
Database, Document, Object, Messaging, Directory, and Security System Interface Standards	Increasing standards-based integration with heterogeneous, network-based information bases and application services	The discussion in Table 7-1 applies equally to the messaging-based workflow market, because both technologies rely on the same general application infrastructure. Relevant standards include ODBC (for database integration), ODMA and DMA (for forms/document management integration), OLE/COM and CORBA (for object management integration), MAPI and VIM (for messaging integration), X.500 and LDAP (for directory integration), and PKCS-7/X.509 (for security integration). Document management systems are being used to index, search, and administer the growing forms libraries built up by users of messaging-based workflow products. Increasingly, the distributed information stores being accessed by messaging-based workflow products are administered under groupware suites such as Lotus Notes and Microsoft Exchange.
Vertical-Market Workflow Application Templates	Increasing development of vertical-market workflow application templates	Once again, Table 7-1's discussion carries over with equal force. Messaging-based workflow vendors and their resellers are providing vertical-market templates that bundle electronic forms, fillers, process models, and other software modules suitable to focused industry-specific applications.

Now that you've reviewed major trends, it's time to see who's doing what in the messaging-based workflow market. The following profiles of leading vendors and their products will give you a good overview. (For a complete listing of messaging-based workflow products, see Appendix A.)

Banyan Systems Inc.

Banyan, headquartered in Westboro, MA, provides electronic forms, database access, and structured routing capabilities with BeyondMail, its rule-based, e-mail client software.

BeyondMail

BeyondMail presents a *routing slip* addressing form to e-mail users, enabling sequential and cycle-to-originator routing. The product provides its own forms-design tools, includes several administrative forms templates, and imports forms created with various third-party applications. Any forms routed by BeyondMail are carried within the e-mail message, rather than, as with many messaging-based workflow products, as a file attachment to a message. Forms' contents can be encrypted before transmission.

BeyondMail's e-mail-enabled workflow scripting language allows users to automate many actions, such as the following:

- Calculate and execute routing rules based on values input into form fields
- File, forward, delete, and respond to messages fulfilling various criteria
- Launch predefined tasks upon receipt of a form in an application mailbox
- Send several forms to predefined users in response to an inbound form sent to an application mailbox
- Update corporate databases from data contained in form fields
- Track responses to forms and alert the originator when all responses have been received
- Produce and route database reports in response to queries contained in inbound e-mail forms
- Poll a user or application's new inbound messages and run that user's rules without opening his or her copy of BeyondMail
- Automate transmission, storage, and searching of forms using Intelligent Messaging extended attributes

BeyondMail, which installs on the desktop only, integrates with Banyan's Intelligent Messaging e-mail system and StreetTalk directory services, as well as with back-end MHS- and SMTP-based messaging systems. The BeyondMail client runs on MS-DOS, Windows, Macintosh, and UNIX desktops. Forms created with its design tool can query, retrieve, and write data on ODBC-compliant SQL databases such as dBASE, Paradox, Oracle, and Sybase. Scanned and faxed *thumbnail* images can be embedded in BeyondMail messages and forms through an embedded version of the FileNet/Watermark Explorer edition image-manipulation software. Data can be imported into BeyondMail forms from other Microsoft Windows applications through DDE calls.

BeyondMail also integrates into the Lotus Notes environment, serving as an alternate e-mail environment for Notes desktops. All Notes menu items relating to mail can be set up to bypass NotesMail and be executed entirely within BeyondMail. Multiple Notes databases and document stores can be queried with a single formatted BeyondMail message, via the Beyond Notes Connection software module.

Enhancements to the cornerstone

Banyan regards BeyondMail as the cornerstone for an e-mail-based electronic-commerce product strategy that it calls *Business on Mail*. BeyondMail will be upgraded to support Web/HTML forms and a wide range of third-party e-mail-enabled forms, developed with Visual Basic and OLE controls. BeyondMail's rules-scripting language will allow developers to write applications that can either take input from a Web site or query a Web site and return the response to a user by e-mail — similar to the query-by-mail capability currently supported with Lotus Notes servers.

Other planned enhancements to BeyondMail include more powerful server-based automated agents, database manipulation capabilities, and more complex workflow processes. The product will be ported to Windows 95, Windows NT, and OS/2 clients; Windows NT and UNIX servers; and Microsoft Mail, Lotus cc:Mail, and UNIX Mail message systems. The forms designer will be extended to support drag-and-drop database field definition, in which the database schema is displayed and the developer can easily select database fields for forms.

FileNet

Branching out into messaging- and suite-based workflow, FileNet — profiled at length in Chapter 7 — released its Ensemble product in 1996 (see Figure 8-1). The package, co-developed with Novell, transmits workflow items over messaging systems within users' existing Novell Groupwise and Microsoft Exchange groupware environments, or via Microsoft Mail. Ensemble enables workflow users to locate, retrieve, attach, route, and automatically launch a wide range of electronic documents from across the network, thanks to ODMA-compliant interfaces to users' existing document management systems. The workflow system can route any type of electronic object, including text, scanned images, faxes, spreadsheets, graphics, electronic forms, CAD drawings, and video clips. It can also exchange work items with Visual WorkFlo production applications.

Filenet's workflow system can route any electronic object, including text, scanned images, faxes, spreadsheets, graphics, electronic forms, CAD drawings, and video clips.

Ensemble users can build sophisticated workflow definitions graphically from their desktops, using an address-driven modeling technique to link recipients (either individually, in groups, or by functional roles), define participants' roles and privileges, create and assign manual or automated tasks, and specify routing and handling rules, including instructions, priorities, deadlines, reminders, and notifications. Users define workflows by dragging and dropping graphical icons that represent participants and by drawing routes to connect the icons. Participants' addresses are retrieved from address books of the underlying e-mail systems and linked to icons that represent people's functional roles. Sequential, parallel, concurrent, and conditional routes can be specified. Workflow application developers can drag and drop preexisting Visual WorkFlo process models into Ensemble workflow designs. Ensemble process definitions can be saved and reused in future workflows.

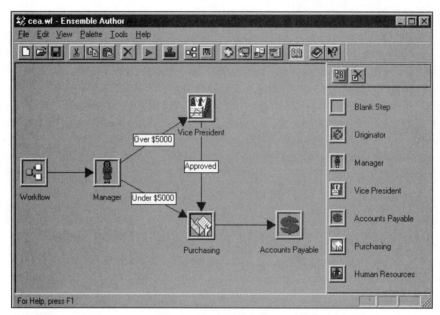

Figure 8-1
Ensemble is a messaging-based workflow product from Novell and FileNet.

Ensemble displays inbound work items in users' e-mail inboxes, from which the file attachments can be launched into associated applications. Users can be given the flexibility to reroute work items dynamically. A graphical status-tracking module, WorkFlo Central, allows users to view all pending work items for them, as well as follow the status of all workflows in which they are a participant.

FileNet and Novell have developed equivalent messaging-based workflow capabilities for the latter's GroupWise groupware suite, which is profiled in Chapter 10.

IBM/Lotus Development Corp.

IBM offers two messaging-based workflow products: its legacy FormTalk package, geared primarily for OS/2 desktops, and the Lotus Forms product, acquired in Big Blue's 1995 acquisition of Lotus Development Corporation. At this writing, IBM had not indicated whether or how it plans to integrate or merge the two products. (Lotus Notes — the company's popular groupware environment — also has workflow capabilities (discussed further in Chapter 10).

Lotus Forms

Lotus Forms is a more sophisticated workflow solution than IBM FormTalk. Lotus Forms' forms/workflow designer and filler both run on Windows desktops, with support planned for UNIX, Macintosh, and OS/2 platforms as well. It integrates with most popular e-mail systems through MAPI and VIM APIs, accessing the mail address book to build routing lists. Various image and graphics formats can be placed in forms fields, including TIFF, PCX, BMP, CGM, HPGL, AmiDraw, DrawPerfect, and Freelance Graphics. Form fields can be populated with text data from most SQL-based RDBMSs through ODBC drivers and ASCII file exchange. Of course, it can access data maintained in Lotus' popular Notes groupware product, as well as information contained in third-party applications through the Notes/FX module. It can also maintain enterprise forms libraries in distributed, replicated Notes document stores and Lotus cc:Mail bulletin boards.

As with most messaging-based workflow products, Lotus Forms has a client-centric architecture, placing all routing logic in the electronic form itself. The form invokes the appropriate commands on the user's e-mail client to route itself automatically to the next designated recipient, even across diverse e-mail systems. The form can also be configured to send notification messages to its originator in the event that it is forwarded, rejected, or otherwise processed. An alternate tracking technique is for the form to report its status periodically to a central database, maintained under Notes or any ODBC-compliant database, that can be queried directly or through forms-oriented messages.

The Forms Designer supports forms and workflow definition through graphical layout tools and an editor and debugger for the powerful LotusScript cross-application scripting language. A set of 12 form templates is provided to jump-start the development process for purchase orders, travel requests, employment applications, quotations, and other standard business documents. Each form has four configurable layers: the graphical layout, routing logic, execution scripts, and menu bar. Sequential or parallel routing lists can be built from e-mail addresses of individuals or from defined *roles* or job titles within the business process. Tables in any supported RDBMS can be created or edited from within the Designer. The product supports Lotus' customizable SmartIcons and SmartStatus bars, allowing developers to build applications exploiting the common look and feel of Notes, cc:Mail, and SmartSuite.

The Forms Filler, installed on user desktops, provides features for receiving, launching, inputting, editing, highlighting, annotating, and tracking electronic forms. From within their standard e-mail boxes, recipients receive filled-out forms as attachments to messages and can automatically launch the Form Filler by clicking on the attachment. Highlighting is supported through an on-screen *red pen* icon tool and editing and annotation through a pop-up note tool. Embedded RSA public-key technology enables forms or any field value therein to be locked, tamper-proofed, and authenticated to recipients. When the user selects the send function from within the form, the item is automatically forwarded to its next designated recipient.

FormTalk

IBM FormTalk is more limited in platform support, running only under the company's OS/2 operating environment (though Windows support is planned) and integrating only with VIM-compatible e-mail systems such as cc:Mail. However, FormTalk forms have the ability to collect information and invoke business processes running under

FlowMark, which is IBM's production workflow solution (see Chapter 7). FlowMark can then perform complex processing on the data fed into it by a FormTalk application.

The FormTalk architecture provides an integrated design and filler tool to every user, supporting grass-roots, peer-to-peer workflow application development. Object-oriented design capabilities allow users to define reusable entry fields, calculations, fixed text, help text, bitmaps, and routing lists that may be added — through icon drag-and-drop — to new electronic forms. Routing and approval lists, constructed from entries in the e-mail address book, may be associated with the form either at design time for all future copies of the form, or at fill time for a particular instance of the form. Sequential, parallel, and cycle-back-to-originator routing chains are supported. Form data can be made available to other applications, through updates to network databases, at the end of the approval process — or can be exported to FlowMark for more complex workflow processing.

FormTalk allows users to display and fill multiple forms at the same time. Forms originators can receive tracking messages that allow them to be kept informed of a form's location in the approval chain. Rejected forms are automatically returned to the originator, who may choose to change field data values and resubmit the form through the same or different routing chain. Read-only *FYI* copies of completed forms may be sent automatically to some e-mail users, who in this case would not need to have FormTalk installed on their desktops.

JetForm Corp.

JetForm, headquartered in Ottawa, Ontario, Canada, is one of the market leaders in forms-based, e-mail-enabled workflow. The company's products run on third-party e-mail systems accessed through MAPI and VIM standard interfaces, as well as in conjunction with most popular Web browsers and servers (more on this in Chapter 9). JetForm is one of the few firms in the messaging-based workflow market without an e-mail product of its own.

In September 1996, JetForm solidified its position in the messaging-based workflow market with its acquisition of Symantec Corp.'s Delrina Group Electronic Forms Division, its longtime rival. JetForm has added Delrina's workflow and electronic forms products — FormFlow and PerForm — to its own stable of workflow products.

The following section discusses the respective architectures and features of the company's JetForm and FormFlow brand products.

JetForm brand products

The JetForm product family is a rich suite of products for many LAN and WAN environments, including the Web (see Chapter 9 for discussion of their Web-based workflow tool). It consists of several components: a forms/workflow design tool (JetForm Design), forms-filler client software (JetForm Filler and Filler Pro), forms dictionary (JetForm Central), and forms routing and tracking server software (JetForm Workflow). JetForm Design runs on Windows 3.1, 95, and NT systems, as well as under Netscape Navigator. JetForm Filler and Filler Pro run on Windows, Macintosh, and OS/2, and MS-DOS desktops. The server-resident JetForm WorkFlow and Central products run on the same operating environments, as well as UNIX and many third-party Web server software packages. The product family integrates with any MAPI- or VIM-compliant e-mail system, including Microsoft Mail and Exchange, Lotus cc:Mail and Notes Mail, Banyan Intelligent Messaging and BeyondMail, Novell GroupWise, and Hewlett-Packard OpenMail.

Routable JetForm electronic forms can pull data from existing applications through DDE and OLE calls and from most industry-standard SQL databases through various ODBC drivers. The JetForm client includes imaging software from FileNet/Watermark, enabling users to embed scanned images and graphics in electronic forms, including such formats as TIFF, PCX, BMP, and PostScript. Various bar-code formats can also be embedded in JetForm forms.

The company's products are designed both as stand-alone forms-routing solutions and as back-end network services that can be called transparently by custom desktop applications. The JetForm application developers toolkit provides dozens of APIs that can be called by any Windows-based application, supporting such functions as form display, filling, calculation, printing, and routing. Third-party design tools such as Visual Basic and PowerBuilder can also be forms-enabled, using the APIs to trigger forms creation, routing, and output.

JETFORM DESIGN

JetForm Design lets you create new, customized electronic forms, which may be up to 99 pages long. At the lowest level of forms design, you can lay down such graphical elements as lines, boxes, circles, colors, and grayscaling, as well as such text features as font, point size, and variable leading. User-defined grids allow you to place graphics and text precisely on the From and To position data fields, tables, checkboxes, and radio buttons correctly.

To speed up the design process, you can invoke JetForm's AutoTrace function to generate computerized graphics over the features of scanned-in forms. Any of 25 pre-designed business forms can be used as a template for your custom form. In addition, designers can build new forms from any of the forms components contained in JetForm's server-resident Form Dictionary software module.

Form fields can support intelligent-forms capabilities unavailable with traditional paper forms.

After the basic layout of a JetForm business form is established, designers can begin to define the data links, internal validations and calculations, and processing logic needed to transform it into a routable object. On a single form, data fields can be set up to pull data from various third-party applications and databases, or simply read and display external data records. Data field definitions can be kept consistent across dozens of corporate forms, thanks to the object-oriented Forms Dictionary. Designers have the option, when changing the master definition of a field, to propagate that change across forms where that field is used.

Form fields can be set up to support intelligent-forms capabilities unavailable with traditional paper forms, such as to:

- Provide custom views for each user, determining the form fields that can be viewed, filled in, printed, and/or faxed

- Enforce mandatory data-field entry

- Limit input data to *legal* values

- Perform spell checks and data validation

- Fill some fields automatically based on cross-field calculations or system-generated information (for example, date, time, username), using any of 90-plus arithmetic, financial, date, and logical functions

- Replicate data in recurring fields on separate pages of a multipage form

- Authenticate and lock some data-field entries with electronic signatures

- Define sequential, parallel, and conditional routing paths, tying conditional routes to user-input data values

- Automatically update underlying databases and indexes at the end of the workflow

JETFORM FILLER

Workflow process logic is embedded within a JetForm form and implemented by the JetForm Filler software, which is installed on each desktop. The Filler allows users to complete, annotate, sign, print, and route forms over existing local- and wide-area e-mail systems through seamless desktop integration with third-party mail-client software. A form's originator automatically receives a tracking message whenever anyone sends the form to its next recipient. Users can return an electronic form to anyone on the routing list preceding them. Users may also be allowed, when a form does not have a fixed route, to define new routes on the fly through access to the e-mail address book.

Integration with the JetForm Form Dictionary enables the Filler to organize business forms into logical categories (such as expense forms, purchase orders, and personnel forms) and locate them quickly when needed. Forms can be grouped into linked sets that update each other automatically when any one of them is populated with data.

As just noted, the run-time workflow logic in a JetForm application is embedded in the electronic form and executed by the Filler client — in contrast to production workflow systems, in which servers wield all process control. The server-resident component of a JetForm solution manages client access to network databases, tracks form location and status, distributes updated forms to all desktops, and interfaces to shared network printers and fax machines.

The server-based Tracking Director module maintains a database that allows users to query the current location and status of forms in process, according to such criteria as date sent, originator, form type, and user-defined attributes.

The Distribution Director integrates with JetForm's Forms Dictionary to distribute and install new or updated forms automatically to all the authorized network users, sparing administrators the logistical hassle and expense of manual or alternate electronic forms distribution.

Changes on the way

JetForm's server-based workflow capabilities are sure to grow as it explores greater integration with third-party production workflow solutions. According to company marketing vice-president Brownell Chalstrom, JetForm is seeking to integrate its environment more tightly with leading production workflow solutions so that users can route and track work items transparently across different domains.

JetForm is maintaining its client-centric electronic-forms-routing architecture, says Chalstrom, but the company has also developed a server-based routing engine to support more sophisticated rules and role-type databases. JetForm now supports an alternate messaging-based workflow system configuration that takes the process logic out of the form and manages it in a central server, similar to the architecture of production workflow applications. Further blurring the distinction between messaging-based and production workflow, JetForm by early 1997 will also support *in situ* file routing, allowing files to be kept on the server and accessed through logical pointers embedded in mail-enabled electronic forms.

JetForm's application development toolkit includes APIs to support *intelligent forms* functions within Web browser clients, including such capabilities as multifield calculation, data validation and verification, display control, and multiple pages. A version of the JetForm Filler can be invoked from within most popular Web browsers to populate HTML forms. Scripting tools enable forms-input HTML data fields to be integrated with legacy corporate databases, via the Web Connectivity Pak for JetForm Central. (More on JetForm's Web-based workflow capabilities is presented in Chapter 8.)

If JetForm has plans to implement Microsoft's MWF, it is keeping them close to the vest. JetForm has participated in the MWF definition effort since fall 1995 but has not yet gone on record as endorsing the standard or announcing plans to implement it in products.

FormFlow brand

FormFlow was the pioneer product in the messaging-based workflow market, setting the stage for JetForm and other vendors. Delrina introduced FormFlow in 1988, integrating the product with most popular third-party messaging systems.

FormFlow's most distinctive feature is its object-oriented enterprise-wide forms library, which can be distributed transparently across multiple operating environments on LANs or WANs. This library enables developers to define forms and workflows quickly from reusable software objects; propagate changes immediately across all networked desktops; and organize stored forms into logical categories to facilitate user search and retrieval. Forms and process-definition libraries can be stored in Internet FTP sites, local or network-based file systems, relational databases (where forms are stored as binary large objects), and Microsoft Exchange folders (either private, public, or global). Around 100 forms templates are bundled with FormFlow, jump-starting creation of user-customized forms libraries.

FormFlow's forms/workflow design tool runs under Windows 3.1. Developers use FormBasic, an object-oriented visual programming language with more than 500 functions, to define form layout, calculations, database linkages, routing rules, and user roles and privileges. Sequential, parallel, conditional, and cyclical (that is, back-to-originator) routes can be defined through simple drag-and-drop graphical definitions. Users can be provided with different access privileges on forms, fields, and databases. Digital signatures can be used to authenticate and lock data in fields, whole forms, or forms and attached files. User roles can be imported from existing corporate databases, eliminating the need to build special new databases to support forms routing.

FormFlow forms can invoke existing applications through ActiveX calls and retrieve data from most industry-standard SQL databases through various ODBC drivers. Databases can be queried, read, written, and manipulated directly by FormFlow without the need to first open a linked form. Forms can be created automatically from database tables, and tables can be created from form fields. Forms can pull data directly from Lotus Notes databases and, through Notes Field Exchange (Notes/FX), from external applications, taking advantage of Notes' document- and field-level security.

If users already have access to form-linked databases, developers can specify that only the form itself — minus contents — be routed, minimizing the amount of data that gets shipped over the network. Alternately, both the form and data contents can be packaged for transit to recipients. For superior performance on database transactions, FormFlow interfaces in native non-ODBC mode to various industry-leading RDBMSs, including Microsoft SQL Server 6, Oracle 7, and Sybase 10 and 11.

Forms are routed over any MAPI-, VIM-, and MHS-compliant e-mail system, including Microsoft Exchange. FormFlow's form-filler client software runs in Microsoft Windows 3.1, MS-DOS, Silicon Graphics Irix, SunSoft Solaris and SunOS, and Macintosh, with IBM AIX, HP/UX, Windows NT, and Windows 95 in the works. Server software runs on the same platforms. The product also routes forms through Delrina's WinFax Pro fax product, by means of the company's Forms Data Interchange specification.

The FormFlow filler's inbox can be set up to automatically process incoming workflow items according to prespecified handling rules. Inbox workflow items are displayed in a hierarchical, folder-style interface, alongside other e-mail messages. The client also allows users to track the current status and location of all workflow items that they originate. Forms-tracking databases can be supported on any ODBC-compliant network database and queried through formatted e-mail messages.

FormFlow has been integrated with DOCS Open, the popular enterprise-wide document-management system from PC DOCS Inc. FormFlow forms can now be organized, searched, and retrieved in an integrated DOC Open repository alongside all other business documents.

Keyfile

Keyfile, one of the leading production workflow vendors (profiled in Chapter 7), released its new messaging/suite-based workflow product, Keyflow, in 1996. (See Figure 8-2.)

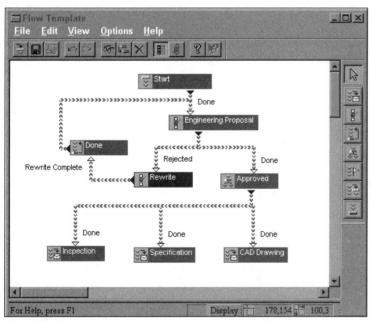

Figure 8-2
A workflow process model created with Keyfile's KeyFlow product.

Keyflow provides workflow functionality comparable to Keyfile's production work-flow product (featured in Chapter 8), but operates entirely over the Microsoft Exchange groupware suite. Exchange's replicated public folders are used to distribute Keyflow electronic forms and process definitions throughout an enterprise. Keyflow users can construct workflow routes graphically using Exchange's *Compose.Newform* menu, pull user names and roles/relationships from Exchange's address book, and route documents through Exchange's messaging transport agents. New work items and attachments appear in user's Exchange e-mail inboxes. Users can view the status of active workflows in public folders and, as necessary, reroute active workflows in process, subject to security controls provided by Exchange.

"We believe that Exchange will be a successful product for wide-area collaboration," says Stephen Marchesano, Keyfile senior product manager. Keyfile has no plans, he says, to port Keyflow to competing collaboration environments, such as Lotus Notes and Novell GroupWise.

Microsoft Corp.

Microsoft, headquartered in Redmond, WA, has geared its Electronic Forms Designer workflow tool for an all-Microsoft desktop, server, and networking environment. This is a product strategy that can succeed only for a vendor that has the pervasive market presence and clout of Microsoft. Electronic Forms Designer allows developers to build rule-driven electronic forms in the Microsoft Visual Basic development environment and route them over Microsoft Mail/Exchange and other MAPI-compliant e-mail systems. (Microsoft Exchange's workflow capabilities are discussed further in Chapter 10).

Electronics Forms Designer

Electronics Forms Designer's designer and client software run only on Windows 3.1, 95, and NT systems over any network that supports MAPI-based messaging (a de facto industry standard mail interface developed by Microsoft). Forms can retrieve and incorporate information from RDBMSs that support ODBC database-access technology (another Microsoft-developed de facto industry standard), such as the vendor's own SQL Server, FoxPro, and Access RDBMS products. Forms can also use OLE (yet another Microsoft-developed industry standard) to retrieve and incorporate text, charts, graphs, and multimedia objects from other desktop applications.

Electronic Forms Designer is a powerful development environment that can integrate workflow-enabled forms tightly with Microsoft Mail's desktop client software, with Windows, and with any applications developed for the Windows environment. Forms are sent as custom messages within Microsoft Mail, indicated by a special in-box icon. Forms are stand-alone Visual Basic executables that can be run from within Mail using the bundled E-Form Browser, invoked from custom commands on the Mail client menu, or invoked from the Windows Program Manager. ActiveX and Visual Basic controls allow developers to integrate electronic forms with other Windows applications.

To jump-start forms/workflow development, Microsoft includes a generic forms/workflow template and several customizable business forms with the Electronic Forms Designer, including templates for supply order, help-desk request, travel reservations, remote-query, and telephone-note applications.

Designers can add new visual elements, routing rules, and other capabilities (for example, pen support, database access, encryption) to existing forms by visually dragging and dropping Visual Basic controls onto the form template. Complex workflow process definitions — and even applications that process forms without manual intervention — can be defined with the procedural BASIC language. Developers can grant different read/write privileges to different users on the same form, depending, for example, on user roles and stages in the routing cycle. Form graphical elements can even be rendered in text so that they can be routed to and read by users on other non-MAPI mail systems.

Similar to Microsoft Mail

Users can compose, read, and address an electronic form as if it were a standard Microsoft Mail message. Blank forms can be retrieved locally from a user's hard drive, from a shared Microsoft Mail bulletin board, or from a file server directory. Forms are presented as formatted mail messages with a mix of structured and unstructured text fields and other information objects. Users are presented with familiar mail-like commands and on-screen buttons such as Address, Send, and Reply. Sequential routes can be defined through a routing-slip dialog box, which may be accessed from within the Microsoft Mail client or from the user interface of any Windows application.

Usually, only a form's data contents and process rules — not its visual format — are routed. Forms are typically preinstalled on a user's desktop and are invoked automatically when data fields instantiating that message type are received and opened. Essentially, the form serves as a viewer on data fields — an architecture that saves bandwidth for LAN/WAN-connected users and dial-up connect time and charges for remote users.

Novell Inc.

Novell, headquartered in Provo, UT, provides a feature-rich electronic forms, database access, and workflow product called *InForms*. The product is one of several network-enabled applications — including the GroupWise e-mail/groupware environment and SoftSolutions document management software — that Novell retained when it sold its desktop applications products (including WordPerfect and Quattro Pro) to Corel Corporation in early 1996. (GroupWise's current and planned workflow capabilities are discussed further in Chapter 10.)

InForms

InForms is a versatile, multiplatform forms-routing solution that integrates with network software environments as follows:

- **Forms-designer client software:** InForms forms-designer software runs on Windows desktops

- **Forms-filler client software:** InForms forms-filler software runs on Windows, Macintosh, and MS-DOS desktops

- **Network operating systems:** Runs under NetWare, VINES, Windows for Workgroups, and any NetBIOS-based LAN

- **Messaging services:** Works with GroupWise, and any other MAPI- or VIM-compliant e-mail system

- **Directory services:** Reads user mail addresses and other information from the NetWare Directory Services or the address books of the various e-mail systems with which it integrates

- **Document management services:** Integrates via ODMA calls with SoftSolutions, using that package to support profile-based forms searches, version controls, and other forms management functions

- **Database management systems:** Reads and writes data on a score of ODBC, ODAPI/IDAPI, and other databases, including NetWare SQL, Btrieve, DataPerfect, dBASE, FoxPro, Paradox, DB2, Informix, Microsoft SQL Server, NetWare SQL, Oracle, OS/2 DBM, SQLBase, Sybase, XDB, and Lotus Notes

- **Application object/data sharing:** Uses OLE and DDE to integrate with other Windows applications, and Notes/FX to pull data from other desktop applications in the Lotus Notes environment

- **Graphics file formats:** Handles BMP, CGM, DHP, DXF, EPS, GEM, HPGL, IMG, MSP, PCX, PIC, PNTG, PPIC, TIF, WMF, WPG, text boxes, and many bar-code formats

- **Fonts and page-description languages:** Handles Adobe Type Manager, Bitstream TrueType, Adobe PostScript, HP PCL 4 and 5, and all Windows-supported fonts

InForms enjoys a special level of integration with Novell GroupWise: Within GroupWise, InForms forms are managed as custom messages and are distinguished from standard e-mail in the GroupWise inbox and outbox by an InForms icon. Forms routed as custom messages may be opened directly into the InForms Filler through double-clicks from the GroupWise inbox (a capability also available with MAPI-compliant e-mail systems). Forms may be managed and tracked as task assignments in the GroupWise environment. On e-mail systems that have no custom-message integration feature, InForms forms must be routed as file attachments, which requires users to open the e-mail message, save the attachment to a local or network directory, and then finally launch Filler to open the form.

InForms Designer

The InForms Designer provides a visual environment for creating complex electronic forms and defining sequential, parallel, and conditional process models. Single- and multipage forms can be built from a wide range of drawing tools, drop-down list boxes, checkboxes, radio buttons, data entry/lookup fields and tables, arithmetic and logical calculations, and file viewers. Calculations can be embedded in forms to automatically process information or activate conditional routing rules.

Form fields can be linked to fields in one or more desktop or server databases. Each field can be linked to multiple databases in a fashion transparent to users who are viewing or filling in the form, with data conversion and joining operations being performed in the Form Filler. Multiple database files can share the same form field as a key field, and, if the values do not match in all linked fields, an error is reported and InForms asks which of the values is correct. Forms designers can control users' read/write access into linked databases. A new SQL database can be created at the time of forms definition, provided that the designer has a copy of the appropriate RDBMS software.

Workflow routes can be defined by calling up the addressing template for the appropriate e-mail system. The form/workflow designer can include any number of users as primary, carbon copy, and blind carbon copy recipients. Rules can be defined that automatically send or route a form when certain conditions exist or when certain actions are taken on the form or any of its fields.

Close to two dozen business forms templates are bundled with the InForms Designer, enabling the product to be used out of the box for many applications with minimal redesign or programming. To speed up subsequent forms/workflow definition, InForms provides an object library of prebuilt form parts, enabling designers to build new forms by simply copying common elements from the library instead of recreating and debugging new objects. Objects can include graphical components as well as items that contain intelligence, such as formulas and data-retrieval operations.

InForms Filler

After a form is designed, it can be processed at any Windows, DOS, or Macintosh desktop using the InForms Filler client software. The form can be filled in and routed according to embedded workflow rules, or used as a template for querying any linked desktop- or server-based RDBMS. When data satisfying the query is displayed in Filler, it can be retrieved into the form, modified, and then saved back to the database (if the user has been granted that privilege). Embedded file viewers may also allow users to preview and copy text, graphics, or other objects from external files into an open InForms form.

Recognizing that electronic forms are often sensitive business documents, Novell provides powerful security services, such as digital signature, encryption, and tamperproofing. A security profile is defined for a form at design time and enforced by the InForms Filler when the form is received at the desktop. Digital signatures may be applied to entire forms or selected fields, verifying that the contents were originated or approved by particular persons and have not been modified since they were signed. Likewise, selected field contents may be encrypted so that only one or a few recipients may read them during the routing process. The TamperSeal feature allows only those users with higher *approval levels* than the originator to alter protected data.

Summary

This chapter has presented an overview of major trends and vendors in the messagingbased workflow market. A more complete vendor list is provided in Appendix A.

As evidenced by inclusion of FileNet and Keyfile in this survey, major production workflow vendors are getting into the messaging-based niche, a trend that should accelerate in coming years. Ad-hoc, messaging-oriented process definition, and execution are critical features for workflow products that aim at the mass business market. One safe prediction is that by the year 2000 you'll be hard-pressed to identify a production workflow vendor without a messaging-based version of its product — or a messaging-based workflow vendor without strong production-like features in its product.

Inexorably, production and messaging-based vendors are also branching into Web-based workflow. Already, you have looked at the *Web-enabling* of one messaging-based product family, JetForm, which allows participants to access workflows from any Web browser and can process information gathered from many Web servers. The next chapter focuses on this new market segment, which is populated both by established workflow vendors (such as Action and JetForm) and by ambitious startups.

CHAPTER NINE

WEB-BASED WORKFLOW MARKET

Today's Web-based workflow vendors generally approach the market from either of three angles: as an extension or offshoot from an existing production, messaging-based, and/or suite-based workflow product (as with Action, Banyan, JetForm, Novell, and Viewstar); as a stand-alone Web-based workflow offering (as with OpenText and Ultimus); or as an extension to a distributed document management product (as with Documentum).

The Web-based workflow segment is young and growing fast. This chapter provides profiles of most Web-based vendors at the time of publication. For guidelines on when to choose a Web-based solution over other workflow technologies, refer to Chapters 3 and 12. Table 9-1 shows the general trends in Web-based workflow.

TABLE 9-1: WEB-BASED WORKFLOW MARKET TRENDS

CATEGORY	TREND	EXPLANATION
Operating Platform	Industry support for Netscape and Microsoft Internet/intranet product architectures	Netscape and Microsoft have established themselves as the dominant providers of Web browsers, servers, authoring, and security tools, as well as most Internet/intranet software providers either follow their lead or pay close attention to their moves. Most Web-based workflow products are geared primarily to work with Netscape and Microsoft's Internet/intranet software environments. Netscape has developed an Internet/intranet interoperability framework — called *Netscape Open Network Environment (ONE)* — that specifies such open industry standards as HTTP (basic browser-server protocol), HTML (page formatting), Java (downloadable applets), SSL and SHTTP (transaction security), SMTP and MIME (messaging), S/MIME (messaging security), IIOP (object interoperability), X.509 (public-key certificates), and NNTP (distributed discussion groups). Microsoft also supports these open standards but, of course, promotes its own operating systems, development tools, and applications as the preferred environment for all things Internet/intranet.
Workflow Management Standards	Vendor compliance with emerging workflow industry standards	Given the Web community's innate embrace of open standards, we can expect Web-based workflow vendors to rally behind the WfMC's technical standards, at more or less the same rate at which these standards are adopted by production workflow vendors. WfMC's standards do not depend on any one type of network platform (such as distributed filestores, messaging, or the Web). Microsoft's MAPI Workflow Framework will make no inroads into the Web-based market, due to that standard's explicit orientation to messaging environments.
Architectures	Integration with production, messaging-based, and suite-based workflow products	Already, we're seeing Web-based products that function as extensions to existing production (e.g., Action, FileNet, Reach, ViewStar), messaging-based (e.g., Banyan, JetForm), and suite-based (e.g., Novell) workflow products. Web-based products usually figure into these other workflow environments as a new type of client interface (i.e., a browser instead of dedicated workflow inbox, a la production workflow, or e-mail inbox, a la messaging- and suite-based products), a new type of filestore (i.e., a Java/HTML-compliant Web site instead of a traditional LAN/WAN document/database repository), and/or a new type of backbone network protocol (i.e., HTTP over TCP/IP, instead of other application, transport, and network-layer protocols that companies may have running on their internal networks).

CATEGORY	TREND	EXPLANATION
Application Development Tools	Universal adoption of HTML V. 3, Java, and JavaScript to support development of smart Web forms	Web-based workflow solutions implement HTML forms to the almost complete exclusion of proprietary electronic forms formats, such as those traditionally bundled with production and messaging-based products. HTML has become the first truly open electronic forms standard in the world. Web-based workflow products are providing browser-based forms-processing functionality through embedding of JavaScript commands and downloading of Java applets. Some Web-based workflow vendors (such as JetForm) also provide *plug-in* browser software modules that beef up the display, calculation, and output features of their intelligent HTML/Java-compliant forms.
Database, Document, Object, Messaging, Directory, and Security System Interface Standards	Increasing standards-based integration with heterogeneous, network-based information bases and application services	The discussions in Tables 7-1 and 8-1 apply equally to the Web-based workflow market. As noted previously, Netscape and Microsoft are spearheading standardization on the network protocols and application services available to Web-based applications in general and workflow applications in particular. Web-based workflow products can tap into the standard Internet/intranet application infrastructure services outlined earlier, plus the vast range of other standards described in Chapter 6.
Vertical-Market Workflow Application Templates	Increasing development of vertical-market workflow application templates	Table 7-1 and 8-1's discussions also carry over to the Web-based market. Web-based workflow vendors need to provide application templates that are as close as possible to *shrink-wrapped* (i.e., require minimal modification or integration by the customer) in order to appeal to a mass market. Vertical-market application templates or packages will become standard in the Web-based workflow market.

Now that you've reviewed the major market trends, you can plunge into the profiles of today's Web-based workflow vendors (contact information for these companies is in Appendix A):

Action Technologies

Action is a pioneer in deploying workflow applications over the Web. Introduced in December 1995, ActionWorkflow Metro enables any Web browser supporting the SHTTP security protocol (for example, Netscape Navigator) to function as a forms-oriented workflow client, without the need to distribute workflow-specific client software. Bundled with Metro are Action's existing graphical process-flowcharting and development tools, as well as sophisticated Web authoring tools and customizable forms supporting customer service, sales and marketing, human resources, finance and accounting, and engineering applications (see Chapter 7 for a discussion on Action's production workflow products). Metro is aimed at firms interested in building Web-based applications or using the Web for workflow applications within a corporate intranet firewall.

Metro appears to users as a set of forms that can be launched from a company's home page. Under Metro, browsers can initiate, process, and monitor work items by downloading appropriate HTML 3.0/JavaScript forms from an ActionWorkflow Metro server, which runs on Windows NT in conjunction with ActionWorkflow Manager (the company's production workflow-engine software), Netscape Commerce Server, and Microsoft SQL Server. A WorkBox Form provides a unified view of a particular user's new, pending, and in-process work items, which is updated in real time. Initiation Forms allow users to initiate workflows — for example, by filling out and submitting a Purchase Order form. Status and Interaction forms allow users to track outstanding work items and respond to work items routed from other people.

Implementing Metro workflow applications can require considerable custom programming and integration by users. It is a high-end, complex development environment on a technical par with production workflow systems in general and Action's production tools in particular. Metro works as follows:

1. From within their Web browsers, users log into Metro, which is installed on an intranet Web site running Netscape Commerce Server software.

2. Upon successful login, users download their personal WorkBoxes, which are HTML 3.0/JavaScript pages listing each user's personal work items.

3. The user clicks on the hyperlink to a particular work item, which causes the HTML/JavaScript form and contents corresponding to that item to be downloaded from the Web site into the user's browser.

4. The user then pulls down menu options embedded in the HTML/JavaScript form to take such workflow actions as approving, declining, or requesting additional information from the form's originator.

5. After the user finishes his or her work on the HTML/JavaScript form, the user indicates this by clicking on the appropriate on-screen *button* and thereby transmits the filled-in or modified form back to the Web site.

   Embedded in the HTML/JavaScript form are Common Gateway Interface (CGI) commands. These commands, after the form returns to the Web site, invoke Metro CGI programs running under Netscape Commerce Server and tell the CGI programs the name of the business process involved, which form fields are to be processed, and how to process them.

6. The Metro CGI program extracts the data from HTML/JavaScript form fields, writes the data to a relational database running on the Web site under Microsoft SQL Server for Windows NT (Metro's native data repository), and, to facilitate failure recovery, records the data in an SQL Server transaction log.

7. The Metro CGI program invokes a custom-built application script to command Metro's Process Manager workflow-engine module (on the Web site) to pass on to a legacy corporate database (usually on a separate computer somewhere on the company's private network) only those workflow-relevant key data fields associated with the work item.

8. Metro's Process Manager determines whether the work item has been validated against the legacy database and processes the item according to a process model that had previously been defined under Action's Process Builder workflow-definition tool.

9. Process Manager uses workflow-relevant form fields to decide how to route or process the work item next, according to the aforementioned process model.

10. Hyperlinks representing this work item are added in turn to the WorkBoxes of each subsequent user in the routing list, as the workflow proceeds.

11. When each subsequent user clicks the hyperlink, his or her browser will send a command to Metro (on the Web site) to extract the updated form fields from the legacy corporate database, regenerate the HTML/JavaScript form, and download it to the appropriate browser.

Action has also extended Metro to support user authentication by means of Kerberos, an industry standard developed originally at the Massachusetts Institute of Technology and now incorporated in commercial network/systems security products from many companies. Kerberos supports centralized key management; distribution of tamper-proof credentials; mutual authentication between clients and services; and encryption of all user passwords, session keys, and transmissions on distributed data applications. Metro recognizes Kerberos user IDs and passwords and can pass them automatically to back-end Kerberos authentication servers.

Action's technical approach to Web-based workflow is similar to its competitors in most aspects. Web-based workflow products are comparable, in complexity and sophistication, to traditional production workflow tools. Building and integrating Web-based workflow applications is no mean feat, seldom the sort of application that one can expect the average, nontechnical end user to develop.

Banyan Systems

Banyan has announced plans to develop a Web-based access to its BeyondMail workflow/e-mail product, profiled in Chapter 8. BeyondMail will be upgraded to support World Wide Web/HTML forms and a wide range of third-party e-mail-enabled forms, developed with Visual Basic and ActiveX. BeyondMail's rules-scripting language will allow developers to write applications that can either take input from a Web site or query a Web site and return the response to a user by e-mail — similar to the query-by-mail capability currently supported with Lotus Notes servers. No further technical details or availability timeframes were provided by Banyan.

Documentum, Inc.

Documentum provides Web-based access and workflow capabilities in its Enterprise Document Management System (EDMS). EDMS allows users to create, index, organize, search, access, view, edit, route, secure, control versions, and print documents in a distributed repository that spans local and wide-area networks. EDMS' searchable document repository, called *Docbase*, can include almost any type of application file, including HTML/Java-based Web pages on the Internet or corporate intranets. Double-clicking on a document's filename or icon automatically opens the document and the applications associated with it.

Documentum's Accelera software enables users to access EDMS functionality and the Docbase through standard Web browsers, with special workflow and document-management functions downloadable to Java-compliant browsers. Web-based users employ Accelera to route any EDMS-managed documents, folders, and other objects — including HTML/Java-compliant Web pages — over corporate intranets, employing a routing-slip interface for definition of simple and complex workflows. Routing of an object displays its filename or icon in the recipient's EDMS/Accelera folder, but does not transfer it physically to that user's hard disk. Links between EDMS/Accelera and MAPI or VIM e-mail systems enable automatic notifications to be sent to Web-based users when workflow items arrive in their folders for review (a delivery-notification feature very similar to that found in production workflow systems) or to report important process events, such as document revisions or approvals.

The Virtual Document Manager (VDM) feature within EDMS/Accelera enables Web-based users to build a hierarchical view of compound documents, showing their high-level structure, separate component files (such as text, graphics, and image files), annotations to those files, master and alternate versions of the files, and any associated workflows. VDM allows users to quickly reorganize the compound document, flag sections that have been changed, and track the revision histories of all sections.

Web-based workflow administrators use EDMS/Accelera to assign users and groups, define permissions, track processes, identify bottlenecks, and generate process-metrics reports.

JetForm

JetForm's Web-based products enable Internet/intranet users to participate in the same automated workflows with users of the company's JetForm-brand products (profiled in Chapter 8). As yet, the company has not yet Web-enabled its FormFlow messaging-based workflow products, recently acquired from Symantec Corp.

JetForm has extended its workflow reach to the Web with new server- and browser-based software modules. At the Web server, JetForm's Web Connectivity Pak supports integration of HTML forms data fields with legacy corporate databases. The Web Connectivity Pak integrates closely with Microsoft's Internet Server and Process Software's Purveyor Web server products through an Internet Server API (ISAPI) interface.

At the browser, the JetForm Filler for the Web supports such *intelligent forms* capabilities as multifield calculation, data validation and verification, display control, and display of multiple pages. The filler can be invoked from within most popular browsers to populate HyperText Markup Language (HTML) forms after they have been downloaded from the Web site.

A JetForm-developed *plug-in* software module in Netscape Navigator enables users to view, edit, save, and route native-format, non-HTML, JetForm-proprietary forms (Netscape plans to develop similar modules for other commercial browsers, such as Microsoft Internet Explorer). JetForm touts its own proprietary format over HTML as a more efficient approach for inputting form-field data into legacy databases, merging data with a format for printing or faxing, or initiating workflow processes. The company says its format and Netscape plug-in do away with the complex CGI scripts (such as those previously described under "Action Technologies") that are necessary to upload HTML forms data to legacy databases.

In another move aimed at improving Web forms integration with legacy databases, JetForm in July 1996 licensed an ODBC driver from DataRamp, Inc. (a subsidiary of PC DOCS Group International Inc.) to be included in future releases of JetForm's Web-based filler. JetForm will use DataRamp's technology to enable its filler to retrieve data over the Internet or intranets from any ODBC-compliant database, such as Oracle, Informix, Microsoft SQL Server, and Microsoft Access. Users will be able to perform live ODBC database lookups when filling in JetForm electronic forms. Public-key encryption technology in DataRamp's ODBC driver will protect queries, passwords, and other sensitive data from eavesdropping, theft, and tampering during transmission across the Internet or intranets.

Novell

Novell's GroupWise WebAccess lets users access their GroupWise inboxes from any Web browser. As discussed in Chapter 10, GroupWise is Novell's groupware suite that presents users with an integrated, replicated multimedia repository — distributed over one or more servers — that contains messages, documents, forms, faxes, graphics, task assignments, and, eventually, voice and video objects as well. Documents are presented through a shared-folder interface similar to Lotus Notes and Microsoft Exchange.

Just as with traditional GroupWise desktop clients, GroupWise WebAccess lets users open shared folders, retrieve and send Internet e-mail, receive and display pending workflow items, assign workflow items to other users, track the status of those items, view calendars, schedule meetings, and access the GroupWise address book. The product allows users to participate in GroupWise workflows when traveling, working from home, or surfing over the corporate intranet. Users simply point their browsers at the appropriate WebAccess home page addresses, log in, and enter their passwords. Upon authentication by the GroupWise WebAccess site, users automatically download their GroupWise Universal Mailbox formatted as an HTML page (with Java applet support planned for the first half of 1997).

GroupWise Web Access is installed on a NetWare 4.X server and can coexist locally with the NetWare Web Server and GroupWise message server. Using HTML hyperlinks in the WebAccess home page, users can navigate back and forth flexibly between GroupWise and other services on the Web.

Open Text

Open Text Corp.'s Livelink Intranet is a Web-based groupware suite that includes a workflow module, so, in that sense, it spans the boundary between Web- and suite-based workflow products.

The Livelink Intranet suite can be accessed from any Web browser. Workflow capabilities integrate with the following suite applications:

- **Livelink Library for Document Management:** The suite revolves around a shared multiformat document library that supports Web-based document check-out/in, automatic version control, and access controls.

- **Livelink Search:** Search and indexing tools enable users to rapidly locate the documents they want across a multisite corporate intranet by file contents and attributes.

- **Livelink Project Collaboration:** Project managers can establish shared document libraries and discussion groups, designate group and individual team members, define members' roles and privileges, assign tasks to personnel, specify task deadlines and priorities, and track progress.

Managers access the Livelink Workflow application module to graphically map, modify, manage, implement, and track serial, parallel, concurrent, or conditional workflows — no programming skills are needed to define process models under Livelink. Any objects in the document repository — including folders and individual files — can be routed in the workflow. Icons representing workflow activities can be dragged, dropped, and linked in a browser-based Workflow Painter module. On-screen entry fields support definition of workflow attributes (including initiation, routing, notification, termination, and auditing conditions), activity attributes (including activity-related forms, documents, instructions, comments, due dates, priorities, and durations), and roles (including document read/write, dynamic rerouting, and approval/rejection privileges).

> *Downloading a status page shows a work package's location in the entire workflow route.*

Users retrieve their Livelink Workflow *In Boxes* into their browsers as HTML-formatted pages. Double-clicking on a work item's hyperlink in the In Box page downloads the complete work package, including documents, instructions, due dates, and previous recipients' comments. Users can be notified when they have new items in

their Livelink Workflow In Boxes through notifications sent, through a MAPI interface, and to their e-mail inboxes.

Authorized users can view work status through the same map interface used to
define workflows. Downloading a status page shows a work package's current location
in the context of the entire workflow route, with color coding to indicate whether the
entire workflow is completed or late, an activity is on schedule or late, or a milestone
has been missed. The status page displays an audit trail that lists responsible personnel,
descriptions, dispositions, due dates, completion dates, and participant comments for
each activity.

Ultimus

Ultimus's workflow product family, called Ultimus, is a hybrid Web-, messaging-, and
suite-based solution — a true boundary-spanning workflow product the likes of which
will become the norm rather than the exception over the next few years.

The product is classified as Web-based in this book simply to call attention to its
innovative client/server workflow architecture. Ultimus' hybrid nature may be seen
most clearly in the range of Windows-based client environments that can participate
in workflows. The product supports popular Web browsers, e-mail clients (MAPI,
VIM, and/or MHS-compliant), Lotus Notes clients, ODMA-compliant document
management systems, and popular desktop applications such as Microsoft Word and
Excel, WordPerfect, and Lotus 1-2-3. Files and data can be routed by Ultimus to and
from any supported desktop application. Automated agents can be developed within
Ultimus to query, retrieve, process, and otherwise manipulate data in any supported
application.

The Web browser is the most feature-limited client in the Ultimus architecture.
Ultimus' WebFlow module only allows users to initiate workflows. HTML electronic
forms are downloaded to Web browsers from the Ultimus Engine module running on
a Netscape Web site. The user completes the form and uploads it back to Ultimus
Engine, which, based on the process definition and on workflow-relevant data contained in the form's fields, routes it to recipients' e-mail inboxes. Routing is accomplished through the Ultimus Engine's interfaces to MAPI, VIM, and MHS messaging
systems, from which the routed items may be retrieved by e-mail clients or messaging
clients embedded in Lotus Notes and any supported desktop application. When each
recipient completes work on an item, it is automatically e-mailed back to the Ultimus
Engine (one engine only in Ultimus 2.0, though the company has promised multi-
engine support in Version 3.0). All work items, notifications, and status updates are
sent to users' e-mail inboxes, not their Web browsers.

*There is a clear trend for workflow vendors to implement Web-based
client access and allow workflow data to be hosted on Web sites.*

Ultimus' design tool, called *Designer*, supports graphical workflow mapping and forms creation, on a par with the current industry state of the art. The tool lets users design and simulate new workflows graphically by defining the following:

- Icons that represent activities

- Links between activities

- Routing rules associated with links

- Electronic forms, spreadsheets (with embedded formulas), documents, and comments/instructions to be routed over links between activities

- External applications (for example, Microsoft Word for Windows, Lotus 1-2-3), documents, and ODBC-compliant databases that will be accessed, retrieved, and invoked automatically at each activity

- Organizational chart with associated position titles, workflow roles, and privileges

- User names and e-mail addresses associated with each position title

Ultimus Administrator, running under Windows, allows managers to automate installation and deinstallation of workflows on participating desktops; monitor workflow status; generate workflow performance statistics; and define and maintain organization charts used for process mapping.

Summary

This chapter has presented an overview of major trends and vendors in the Web-based workflow market. The complete vendor list is provided in Appendix A.

Web-based workflow is an application that makes the most of companies' investments in region, nation, and globe-spanning intranets, especially for electronic commerce and administrative transactions that utilize electronic forms. Web-based workflow tools also enable companies to extend their installed base of production, messaging-, and/or suite-based workflow tools by providing workflow access from any authorized browser, on the intranet or Internet. As this market survey has shown, there is a clear trend for workflow vendors to implement Web-based client access and allow workflow data to be hosted on Web sites.

The next chapter surveys the market for suite-based workflow products, which leverage users' investments in another critical piece of the network application infrastructure: groupware and desktop application environments, such as Lotus Notes, Microsoft Exchange, and Novell GroupWise.

CHAPTER TEN

SUITE-BASED
WORKFLOW MARKET

Today's suite-based workflow products are marketed either as components of desktop application suites (such as Microsoft Office, Lotus SmartSuite, or Corel Perfect Office) or as the forms-routing services within groupware environments (such as Lotus Notes, Novell GroupWise, and Microsoft Exchange). This market segment overlaps the other three considerably, insofar as suite-based products may route work items over distributed filestores (such as the replicated document databases in Lotus Notes and Microsoft Exchange), messaging systems (all desktop and groupware suites), and/or Web-based intranets (such as Notes and GroupWise). What distinguishes suite-based workflow products from their counterparts in other segments is their reliance on the suite's application infrastructure, including messaging, directory, security, database, and document management services.

Suite-based workflow tools are pitched at users with minimal technical expertise in process definition and application development.

This chapter provides an overview of leading vendors and solutions in the suite-based workflow market. For guidelines on when to choose a suite-based solution over other workflow technologies, refer to Chapters 3 and 12. Table 10-1 details the general trends in suite-based workflow.

Table 10-1: Suite-based Workflow Market Trends

CATEGORY	TREND	EXPLANATION
Operating Platforms	Increasing convergence of mass-market workflow applications around industry-standard groupware suites	As noted in Tables 7-1 and 8-1, many production and messaging-based workflow products are being adapted to run on one or more of the three principal groupware suites: Microsoft Exchange, Lotus Notes, and Novell GroupWise. These suites provide a full range of development tools and application services to support workflow, including filestores, messaging, directories, security, and communications services, including access to the Web.
Workflow Management Standards	Increasing vendor compliance with emerging workflow industry standards	Before the millennium turns, expect to see near-universal compliance with WfMC and/or MAPI Workflow Framework (MWF) standards in the suite-based workflow market. WfMC's technical interfaces will be adopted by suite-based workflow products as a standard means of linking to third-party client applications, process-definition tools, infrastructure services, and enactment services — especially those internal to production and Web-based workflow environments. MWF-compliance will become standard in Microsoft's Exchange, Office, and BackOffice suites by the end of 1997, as well as in many third-party production and messaging-based workflow products that have already committed fully to a Microsoft-centric networking environment. It remains to be seen whether and when Lotus and Novell will capitulate to Microsoft's workflow industry standard-in-the-making and make their respective suites (Lotus Notes and SmartSuite; Novell GroupWise) MWF-compliant.
Architecture	Increasing re-architecting of suite-based workflow products to adopt some features typically associated with production and Web-based workflow	The discussion from Table 8-1 applies here as well. MWF-compliance will migrate suite-based workflow products to more closely resemble production workflow solutions, making suite-based products less client-centric and performing more workflow enactment, object management, and tracking services at network servers. At the same time, suite-based products will follow the suites themselves out onto the World Wide Web, so that workflow data can be published and replicated automatically across the Internet and corporate intranets, and so that users will be able to access worklists from Netscape Navigator and other off-the-shelf browsers.
Application Development Tools	Increasing reliance on graphical, industry-standard, object-oriented form, application, and process-design tools	The discussion in Table 8-1 applies equally to the suite-based market, with an important caveat. Suite-based workflow tools are pitched at a broad mass market of average users with minimal or no technical expertise in process definition and application development. Consequently, suite-based workflow

CATEGORY	TREND	EXPLANATION
Application Development Tools *(continued)*		vendors will have to provide very user-friendly, almost no brainer, graphical forms and process-design tools targeted at the average office worker. No one expects the average workflow user to spend the time to learn high-end development tools such as ActiveX and Visual Basic.
Database, Document, Object, Messaging, Directory, and Security System Interface Standards	Increasing standards-based integration with heterogeneous, network-based information bases and application services	The discussion in Table 8-1 applies equally to the suite-based workflow market, since all workflow technologies rely on the same general application infrastructure. More and more of the database, document, forms, object, messaging, directory, Internet/intranet, and security services in workflow applications will be provided from industry-standard groupware suites such as Lotus Notes and Microsoft Exchange.

These trends are compelling, but you'll better understand the strengths of work-flow-enabled applications when you consider the following survey of the market's leading vendors and their products. (For a complete listing of workflow-enabled products, see Appendix A.)

Digital Equipment Corp.

Digital Equipment Corp. (DEC), headquartered in Maynard, MA, provides mail-enabled workflow capabilities within two network application suites. One — LinkWorks — is regarded as a loosely integrated suite linking third-party applications, while the other — TeamLinks — provides a more integrated assemblage of DEC-developed group-collaboration tools.

LinkWorks

LinkWorks is designed to integrate with and workgroup-enable various off-the-shelf applications developed by DEC and third-party software developers, using OLE/COM interfaces. The product provides users with a complete desktop environment in which to work with applications and documents. Unlike Lotus Notes, which requires that applications be written or retrofitted to the Notes APIs, scripting language, and graphic user interface, LinkWorks easily integrates third-party applications into its environment. It provides workflow services that bind external applications into the following:

- A complete document routing and tracking environment, offering graphical, object-oriented work-process design

- Integrated e-mail; electronic forms

- Sequential, parallel, and conditional document routing

- Document tracking through on-screen organization charts
- Document access and version control
- Content-based document retrieval
- Electronic approval and signature

To users, the LinkWorks desktop consists of a set of icons representing shared applications, folders, and data files, which are arranged in the same way in all desktop operating environments. Workflow items appear in the LinkWorks inbox as single documents or hierarchically organized *intelligent containers* that consist of multiple documents and pointers to associated applications.

Released in 1994 and now in its third generation, LinkWorks runs on MS-DOS, Windows, Windows NT, Macintosh, OS/2, SunOS/Motif, Solaris, HP-UX, and AIX clients. On the server side, LinkWorks is available for systems running AIX, HP-UX, DEC OSF/1, OpenVMS, Ultrix, and SCO UNIX. It works on DECNet, NetWare, and TCP/IP LAN/WANs, and it routes work items via DEC ALL-IN-1 and IBM MEMO mail transports. It can access workflow-relevant data in Oracle, Ingres, Informix, and DEC Rdb RDBMSs and can also store *metadata* (such as object relationships and pointers) in these databases.

TeamLinks

TeamLinks is a functionally similar workgroup suite that consists primarily of DEC-developed applications and is designed for a more homogeneous DEC LAN/WAN environment. In addition to workflow routing and tracking, it supports secure messaging, group calendaring, group authoring, document management and conversion, desktop conferencing, and data access and reporting services.

TeamLinks runs on a DEC VAX/OpenVMS server under DEC's PATHWORKS LAN operating system, Novell NetWare (via DEC's NetWare Coexistence product), TCP/IP networks, or asynchronous dial-up connections. It can be accessed by DEC VT100 terminals, PCs in VT100-emulation mode, Windows, or Macintosh clients. It integrates with legacy mail and office systems (for example, X.400, DEC ALL-IN-1, and IBM's Professional Office System and Systems Network Architecture Distribution Service) via DEC's MAILworks multivendor messaging backbone. The TeamLinks e-mail/workflow directory synchronizes with external mail directories via DEC's Distributed Directory Services. DEC's database integration products enable TeamLinks applications to access data from various SQL RDBMSs, including those from DEC, IBM, Oracle, Microsoft, and Novell. OLE and DDE support tight integration with various third-part applications.

TeamLinks' workflow component — called *TeamLinks Routing* — can route electronic documents in many formats, such as electronic forms, word-processing documents, images, CAD drawings, and spreadsheets. It allows users to build and route multidocument, multiformat packages. It comes with 11 sample applications that can be used straight out of the box, including delegating and tracking action items, processing travel requests, and logging, tracking, and distributing versions of PC software in use. These templates can be modified — or new ones built from scratch — using the TeamRoute Software Development Kit for Visual Basic, which supports C and C++ function calls. APIs enable third-party applications to store documents in any of the *drawers* or *folders* in the TeamLinks File Cabinet repository, or in DEC's legacy ALL-IN-1 environment. Electronic forms designed with third-party Windows-based packages can be integrated with TeamLinks applications.

IBM/Lotus Development Corp.

IBM/Lotus provides forms-oriented, mail-enabled workflow capabilities in its preeminent groupware environment — Lotus Notes — and in its application-suite products, SmartSuite and NotesSuite.

Notes

Notes has from its inception been a forms-, document-, and message-oriented application environment, a fruitful platform for custom and third-party workflow applications. The basic element in a Notes database is an individual document, the structure of which is typically defined by a form, which contains a number of structured and unstructured fields. Form fields can contain various formulas and macros that perform calculations and trigger workflow routing and processing.

Notes revolves around two architectural components: a distributed object store and a robust enterprise messaging environment. Notes integrates with any VIM-compliant e-mail system, including its native NotesMail and cc:Mail message transport agents. It runs on Windows 3.1/95/NT, OS/2, Macintosh, and UNIX (HP-UX, AIX, Solaris, SCO) desktops; OS/2, Windows 3.1/95, Windows NT, NetWare/NLM, and UNIX (Solaris, SCO, HP-UX, AIX) servers; and TCP/IP, X.25, SNA, AppleTalk, NetBIOS/NetBEUI, and IPX/SPX networks. It exchanges data with third-party RDBMSs and applications through SQL/ODBC, Notes/FX, OLE, DDE, and the Notes API.

Notes' object store can be replicated transparently across many servers on LANs and WANs, ensuring that all users in the enterprise have access to the same information base. The object store can contain almost any digital information, including application binary files, tabular data, formatted text, posted e-mail messages, scanned document images, and video. Notes' high-level folder/tab interface, hierarchical file structure, and full-text search engine facilitate searches through masses of information within its distributed object store. Notes uses RSA public/private key technology to sign, seal, and tamper-proof documents transmitted over LANs and WANs, either through replication or as attachments to any e-mail messages.

Notes has traditionally participated in workflow applications as a provider of messaging, database, and imaging services to other software products, which more or less sums up its integration with Lotus Forms and Lotus Notes:Document Imaging. Many production and messaging-based workflow vendors boast about their level of messaging, database, and imaging integration with Notes.

Notes' own workflow capabilities have traditionally been limited to the following:

- Embedding an @ *MailSend* formula in form fields, command buttons, icons, and macros to send a document to named users

- Using macros to trigger automated mailing of notifications, documents, and database reports in response to document and database events

- Using macros to enable one database to look up values in another and update the second database based on various events

- Tracking document versions automatically and flagging changes and comments made by different users

- Using the LotusScript procedural language along with Notes/FX, OLE, and DDE to link several applications, files, and databases into a unified workflow solution

NotesFlow

Notes 4.0, released in 1995, provides several new workflow features under the NotesFlow module. The upgrade allows developers to link workflow scripts to on-screen *action buttons*, so that users can submit a form to the appropriate routing chain, depending on their decision to approve, reject, or otherwise dispose of the form.

NotesFlow also allows users to define workflows triggered by background events in the object store. Users can fill out specially designed Notes forms that define the conditions for routing documents or generating e-mail to particular users. They would then submit these messages to the Notes server, which would monitor the object store for the specified events and execute the stipulated actions.

For example, users can instruct the object store to watch for specific keywords in incoming documents or numerical fields that exceed certain values. When the specified conditions occur, the Notes server will perform any actions defined in the originating message, such as e-mailing a document to a distribution list or sending an urgent notification message to a particular remote user.

NotesFlow also provides a library of reusable forms, component objects, and action buttons that trigger structured workflow routing. In addition, Notes already includes a score of ready-to-use forms-based applications, supporting activities such as customer service, project tracking, account management, and group conferencing.

NotesFlow allows developers to create custom workflows that integrate Notes with Lotus InForms and various third-party applications, with Notes/FX and OLE interfaces.

Integrated third-party tools

Unfortunately, NotesFlow lacks a visual tool for defining workflow process models and streamlining creation of workflow-relevant forms, databases, and rules. Several third-party workflow products provide process-definition tools and run-time enactment services that integrate with Notes servers and object stores.

Action Technologies's ActionWorkflow Manager for Lotus Notes provides the ability to workflow-enable all Notes forms and views and to generate Notes databases to support workflows. It provides a graphical process-flowcharting tool and adds sequential, conditional, and parallel forms-routing capabilities to Notes e-mail. The solution requires that an Action workflow software module and databases be installed on Notes servers. Action provides three forms-routing applications — for action items, to-do lists, and meeting coordination — right out of the box. These applications appear as database icons in the Notes tab/folder workspace. The product also generates reports on workflow status and performance, maintained in a separate ActionWorkflow database.

Application Partners's WIT adds a set of workflow commands to the Notes development environment. WIT's APIs enable applications to poll server-based Notes processes and execute workflow tasks, such as routing documents and updating databases, in the background.

Reach Software Corporation's WorkMAN for Lotus Notes provides visual forms and workflow design tools and a run-time environment that is integrated with the Notes object store. It supports sequential, conditional, and parallel forms routing over Notes e-mail. The solution requires that WorkMAN software and databases be installed on Notes servers and client workstations. Like Action's product, WorkMAN generates the workflow application code to support a visual workflow design and embeds an application icon in the Notes workspace.

WorkFlow's FlowMaker provides a text-oriented approach to developing Notes-based workflow forms, applications, and rules. It simplifies development and modification of workflow applications in Notes environments.

As noted in Chapter 8, IBM is integrating Notes with two of its imaging-oriented production workflow products: FlowMark and ImagePlus. Run-time interfaces are being developed that will allow FlowMark, ImagePlus, and Lotus Notes:Document Imaging to start and stop workflow processes, exchange work items, invoke applications, and track process status within each other's domains. Full server-to-server and client-to-server interoperability will be established between the product platforms within the 1996-1997 time frame. When full interoperability is established, users will be able to migrate any Notes data, documents, or images to ImagePlus VisualInfo servers, eliminating storage constraints associated with the Notes environment.

SmartSuite

Lotus SmartSuite has traditionally been a peripheral player in workflow applications, primarily as a supplier of data — via Notes/FX, OLE, and DDE — to workflow applications running in the Notes environment. It is a Notes-ready desktop-application suite that includes the Word Pro word processor, Lotus 1-2-3 spreadsheet, Freelance Graphics presentation graphics, Approach database, Lotus Organizer personal information manager, and Global Network Navigator's GNNWorks Internet/Web browser. The suite is typically sold with Lotus cc:Mail as the messaging application. It runs on clients supporting Windows 3.1, Windows 95, Windows NT, and OS/2.

In 1995, Lotus began to add new workflow capabilities to SmartSuite applications. Word Pro has been provided with the ability to coordinate document review, revision, and consolidation by many team members across LANs and WANs. The TeamReview capability allows authors to assign access and editing rights for each individual reviewing a document, whether the document is circulated by network or floppy disk. The TeamConsolidate feature lets authors combine multi-edited documents into a single document, automating the process of consolidating multi-edited versions of a document into one final draft.

Other SmartSuite applications are also evolving into workflow-enabled productivity tools. Lotus will add the TeamConsolidate feature to 1-2-3, allowing users to collect multiple sheets into a single spreadsheet. An upcoming version of Freelance Graphics will allow two users to work on the same slide at the same time while allowing each person to keep some information (such as speaker notes) private from the other.

Lotus NotesSuite combines Notes with SmartSuite for Windows, providing access to the workflow capabilities of both environments. It comes bundled with two starter Notes workflow applications supporting creation, routing, and tracking of sales proposals and contracts.

Microsoft Corp.

Microsoft has provided workflow capabilities for several years in its market-leading application suite, Microsoft Office, and plans to support standards-based workflow in its new Microsoft Exchange enterprise e-mail and groupware environment. The standards underlying messaging-based workflow in all Microsoft products will, of course, be defined within the company's own MAPI Workflow Framework, which is well on its way to broad industry acceptance.

Applications can invoke a routing slip dialog box to define sequential, parallel, and cycle-back-to-originator workflows.

Microsoft Office

Microsoft Office provides a simple but powerful document-routing capability to all its desktop applications, which include the Windows 95/3.1/NT versions of its Word word processor, Excel spreadsheet, PowerPoint presentation graphics, and Access RDBMS products. Applications can invoke a *routing slip* dialog box and use it to define sequential, parallel, and cycle-back-to-originator workflows over Microsoft Mail and other MAPI-compliant e-mail systems. Routable objects can consist of MAPI Custom Messages (such as forms defined with Microsoft's Electronic Forms Designer or third-party forms tools; see Chapter 9) or standard e-mail messages plus file attachments. Visual Basic can be used to script workflow applications that integrate objects from Office applications and other Microsoft and third-party applications.

When users finish reviewing or revising Microsoft Office application files, they can automatically forward them to the next recipient by invoking the Send command in the Windows File menu of the appropriate desktop application. Workflow status can be tracked automatically through messages sent back to the originator each time a document is forwarded to the next person in the routing list. Recipients can change the routing order in mid-workflow by moving the name of someone who has not yet received the document up or down in the distribution list.

Document review, annotation, and consolidation features are available to all Microsoft Office applications. Originators can, from within the routing-slip dialog, determine whether reviewers can edit documents, input information only into form fields, and add textual (and even voice) annotations. Reviewers' edits and annotations can be tagged with their names or initials, plus the date and time they were made, and displayed alongside original text. Originators can compare two versions of a document, review and decide whether to incorporate various edits and annotations, and automatically consolidate approved changes.

Microsoft provides over a dozen templates that link its Office suite and other applications (such as the Electronic Forms Designer and Schedule+ calendaring package) into various workflow-enabled solutions. Templates support such business processes as service request processing, project coordination, status tracking, report consolidation, and expense reporting.

Microsoft Office 97, the latest upgrade to the suite, includes a new electronic forms-definition tool, called *Forms³*. Office 97 with *Forms³* allows users to employ Visual Basic and OLE Custom Controls in writing forms-based applications. Office 97 also includes a powerful text indexing and searching engine, strengthening the suite's ability to support network-based document management capabilities.

Exchange

In March 1996, Microsoft released Version 1.0 of Exchange, its long-awaited enterprise-wide collaboration environment that combines standards-based e-mail, rule-based message handling, electronic forms, directory services, information store, replicated public folders, group scheduling, message database, and built-in Internet browsing capabilities. Microsoft Exchange is designed to fend off competition from established groupware products such as Lotus Notes and Novell GroupWise.

Exchange is part of Microsoft's formidable BackOffice family of server-based software infrastructure products, including the Windows NT Advanced Server network operating system, SQL Server database, Systems Management Server network-administration package, and SNA Server terminal-to-host communications product. The Exchange Server runs only on Windows NT, but the Exchange client runs on a wider range of operating environments, including MS-DOS, Windows 3.X/95/NT, Macintosh, and UNIX.

Exchange services are accessible from any MAPI client, including existing Microsoft Mail desktops. The Exchange Client presents a *universal inbox* that allows users to store, access, and send messages, forms, faxes, and meeting requests from a single location. Exchange is built on an enterprise messaging backbone with support for X.400 and Internet SMTP/MIME/UUENCODE (RFC821, RFC822, RFC1521, and RFC1154) transports, as well as other messaging environments such as Microsoft Mail, IBM PROFS, and Lotus cc:Mail. It supports sporadically connected remote users through selective replication and transfer of messages, folders, and files upon connection. It also allows users to automatically invoke Web browsers and dialers by clicking on Uniform Resource Locators (URLs) contained in e-mail messages.

Exchange's enterprise-wide directory service is based on the hierarchical, object-oriented X.500 standard and supports definition of complex workflow roles. Complex applications can be built for Exchange with tools such as Microsoft's Visual Basic and Visual C++, using interfaces such as MAPI and OLE Automation.

Missing from the first release of Exchange are server-based workflow enactment and tracking services, such as those defined in the MAPI Workflow Framework, according to Microsoft program manager Steve Silverberg. These capabilities will be incorporated in the next major upgrade to Exchange, slated for late 1997.

MAPI Workflow Framework

A first public draft of MAPI Workflow Framework was published around the same time that Microsoft Exchange 1.0 was released. Microsoft developed the document with assistance from Wang and other production and messaging-based workflow vendors and in consultation with the Workflow Management Coalition (WfMC). The document defines APIs, message classes, and conversational dynamics needed for client applications to request and track workflow-engine services in the MAPI messaging environment.

The MAPI Workflow Framework supports sequential, parallel, and conditional routing of work items over MAPI-compliant e-mail systems. Workflow-enabled applications will be able to route formatted work items transparently through MAPI-compliant message transfer agents to workflow engines, which function as specialized inbox processors. The specification defines mechanisms for connecting multiple workflow engines through MAPI-compliant e-mail systems. It also supports the tracking of message locations and status, as well as the consolidation of recipient responses into the original message or a public folder.

In placing its considerable clout behind workflow standardization, Microsoft is performing a great service to the industry.

In the MAPI Workflow Framework, Microsoft has adopted a workflow nomenclature consistent with that contained in the WfMC's Workflow Reference Model and has endeavored to make its specifications consistent with those being developed by the WfMC. At Microsoft's urging, the WfMC modified its reference model to make the cross-platform workflow interoperability specification independent of underlying communications transports, be they synchronous (such as remote procedure calls) or asynchronous (such as store-and-forward messaging systems).

In placing its considerable clout behind workflow standardization, Microsoft is performing a great service to the industry. The MAPI Workflow Framework will contribute to the workflow-enabling of all desktop applications throughout the business world and to the establishment of basic interoperability between previously incompatible messaging-based and production workflow environments. The framework takes much of the routing logic away from the workflow client application and electronic forms, invests it in a background service process, and increases administrators' abilities to monitor and control e-mail-enabled workflow in real time. In future upgrades to Exchange, says Silverberg, the product will support quasi-production workflow capabilities such as leaving application data in place on public folders and simply routing access pointers and privileges that reference appropriate folders.

Many third-party messaging-based workflow products are being ported to run on top of Exchange 1.0, well before Microsoft rolls out support for MAPI workflow specifications. According to Silverberg, vendors are recasting and registering their electronic forms and folders as custom message classes under the MAPI Forms Subsystem, which is supported within Exchange 1.0. The Exchange mail client will automatically activate the appropriate forms/folder viewer and inbox icon when a work item embodying a registered message class has been received. Exchange 1.0's form registry also supports automatic replication of new forms definition across connected servers.

Novell Inc.

Novell is focusing its workflow strategies on GroupWise, which — along with Lotus Notes and Microsoft Exchange — is one of the top three groupware environments on the market today.

GroupWise, created in 1987 as WordPerfect Office, is an e-mail-centric collaboration environment that provides a *universal inbox* for retrieving text messages, electronic forms, task assignment, faxes, and almost any other digital item that can be wrapped in or attached to an e-mail envelope. It also provides a *universal outbox* for tracking the status and location of all items that either originated on a desktop or were routed through it.

GroupWise

The current version, GroupWise 5, integrates rule-based messaging, electronic forms, workflow, task management, group scheduling, document management, and asynchronous discussion functions. GroupWise 5 is a broad suite that integrates tightly with Novell's InForms messaging-based workflow solution (discussed in Chapter 9) and SoftSolutions document management product. It supports both production workflow (in which documents remain on the server and only pathnames are routed) and messaging-based workflow (in which documents are physically transferred as e-mail file attachments).

The product supports the following workflow functions:

- Sequential, parallel, and conditional routing of documents and e-mail messages

- Tracking document/message location and status through the e-mail outbox

- Group editing, annotation, version control, and consolidation of routed documents

- Submitting task assignments (via e-mail) to other users, specifying applicable deadlines and priorities

- Determining whether task assignments have been accepted, rejected, delegated, or completed

- Building automated *context trails* that link objects of a given type to actions performed on them (for example, linking messages with a particular subject to schedule requests, electronic forms, and discussion groups that also mention that subject)

GroupWise operates over a wide range of clients, servers, mail systems, and connectivity services supported by Novell's market-leading NetWare network operating system. GroupWise client software runs under Windows, Macintosh, MS-DOS, and various UNIX operating environments. Servers run the NetWare 4.X network operating system over Windows, OS/2, MS-DOS, and several UNIX variants and speak the TCP/IP and IPX/SPX protocols internally and various asynchronous modem protocols to remote dial-up users. The product hooks into MHS (Standard Message Format 70 & 71), MAPI, VIM, and CMC-compliant mail systems and connects through messaging gateways to Internet/SMTP, X.400, Lotus Notes, SNADS, VMS Mail, OfficeVision/VM, pagers, and touch-tone telephone services. It piggybacks on the NetWare Directory Service, which enables administrators to manage GroupWise, InForms, and NetWare users and services from an integrated console.

Ensemble

GroupWise's production workflow capabilities are provided by Ensemble, a new package of sophisticated workflow and imaging functions that Novell co-developed with FileNet Corp. Ensemble can route workflow items to and from FileNet's production workflow environments: Visual WorkFlo and WorkFlo Business System. Workflow application developers can drag-and-drop pre-existing Visual WorkFlo process models into Ensemble workflow designs. Ensemble has also been integrated with Corel Corp.'s PerfectOffice application suite (recently divested by Novell) and is being marketed as a stand-alone product by both Novell and FileNet.

Ensemble introduces visually oriented workflow to GroupWise's extensive customer base. In the GroupWise environment, Ensemble consists of a graphical workflow design tool integrated with the GroupWise client (under Microsoft Windows 3.X, Windows 95, and Macintosh); run-time client workflow and imaging software; Visual

WorkFlo for NetWare (a NetWare Loadable Module version of FileNet's workflow engine), and the Ensemble Server Access Module (a server add-on that integrates the Ensemble client and Visual WorkFlo Server).

Multimedia and the Web

GroupWise presents users with an integrated, replicated multimedia repository — distributed over one or more servers — that contains messages, documents, forms, faxes, graphics, task assignments, and, eventually, voice and video objects as well. Documents are presented through a shared-folder interface similar to Lotus Notes and Microsoft Exchange. The object store maintains security and version controls and supports intelligent data search and retrieval across multiple servers. What the browsing user actually sees may simply be a pointer to a remote file, which is retrieved and displayed only upon demand. Users can program automated agents to automatically retrieve and mail them new documents that meet various criteria.

The product operates over the Web, thanks to GroupWise WebAccess (discussed in Chapter 9). WebAccess enables users to access their GroupWise inboxes from any Web browser to retrieve and send Internet e-mail, receive and display documents, open shared folders, view calendars and schedule meetings, and access the GroupWise address book. The product allows users to participate in GroupWise workflows when traveling, working from home, or surfing over the corporate intranet. It is installed on a NetWare 4.X server and can coexist locally with the NetWare Web Server and GroupWise message server. By using HTML hyperlinks in the WebAccess home page, users can navigate back and forth flexibly between GroupWise and other services on the Web.

Summary

This chapter has presented an overview of major trends and vendors in the suite-based workflow market. A more complete vendor list is provided in Appendix A.

Suite-based workflow represents the emerging horizontal, mass market for workflow technology, in which workflow capabilities are embedded as menu options, icons, or buttons in most everyday business applications. Workflow capabilities are becoming a ubiquitous, background component of the everyday office application, just as mundane a feature set as the e-mail commands, spell checkers, drawing tools, and printing drivers (and, just recently, Web browsers and HTML authoring tools) embedded in most Windows-based applications.

Conceivably, all the other workflow technology segments — production, messaging-based, and Web-based — could merge into the suite-based segment in the next few years, as these other tools tap into the application services (for example, databases, document/image repositories, directories, messaging, Internet/intranet, and security) provided by the suites. Already, major workflow vendors (such as Action, FileNet, Keyfile, ViewStar, and Wang) have either already released products that tap into Microsoft Exchange and/or

Lotus Notes, or have announced intentions to do so. Other, lesser-known workflow vendors are probably following suit, both recognizing the industry trend and seeing an opportunity to speed workflow product development over industry-standard application environments.

This marks the conclusion of Part III, a survey of the production, messaging-based, Web-based, and suite-based workflow market segments. Of necessity, this survey has been limited to commercial workflow solutions on the market or announced at the time this book went into print. The market and underlying technologies are changing so fast that this survey may have already grown a tad dated by the time you pick up the book. If you take away one impression from the preceding survey, it should be that these market segments are rapidly converging into each other, erasing platform-specific distinctions between workflow technologies. Within the next few years, all the major workflow vendors will provide products that can work over whatever environment makes best sense for your target application: distributed filestores, messaging systems, Web-based intranets, or groupware and desktop-application suites.

You now move into the final major section of the book, Part IV, in which you learn about the guidelines for users to evaluate, implement, and administer workflow applications. The just-concluded tour of today's workflow market puts you in a good position to understand the range of alternative commercial solutions. The remaining chapters help you cut through the complexity to identify and select those solutions that best meet your company's workflow and process-reengineering needs.

PART IV

Evaluation and Implementation Guidelines

Realizing Organizational Payback from Workflow

This part presents management guidelines for evaluating, planning, acquiring, implementing, and administering workflow applications within small and large organizations. The section is organized according to the following phases in the life of a workflow project: project planning and justification, operations review and analysis, market survey and product selection, application development and implementation, and user training and support.

CHAPTER ELEVEN

JUSTIFYING WORKFLOW-REENGINEERING PROJECTS

Talking the board of directors, the boss, or even yourself into spending money and staff-hours on new software and work procedures can be as daunting as implementing the project itself. This chapter provides some practical guidelines for selling your workflow-reengineering proposal to the corporate *movers and shakers* and gaining broad-based support from the organizational grass-roots. The discussion draws on perspectives introduced in Chapter 2 and relates them to concrete steps you can take to gain acceptance for specific workflow proposals.

Few sensible managers will bet the business on processes cobbled together on the fly by grass-roots personnel. The more mission-critical the business process, the greater the need for careful process planning, analysis, and redesign. In such cases, you should have a solid justification and implementation plan for your workflow solution, because so much will be riding on your recommendations.

Still, it's not uncommon for big companies to make expensive investments with only a shred of a business case and no clear implementation plan. Only 14 percent of all workflow purchases involve a formal and successful cost justification, according to Thomas Koulopoulos[1]. Over 65 percent of process-reengineering projects fail to meet their goals, according to groupware expert David Coleman[2]. The lackluster performance of BPR projects may be attributed in part to the failure of companies to adequately define the business case, goals, and objectives of workflow-reengineering investments in advance. To ensure your company stays in that successful 35 percent, follow these general pointers for justifying high-cost, high-stakes workflow investments.

Locate Management Sponsors

The fastest track for any workflow-reengineering project is to have the complete, enthusiastic support of your company's entire senior management team from Day One. In this most wonderful of all scenarios, the need for your project is unquestioned, long-term funding is available, and corporate resources are allocated without a formal justification or implementation plan.

To win quick support for your workflow application, limit it initially to one department that manages a critical process.

You can dream if you want, but this scenario is about as likely as hitting a multi million-dollar lottery jackpot. Workflow applications tend to impact many users, workgroups, and departments, making them just as likely to ruffle feathers as win supporters. Any project that even hints at overturning the way things are done or shifting responsibilities will be seen as a threat by many staff members. Enterprise-wide workflow-reengineering projects can easily degenerate into prolonged political trench wars.

Sow a seed

One way to win quick support for your workflow application is to limit it initially to a single department or workgroup that manages a critical process or subprocess. Concentrate your lobbying efforts on a single manager who has responsibility for all or most of the group.

For example, your company may have a critical need to automate routing, tracking, and version controls on a wide range of product documentation, including product descriptions, functional specifications, software and firmware source code, electro-mechanical drawings, test procedures, manufacturing bills of materials, and user documentation. Trying to automate document preparation on the entire product life-cycle would be a difficult endeavor, because you would have to lobby several supervisors — including engineering, manufacturing, materials, and training and documentation — for their concurrent support. On a normal day, several of these people may not be on speaking terms with each other, and they would almost never band into a common cause except under the most extraordinary circumstances.

Your best initial approach might be to lobby the supervisor — perhaps engineering — who seems most open to the idea of *workflow-enabling* his or her group's operations. You may be able to convince this manager of the need for a limited pilot, perhaps involving workflow-enabling of one important, highly visible document, such as quick-turnaround engineering change requests. This manager-advocate will be able to pull strings to authorize, at the very least, a prototype or *seed* pilot application of your idea within his or her operation. The manager may also be able to provide you with necessary funding, staff, computers, network connections, and office space. In this way, you may be able to bring your workflow idea to fruition in a hands-on *incubator* environment with direct feedback from end users.

A successful seed pilot will increase your chances of enlisting managers from other departments as participants in your workflow-reengineering project. Seeing positive results from the initial workflow application, the original manager-advocate will ask you to put other documents on the system — it's a short step from workflow-enabling an engineering change request to doing the same with other R&D documents such as mechanical drawings, block diagrams, and source code. The initial advocate will be encouraged to spread the word among his or her peers in the organization. Higher-level executives may insist that the management team study the pilot and evaluate its applicability to their operations.

Even if your seed pilot is a smashing success, you may experience some difficulty in extending, replicating, or transferring it to other groups, for many reasons:

- The original manager-advocate may not carry much clout with his or her peers.

- The original application may not have much obvious relevance to work done in other groups. For example, engineering change requests, which travel a fixed sequential route through the organization, are distinctly different from functional specifications, which may zigzag through the organization several times with no clear-cut routing path before they arrive at a state acceptable to all product managers.

- Existing business processes in other groups may be adequate and not require an expensive technical solution. For example, training and documentation may involve three people sitting in the same office, whose existing paper/diskette-based workflow suits them just fine.

- Your proposed workflow application may be regarded as *bleeding edge* and not ready for full-scale deployment. For example, other managers may not be ready to start designing processes with a visual flowcharting tool. They may not fully understand the art of process design, or fear giving staff the impression that they are trying to dictate processes that have traditionally coalesced from the collective activities of ground-level staff.

- Skittish end users may torpedo the whole exercise as a ruse to pave the way for future layoffs. Workflow management may strike cynical users as a synonym for business-process reengineering, which has been tagged widely as synonymous with *downsizing* or *rightsizing* — in other words, a euphemism for throwing people out of jobs in pursuit of profits.

Educate the reluctant

You may need to wage a determined education and marketing campaign to win acceptance for workflow automation within a reluctant corporate culture. Often, the best way to win support is through education, which removes the apprehension that people naturally feel toward any fundamental new technology or discipline of which they know little.

For example, you might persuade the engineering supervisor — your original manager-advocate — to join you in presenting *dog and pony shows* to familiarize other departments with the details of the seed pilot.

You could also organize a special demonstration of the application during the lunch hour — catered with pizza and soft drinks — in the manager-advocate's department. In conjunction with this demonstration, lessons learned from the pilot could be published throughout the company. Workflow and business-process-reengineering consultants could be brought in to deliver informal *brown-bag* presentations to management and users. Sample out-of-the-box workflow applications could be installed on the corporate network, making them available for perusing by any interested user. Seminars could be held to familiarize business and technical staff with unfamiliar workflow technology and terminology.

Keep your proposal simple and plugged into the corporate mission statement, so that the potential bottom-line contribution is obvious.

If you want to roll out enterprise-wide workflow applications, you're going to have to marshal all your politicking skills. You're going to need a preliminary proposal to distribute to interested parties, preferably with high-level process flowcharts that can be reviewed quickly by nontechnical personnel. You will want the original manager-advocate to accompany you to as many *marketing* presentations as practical, to reinforce your message that the technology works, has been accepted by initial users, and has delivered hard-dollar payoffs.

Keep your proposal simple, to the point, and plugged into the corporate mission statement, so that the potential bottom-line contribution is obvious to all. You'll have to make your presence felt throughout the company, communicating your ideas forcefully in every appropriate forum and channel. One good way to catch people's attention is to publish a workflow-related article in a trade magazine or paper read widely in your organization. The act of getting published suddenly elevates your ideas, previously shared only with immediate colleagues and kindred spirits, to a new level of perceived legitimacy. Acceptance by a publisher is a sign that your ideas are worthy of being shared with a wider audience.

In addition, you'll need to work your corporate connections extensively, building coalitions of workflow advocates in all departments likely to be impacted by your proposed application. One effective way to build coalitions for your ideas is to circulate widely within your organization, become known as the in-house workflow expert, and spare no occasion to relate workflow to pressing business issues and challenges. The workflow paradigm and your proposed new applications will gain acceptance over time as they become more familiar and relevant to everyday business concerns.

Campaign for commitments

Your first objective is to obtain the funds and resources needed to activate the project. However, you will need to make it known that successful workflow implementation depends on long-term, broad-based commitment by all levels in the organization.

Make management aware of the fact that a stable budget is critical for a workflow project's success, but that throwing technology at a problem does not necessarily cure it. You will need their ongoing support to weather the near-inevitable turf battles that surround the average workflow project. You will also need their clout to help you prevent lower-level managers from balkanizing, compromising, and watering down your enterprise-wide workflow-reengineering vision.

The coalition-building exercise will help you identify sources of support and resistance for your workflow project — and you may find them to be distributed, scattered, and fast changing. You may need many sponsors, designers, and facilitators to see your workflow project through to fruition. To elicit the support of other managers and supervisors, you will need to prepare a strategic plan showing how workflow-enabled applications can support those individuals' particular operations. Absent such a *workflow development roadmap*, managers can easily walk away from your ideas, seeing nothing of immediate benefit or relevance to them.

In building your coalition, you will be shaping organizational expectations for the success of your workflow project. To gauge these expectations, you will need to meet regularly with and listen to the concerns and preconceptions of the people who you're trying to sell on your ideas. You should be gearing your workflow development roadmap to satisfy, first, your target market.

Prepare a Project Justification

At some point, you may be called upon to produce a business justification for your workflow project, complete with competitive, cost-benefit, and risk analyses. Depending on how things get done in your company, the justification may be either a formal document or one or more executive-level presentations. If you're fortunate to already have high-level management buy-in, this formal business review may be omitted altogether or transformed into a rubber-stamping exercise.

The more expensive, risky, and mission-critical the project, the more involved, rigorous, and time-consuming the justification process.

At the risk of appearing submissive, you may find it expedient to invoke whatever strategic vision has been proclaimed or endorsed by your superiors (chances are that it will be one of the popular business theories or buzzwords presented in Chapter 1 of this book).

As a rule of thumb, the more expensive, complex, risky, and mission-critical the project, the more involved, rigorous, and time-consuming the justification process — especially if it demands extensive upgrades or modifications to existing systems. This being the case, expect production workflow systems to be the most difficult investments to justify, messaging-based and Web-based workflow products to be less difficult, and suite-based applications to be the easiest. Production workflow solutions often involve installation of dedicated document-image processing workstations, file servers, optical jukeboxes, local-area networks, high-resolution scanners, color printers, and other expensive hardware and software for stand-alone applications, while the other workflow solutions usually piggyback applications on top of users' existing infrastructure.

It's usually easier to justify a new investment that leverages or realizes the promise of a prior investment than to lay out funds for a new stand-alone capital acquisition.

Stress quantifiable payback

The most persuasive business justifications are built on quantifiable payback calculations. To sell a workflow project to an unsympathetic corporate status quo, you will need to stress the revenues to be generated, costs reduced, errors eliminated, and time saved from a process redesign. The workflow case studies in Chapter 14 and the consulting/research firms listed in Chapter 15 will give you fodder for your business justification.

The more cost-effective your proposal is, the better. Consequently, as noted in the preceding text, it's a good idea to stress the extent to which your workflow application will integrate with existing corporate technology assets (such as PCs, file servers, databases, e-mail systems, and directory services). You should also highlight the extent to which the workflow solution is based on open industry standards, since this will maximize your ability to acquire interoperable technologies from multiple sources, thereby holding down the life-cycle ownership cost of the workflow application.

Be careful not to oversell your proposed workflow application, exaggerate its benefits, or downplay its costs and risks. If you build expectations too high, you may be setting yourself up for failure down the road as reality comes home to roost. Any *hard dollar* cost/benefit estimates you produce may be used as the benchmark against which project success is measured. Make sure to factor *soft* benefits (such as increased flexibility, quality, and customer satisfaction) into your justification; they may hold the key to corporate competitive advantage.

One way to get senior executives' attention is to point out case studies of direct competitors that used workflow to cut costs, reduce cycle time, or achieve some other strategic advantage. Never underestimate the power of the *me too* instinct in corporate decision making. Suddenly, workflow will achieve instant legitimacy as a corporate agenda topic, and workflow experts will be in big demand to explain how the company can respond to this new threat-cum-opportunity. However, this tack represents a double-edged sword, because you may have to explain how your direct competitor was able to beat you off the starting block with a mission-critical workflow application.

Another way to appeal to upper echelons is to illustrate how workflow applications will increase management's ability to control and monitor the organization in real time. Workflow systems should appeal to the same managers who have invested serious resources in executive information systems to feed them with operational performance statistics. Show managers the amount of status reports they will be able to obtain on organizational workloads, bottlenecks, resource allocation, throughput, efficiency, and productivity. Ideally, you should have a working demo of the desired workflow product set up in the corporate boardroom, displaying real-time process status and operational indicators in simple, user-friendly graphics for interested senior executives.

Stay focused and in familiar territory

You won't usually need a fully developed technical implementation plan to get high-level corporate approval, sponsorship, and funding for your workflow project. However, you will need a project plan that identifies what ails current business processes, with such criteria as speed, cost, accuracy, quality, customer satisfaction, and flexibility. You will have to define the project's impact on business processes, users, and information and networking systems. More importantly, you'll have to identify project costs and benefits, in hard dollars if possible, and how soon the company can expect to recoup its investment and realize a positive return. Competing for scarce budget, you'll have to define how this project should take priority over other proposals on the table, based on its relationship to critical success factors, strategic imperatives, and/or core competencies.

You may also be required to justify your choice of workflow platforms, technologies, or vendors. You can improve your chances of approval if you propose to base your application on existing corporate network and computer platforms, such as Novell NetWare, Lotus Notes, cc:Mail, and Windows. Some managers may be more inclined to approve acquisition of workflow solutions from well-known vendors (such as Microsoft, Novell, IBM, and DEC) than from equally deserving but relatively obscure workflow companies.

Recruit a Core Project Team

At the same time you market your workflow-reengineering idea to the management team, you should be building a project team to help you translate your proposal into a real application.

You'll need to identify lead business and technical analysts as well as key managers and staff from all impacted business units and workgroups. Chapter 15 provides a list of the types of personnel you should have on your team, which should always include supervisors and analysts who are intimately familiar with the business processes that will be *workflow-enabled*. Having these people fully on-board will help you make sure that you don't misdesign the workflow application and will buy your project instant credibility and support throughout the organization.

Involve end users directly in the process of workflow redesign.

To maintain broad-based support for your project, you will need to involve many levels of the organization, recognizing that this may diffuse the project's focus or dampen its momentum to some degree. This is the price you may have to pay to ensure project success and fit your workflow application to the twists and turns of corporate business processes.

Involve end users directly in the process of workflow redesign. This will become a complex multisided role-playing exercise, as people define new functional responsibilities for themselves and their workgroups and then endeavor to retool their thinking along those lines. Without this level of participation, users will resist change and fight workflow technology by clinging to traditional ways of doing things. Ultimately, your workflow application must be justified to each person who will be required to participate in it.

Take heart, however. The need for formal workflow project justifications will diminish as the technology becomes a standard feature of ubiquitous application suites. Your boss will not question your use of workflow any more than he or she will ask you why you use e-mail, group scheduling, spell checking, or any other feature provided by the suite. You and your colleagues will route messages, forms, and documents among each other naturally and spontaneously, as an extension and expression of your jobs. You will be able to improvise new business processes without needing to establish formal process review, redesign, and reengineering projects.

Summary

This chapter took you through the organizational obstacle course that could stymie your workflow application before it can get off the ground. You are now ready to turn to the all-important issue of how best to *workflow-enable* current business processes to make good on the technology's promise — the topic of Chapter 12.

CHAPTER TWELVE

RETHINKING CURRENT
WORKFLOWS

Before you bother with the details of application development and software integration, you must rethink your company's workflow in fundamental business terms. This chapter helps you look at your current business process with fresh eyes, using the three-dimensional workflow paradigm — involving collaborative platform, structure, and media — introduced in Chapter 3. This chapter also examines candidate processes for production, messaging-based, Web-based, and suite-based workflow. You are shown how to parse your business processes into their three structural dimensions: routes, roles, and rules. You are provided with guidelines for mapping your restructured workflows to your network platform. Finally, you are given pointers for assessing your company's requirement for staff to develop and administer your new workflow-enabled business processes.

Define the Structural Dimensions of Your Business Process

Job number one for your workflow/reengineering project team should be to diagnose precisely what ails the process in question. Even the user of a low-cost workflow-enabled application must think about why certain people should be included in a document's routing list, in what order, and with what responsibilities and access controls. This involves focusing on the current and ideal structure — the routes, roles, and rules — of your organization's business processes.

Zero in first on existing processes that are fairly well defined and for which the benefits are likely to outweigh the costs and near-term work disruption associated with reengineering. As discussed in Chapter 1, you should benchmark your processes with any or all of the perennial business criteria: speed, cost, accuracy, quality, customer satisfaction, and flexibility.

Time-based project analysis

Speed is an important concern for most business processes. One of your first actions should be to perform a time-based analysis of your process. Define for yourselves the final customer's expectations for timely response, turnaround, delivery, and service. Break the process down into subprocesses, activities, dependencies, and participants. Gather data, through historical records and current observation, on the duration of every discrete activity, as well as the amount of time that work spends in transit and in users' in- and outboxes. You may want to organize this data in a standard, well-understood format, such as a PERT chart, Gantt chart, or work breakdown structure.

A *PERT chart* is a flowchart that highlights logical dependencies among activities, including the critical path. This latter concept is very important for time-based workflow analysis, because it shows the sequence of activities that directly determines the minimum time needed to complete the entire process. Shorten the critical path — for example, by eliminating several unnecessary management reviews — and you can chop significant time off the process.

A *Gantt chart* is a timeline that highlights the durations of many parallel or sequential tasks. This chart allows analysts to get a quick reality check on the durations of various activities and determines whether additional activities can be run in parallel.

A *work breakdown structure* is a matrix that provides a hierarchical listing of all subprocesses and activities and, possibly, includes task duration, start/stop dates and times, and responsible parties. The work breakdown structure is a logical outline that allows managers to ascertain whether the process includes unnecessary or redundant activities that can be deleted or consolidated, thereby shortening process duration. It allows managers to group activities logically, allocate resources to them, and get a high-level view of costs. By associating labor categories with particular activities, process designers can begin to define roles and privileges that will be enforced with automated workflow tools.

Business processes are multidimensional and difficult to grasp completely in a single chart, outline, or matrix. Consequently, you may want to use all three of these formats — or any number of other charts presented in popular BPR books — when doing your analysis. The end result of your analysis should be detailed maps of the business process as currently constituted (that is, your baseline workflow) and the new process you want to institute (that is, your target workflow).

Process building blocks

The art of process redesign involves modeling and simulating many alternate work-flows, evaluating them by criteria contained in your project justification. Although the variables involved in the basic process building blocks were discussed previously in Chapter 5, a review is in order before you start your redesign. The key five are activities, roles, conditions, workflow-relevant data, and rules.

The first two are easy to explain. Performed by a single individual, an *activity* is a unit of work that has defined initiation and termination conditions. Upon completion of the activity, the resultant work product will generally be routed to other participants. An activity may be further subdivided into individual work steps performed by a given staff member, according to a standard corporate practice or procedure. A *role* describes the activities that may be performed and privileges enjoyed by a process participant.

Conditions are a bit more involved. A *condition* describes a context or set of trigger-ing events within which a business process will be implemented. Conditions fall into several categories, as described in Table 12-1.

TABLE 12-1: WORKFLOW CONDITIONS

WORKFLOW CONDITIONS	DESCRIPTION
Initiation	Conditions under which the process begins. The most common initiation condition in most business processes is for an employee to fill out and route a standard form.
Scheduling	Conditions that describe the maximum and minimum time allotted for each activity, including in-queue time, processing time, and out-queue time. For example, corporate policy may require that new service requests spend no more than 30 minutes in a customer service representative's inbox and be fulfilled within four hours of submission.
Pre-activity	Conditions that describe when a particular person is allowed to begin a particular activity, such as reviewing and editing a document. For example, most sequential processes require a prior reviewer to formally sign off on a document before the next reviewer can begin his or her work.
Execution	Conditions that describe the kinds of tools, applications, methodologies, and techniques used to process a given work item. This refers to all the activities that, from the user's point of view, add value to the end product.
Notification	Conditions under which people will be notified of a process event, such as document approval, rejection, or return to originator.
Post-activity	Conditions that describe when a particular person is allowed to complete a particular activity and what happens when the activity is complete. A workflow routing chain can be described as a concatenation of post-activity conditions, such as sequential, parallel, and conditional routing. Typically, the post-activity conditions involve approving a work item and forwarding it to the next person in the chain. Conditional processes forward the work item to different recipients, depending on some activity performed or data value entered in a field of a business form.

(continued)

TABLE 12-1: WORKFLOW CONDITIONS *(continued)*

WORKFLOW CONDITIONS	DESCRIPTION
Security	Conditions that describe which people will be allowed to participate in the process, what functions they will be allowed to perform, and what information they will be allowed to access. Usually, these conditions are defined by a person's job title, position description, or location in the organizational structure.
Audit	Conditions that describe which process events will be logged, in how much detail, how often, and in what locations. Many business processes use a transmittal sheet as a log, attached to a workflow item, that records who reviewed and approved the item on what dates.
Termination	Conditions under which the process will be completed or aborted, notifications issued to appropriate personnel, and process information archived or otherwise disposed. The most common termination condition is for a form to reach its final approver, who then takes or directs someone else to take the requested action.

Workflow-relevant data is any information that is used throughout the process to evaluate conditions (for example, initiation, security, execution, and post-activity) and determine how to route, process, and otherwise handle a work item. The prototypical type of workflow-relevant data is a standard business form. The values input into fields of a business form often determine who will review it and whether they will approve it.

Rules are conditional statements that describe how workflow-relevant data is to be processed, routed, tracked, and controlled. For example, business forms usually come with a set of rules specifying legal input values, mandatory fields, routing procedures, and authorized approvers.

Look for ways to improve your process

Having defined the dimensions of your current business process, you'll start to look for ways to improve it. This is a complex proposition, to say the least, playing with many process variables as well as a plethora of human, management, and technical considerations. Fortunately, others have struggled with this dilemma before you, so you can follow some well-tested guidelines for streamlining, tightening, and refocusing business processes (drawing on the process-optimization framework presented in Chapter 3).

MAXIMIZE WORKFLOW-RELEVANT DATA CAPTURED AT PROCESS ORIGINATION

Processes exist to capture relevant data and transform it into business results. You can speed a process along by giving the person who originates the tools to locate, retrieve, and enter as much relevant information as possible, so that subsequent personnel can simply review, approve, and route the work item. For example, front-line personnel (such as account representatives) should be able to call up a complete client profile, transaction history, and credit status in an on-screen form, based on a simple identifier (such as the customer's name or phone number). The rep should have immediate access to all relevant documents and databases (such as product features, price lists, financing options, inventory, backlog status, and technical questions) so that a sale can be closed and a shipment can be scheduled while the customer is still on the phone. A completed purchase order with no anomalous entries will usually breeze through the fulfillment and invoicing process.

MAXIMIZE NUMBER OF WORKFLOW ACTIVITIES COMPLETED AT PROCESS ORIGINATION

Equip the person who originates the workflow to perform many activities that previously were handled by several staffers or contractors in sequence or parallel. For example, a skilled customer service representative may be able to respond in detail to many technical inquiries that previously required time-consuming referrals to other personnel. The rep may also be allowed to enter customer orders, specify appropriate technical solutions, and issue work orders to have the solution configured, delivered, and installed. Complex transactions need not involve complex workflows if a single, multifunctional, empowered staffer can handle the bulk of it.

If one person cannot handle all upfront functions, another approach would be to place that person in close physical proximity to people with the required skills and expertise. If your departments are far-flung, keep your employees in virtual proximity, via computerized bulletin boards, conference calling, or paging.

MAXIMIZE NUMBER OF ACTIVITIES RUNNING IN PARALLEL

More business processes can be accomplished in parallel to a greater degree than people realize, crunching the critical path down considerably. Processes that have been sequential because they required several people to access a single master paper document — one at a time — can be radically shortened by providing everyone with concurrent read-only access to a computerized version of that document. Different sections of a proposal can be written at the same time by various personnel, depending on their areas of expertise, and then recombined and smoothed out by a technical editor.

Reducing paperwork helps companies cut costs, speed up processes, and utilize staff more efficiently.

MINIMIZE PAPER DOCUMENTATION

Business processes should run on digital information, not pulp. Paper is a big money-, time-, and space-waster. It is an expensive medium to acquire, process, file, organize, transport, store, archive, retrieve, and dispose. Paper documents must be transferred physically from point A to point B, sorted and distributed by hand, located through tedious reading and skimming, and retrieved from cumbersome filing systems and overstuffed inboxes (assuming the documents weren't lost or mislaid, as often happens). Paper also takes up precious office, filing, and storage space that could be better put to other uses. Eliminating or reducing paperwork usually helps companies cut costs, speed up business processes, and utilize staff and facilities more efficiently.

MINIMIZE NUMBER OF ACTIVITIES OR PARTICIPANTS IN A PROCESS

Many processes include activities that are redundant, are marginally useful, or can be logically combined with other activities. Your initial temptation in redesigning processes may be to go at them with a weed-whacker, pruning out activities that nobody can justify in 25 words or less. For example, one way to speed up action on engineering change requests is to require technical reviews only by engineering managers whose particular subsystem or component (for example, software, firmware, enclosures, and packaging) is affected. However, this can be a politically sensitive issue, because people's jobs and core responsibilities may sometimes be placed on the chopping block. One sad fact of the business world is that some people's jobs are 90 percent make-work. Instead of the weed-whacker approach, snip and prune away unnecessary processes gently to avoid bruised egos.

MINIMIZE NUMBER OF FORMS IN A PROCESS

One of the symptoms of a sick process is a half-dozen or more specialized forms where a single, integrated form would suffice. Confusion often ensues from the multiple-form scenario, with people frantically chasing down and trying to reconcile several related forms that may have incomplete, conflicting, or outdated information. It's usually better to have a single multipart form that provides a complete process overview and status, saving everybody time and needless heartburn.

MINIMIZE TIME THAT WORK IS QUEUED AWAITING START

One way to kill a good process is to let reviewers sit on documents and folders, doing nothing, as long as they want. This problem can be eliminated by decreeing that reviewers must take some action (such as start work, complete work, and/or forward the work item) by a specified date or forfeit the item altogether. Another approach is to allow the document originator to escalate the matter to the reviewer's supervisor, who, hopefully, would be able to apply some muscle to unclog the jam.

MINIMIZE SIZE OF INBOUND WORK QUEUES

Many process bottlenecks crop up because people have too much in their inboxes and just so many hours in the day. One remedy is to allow supervisors to transfer inbound work items, as necessary, between overworked and underworked staff. Or personnel could be allowed to transfer items back and forth on a peer-to-peer basis. Or they could all retrieve inbound work items from a single office-wide queue on a first-come, first-served basis.

MINIMIZE TIME REQUIRED TO LAUNCH APPLICATIONS ON USER'S DESKTOP UPON RECEIPT OF WORK ITEM

The whole point of a business process is to add value to some work item or end product. Value-adding activities bring shape, substance, and coherence to the end product. Within business processes, they correspond to the productivity applications (for example, electronic forms readers, computer-aided design tools, and spreadsheets) that are used to facilitate each step in the processing of a work item. One of the irritations of computerized work is the proliferation of file formats and the need to open separate applications to work with them (not to mention the frustration of toggling among applications and running into incompatible formats).

Ideally, users should be launched into the appropriate application when they accept a work item (a capability supported by many of today's workflow products). They should be able to read, edit, and manipulate all associated documents and data from within that application (possible with OLE, also an increasingly common feature of workflow products). And the applications should default to corporate-standard stylesheets and analytical tools, ensuring that all work is done in approved formats and minimizing the need for items to be returned to people for rework. An integrated, consistent, standardized tool set will increase staff efficiency and reduce unproductive time spent wrestling with the mechanics of launching and using diverse applications.

MINIMIZE TIME REQUIRED FOR PARTICIPANTS TO ACCESS DOCUMENTATION AND DATABASES

Much of the time spent processing a typical work item is wrapped up in searching for basic information needed to evaluate the item fully. Business forms are often little more than *transmittal sheets* — cover pages attached to a substantial file that constitutes the supporting material used by analysts to evaluate a case. Sometimes, all supporting information is included with the form, but quite often it resides in scattered documents, files, databases, and reference books — as well as in the heads of various people. Workflow participants require on-line access not just to relevant corporate documentation but also to search engines needed to locate the needle in this haystack of overwhelming information. It may also be necessary to provide staff with access to the Internet and World Wide Web, which have become the universal, shared *virtual library*.

MINIMIZE COMPLETION TIME OF EACH ACTIVITY

Obviously, you can shorten an activity's completion time by making users more efficient and productive. As you know, however, work tends to expand to fill the time allotted for its completion. Consequently, process designers may consider imposing a deadline for each activity. A procedure could be set up whereby staff will be sent *tickler* notifications reminding them of imminent deadlines, as well as delinquency notifications on missed dates. Users might also be required to report work status and completion percentage at prespecified points within the activity's duration. These notifications and reports could be sent to the appropriate supervisors, who could then take action to ensure successful, on-time completion or reassign work to other employees.

MINIMIZE TIME NEEDED TO TRANSFER WORK BETWEEN ACTIVITIES

Protracted work-transfer times have long been the bane of paper-based processes, which depend on mail, courier, and overnight-delivery services. Fortunately, information technologies allow you to crunch transfer time to split-second intervals, if you want. Some processes may be set up for deferred delivery, so that items are forwarded to the next recipient — typically via e-mail or fax — after a prespecified interval. Until that time, the item would sit in the previous participant's outbox, awaiting the time when the next person is available or ready to receive and process the item. Minimizing the time spent transferring work items increases the time available for value-adding activities.

MINIMIZE TIME PARTICIPANTS AND ADMINISTRATORS NEED TO OBTAIN STATUS OF WORK ITEMS

Another problem with paper-based processes is the difficulty of tracking the status of an item in real time. People have to walk from office to office or place several phone calls to determine who has a particular document and how soon they'll be done with it. Managers cannot easily control their organizations if they have no way to track the real-time status of work items. Many workflow management tools provide strong location/status tracking features that enable managers to tighten their process oversight and control. Workflow applications can also be set up to issue immediate notifications of workflow events to appropriate participants, thereby easing the anxiety that comes from feeling that, after you have submitted a document for review, the matter is out of your hands. Minimizing the time spent in monitoring workflows increases the time available for value-adding activities.

ENSURE THAT STANDARD WORKFLOW ROUTES, ROLES, AND RULES ARE APPLIED AUTOMATICALLY

Standard operating procedures have, unfortunately, become casualties in an increasingly dynamic business environment. Many firms have become true *adhocracies* that seem to have a new way of doing things every week or day. Even worse, there is little consensus among employees at any point as to how even the simplest of procedures is to be carried out. Rapid employee turnover destroys the last shreds of institutional memory, resulting in a workplace where fundamental business processes are improvised and revised on the fly. This is perhaps the greatest challenge facing process reengineers: the possibility that any new workflow they design will be ignored, misconstrued, and abandoned almost from Day One.

Workflow management tools have the great advantage over paper processes of constraining users to follow the automated procedure as defined. New employees don't have to ask around or pore through thick books to identify the procedures they should follow. All they have to do is bring up a predefined electronic folder or form on their computer screen, fill in the appropriate fields, forward the item, and — voila — they're participating in a standard operating procedure (the details of which they may not have to bother with). Minimizing the time spent getting up to speed on business processes increases the time available for participating in them.

ENSURE THAT AUTHORIZED PERSONNEL CAN MODIFY PROCESSES RAPIDLY

Standard operating procedures become standard because some corporate official decrees, publishes, and enforces them. Controls are needed on process definition to prevent the company or workgroup from sliding back into pure adhocracy. Clearly, workflow management systems provide powerful tools for locking organizations into rigid procedures; this is an approach that may work well with highly structured, repetitive activities, such as managing administrative casework. However, many business processes are more provisional in nature, subject to change without notice due to exceptional circumstances or dynamic business conditions. Workflow tools increasingly support dynamic rerouting and process redefinition, capabilities that allow organizations to adapt without totally abandoning standard procedures.

ENSURE CONTINUOUS INVOLVEMENT OF ALL PERSONNEL IN WORKFLOW

Effective business processes depend on the active participation of all individuals. People who are seldom in the office or frequently out of contact become a serious bottleneck, especially if they are senior approval authorities or have unique skills and expertise. One way to get around this is the time-honored practice of designating alternates and backups for various individuals. Another way is to provide users with remote access — via laptops, modems, and dial-up connections (POTS, wireless data, Internet, and so on) — to automated workflow environments. People need not be out of touch or unavailable for work if they can always dial in to access their worklist and upload completed work items.

Identify Workflow Technology that Best Supports Structure of Target Process

After rethinking your business process structurally, you will want to identify the best type of workflow solution to support your target, redesigned process. As illustrated by Table 3-5 in Chapter 3, today's commercial workflow solutions differ greatly in their support for collaborative structure, platform, and media. The following discussion will help you determine whether your target workflow is best supported by a production, messaging-based, Web-based, or suite-based product.

> *Think of the most repetitive, paper-laden administrative processes in your organization, and you've found prime candidates for production workflow reengineering.*

Processes best suited to production workflow

What best distinguishes production-grade workflow products is their support for the classic bureaucratic process: a complex, unchanging, high-volume workflow involving multiple participants with diverse roles and responsibilities. These tools are sometimes referred to as case management systems, because they have been adopted by government agencies, insurance companies, and other bureaucracies to automate handling of routine customer and constituent casework.

Traditionally, the initial application of production workflow systems within organizations has been a *no brainer* exercise in paperwork reduction. Take an existing, manual, paper-intensive process and remove the paper, preserving the process more or less in its current state. This process can be done by scanning paper documents into optical storage at the beginning of the process and then routing and processing digital images from then on. It can also be done by removing paper altogether and routing electronic forms, files, or work items from end to end.

Think of the most mundane, repetitive, paper-laden administrative processes in your organization, and you've found prime candidates for production workflow reengineering. You can cut processing time, staffing requirements, and paper processing, storage, and retrieval costs in one bold stroke.

A COMPLEX PROCESS

In many organizations, one juicy candidate for production workflow is the procurement process, which typifies bureaucracy in its classic paper-devouring, time-wasting form. Table 12-2 illustrates the typical steps in a large company's purchasing process.

The following hypothetical (but very plausible) procurement process illustrates the sort of complex, conditional workflow that is best suited to production workflow applications. The basic steps are request origination, management review, order placement, order fulfillment, and payment. This chapter first describes the complex process in considerable detail, and then it shows how it can be rethought, modeled, and routinized in a complex production workflow application.

TABLE 12-2: A COMPLEX PROCESS

ACTIVITY	DISCUSSION
Request Origination	In the first phase of the process, employees fill out multipart, multipage purchase request (PR) forms and submit them to their immediate supervisors. PR originators must use the current version of the company's PR form, order items only from catalogs of company-approved vendors, and determine whether sufficient funds remain in the current year's budget to cover the purchase. To run the bureaucratic approval gauntlet, the PR must include a unique identifying number, priority level, request date, accounting charge number, requested delivery or performance date, recommended source company name, recommended source point-of-contact (name, address, and phone number), shipping/receiving point-of-contact (name, address, and phone number), items requested (makes, models, vendor stock numbers, descriptions, quantities, estimated unit prices, and estimated total prices for each item), and estimated total cost of request. The PR must also include a transmittal form indicating the appropriate review/approval chain.
Management Review	The originator's immediate supervisor reviews the PR. If the request is below a certain dollar threshold (e.g., $5,000) and for a limited category of items (e.g., office supplies, simple furniture, and company-standard PCs and peripherals), the immediate supervisor can approve and forward it directly to a procurement specialist. Otherwise, the supervisor must, after approving it, forward it to his or her supervisor, to a technical specialist, or to both in parallel or sequence. In authorizing a large-dollar-amount PR, managers certify that it fully and correctly represents the needs of the company and/or client on whose

ACTIVITY	DISCUSSION

Management Review *(continued)*

behalf the items will be purchased. This may involve including a brief rationale that justifies the purchase through reference to the corporate business plan or customer contract. In authorizing PRs that request nonstandard items, technical specialists certify that the requirements represent an unusual case that cannot be satisfied fully by standard products or solutions. In any case, management's approval of a purchase certifies that sufficient funds are in the designated budget account to cover the payable dollar amount. After all necessary management approvals have been obtained, the PR is forwarded directly to the head of procurement, who assigns it to the appropriate procurement specialist. Different procurement specialists will be assigned to the case, depending on the nature of the procurement and workloads at the time the PR is received. If the PR is rejected at any step, it is returned to the originator with attached comments indicating why it was rejected. The originator may resubmit a revised PR that responds to reviewers' comments.

Order Placement

The procurement specialist reviews the purchase request and provides a *reality check* on the justifications, requirements, specifications, source recommendations, and cost estimates, based on his or her knowledge of company or client requirements and availability of suitable goods or service in the marketplace. Requested items may be available in corporate inventories or through transfer of surplus property from another department or region, which the procurement specialist could determine by looking up the appropriate databases or making a few phone calls. On recurring small procurements for which there are established vendors, the procurement specialist will prepare a corporate purchase order and submit that to the vendor. On some large-dollar-amount, technically complex, capital-equipment procurements for which there is no existing contractual procurement vehicle, however, the PR may be assigned to a contracting specialist who will define an acquisition plan, manage the procurement, oversee source selection, and administer the new contract. The acquisition plan will contain as much detail as warranted by the size and complexity of the acquisition. A fully developed acquisition plan would include a written justification, requirements statement, functional and technical specifications, market survey, cost projections, milestones, participants, delivery or performance periods, risks, source selection approach, solicitation type, contract type, funding source, financing approach, and acceptance criteria. The contracting officer presents the final acquisition plan to the originator and the authorizing manager for their review and approval. Signed approval of the acquisition plan by the originator and/or manager represents that person's concurrence and approval that the acquisition plan addresses his or her requirements. Receipt of the signed concurrence and approval authorizes the contracting officer to commence the proposed contracting action and begin development of necessary solicitation documents. A large procurement may spawn one or more Requests for Proposals (RFPs), each with their own contracting officers, source selection panels, and vendor negotiations. Ultimately, procurement specialists will establish one or more contracts — in consultation with corporate legal counsel — which will result in submission of one-time or recurring purchase orders, delivery orders, or similar ordering vehicles. The originator of a purchase request will be notified when an order is placed.

Order Fulfillment

After the order has been placed, the procurement specialist will request periodic updates from the vendor on the anticipated delivery or performance date, which will be forwarded to the request originator and to the designated shipping/receiving point-of-contact. When the shipment arrives, shipping/receiving will check the packing slip against what was delivered and then send the packing slip to accounts payable. The shipment will either be

(continued)

TABLE 12-2:   A COMPLEX PROCESS *(continued)*

ACTIVITY	DISCUSSION
Order Fulfillment *(continued)*	forwarded directly to the designated recipient (which may or may not be the originator), or the designated recipient will be notified to pick it up in shipping/receiving. The invoice will be sent directly to accounts payable, which will verify it against the packing slip and purchase order. Accounts payable will contact the vendor to report damaged or incomplete shipments and inaccurate invoices. The procurement specialist will notify the PR originator of any delays associated with return of goods.
Payment	Finally, accounts payable will issue payment to the vendor for shipments against authorized purchase orders, pending acceptance or inspection testing. The funds will be taken from the appropriate corporate account.

A PARSED, COMPLEX PROCESS

This everyday purchasing workflow seems straightforward until you put it under the proverbial microscope and attempt to model and automate it. Suddenly, you notice all the people involved, the myriad pieces of paper that change hands, and the complex routing and handling rules. Returning to the framework presented in Chapter 3, you can parse this workflow into the collaborative structure and media described in Table 12-3 (ignoring, for the time being, the computer and network platform used by participants, as well as their physical locations with respect to one another). This parsing can serve as the basis for a production workflow process model.

TABLE 12-3:   A PARSED, COMPLEX PROCESS

COLLABORATIVE DIMENSION STRUCTURE	DISCUSSION
Routes	This is no administrative assembly line, which would imply a cut-and-dried, one-way, unconditional workflow. Depending on the nature, scope, and complexity of the purchase, the process may expand and sweep in an ever-widening circle of participants, tasks, milestones, forms, documents, and databases. A PR may be routed across the desks of several management reviewers, technical specialists, and procurement personnel — not to mention the many vendor personnel who will handle the resultant purchase order. Several reviewers may be looking at the PR concurrently or in strict sequence. Reviewers may bring in additional personnel to determine the technical appropriateness of the request, as well as to determine the availability of comparable solutions within the company. At any point in the intracorporate review process, someone may reject the PR and return it to the originator with comments and suggestions. The originator will also receive notifications on the status of the procurement. Delivery and installation of the requested item may entail a complex ballet of message passing between the originator, vendor, procurement specialist, shipping/receiving, accounts payable, facilities administrator, information systems administrator, and transport carrier.

COLLABORATIVE DIMENSION	DISCUSSION
STRUCTURE	

Roles

Workflow participants vary in their ability to facilitate, complicate, delay, or cancel pending purchases. People's roles may be defined by their ability to create, revise, or influence the evolving procurement documentation package. Only a limited group of employees may originate PRs. An originator prepares the initial draft of the PR but must respond and/or yield to comments and suggestions from internal reviewers. The originator reserves the right to withdraw or revise the PR. The direct supervisor may summarily reject the PR, postpone it pending funds availability, sit on it indefinitely, or return it with pointed instructions. Technical reviewers may be allowed to revise requests unilaterally to bring them in line with corporate standards, or simply flag nonstandard items and return the PR with suggested alternatives. Procurement specialists make sure that the documentation package includes all necessary sections and signatures, conforms to the correct format, contains no inaccuracies, and specifies company-approved vendors and solutions.

Rules

An intricate web of business rules defines the rhythm by which the PR and associated documentation ping back and forth between workflow participants. PR routing and handling procedures vary with the type of procurement, dollar amount, priority level, and requested delivery date. Processing turnaround times are shorter on high-priority requests. PRs will not be approved if they can be satisfied by internal inventories or cannot be covered by remaining budget allocations. Invoices will not be honored unless they correspond to an authorized purchase order number and are accompanied by an accurate packing slip or bill of lading. Status notifications will be returned to the originator only when a purchase order is placed and the requested item is delivered.

COLLABORATIVE DIMENSION	DISCUSSION
MEDIA	

Information Base

Workflow participants must consult and generate a wide range of files, records, and documentation in order to process the procurement. Originators must obtain the current corporate PR form, vendor catalogs, price lists, accounting charge number lists, and technical standards documents. On larger, more complex purchases, originators may be required to include with the PR any or all of the following separate documents: rationale, requirements statement, technical specifications, market survey, and statement of work. Management and technical reviewers may participate in developing some of this documentation. Managers will look into their budget balances before authorizing the purchase. Procurement specialists will make use of corporate purchasing guidelines, contract files, vendor histories, bidders lists, and inventory databases.

Messaging

Workflow participants use various messaging options (e.g., hand-carried paper, interoffice mail, e-mail, fax, voice mail) to route procurement documentation, reminders, notifications, and other necessary information.

Conferencing

The more complex and costly the procurement, the greater the need for internal meetings involving the originator, reviewers, and procurement specialist. If the procurement leads to an RFP and vendor negotiations, add more meetings to the process. Meeting coordination demands more interpersonal messages, agendas, status reports, and other overhead documentation.

A WORKFLOW-ENABLED, PARSED, COMPLEX PROCESS

Someone unfamiliar with production workflow process modeling tools would find this complexity daunting. Surely, they would argue, the process just parsed doesn't exactly sound like anything that can be routinized in an automated workflow management system.

By contrast, a business-process analyst looks at this parsed, complex process and sees the outlines of an implementable production workflow solution. The process model could be blocked out with visual flowcharting tools included with most production workflow products. The model would include the following principal elements in Table 12-4:

TABLE 12-4: A WORKFLOW-ENABLED, PARSED, COMPLEX PROCESS

ELEMENT	DESCRIPTION
Routes	The analyst blocks out a process that has a predominantly sequential flow but includes some concurrent routes (for overlapping technical reviews), conditional routes (for reviews that depend on attributes of the proposed purchase), cyclebacks (for rejected requests), and notifications (for informing the originator of the request's location and status). The flow of the purchase request would be defined as taking place entirely inside the originator's company. If the originator's company had establish interorganizational workflow connections with trading partners, the process could be extended to include supplier personnel who respond to the resultant purchase order.
Roles	The analyst defines some basic roles and associated privileges in the process. Originators are allowed to create, submit, and withdraw purchase requests, and are notified on the status and location of purchase requests they submitted. Supervisors are allowed to review, revise, annotate, approve, postpone, return, and kill purchase requests from persons in their workgroups. Technical reviewers are also allowed to review, revise, annotate, approve, and return purchase requests, but may not postpone or kill purchase requests. Procurement specialists are allowed to review, annotate, approve, and return purchase requests, but may not revise, postpone, or kill them; they may also issue purchase orders pursuant to approval. Receiving personnel are allowed to issue, receive, and forward bills of lading in response to approved purchase orders, and to notify originators of inbound shipments. Accounting personnel are allowed to issue and pay invoices on approved purchase orders, subsequent to receipt and acceptance of the order of goods by the originator.
Rules	The analyst defines conditional routing and handling rules for the procurement package that depend on the values input into the fields of the Purchase Request form, which functions as an electronic *transmittal sheet* on a procurement package *folder* that may include many files. Conditional routes may be activated totally on the basis of information contained in the Purchase Request form (e.g., routing to a particular technical reviewer based on the request's categorization) or based partly on a system lookup of relevant records contained in a corporate database (e.g., automatically killing a purchase request for an item found to be in inventory).

ELEMENT	DESCRIPTION
Information Bases	The analyst defines links from the fields of the electronic Purchase Request form into several existing corporate databases on the network, ensuring that the most current data is used by originators, supervisors, and technical reviewers to populate the forms. The form's contents are set up to automatically write to a new shared database pertinent to purchase requests. In defining an electronic procurement folder to be routed, originators are allowed to attach any electronic file from their computers or departmental servers. Access controls are defined for the workflow-relevant databases, records, and fields, associated with various roles.
Messaging	The analyst defines e-mail, voice mail, voice, and/or paging notifications to be triggered by various events in the workflow. Many notifications are sent to originators to alert them to the current location and status of outstanding purchase requests.
Conferencing	The analyst can set up the process to automatically post relevant documentation, notifications, and participant messages to a shared network bulletin board, so that all personnel can stay current on the procurment's status and perhaps engage in a near-real-time discussion of critical technical and coordination issues.

The object of this exercise has been to show how an analyst can take a process of considerable complexity — either an existing procedure or a desired new procedure — and boil it down to functional specifications that can be mapped straightforwardly into a production workflow application. After the business process has been functionally decomposed in this fashion — specifying both its collaborative structure and media — the next steps are to roll up your proverbial sleeves and develop the target workflow application.

Many of the process-modeling techniques discussed in Chapter 4 can be used to develop complex production workflow applications similar to the one just presented. Before venturing into the market for process-modeling tools, you will need to clearly analyze and parse your business processes, so that you can gauge their complexity and logical flow. You don't want to invest in tools that force you to oversimplify your workflow or deny you the flexibility needed to reengineer processes for maximum business advantage.

Processes best suited to messaging-based workflow

Messaging-based workflow systems often represent a low-end, entry-level *proof of concept* solution for organizations unfamiliar with this technology. These products — sometimes referred to as *administrative workflow systems* — usually automate processes that possess neither the complexity nor document-image processing requirements associated with traditional production workflow applications. As noted in Chapter 3, they typically support the following collaborative dimensions as shown in Table 12-5.

TABLE 12-5: COLLABORATIVE DIMENSIONS SUPPORTED BY MESSAGING-BASED WORKFLOW SYSTEMS

COLLABORATIVE DIMENSION	DISCUSSION
Platform	Messaging-based workflow applications run over users' existing local- and/or wide-area e-mail systems, as compared with distributed document/database systems, or *shared filestore*, used to support production workflow applications.
Structure	Messaging-based tools support simple process models that can be defined with *routing list* dialog boxes similar or identical to e-mail addressing functions, as compared with complex process models, defined with visual flowcharting tools, used to develop production workflow applications. Routing options on messaging-based solutions are usually limited to sequential and parallel paths, with some support for conditional routing based on user inputs into electronic form fields.
Media	Messaging-based products primarily route electronic forms as file attachments over users' e-mail systems, as compared with the complex, multidocument folders — including electronic forms, document images, database extracts, and various application files — that are routed *logically*, through transfer of access privileges, by production workflow applications. Electronic forms on messaging-based workflow systems are primarily used to query and update back-end database management systems.

Business processes possessing any of the features presented in Table 12-6 are good candidates for messaging-based workflow applications.

TABLE 12-6: FEATURES OF BUSINESS PROCESSES BEST SUITED TO MESSAGING-BASED WORKFLOW

PROCESS FEATURE	DISCUSSION
Forms Orientation	Any process oriented around a single form with little or no additional documentation is a prime candidate for messaging-based workflow support. For example, requests to install an office telephone, move an existing phone line to a new floor, or set up a voice mailbox for a new employee can usually be handled with an administrator's signature on a filled-in business form. Likewise, low-dollar-amount purchase requests for office supplies almost never need supporting documentation.
Simple Routing between E-mail-Connected Participants	Document-routing procedures that previously have been supported by standard e-mail could be given additional structure through messaging-based workflow. For example, the same five individuals may be involved in preparing monthly status, financial, and operational reports for your company. Traditionally, a draft report is prepared by a single individual with a standard style sheet and e-mailed to the others for review. The others make revisions or append comments and e-mail the marked-up drafts back to the originator, who is responsible for reconciling and merging them into a final master report. The document originator has the tedious job of tracking how far the recipients have got in reviewing the drafts and reminding them to return their comments and changes before the deadline.

PROCESS FEATURE	DISCUSSION
Dynamic Process That Changes Frequently and Shows No Signs of Settling into a Predictable Pattern	Standard operating procedures are luxuries for companies in fast-changing, volatile competitive environments. Business routes, roles, and rules may be in total flux — an environment in which some people thrive and others burn out. Many high-technology companies are *adhocracies* that suffer from the *process of the week* syndrome. Nevertheless, even the most egregious adhocracy may see the need for standard procedures — even if they're often observed in the breach — to be implemented rigorously at some indefinite future date when *things settle down*. Messaging-based tools would allow the standard procedure to be redefined continually as conditions change.
First, Rough, Trial-and-Error Cut at Formal Process	Companies may see a clear-and-present need for a formal process but not be sure what the outlines of the ideal process might be. Messaging-based tools would allow the process model to be defined and refined operationally through successive trials and *reality checks*. One real-world run of a proposed process can provide more useful feedback than a year's worth of reengineering meetings and tool-based simulations.
Temporary Process with Few Expected Runs	Temporary workgroups may have a clear-cut process in mind and want to implement it rapidly with off-the-shelf tools. The resultant workflow may be run just a few times, but each of these process instances might be critical to some high-stakes operation, such as facilitating a corporate acquisition or responding to an environmental disaster. Messaging-based workflow tools allow temporary projects to be managed with clockwork precision.

The typical process for messaging-based workflow is one defined and redefined by participants *on the fly*, in contrast to the top-down orientation of production workflow. The comparative low-cost and simplicity of messaging-based workflow tools encourages users to experiment with the grass-roots process reengineering, rather than wait for hard-coded new workflows handed down by a high-level corporate process architect.

Processes best suited to Web-based workflow

Web-based workflow applications are best suited to forms-oriented processes that involve participants at several sites. As noted in Chapter 3, Web-based workflow solutions typically support the following collaborative dimensions, as shown in Table 12-7.

TABLE 12-7: COLLABORATIVE DIMENSIONS SUPPORTED BY WEB-BASED WORKFLOW SYSTEMS

COLLABORATIVE DIMENSION	DISCUSSION
Platform	Web-based workflow applications run over the Internet or corporate intranets, are served from users' Web sites — a very specialized type of shared filestore — and are accessed through users' Web browsers. Information is routed physically between user browsers and through intermediary Web sites.

(continued)

Table 12-7:   Collaborative Dimensions Supported by Web-based Workflow Systems *(continued)*

COLLABORATIVE DIMENSION	DISCUSSION
Structure	Web-based workflow tools support process models that range from complex to simple, using visual development tools similar to those long associated with production workflow.
Media	Web-based products primarily route stand-alone HTML-formatted electronic forms (lacking support for the multidocument folders and file attachments associated with production and messaging-based workflow, respectively). The forms populate external databases accessed by Web sites. The forms can also incorporate considerable image, audio, and other multimedia content, owing to the rich document formats inherent to Web applications in general.

The typical Web-based workflow application is more top-down than bottom-up in orientation. It is preplanned in considerable detail, like a production workflow application, and does not generally sprout up from grass-roots users. This application automates an enterprise-wide process that needs to be made available to the broadest range of corporate users, and possibly to remote sites dialing in through a security firewall gateway. Web-based environments will be ideal for interorganizational EDI workflow (that is, when companies decide to get serious about it).

Processes best suited to suite-based workflow

Suite-based workflow solutions, by contrast, support the most grass-roots, spontaneous, ad-hoc routing decisions. They are appropriate for any process, initiated by a single user on a single occasion, that involves review and mark-up of a particular document. The originator will usually place any or all of the structural controls (shown in Table 12-8) on the process.

Table 12-8:   Structural Controls on Document Routing and Processing Typically Associated with Suite-based Workflow Applications

STRUCTURAL CONTROL	DISCUSSION
Cycle Back to Originator	Typically, users route application files in order to receive them back — with comments, annotation, and/or revisions — at the end of the process. The originator may also be able to specify when the document must be returned to him or her. Contrast this with standard e-mail, in which the originator typically cannot require recipients to return the document.

STRUCTURAL CONTROL	DISCUSSION
Prespecified Routing Order	Suite-based applications allow originators to specify the precise order in which recipients will review a document. A recipient may only route the message containing the document to the next person in the chain and may not forward it to anyone else.
Document Location and Status Updates	Suite-based applications usually allow originators to indicate whether they want to receive regular or event-driven updates on the location and status of routed documents. Recipients' mail clients automatically return requested notifications to the originator when a document is received, read, altered, and routed.
Comment Traceability	Different reviewers' comments or annotations on the master document may be highlighted by special colors, fonts, or other visual indicators.
Version Control	Several reviewers' changes to the master document may be entered and displayed in various ways. One approach is to enter changes in on-screen insert boxes linked to the appropriate areas of text, allowing the originator to determine who made what change and providing the option of accepting or rejecting a suggested change later on. Alternately, each reviewer's changes may be written to a new file with a different filename.

Suite-based applications represent the future of distributed computing, in which workflow capabilities will be embedded within e-mail clients, word processors, spreadsheets, and other desktop and workgroup productivity tools. Functionally similar to messaging-based tools, suite-based applications provide convenient document-routing capabilities to the mass market.

Define Network and Information Systems Requirements of Your Reengineered Workflow

After you have defined your workflow functional requirements, you can begin to delve into the system requirements associated with implementing the desired new process on your company's network and computing platform. Your workflow system requirements will be shaped by the platform considerations presented in Table 12-9.

TABLE 12-9: NETWORK PLATFORM CONSIDERATIONS FOR WORKFLOW APPLICATIONS

NETWORK PLATFORM CONSIDERATION	DISCUSSION
Geographic Range	How widely are workflow participants and the requisite information-processing resources scattered across the map? If all users are in a single office and rarely travel, you should explore using their current e-mail system or groupware or desktop application suites as the platform for the workflow application. The greater the concentration of users in a particular building, the more feasible it is to support them all from a single workflow engine and/or mail server/store. As multiple workgroups, buildings, cities, and time zones are brought into an application, the greater your requirement for workflow products that run across distributed workflow engines, databases, and document/mail stores. As users spread out across the map, you should strongly consider hosting your workflow application on the corporate intranet, which deploys distributed file stores — known as *Web sites* — on a wide-area basis.
Mobility	How extensively do workflow participants move or roam during execution of the business process? If users travel frequently and require continuous involvement in the business process, you should consider workflow products that provide remote dial-in/dial-out capabilities via standard voice lines, cellular telephone services, packet radio services, or the Internet/Web. Messaging-based and suite-based workflow products may be the preferred choice for mobile personnel, many of whom carry modem-equipped laptops and remote e-mail access and file-transfer software. Web-based workflow solutions will not be a good solution for mobile professionals until wireless data services (increasingly, the preferred mobile data communications technology) support the faster data rates needed for graphics-intensive home-page downloading.
Access Terminals	What types of shared, desktop, or portable terminal equipment and application software are available to workflow participants? All workflow solutions run on networks of desktop PCs and, increasingly, portable computers. However, your business process may also involve communications with users equipped with voice mail boxes, fax machines, cellular phones, and pagers. In this case, you would only want to consider those workflow solutions that include gateways to those communications systems.
Operating Environments	What operating systems, network operating systems, distributed file and database systems, e-mail transports, directory services, and communications protocols are used to provide application services to workflow participants over the network? You always need to make sure a workflow solution runs across the application infrastructure of the intended process, be it wide- or local-area in extent. Of course, your choices of messaging- and suite-based workflow products will be constrained by your existing e-mail systems and application suites. And, depending on the particular Web browsers and servers used in your company, you may encounter some difficulty in achieving full interoperability from some Web-based workflow products.

Communications Networks

What departmental, corporate, public, and international communications facilities are used to physically connect workflow participants to each other and to various application resources? You need to make sure that a proposed new workflow application does not chew up inordinate amounts of network transmission capacity, also known as *bandwidth*. Imaging-based workflow applications can make great demands on network bandwidth, so you will usually need to run the applications only over local or campus-area networks, which generally provide 4-100 megabit-per-second data rates, or over high-capacity wide-area networks based on asynchronous-transfer-mode (ATM) or frame-relay technology. Corporate intranets are increasingly being implemented with ATM and frame relay technologies, but the public Internet seldom provides more than 28.8 kilobits per second (kbps) on an end-to-end basis. Wireless data services — such as cellular digital packet data (CDPD) and Mobitex — are even more bandwidth-poor, rarely providing more than 9.6 kbps of sustained application throughput. From a workflow user's point of view, raw network speeds may not be very important, since most workflow routing procedures are performed on a store-and-forward, not real-time, basis. However, from a network administrator's point of view, the size of the network *pipe* is very important, because a bandwidth-hungry workflow application will slow down the performance of other applications on the network.

Define Development and Administration Responsibilities for Workflow System

After identifying the broad structural and platform requirements for your workflow application, you'll be able to define general responsibilities for developing and administering the application. You must always keep the endgame in mind: How, and by whom, will the application be modified, maintained, and supported in the target environment? After all, an integral part of any workflow is the range of activities needed to sustain, control, and extend it on an ongoing basis.

> *You need the shmoozing skills of a career politician to manage an enterprise-wide workflow implementation.*

Your analysis should help you to identify the specific users, managers, analysts, and technical personnel who will attend to the care and feeding of your workflow application. You will need the shmoozing skills of a career politician to manage an enterprise-wide workflow implementation, due to the inherently sprawling, boundary-spanning nature of this technology. The more complex your workflow application — according to the three principal collaborative dimensions — the more difficult and expensive it will be to coordinate all involved personnel, departments, and functions, per Table 12-10.

TABLE 12-10: WORKFLOW APPLICATION DEVELOPMENT AND
ADMINISTRATION SUPPORT REQUIREMENTS

COLLABORATIVE DIMENSION	WORKFLOW APPLICATION DEVELOPMENT AND ADMINISTRATION SUPPORT REQUIREMENTS
PLATFORM	Developing and administering the platform component of workflow applications usually requires assistance from various computer and telecommunications support organizations. These support requirements are discussed under the platform headings of geographic range, mobility, access terminals, operating environments, and communications networks.
Geographic Range	The simplest workflow application involves one server and a small group of users on a workgroup LAN. Under these circumstances, the application could conceivably be developed, installed, and administered by one person, perhaps the LAN administrator. Connect more users, servers, workgroups, buildings, and cities to the application and you steadily increase the cast of characters needed to develop, manage, and maintain it all. Support requirements for workflow are similar to those for network operating systems, electronic software distribution, e-mail, and other client-server applications — they are tied more closely to the number of sites than to the number of users or volume of traffic that must be supported.
Mobility	Workflow application development and support costs also increase with the number of users requiring mobile access. You will need to optimize the application for at least two client operating environments — users' desktop and portable computers — and develop application interfaces to cellphones, pagers, voice mail systems, and other communications services they use on the road. Distributing workflow application upgrades and bug fixes to a fleet of sporadically connected mobile computers can quickly become a logistical nightmare, especially if you've failed to maintain an accurate configuration database covering software and hardware in the field. User training becomes a hit-or-miss enterprise, as it may take weeks to find time on a mobile user's schedule to train them on how to use a new or modified workflow electronic form. To support mobile workflow participants, you may have to bear the cost of maintaining decentralized training facilities and service/support depots in several cities, regions, or countries.
Access Terminals	The greater the range of computers, phones, and other terminals that need workflow access, the more complex the application development, integration, installation, maintenance, and administration effort. For example, you may need to ensure minimum system configurations (such as processor type, memory, free disk space, display dimensions, and communications interface speed) in all connected devices to ensure consistent, optimal application performance. Modifications may have to be made to workflow client software to make it work on some hardware platforms. Some older generation access terminals (e.g., 80386 and earlier CPUs) may be excluded altogether as too slow and resource-limited to run workflow client applications and other critical software (such as mail clients, forms fillers, and image viewers).

Operating Environments	Every infrastructure technology integrated with your workflow application (e.g., client operating system, network operating system, server, database, image repository, messaging system, and directory service) is managed by one or more support groups, with which you will have to coordinate closely throughout the application's life cycle. Changes to a workflow client application, electronic form, routing path, or other feature may have to be cleared with several managers, since these revisions could have serious impacts on their systems' workloads and performance. The workflow administrator may control little or none of the underlying application infrastructure, which places him or her in the unenviable position of having to wheedle or cajole others continuously for support on a wide range of technical issues. Workflow administrators need to maintain especially cordial relations with the people who manage the fundamental application service (filestore, messaging, Web, or application suite) underlying their specific workflow category.
Communications Networks	Likewise, workflow administrators will have to coordinate application development and administration with administrators of the various departmental, corporate, public, and international communications facilities used to physically connect workflow participants to each other and to application resources. This coordination is especially critical when workflow traffic must share network transmission, switching, and routing capacity with other network applications, as is usually the case with messaging-based, Web-based, and suite-based workflow applications. By contrast, traditional production workflow applications run on dedicated networks set up for high-volume document-image processing, which makes cross-application bandwidth-sharing less of an issue.
STRUCTURE	Paradoxically, developing and administering the structure component of workflow applications requires support from a group that views its role as anything but support-related: business, project, and task managers. These support requirements are discussed under the structure headings of routes, roles, and rules.
Routes	In most cases, document-routing procedures are not changed unilaterally by workflow developers and administrators, unless they — Dogbert-style — want to engineer a management coup d'etat and assume total control over the workplace. Usually, the workflow developer/administrator will design and modify the process model to conform with routing procedures handed down by the business manager or supervisor with jurisdiction. Or, in a peer-to-peer relationship, the workflow administrator may recommend altered routing procedures, based on proactive analysis and/or observed process bottlenecks and delays. Under either scenario, business managers — and operational analysts in their employ — need to learn a new discipline: issuing detailed, unambiguous routing procedures that they intend to implement immediately to the letter. Workflow technology cannot be effective in a business environment where managers casually define vague routing procedures on legal pads and never muster enough backbone to put them into practice (rather, they show no commitment to their new procedures and implicitly let the status quo endure).

(continued)

TABLE 12-10: WORKFLOW APPLICATION DEVELOPMENT AND ADMINISTRATION SUPPORT REQUIREMENTS *(continued)*

COLLABORATIVE DIMENSION	WORKFLOW APPLICATION DEVELOPMENT AND ADMINISTRATION SUPPORT REQUIREMENTS
Roles	Similarly, workflow developers and administrators usually define participant roles — and map particular individuals to these roles — based on the organizational chart and responsibilities dictated by business managers. Individuals' workflow roles are often specific to a given project or task to which they've been assigned. Consequently, project and task managers need to communicate these individual role assignments promptly to the workflow administrator. In some cases, the business, project, or task leaders will assume the role of workflow administrator for their particular process and will input role assignments directly into the workflow application.
Rules	Similarly, workflow developers and administrators — in theory — work with the document/forms routing, processing, notification, access control, tracking, audit, backup, and other rules handed to them by business managers. However, it's usually asking too much to expect business managers to define complex process models to the level of specificity required by workflow application developers. In practice, workflow professionals will usually take the initiative in defining detailed executable rules based on their analysis of corporate policies and procedures, much the same way they would define a complex database application based on high-level business requirements. After the workflow application has been defined, the workflow analyst will present it to management decision makers for their concurrence, taking pains to explain the business rules governing the application's behavior.
MEDIA	Developing and administering the media component of workflow applications — that is, the desktop presentation, display, and manipulation of work items — usually requires assistance from various computer and telecommunications support organizations, and from the users themselves. These support requirements are discussed under the media headings of information bases, messaging, and conferencing.
Information Bases	The principal collaboration medium in most workflows is the range of documents, databases, Web sites, and other information bases accessed and used by people doing their jobs. To provide people with access to the necessary information bases, search/viewing tools, and manipulation/analysis tools, workflow developers require extensive assistance and input from end users. Electronic forms design is one area where user inputs are required, because forms — usually implemented as database front ends — are the primary objects routed in many workflows. You should not leave forms and database design entirely up to business managers and systems administrators, because they may never actually use the forms in their jobs. Chances are that they would impose a wrongheaded design that would hinder more than expedite the target workflow. Usability testing — involving the ultimate users — is critical to the well-tuned, workflow-enabled business process.

Messaging	Messaging services are usually transparent to workflow users, who seldom realize or care exactly how items are transported to and from their inboxes. However, workflow developers need to consult with users to determine how best to customize or modify mail-client software to optimize worklist presentation and handling. For example, users may indicate that they would like messages containing incoming work items to be routed to several desktop folders and ranked in various orders, depending on their senders, subjects, priorities, contents, and other criteria. Likewise, users might request that workflow items be distinguished from standard e-mail by special inbox icons. These are critical usability and efficiency issues that business managers and systems developers might overlook or dismiss out-of-hand.
Conferencing	Conferencing, in the context of workflow, usually refers to messaging-based bulletin boards to which participants post general discussion items and the system automatically posts notifications, reminders, and status/location updates. Users need to assist workflow developers in defining the types of process-tracking information to which shared bulletin-board access will be required for effective real-time coordination. Anybody who has managed a high-stakes project under an aggressive schedule will tell you that interpersonal messaging and background documentation are not enough to focus groups of people on critical, short-fuse issues.

Of course, all this discussion begs the question of who exactly are these workflow developers and administrators. You — as workflow champion within your company — may see yourself performing or overseeing this role for one or more applications. Or you may propose that your company designate personnel responsible for these functions in various business units.

If you're not careful, this issue — who defines and administers workflow applications — could become the focus of a power struggle between various groups in your organization. You could find yourself whipsawed between upper management's demands for greater structure, monitoring, and control, and end users' demands for flexible, ad-hoc process definition, rerouting, and customization. You may find yourself mired in the age-old struggle for control of the workplace (at which point you'll be tempted to dust off that old copy of Karl Marx's *Das Kapital* you had to read in college).

Who your company chooses to designate as workflow administrators depends on how the technology is implemented — vertically from the corporate upper echelon on down, or horizontally between various workgroups. If you take the top-down approach, you'll probably want to designate workflow administrators in each business unit, who will be responsible for defining standard processes within their units and forwarding these — as well as change requests — to a central corporate administrator for incorporation into a standard enterprise process model. If you take the horizontal approach, each workgroup or function will define its own process model and then laterally negotiate workflow linkages with other business groups.

Whichever approach is taken to assigning workflow administration responsibilities, your organization's workflow administrators should comply with the following guidelines designed to ensure smooth operations:

- Baseline and revise process models only at regular, controlled intervals (such as once a quarter), lest they succumb to the chaos of operational adhocracy that workflow technology was supposed to help cure

- Adopt a corporate-standard BPR/workflow definition tool, so that all process models conform to the same structure and conventions

- Clear major workflow application changes with the administrators of all impacted systems, including operating environments, networks, databases, image repositories, directories, and messaging systems

- Train, educate, and update users regularly on workflow applications, features, and operating procedures

Summary

In summary, this chapter presents a detailed set of guidelines for defining your workflow functional, system, and staffing requirements, enabling you to begin designing workflow applications, process models, and development/support organizations. It has supplied conceptual tools for determining which category of workflow solution — production, messaging-based, Web-based, or suite-based — is best suited to your requirements. It has also given you a framework for defining the appropriate mix of personnel — management, system administrators, application developers, and users — that will be needed to build, implement, and manage workflow applications in your organization.

After you have thought through your workflow requirements in considerable detail, you will be ready to venture into the marketplace for commercial workflow management solutions. The next chapter supplies pointers for evaluating and selecting the best workflow products to meet your requirements.

CHAPTER THIRTEEN

SURVEYING AND EVALUATING WORKFLOW PRODUCTS AND PROVIDERS

You need to write documents, so you buy a word processor. You need to control your workflow, so you buy a workflow management product. Simple, right? Far from it. Just as some word processors are better suited for short, straightforward jobs and others are suited for complex, heavily formatted documents, not all workflow products will fit your needs. In fact, the best solution may require, at least in part, custom application development and integration. Consequently, your choice of a workflow development partner — the software vendor or a third-party consultant or integrator — is often just as important as your choice of a workflow management product.

This chapter provides guidelines for sorting through the field of commercial workflow solutions. It points you to workflow industry resources such as books, periodicals, trade shows, Web sites, and research firms. And it discusses principal evaluation and buying criteria for finding just the right workflow solution for your needs.

Perform a Market Survey

How do you narrow down the field of commercial workflow products and providers to a choice few that are worthy of detailed examination? You will need to perform a comprehensive market survey, educating yourself on vendors, solutions, standards, and market and technology trends. Several sources can help you.

Reference books

Although this book and similar books present a comprehensive picture of the workflow and BPR markets, remember that reference books are designed to have long shelf lives. Market surveys contained therein are likely to get dated quickly, especially in a fast-changing market such as workflow. In addition, reference books often focus on general market trends and vendor/product overviews. Consequently, you may not find the level of detail you want on candidate workflow solutions. In particular, BPR books tend to skimp on product details and favor lengthy descriptions of the author's project planning and modeling framework.

Trade periodicals

You will probably find more current vendor profiles, product information, and comparison charts in computer and network trade periodicals. Go back through the last 6 to 12 months of these magazines and pull out any article that even remotely pertains to workflow. Read everything. Don't be afraid to contact authors for more details. And don't hesitate to send in response cards or consult listed Web sites for more information on advertised workflow products.

Workflow product, vendor, and application articles can be found intermittently across the full range of mass-market computer and telecommunications periodicals. Some magazines that focus on workflow (primarily imaging-related production workflow solutions) include the following:

- Advanced Imaging (PTN Publishing Co., Melville, NY)
- Delphi Report (Delphi Consulting Group, Boston, MA)
- Document Imaging Report (Phillips Business Information, Inc., Potomac, MD)
- GroupTalk (Collaborative Strategies, San Francisco, CA)
- Imaging Magazine (Telecom Library Inc., New York, NY)
- Imaging Technology Report (Business Research Publications, New York, NY)
- Imaging World (Cardinal Business Media, Inc., Fort Washington, PA)
- Workgroup Computing Report (Patricia Seybold Group, Boston, MA)

On-line information services

An even quicker way to survey the workflow field is to consult the Web, thanks to on-line search services such as Yahoo!, Excite, Alta Vista, and DejaNews. Simply input the search term *workflow* (and any qualifying/delimiting terms), and you'll have quickly compiled scads of recent workflow-related articles plus a long *hot list* of workflow vendors, integrators, consultants, and associations. If you subscribe to an on-line real-time news service, you may request that it send you workflow-related headlines, briefs, and full-text stories via e-mail or fax. You may also want to subscribe to any workflow or BPR-related electronic journals or listservers you encounter. (To see a list of workflow industry Web addresses, refer to Appendix A in the back of the book.)

Industry conferences

Industry conferences are a great venue for making connections and getting the street-level buzz on what products and vendors are hot. Workflow solutions are featured at many leading computer and telecommunications industry shows. However, it's best to consult show exhibitor directories in advance before making arrangements to attend a conference, just to make sure enough workflow vendors will be present to justify your going.

Associations

Associations provide another excellent forum for surveying workflow providers and solutions. You may want to call on (or visit the Web sites of) the following workflow-related industry associations:

- Association for Information and Image Management
  (Silver Spring, MD, 800-477-2446)

- Workflow and Reengineering International Association
  (San Francisco, CA, 800-476-8792)

- Workflow Management Coalition (Brussels, Belgium, +32 2 774 96 33)

Research and consulting firms

In gathering all this workflow information, your head may start to swim unless you can find someone to help you put it all into perspective. There are many research and consulting firms that specialize in workflow and BPR. These firms frequently offer publications, seminars, and training in these subject areas. The following firms will be glad to assist you in identifying workflow requirements and evaluating commercial solutions:

- Aberdeen Group (Boston, MA, 617-723-7890)
- Andersen Consulting (New York, NY, 212-708-4400)
- Bruce Silver Associates (Weston, MA, 617-237-6879)
- Burton Group (Salt Lake City, UT, 801-934-1966)
- Collaborative Strategies (San Francisco, CA, 415-282-9197)
- Connexus Consulting Group (Andover, MA, 508-474-9117)
- Coopers and Lybrand (Boston, MA, 617-478-5000)
- Creative Networks (Palo Alto, CA, 415-326-9926)
- CSC Index (Cambridge, MA, 617-492-1500)
- Datapro Information Services (Delran, NJ, 609-764-4542)
- Dataquest (San Jose, CA, 408-437-8000)
- Delphi Consulting Group (Boston, MA, 617-247-1511)
- Ernst and Young (Chicago, IL, 312-879-2000)
- Gartner Group (Stamford, CT, 203-967-6700)
- Gateway Management Consulting (New York, NY, 212-880-9300)

- Giga Information Group (Norwell, MA, 617-982-9500)
- IDC/Avante Technologies (Framingham, MA, 508-872-8200)
- Meta Group (Westport, CT, 203-973-6700)
- Patricia Seybold Group (Boston, MA, 617-742-5200)
- Rapport Communication (Silver Spring, MD, 301-585-4717)
- WorkGroup Technologies (Hampton, NH, 603-929-1166)
- Yankee Group (Boston, MA, 617-367-1000)

Select a Service-oriented Workflow Provider

While surveying the field, you should be developing a hot list of workflow products that meet your functional, system, and administrative requirements, as discussed in Chapter 12. One of your primary concerns is to find a solid, reputable provider with the resources necessary to help you develop and implement your application. You may choose to acquire the desired solution either directly from the vendor or through a third-party consultant, systems integrator, or value-added reseller.

After your hot list has shrunk to manageable proportions, you should contact each of the prospects, request product information, ask for demo or evaluation software, and schedule visits by sales representatives. Take the time necessary to develop a comprehensive picture of different providers' capabilities, commitment, responsiveness, and understanding of your business. Evaluate companies with an eye toward making one of them your long-term workflow business partner. The following criteria should help you select a solid, reputable, service-oriented workflow provider.

Installed base

You can limit your risk by gravitating toward vendors or distributors with the largest installed bases. Companies with the longest customer lists tend to have the strongest track records, broadest distribution channels, and deepest consulting and service organizations. High-profile workflow vendors frequently offer a wider assortment of vertical-market applications, including ones that could serve as templates for your desired solution (and you will have less trouble finding third-party consultants or programmers with expertise in *brand name* workflow products).

Reputation

Try not to equate size with quality, responsiveness, or professionalism in all cases. Ask workflow users, consultants, and resellers to give you the straight dope on which vendors make the grade — and which tend to promise more than they deliver or otherwise neglect or mistreat customers. Resellers can be your best source of comparative market intelligence; they often distribute, integrate, and support products from multiple vendors. Sometimes, resellers are left holding the bag when the vendor goes out of business or backs away from the workflow market.

Consulting, development, and support services

You may not have the skills, experience, or resources necessary to develop your own workflow applications. If this is the case, you will have to rely on vendors or some third party for application planning, definition, development, integration, installation, and training services. Determine early-on how much of this work the vendor is prepared to perform. In many cases, the vendor will refer you to an authorized reseller or consultant with expertise in your particular industry or environment. Make sure that whichever workflow development partner you choose, that they have the resources to provide ongoing user training, help desk, upgrade, maintenance, and troubleshooting support. Give preference to vendors that have a broad array of third-party distributors, which can provide a safety net of ongoing support in case the vendor or any one distributor goes out of business.

Experience

Determine the provider's level of experience, both with workflow technologies in general and with projects similar in size and scope to yours, preferably in your industry. Ask for user references, relevant case studies, and project summaries. Look at the resumes of principal personnel to determine whether they have the skills necessary to integrate your company's mix of operating environments, networks, protocols, applications, databases, documents, imaging repositories, messaging transports, and other systems. Bombard the provider with a thousand technical questions to determine whether they truly have the depth needed to manage your project effectively. Avoid startup vendors that can only point you to a handful of beta sites for their product; you don't want to be part of their learning curve in the workflow market.

Product breadth

Your workflow requirements may be dynamic, complex, and integration-intensive. Look for providers whose product families cover a broad range of capabilities, supporting your current needs and providing an easy upgrade path as your requirements grow. Some of the larger, more established vendors provide workflow solutions in two or more categories (such as production, messaging-based, and Web-based), which means they may be better able to address your changing requirements over time than vendors with solutions in only one market segment.

Make sure that the provider's workflow solutions conform with established and emerging industry standards.

Another way to tell a broad-based workflow vendor is that it can boast an array of third-party developers and resellers that offer add-on software and hardware for its basic workflow product family. You should query the workflow vendor regarding which of the following add-on capabilities are provided by its strategic partners:

- Visual process definition and scripting
- Dynamic rerouting and reallocation
- Hierarchical folders
- Forms design
- Image management
- Database management
- Document management
- Object management
- Computer output to laser disk
- Product data management
- Electronic messaging
- Directory services
- Internet/intranet services
- Electronic commerce
- Security management
- Event notification
- Administration and monitoring
- Status/location tracking and reporting
- Productivity measurement
- Storage management

Standards orientation

Make sure that the provider's workflow solutions conform with established and emerging industry standards, including the WfMC and/or MAPI Workflow specifications. You wouldn't want your choice of workflow vendors to limit your ability to install whatever operating environments, protocols, databases, messaging transport agents, and other systems you need. If possible, obtain the workflow vendor's explicit assurance of interoperability with the various hardware and software components of your current distributed systems.

Avoid any provider that lacks a coherent development road map.

Development path

Your workflow provider should have a clearly defined architecture and strategy for new product introductions, upgrades, and enhancements over the coming one to two years. Avoid any provider that lacks a coherent development road map. The last thing you want is a strategic vendor that seems clueless about market trends; this could indicate lackluster management, weak technical skills, or insufficient commitment to the workflow market. Every workflow vendor should be grilled on their plans to support third-party BPR tools, visual process flowcharting, distributed object databases, replication, and interfaces to Web browsers and servers. Production workflow vendors should be required to state whether, when, and to what extent they will support routing through store-and-forward messaging transports. Messaging-based workflow vendors should define how they will link to production workflow environments and support Microsoft's MAPI Workflow Framework.

Strategic business alliances

You can gauge a workflow vendor's strength, influence, and staying power by its ability to enlist strategic business allies. Market leaders tend to attract partners interested in joint marketing, application development, and technology transfer. Workflow vendors with development partners are likely to be among the most technologically innovative, aggressively adding capabilities in BPR design, imaging, document management, object management, messaging, and Internet services. Count on these vendors to pursue aggressive upgrade and development strategies and to offer a growing range of interoperable third-party products. Given the rapid rate of technological change in the workflow arena, it's very important that you not saddle yourself with a go-nowhere, backward-looking provider.

Distribution channels

Users with enterprise-wide workflow applications need vendors with widespread sales, service, and support outlets. Determine whether the vendor has a presence in all the time zones, countries, regions, and cities where you intend to install its products. Workflow applications sometimes entail a significant learning curve and ongoing handholding, so it's very important that your vendor be everywhere you are, available when and where you need them. Startup workflow vendors may have breathtakingly wonderful products, but your Nairobi office may not appreciate having to call a help desk half a world away at 3 o'clock in the morning.

Financial stability and resources

Never trust the workflow vendor's placid assurance that it's in business to stay. Approximately 100 large and small companies offer workflow solutions, and no one can say who will be around in a year's time, or whether any given vendor's commitment to the workflow market will evaporate after several quarters of disappointing financial results. If the vendor is publicly traded, ask to see its annual report, prospectus, and other financial documentation. If it is privately owned, inquire into its years in business, ownership, customer base, revenues, profitability, assets, and liabilities. Any workflow vendor that is not willing to disclose its true financial position is one with whom you do not want to do business.

Evaluate Commercial Workflow Solutions

After you find several workflow providers that meet these criteria and are worth further examination, you'll distinguish between providers based largely on the technical merits of their workflow products (not to mention the all-important issue of price). A word to the brochure-weary: In surveying the workflow market, you will need to filter out fluff-intensive marketing buzzwords such as *unique*, *open*, *distributed*, *scalable*, *client/server*, *object-oriented*, *seamless*, and *flexible*. Every workflow vendor will try to tilt the rhetorical playing field in its direction by depicting its solution as the pinnacle of technological achievement.

Hopefully, this book will help you achieve some intellectual perspective, cut through the hype, and extract the kernel of information within every marketing pitch. Apply the following criteria when evaluating commercial workflow solutions.

Operating platforms and environments

The ideal workflow solution should operate on your existing desktops, servers, networks, databases, and messaging systems without requiring modifications to these or any other piece of infrastructure. Most of today's workflow products run in a variety of Windows and UNIX operating environments, with some OS/2, Macintosh, and MS-DOS support occasionally thrown in for good measure. Most workflow products also work over the leading network operating systems and protocols, such as Novell NetWare and TCP/IP (note: TCP/IP is the backbone protocol of the worldwide Internet as well as corporate intranets).

Make especially sure that your company's existing desktop PCs have fast enough CPUs and sufficient memory and disk space to run workflow client software plus all necessary application programs and data files. With production workflow solutions, prepare to invest in powerful new servers to run workflow engines, imaging software, and hierarchical storage subsystems. Messaging-based workflow products are client-centric and should require minimal change to back-end server hardware and software.

Application interfaces and file formats

Before you shop for a workflow solution, make a long list of application interfaces and file formats that the solution will have to support in order to work in your enterprise networking environment. You don't want to invest in a workflow solution that will require expensive integration with existing systems; you would prefer full *plug-and-play* interoperability from the very start. Your interface/format standards list may include any of the following discussed in Chapter 6:

- **Image management:** Raster Groups III and IV, GIF, TIFF, JPEG, MPEG, JBIG, EPS
- **Database management:** SQL, ODBC, IDAPI
- **Document management:** ODMA, DMA, ASCII, ODA, HTML, PDF, PS
- **Object management:** COM/OLE, CORBA, DSOM, OpenDoc

- **Product data management:** IGES, CGM
- **Electronic messaging:** MAPI, VIM, MHS, X.400, SMTP, MIME, CMC, fax, paging, voice messaging
- **Directory services:** X.500, LDAP, Novell NDS, Banyan StreetTalk
- **Internet/intranet services:** HTTP, FTP, SMTP, Java, JavaScript
- **Electronic commerce:** ANSI X12, UN EDIFACT, PKCS-6, PKCS-7, S/MIME, MOSS, PGP, DSA, DES, X.509, SSL

Functionality

You should also compile a list of core workflow application functions, for all the categories listed in the previous section, before you explore the market in earnest. For each commercial workflow solution, identify those functions that are provided out of the box, as opposed to those that must be custom-developed by the provider or your MIS staff.

Ask the vendor or reseller whether they sell a workflow application template geared to your vertical-market needs. Vertical-market templates, incorporating industry-specific user interfaces and process models, are a popular option for rapid workflow application deployment in cases where little client-specific customization is required.

Process-definition tools

Look for workflow products with versatile yet intuitive graphical process-definition tools. Ideally, the tool should allow business managers, analysts, programmers, and end users to use their preferred process-flowcharting paradigm (such as any of the paradigms discussed in Chapter 4), as well as their choice of third-party BPR tools. The tool should serve as a common frame of reference for joint process design by all of these parties. It should support definition of process models ranging from simple to complex and involving sequential, parallel, concurrent, and conditional flows. The vendor may provide sophisticated scripting and macro languages to support the most complex process-modeling requirements. To support fast-changing processes and exception-handling procedures, the tool should allow administrators to reroute processes dynamically without interrupting ongoing work. Production workflow process-definition tools should be able to import process, activity, and role definitions from existing corporate databases. Messaging-based workflow tools and workflow-enabled applications should be able to import user entries from LAN/WAN e-mail user directories.

Forms and folder design tools

Look into whether the solution provides rich tool sets to build the digital workflow *cargo*: electronic forms and hierarchical compound-document folders. Forms-design tools are a standard feature of most workflow solutions. Make sure that the tools allow you both to import fields from existing databases into new forms and to automatically create new databases upon development of a new form. Folder-definition tools should let you integrate different file formats in such a way that users can easily access, display, and manipulate them without worrying about what applications they originated in.

Form and folder definition tools should allow you to create user-friendly routable objects that support sophisticated display, calculation, and database retrieval features. You should also be able to store forms and components in object-oriented libraries that can be reused for future forms. Drag-and-drop forms-creation capabilities are preferred.

Programming tools

Programming is a necessary evil, so look for workflow products that allow you to develop applications quickly and efficiently with as few lines of code as possible. Object-oriented programming tools are becoming standard in the workflow market-place, enabling developers to quickly build new workflow applications from the components of existing applications. Many workflow vendors also provide access to their products' low-level functionality through a range of proprietary macros and APIs. Messaging-based workflow products speed up application development by providing a library of template forms for common business processes.

Your MIS staff should be able to use their preferred programming interfaces and tool sets to build and maintain workflow applications. Most production and messaging-based workflow solutions support C, C++, OLE, and DDE programming interfaces, as well as popular object-oriented programming tools such as Visual Basic and PowerBuilder.

Workflow-enabled applications require no programming at all — just create a file, define a routing list, and send the file on its way — but without the sophisticated routing, tracking, and customization features of more full-blooded workflow solutions.

Ease of use

Usability is a *try it on for size* criterion, hard to define in the abstract but crystal clear when you actually use a product. Obviously, it's important that the workflow client conform to the design conventions of your company's operating environments, so as to capitalize on user familiarity and retain consistency with other desktop applications. Beyond that, the usability of a workflow application depends on several things, including users' ease of access to worklists, ability to work within existing applications, and ability to understand and navigate within on-screen forms and dialogues.

For ease of worklist access, you could argue that messaging-based solutions and suite-based applications are most user-friendly, because they place all work items in users' existing e-mail inboxes (rather than require people to check separate workflow-specific inboxes, as with production solutions). Likewise, they benefit from being integrated into users' familiar desktop applications.

With regards to the usability of workflow-enabled applications and forms, all four workflow market segments are roughly comparable. A workflow system can only be as user-friendly as the applications and electronic forms developed for it. According to one school of thought, the application should speed users through the process of receiving, reviewing, revising, annotating, and approving documents — a throughput-related criterion that entails simplicity and *idiot-proofing* as paramount design considerations.

Talented workflow application designers can work wonders with the basic development tools available with production, messaging-based, Web-based, or suite-based products.

Ease of administration

Workflow administration tasks should blend in with other network administration chores. Look for workflow products that integrate with existing network, server, and desktop administration utilities. Ideally, this would allow workflow application modules to be loaded and unloaded dynamically as needed; existing LAN/WAN and e-mail system directories to be accessed when building and executing routing scripts; and application-level security, audit, and archiving functions to be performed through the underlying operating environment. It's also important that the workflow product use the same visual interface to define, track, and administer workflows, so that process status information is always available at a glance, routing paths and privileges may be redefined on the fly, and work items are shifted between queues as necessary. Where dynamic rerouting is a requirement, users should be allowed to modify executing workflows directly through drag-and-drop operations on the process flowchart. Administrators should be provided with flexible tools to produce real-time and historical reports on workflow status, throughput, and efficiency.

Performance

Performance of any application usually depends on the configuration and loading of the hardware and software environment in which it runs. You will need to establish performance benchmarks or goals before you venture far into the workflow evaluation process. For starters, you might explore using established industry benchmarks for any of the technologies (for example, database management and document-image processing) integrated with your workflow application.

To avoid any nasty surprises, you will have to try before you buy: run candidate workflow products in your network environment, using the servers and clients that will figure into your target application. Simulate the network loading scenarios you expect during normal workflow operations. Use performance monitors to measure loading on the network backbone, servers, and clients. Make sure you have workflow software configured correctly vis-à-vis your network operating system and client-side shells.

If your application involves exchange of imaging and multimedia data, it's best to consider production workflow solutions, which minimize the amount of that traffic that gets on the network backbone. By contrast, messaging-based workflow products move data as file attachments to e-mail messages and will not scale up to high-volume image transfers — instead, they'll quickly saturate the network backbone and slow all network traffic to a crawl.

Think twice before acquiring Version 1.0 of any workflow product.

Scalability

Your workflow management system should be a platform for continued business growth and not a straightjacket that slows down and becomes unmanageable as you bring on new applications, traffic, users, servers, and sites. Workflow products should be judged by their ability to scale up to new usage loads.

Obviously, scaling up your workflow applications requires continuing expansion and optimization of the LAN/WAN backbone. This will be an ongoing challenge for your network and MIS staff, so don't believe workflow vendors when they assure you that scaling up their product will be a snap. Conduct a traffic analysis and projections to get at least a rough order of magnitude on the required throughput of the workflow solution over the next three to five years.

Technical risk

You should think twice before acquiring Version 1.0 of any workflow product; you might become an unwilling participant in a protracted debugathon with an embarrassed vendor. You should also be careful not to commit your company to a product that requires extensive customization and integration, because this exposes you to the risk that myriad technical glitches might delay or derail your workflow application. Find a solution that comes with the requisite core functionality and has been field-tested extensively, giving you greater assurance that it will work more or less out of the box.

Cost

The bottom line on any investment is its life-cycle cost, which includes the costs of acquisition, development, implementation, upgrades, user training, and ongoing administration. You should estimate these life-cycle costs as part of the business justification and analysis exercises described in Chapters 11 and 12.

You may want to price out each candidate product in terms of software and hardware costs per user, including all costs of in-house and/or vendor integration. Expect to pay software license costs of anywhere from under one hundred dollars per user (for low-end forms-routing products) to several thousand dollars per user (for high-end production workflow). Then, if you want to perform a classic cost-benefit analysis, you should weigh a product's life-cycle costs against its anticipated return in increased revenues, lower operating costs, improved productivity and efficiency, and other hard-dollar benefits.

Keep in mind that you may be able to get away with zero in marginal software license fees if you avail yourself of bundled workflow features in your existing application suite or groupware environment. It all comes down to this question: Is a commercial workflow solution worth the cost of acquisition, customization, implementation, and user training, or can similar capabilities be provided more cost-effectively with existing applications?

Do Your Analysis

Ultimately, you'll choose the workflow provider and product that provide the best value for your dollar. The decision may be complex or simple, depending on the depth of your requirements and the range of available solutions. Still, there's no substitute for doing your homework before you venture out into today's exciting, complex, fast-changing workflow marketplace. Good workflow solutions will come to the prepared mind and careful pocketbook.

Summary

This chapter has provided general guidelines for evaluating commercial workflow vendors and solutions. Before you take the plunge and acquire a workflow product, you generally want to check out a vendor's user references. You also want to learn from existing users' experiences with workflow tools, so you can benefit from their insights and avoid making their mistakes. Learning from others' experiences is the subject of the next chapter, which presents workflow user case studies organized by the type of process being automated. The chapter following that will provide guidelines for actually implementing workflow applications in your organization, assuming that you have already chosen the best solution for your needs.

CHAPTER FOURTEEN

PROFITING FROM OTHERS' EXPERIENCES

Case Studies of Successful Workflow Implementors

Learning from other organizations' workflow implementations is always better than fumbling in the dark, especially when your company's future and, perhaps, your career are at stake.

You can be sure that other businesses have walked the workflow-reengineering path before you and profited from the experience. Studying their successes and struggles can be an invaluable source of application ideas. It can also temper your expectations regarding the technology's strategic potential, implementation challenges, life-cycle costs, operational disruption, and grass-roots acceptance. You'll need to immerse yourself in the details of real applications to prep yourself for the rigors of a full-blown workflow-reengineering project.

This chapter presents capsule workflow case studies culled from press accounts, vendor literature, and interviews. When evaluating commercial workflow solutions, you should ask vendors for case studies and references of actual users that you can contact for advice and ideas. Follow up on all references to develop a detailed profile of each user's requirements, why the vendor's solution was chosen to support them, and how well the vendor supported implementation and administration of the resultant workflow application.

Hold vendors' feet to the fire on customer references.

Use this chapter's problem-solution format as a template for developing detailed case studies addressed to your own requirements. Seek out cases closest to your intended application, in terms of the user's business, the type of process that was automated, and the type of workflow application that was developed. Beware of the steady stream of unambiguously successful case studies that vendors may try to send your way. Talented marketing copywriters will polish case studies until they gleam with technocratic righteousness and inevitability, softpedaling the doubtful beginnings, messy implementation details, and uncertain results experienced by the average mortal.

Really hold vendors' feet to the fire on customer references. Vendors reluctant to put you in touch with current customers may not have many to speak of, or many that are willing to speak kindly of the vendor.

The following capsule case studies are organized alphabetically according to the business processes they automate. Hopefully, you will see your organization, requirements, or situation reflected in at least one of these cases.

Administrative Action Request Processing

Problem

The U.S. Department of Energy's (DOE) Sandia National Laboratories, based in Albuquerque, NM, provides engineering, research, and development support for the department's nuclear weapons, energy security, environmental remediation, and other programs. The laboratory's 8,000 employees, working at sites in four states, require prompt processing of requests for new employees' security badges, foreign-travel authorization, and other administration actions. Paper-based processing of such requests typically takes up to 2 weeks, a delay which laboratory staff sought to shorten to 1-2 days. Reductions were also sought in printing, routing, sorting, storage, and searching costs associated with processing requests. The laboratory was interested in automating the processing workflow over its new Web-based intranet; providing round-the-clock access from user desktop computers running Microsoft Windows, Apple Macintosh, and UNIX; and in integrating with legacy human resources, financial, and purchasing databases running on IBM mainframes.

Priorities

The laboratory needed to speed up administrative action request processing, reduce internal workloads and costs associated with such processing, reduce the volume of status-inquiry phone calls, and increase staff satisfaction with the process. The lab's priorities were to minimize process time (that is, speed routing, review, and approval), maximize value-added process content (that is, manage a growing administrative workload with existing staff, legacy information systems, and intranet infrastructure), and maximize flexibility at the initial point of customer contact (that is, enable customers to initiate and track administrative actions anytime, day or night, from any Web browser on their intranet).

Solution

To achieve these objectives, the laboratory implemented Action Technologies' Web-based workflow environment, Metro, to eliminate routing delays and paper handling on travel authorization and access-badge requests. Sandia plans to implement future workflow applications for shop-floor automation, purchase requisitions, employee transfer processing, and expense reporting.

Action Metro allows Sandia's 8,000 employees to retrieve new work items from across the laboratory's intranet through their existing Netscape Navigator browsers, which run on Windows PCs, Apple Macintoshes, and UNIX workstations. Action's workflow server integrates with many pieces of Sandia's intranet infrastructure, including the Netscape Commerce Server, Sybase database on a UNIX file server, SQL Server database on a Microsoft Windows NT server, and legacy human resources, financial, and purchasing systems on an IBM mainframe. Sandia's systems analysts use Action's graphical flowcharting tool to map out workflow routes and business rules.

On foreign-travel requests, the new mode of operations is for managers with approval authority to log into Metro, which is installed on an intranet Web site running Netscape Commerce Server software, and pull down their personal WorkBoxes, which are HTML/JavaScript pages listing each manager's personal work items. Clicking on the hyperlink to a particular travel request causes the completed HTML/JavaScript form corresponding to that request to be downloaded into the manager's browser. The manager then pulls down a menu, embedded in the form, to approve, decline, or request additional information from the form's originator. After the manager approves the form, it is routed sequentially to each of the other Sandia managers whose approvals are also required.

Some custom software integration was needed to connect Action Metro to Sandia's application infrastructure. After all approvals are obtained, the HTML/JavaScript form's data contents are written from Sandia's intranet Web site to a relational database running on Microsoft SQL Server, which copies it to a Sandia business application repository running on Sybase's database. The form's field values are validated records contained in the Sybase database. An application script, linked with the Sybase database, calls Metro's Process Manager workflow engine to pass on only those workflow-relevant key data fields associated with the transaction. Process Manager will use those key fields to decide how to route or process the data next, according to a computerized, run-time process model developed with Action's process-definition tools. Then a hyperlink representing this work item will be added to the WorkBox of the next user in the routing list. When that user clicks the hyperlink, his or her browser will send a command to Metro (on the Web site) to extract the updated form fields from the Sybase database, regenerate the HTML/JavaScript form, and download it to the browser.

Network, application, and data security are critical requirements for an organization such as Sandia entrusted with responsibility for nuclear weapons R&D. The laboratory had already standardized an industry-standard, application-independent security technology known as *Kerberos*, developed at the Massachusetts Institute of Technology. Kerberos supports centralized key management, distribution of tamper-proof credentials, mutual authentication between clients and services, and encryption of all user passwords, session keys, and transmissions on distributed data applications. Action Technologies extended Metro to support Kerberos user IDs and passwords for Sandia's applications.

Constituent Correspondence Management[1]

Problem
The governor of Kansas receives about 250 letters a week. Each of the letters requires a response, and many must be reviewed by several staff members. Under such heavy workloads, manual routing often resulted in process bottlenecks, administrative delays, and mislaid correspondence. An outdated Wang minicomputer, used primarily as an expensive word processor, did not support the tools to distribute documents or track their locations.

Priorities
The governor's office needed to speed up correspondence processing and ensure necessary reviews without bringing on additional staff. Its workflow priorities were to minimize process time (that is, speed routing, review, and response preparation) and maximize value-added process content (that is, manage a growing correspondence workload with existing staff and assure that letters are reviewed by the appropriate staff).

Solution
To achieve these objectives, the governor's office replaced manual correspondence routing with automated document-image routing. It chose Keyfile's workflow/document management product, also known as *Keyfile*, for this application. The system works with the office's new Novell NetWare local-area network, which supports 100 PC users with WordPerfect word processors and Microsoft Access databases. Incoming correspondence is scanned into the Keyfile system, linked with WordPerfect documents, and tracked through an application built with Access. Workflows revolve around categories that are assigned to correspondence at the time it is scanned into the system. A document's category determines the staff routing list to which it is forwarded. "It's hard to put a dollar figure on the confidence level the staff has in knowing a document will get to where it's supposed to," says Warren Neudorff, information resources management for the state of Kansas' division of information systems and communications.

Defective Material Reporting

Problem
Dana Corp. is an automotive supplier with 17 manufacturing plants across the United States. According to Dennis White, Dana Corp.'s operations manager and forms administrator, the company's Marion, Indiana-based driveshaft division began, in

1992, to search for ways to speed up the process by which dispersed staff members were notified of customer-reported product defects. The standard notification procedure at that time was for one location to fax defect reports to all other locations. The fax method became administratively more time-consuming and burdensome as the number of interested users and variety of defect reports grew.

Priorities

In searching for an alternative, the company's workflow priorities were to minimize process time (that is, forward defect reports immediately to all relevant personnel) and maximize value-added process content (that is, automate the manual, paper-intensive, time-consuming report-hand-off process).

Solution

Dana Corp.'s strategy was to replace faxed defect reports with an e-mail-based electronic-forms application. Fischer International's Workflow 2000 product was selected, in no small part because it worked with Dana's EMC/TAO mainframe-based e-mail system, also from Fischer.

Under the new system, staff members input product defect information into on-screen forms. Other data is pulled from a mainframe IDMS database for input into forms. Completed defect reports are posted to any of several company e-mail distribution lists, depending on the part numbers and customer codes entered. Defect reports are also posted to e-mail-based discussion groups, where their status (outstanding or resolved) is tracked. Every time that an update is made to a defect report's status, the report originator is notified by e-mail. The application allows everyone in the division to be notified immediately of customer-reported defects, because reports are sent directly to their e-mail inboxes.

"There was a fast learning curve for users," says White. "If the user was familiar with e-mail, it was nothing to learn to use the forms."

Engineering Problem Tracking and Resolution

Problem

The U.S. National Aeronautics and Space Administration has a mission-critical requirement for real-time problem tracking and resolution on space shuttle operations, as on all its missions. Tight coordination is required among more than 500 government and contractor personnel in California, Texas, and Florida on each shuttle mission. Strong authentication, security, and auditing capabilities are essential.

Priorities

The agency's workflow priorities were to minimize process time (that is, speed identification, isolation, and resolution of technical problems by a distributed project team) and maximize value-added process content (that is, support complex document searches and ensure tight security, authentication, and auditing of all activities).

Solution

To achieve its objectives, the agency implemented a wide-area workflow application that routes engineering problem documentation in electronic *folders* within and between dispersed project sites. NASA selected Identitech Corp.'s FYI Enterprise workflow management system for this application. The system integrates with various desktop operating systems, Structured Query Language (SQL) databases, network protocols, optical disc jukeboxes, scanners, and printers. It uses digital signature technology to authenticate trouble-report originators, multilevel access controls to prevent unauthorized document modifications, and version controls to track what changes were made when and by whom. Users can simply view a trouble report or launch the originating application — if permitted — to modify it. NASA credits FYI Enterprise with trimming 33 percent off the time needed to resolve technical problems with shuttle operations.

Enrollment Processing

Problem

A large regional Health Maintenance Organization (HMO) sought to automate the preenrollment Medicare application and approval process to keep administrative costs under control. Medicare regulations require that HMOs maintain stringent operational controls, prepare ample paperwork, and submit themselves to thorough oversight by the Health Care Funding Agency (HCFA).

Priorities

In automating its Medicare-related operations, the HMO's workflow priority was to maximize value-added process content by automating the Medicare application process, verifying accuracy and validity of input data, and controlling administrative costs.

Solution

As a solution, the HMO designed an electronic forms application to run on top of Logical Software Solutions Corp.'s FlowMan product. The application verifies an applicant's eligibility, guides enrollment specialists through applicant telephone interviews, uploads a list of eligible applicants to HCFA, receives approval/disapproval from HCFA, transfers approved applicants to the HMO's legacy computer systems, and sends out letters to applicants.

FlowMan runs on the organization's existing computer systems, which include the Microsoft Windows client operating system, Novell NetWare network operating system, and Oracle database server. Enrollment specialists can use the application to display a list of data-input discrepancies and then autodial the applicant to clear up these problems one by one. FlowMan's automated routing feature enables applications to be located at any point in the process and an audit trail to be generated for regulators.

Facilities Regulation and Code Compliance[2]

Problem

The University of North Carolina-Chapel Hill's Physical Plant Department manages all facilities, utilities, and telecommunications systems on campus. Each year, department staff handle thousands of forms and documents that deal with various university departments, utility companies, regulatory agencies, contractors, suppliers, and other organizations. Staff must often retrieve documentation from archives to comply with requirements of research grants, government regulations, and building codes. "Everything has to be saved; even seemingly useless notes," says department IS manager, Toby Considine.

Priorities

The department needed a way to manage the growing regulatory paperwork burden without adding new staff. In exploring potential approaches, the department identified its workflow priorities as minimizing process time (that is, speed the location, retrieval, routing, and review of required documentation from archives), maximizing value-added process content (that is, manage a growing workload without adding administrative staff or filing cabinets), and maximizing flexibility at the initial point of customer contact (that is, enable construction project managers to define ad-hoc workflows involving select individuals).

Solution

To achieve these objectives, the department implemented an imaging-based workflow application that can scan, run optical character recognition, index, file, retrieve, share, route, fax, annotate, mark-up, and e-mail any document to other campus users. It chose Keyfile Corp.'s workflow/document management product for this application. Keyfile runs in conjunction with the department's existing Microsoft Windows-based PCs, Novell NetWare 3.11 network operating system, DaVinci e-mail system, and various desktop application packages. The application enables users to route *folders* consisting of image-based documents, binary application files, and text files to others' workflow inboxes, which are separate from their e-mail inboxes. Recipients retrieve the folders and can attach their input in the form of textual annotations and various binary application files, such as AutoCAD drawings, Excel spreadsheets, and Microsoft Word documents. Ultimately, a document with sundry annotations and attachments can be routed back to its originator, who can then revise it accordingly.

"For us, [implementing the Keyfile workflow application has been] a cost-avoidance issue," says Considine. "By avoiding adding even two people to our staff, we've recouped our investment in hardware and software in a year."

Magazine Publishing[3]

Problem

Until 1995, *TV Guide*, the largest circulation periodical in the U.S., used manual, paper-based layout and production methods in 10 regional offices to prepare 120 different weekly local editions.

The pre-workflow *TV Guide* editorial cycle involved weekly entry of regional television schedules by staff members in the regional offices. This data was transmitted electronically to a central UNISYS mainframe database in company headquarters in Radnor, PA, where it and various authored articles were compiled. The mainframe then transmitted the text back to the regional offices, where it was printed out in the proper format. At the regional offices, the final camera-ready pages were pasted up manually, integrating the text with graphics and local advertising content.

Manual paste-up had long ago become an anachronism with the advent of computerized editorial, layout, and printing technologies. *TV Guide* management had for many years been evaluating the total computerization of their costly, labor-intensive, time-consuming weekly workflow, with an eye toward closing the regional offices and performing all functions at headquarters. Producing any one local edition involved over 10,000 separate manual and automated tasks operating under exceedingly tight schedules, which makes workflow automation a dauntingly complex project. Production of each edition, which sometimes exceeds 200 pages in length, must happen in only two days from the point at which the last schedule changes are accepted for publication from local TV stations. The magazines are, of course, complex work products that include authored text, compiled directory listings, photographs, color graphics, and black-and-white features such as crossword puzzles.

Automating this complex production workflow would involve building process models that execute across hundreds of UNIX servers and workstations from vendors such as Silicon Graphics, Sun Microsystems, and Hewlett-Packard, plus some networked PCs and Apple Macintoshes. The process model would include both manual and automated activities linked into intricate conditional routing and handling procedures. It would tap into many information bases containing data, text, images, and other graphical elements.

On the human side, workflow reengineering would also require laying off personnel from the regional offices when those facilities were closed, taking on new staff at headquarters, and retraining headquarters staff in the new automated and semiautomated procedures.

The publisher estimates that it will recoup investment in workflow technologies over 3 to 5 years.

Priorities

The publisher's workflow priorities were to minimize process time (that is, speed up the weekly compilation, writing, editing, layout, production, printing, and distribution of the many local editions), and maximize value-added process content (that is, manage this tremendous workload from a single facility while improving quality, increasing the volume of information and advertising on each printed page, and reducing staff, equipment, and space requirements).

Solution

TV Guide chose to consolidate and reengineer its processes using XSoft Inc.'s InConcert production workflow management system. InConcert was chosen for the sophistication and flexibility of its workflow process-definition and application-development tools, and for its ability to manage the publisher's heavy workload with acceptable performance. InConcert supports efficient utilization of *TV Guide*'s headquarters computing infrastructure by balancing workloads among available servers.

Upon consolidating and workflow-enabling all 10,000 tasks in headquarters, the publisher closed the regional offices. To minimize business risks during the five-month phase-in to the new workflow system, *TV Guide* converted a limited group of local editions each week and for a few weeks produced each edition both manually and electronically. This allowed the publisher to make its weekly deadlines with traditional methods, in case the electronic method ran into a serious glitch.

The publisher estimates that it will recoup its investment in workflow technologies over 3 to 5 years, based on savings from closing regional offices and, thanks to efficient electronic layout, from reducing the number of pages per edition needed to carry the same editorial and advertising content. Training staff on the new system has added to the cost of implementation, but, according to TV Guide management, staff have accepted workflow automation as a welcome and much-needed innovation.

Mortgage Loan Processing

Problem

Western Bank's mortgage-loan group processes over 30,000 pages of documentation a month. The bank had difficulty managing a growing workload with its traditional, labor-intensive, paper-based process. Information was being rekeyed at different processing steps and files were difficult to maintain and retrieve. The bank sought to increase the productivity of loan-processing personnel while meeting tight internal and regulatory timelines in the loan-origination process. For example, Real Estate Settlement Procedures Act (RESPA) disclosures must be generated within 72 hours of loan origination.

Priorities

The bank's workflow priorities were to minimize process time (that is, speed the generation, retrieval, routing, review, and approval of loan documentation) and maximize value-added process content (that is, manage a growing workload and maintain high accuracy with minimal growth in staff and storage space).

Solution

The bank implemented Intelus Corp.'s MortgageFlo, an imaging-based workflow application that enables processing to begin when initial loan documentation is faxed in from a branch office. MortgageFlo runs on 16 Microsoft Windows PCs on a Novell NetWare LAN with a file server, a 286-gigabyte optical jukebox, two optical scanners, and a dedicated print server. The faxed-in application form is scanned into the system, automatically assigned a bar code, and routed to a loan-processing staffer for initial review. When the complete documentation arrives in the mail, it is scanned into an on-line loan *folder* linked to the initial form, and then made available simultaneously to loan processors, administrative staffers, and the loan underwriter. Intelus' software keeps track of whether all required documentation has arrived, whether it has passed all necessary reviews, and whether critical milestone dates have been met. The application also produces necessary documentation for loan resale and uploads information on approved borrowers into the bank's mainframe databases.

"Ninety days after implementation," says bank vice president Patricia Rumbaugh, "MortgageFlo has already eliminated seven days off our loan cycle."

Rehabilitation Service Request Processing

Problem

The state of Ohio's Rehabilitation Services Commission (RSC) provides job training, placement, and other services to over 30,000 Ohioans with physical or mental disabilities. Services are authorized pursuant to rehabilitation plans developed by staff counselors, processed at field offices, and signed and returned by clients. The traditional paper-based rehabilitation plans slowed down the process of authorizing service delivery, because it required counselors to write up plans in the field, return them to the field office for typing and processing, mail them to the client for a signature, and then wait for the document to be mailed back.

"Counselors in the field were authorizing services before they knew they were out of money," stated Karen DeLong, MIS Manager for the RSC. "There was no real-time budget information. Counselors had to wait weeks for paperwork to be processed before they could activate a service plan. This was time that could have been put to better use making Ohioans with disabilities employable."

Priorities

As a first step towards rectifying the situation, the state of Ohio RSC decided its workflow priorities were to minimize process time (that is, ensure prompt development, submission, and authorization of rehabilitation plans), maximize value-added process content (that is, automate the routing/approval cycle and minimize the paperwork hand-off needed to initiate service delivery), and maximize flexibility at the initial point of customer contact (that is, enable field counselors to develop plans at client sites and coordinate promptly with dispersed colleagues via computer conferences).

Solution

RSC provided counselors with notebook computers that support dial-up access to workflow, e-mail, and conferencing capabilities on the commission's wide-area computer network. Rounding out the new workflow system was Digital Equipment Corporation's TeamLinks Routing and TeamRoute software, which enable documents to be developed in the field and promptly submitted for immediate processing.

"We've calculated that we will save the taxpayers approximately $2 million per year with the full implementation of this system," stated DeLong. "We will be able to speed up the rehabilitation process, generate taxpaying workers sooner, and redeploy clerical staff to other assignments."

Sales-Lead Referral Management

Problem

Firstcom Cato Johnson manages sales, promotion, and direct-marketing campaigns for Fortune 500 clients. The 75-person firm, based in Toronto, is a subsidiary of advertising giant Young and Rubican Inc. One project involved provision of inbound call management for logging, tracking, and routing sales leads to Canadian Ford, Mercury, and Lincoln dealers in response to a televised *infomercial*. It was critical that sales leads be routed as soon as possible to the most appropriate dealer, which may be the one with which the customer was currently dealing or the one nearest the prospect.

Priorities

Firstcom Cato Johnson's workflow priorities were to minimize process time (that is, send the lead sheet at the time of customer contact), maximize value-added process content (that is, introduce electronic transmission in the lead-sheet hand-off process), and maximize flexibility at the initial point of customer contact (that is, route the lead sheet automatically to the most appropriate dealer, before the lead grows cold).

Solution

To achieve these objectives, the company sought to match dealer locations contained in an existing database with customer postal codes and phone numbers entered by telemarketing operators, and to fax customer lead sheets automatically to dealers throughout Canada. The firm chose Delrina Corp.'s FormFlow and WinFax Pro for Networks products based on their ability to support rapid electronic-forms creation and work with Windows, dBASE, and an outgoing facsimile server. It took about one day to set up the entry forms, design lead-sheet output formats, and build links between the database, FormFlow, and WinFax Pro. The application was a success for Firstcom and its client, generating more than 30,000 leads, 8,000 dealership appointments, and 1,300 sales — a conversion rate of 15.23 percent — in the three-month marketing campaign.

Summary

As the case studies in this chapter suggest, successful workflow-reengineering projects frequently begin with clearly defined business requirements. Harking back to the justification approaches presented in previous chapters, you should be able to justify your project based on the time saved, value added, and flexibility gained in your business processes. The better able you are to quantify the expected return on investment, the easier the project will be to sell to the corporate power brokers.

One good approach for focusing your workflow project is to write a future case study, assuming that one year has elapsed, the project is a success, and you are now in a position to boast of your accomplishments in print. How would you summarize your future successes in terms as crisp, succinct, and quantitative as the case studies just presented? Visualizing a successful project, in all its major details, is one of the best ways of motivating yourself and others to make it happen.

A very important lesson to draw from these cases is that it may be best to focus initial workflow-reengineering efforts on a single high-visibility process. After that application has taken root and delivered tangible benefits, you should then attempt to workflow-enable other business processes. Grand plans to reengineer the entire company or divisions thereof should be held in abeyance until workflow technology has proven itself in a series of limited grass-roots applications. Even an ambitious case study, such as that of *TV Guide* magazine, concerns innovations to one well-defined process — in that case, magazine layout — and associated changes in other subprocesses needed to achieve the full fruits of reengineering. Big dreams often sprout from soil fertilized by many incremental victories.

The following chapter shows you how to till the soil of a successful workflow project. It provides practical guidelines for implementing and administering workflow applications in your organization. Your investment in workflow technology will be wasted if you can't automate a simple business process and get users to intuitively recognize the application's benefits to themselves and the organization as a whole.

CHAPTER FIFTEEN

IMPLEMENTING AND ADMINISTERING WORKFLOW APPLICATIONS

You map out a new business process, buy a workflow product to implement it, and then scratch your head wondering how best to develop the application and introduce it to users.

This chapter provides guidelines for planning, designing, developing, rolling out, and administering workflow applications in your organization. Whether your company gets its money's worth from the technology depends on how well you implement and fit it into the organization's work style and operating procedures. Even the best-intentioned application can fail miserably if implemented over budget, behind schedule, full of technical problems, lacking even basic user training, and with total disregard for staff requirements and sensitivities.

The following discussion primarily addresses the implementation cycle — planning, design, development, integration, pilot installation, formal rollout, ongoing operations — of a complex, high-end workflow application designed to support enterprise process reengineering. High-end workflow/reengineering projects usually entail a considerable investment of money, personnel, and systems, and involve considerable technical and business risk. Typically, they rely on production workflow systems and, to a lesser extent, messaging-, Web-, and suite-based solutions.

Low-end workflow solutions — those used to automate simple, one-time, ad-hoc processes — may allow you to dispense with most of the planning, analysis, and implementation tasks described in the following discussion. Beware, however, of low-end applications' tendency to climb the corporate ladder: a *one-time* originator-defined process, found to succeed, may quickly turn into an organizational standard, in which case it will have to be planned, maintained, and administered using the same procedures appropriate for ambitious *top-down* workflow applications.

Project Planning

Complex workflow applications — supporting corporate operations such as the hypothetical procurement process presented in Chapter 12 — do not coalesce spontaneously out of the atmosphere. They are developed by multidisciplinary project teams over several weeks or months of concerted effort. Coordination — or lack thereof — among the development and implementation teams will spell the difference between the success and failure of your workflow application.

> *The schedule should define a phased approach for implementing the application over a manageable timeframe.*

The basic outlines of the workflow application should be defined in a well-thought-out implementation plan, which flows from an approved project justification (see Chapter 11), business process analysis (see Chapter 12), product recommendation (see Chapter 13), and review of user case studies similar to your intended application (see Chapter 14). The plan needs to define the project's objectives, schedule, technical approach, test and acceptance procedures, budget, and the following critical resources:

- A project manager with strong organizational, interpersonal, and marketing skills
- A team of business analysts familiar with all impacted business functions
- A team of technical analysts and programmers with expertise in all impacted computing and telecommunications systems
- A team of trainers and support personnel able to help end users master the new workflow without disrupting their jobs
- Software and hardware resources to support development work, pilot implementations, and the final workflow application rollout

The project schedule should define a phased approach for implementing, debugging, and refining the application over a manageable timeframe, such as 3-6 months. Pilot projects — which often run between 1-6 months — are a good way of implementing workflow in a controlled, limited environment with intense, unvarnished user feedback. Only when the new workflow has been field-tested and refined by a representative workgroup (a process that may take up to a year) should it be rolled out across the enterprise.

Application Design, Development, and Integration

Your workflow application development team should already have a comprehensive functional specification from which to work, based on the business process analysis described in Chapter 12. Review the hypothetical procurement process in that chapter and use the same technique for parsing your workflow down to its basic platform, structure, and media elements, and for reengineering the process to improve its performance.

This parsed, reengineered business process will be the storyboard that your development team uses to build a workflow application. Think of workflow as music and your team as the band that will bring it to life. Every member of the team must have the rhythm of the new workflow imprinted on their consciousness from Day One. At the very first team meeting, a detailed flowchart of the new business process should be spread out on a conference table, whiteboard, or wall. The chart should depict all participants, activities, durations, queues, dependencies, documents, databases, servers, and other resources involved in the new process. Most important, it should present — in bold lines available to a single glance — the end-to-end flow of the new process. Any of the process-modeling techniques discussed in Chapter 4 may be used, depending on your preference and the nature of the process being reengineered.

After the new workflow has been grasped in its entirety, the development team will need to break it down into atomic steps that will be mapped to separate application functions. The particular development tools at your disposal will determine your method of specifying low-level workflow application functions, such as form-field calculations, data retrieval, worklist handling, conditional routing, notification, and event logging. As you delve deeper into the details of the workflow, the same division of labor and tool sets will likely emerge in your development team as it does in most companies. Business analysts will use process-definition flowcharting tools to define high-level workflow process models consisting of activities, roles, and routing rules, while visually oriented programmers will use forms-design and object-oriented development tools (for example, Visual Basic) to create workflow application user interfaces and data retrieval/manipulation features. At the same time, systems programmers will use scripting languages, traditional programming languages, vendor APIs, and industry-standard system interfaces (for example, SQL/ODBC, OLE, DDE, and MAPI) to integrate workflow applications with desktop operating environments and back-end corporate information and communications systems.

Your development team should consult with end users regularly to get a reality check.

Developers will need to define a common set of workflow rules, which consists of conditions (sometimes known as *states*) and the actions they trigger automatically. Remember Chapter 12's key conditions categories: initiation, scheduling, preactivity, execution, notification, postactivity, security, audit, and termination. Depending on the tool set, these may be defined through nodes and links on a graphical flowchart, programming scripts, or some combination of the two techniques.

Developers will also need to define a common set of workflow-relevant data, which provides basic information that the workflow system will use to evaluate conditions and trigger rules. Typical examples of workflow-relevant data include the contents of a form field or a user mouse-click indicating approval of a document. Any digital information handled by the application (for example, databases, documents, images, objects, messages, and audio streams) may serve as workflow-relevant data, provided that its attributes can be retrieved and interpreted by the workflow engine or client application. The desktop or server system clock will also provide workflow-relevant data needed to monitor work queuing and processing times, as well as to determine when notifications are to be sent and work items reassigned among available users.

Your development team should consult with end users regularly to get a reality check on whether the application meets their needs. Developers should show work-in-progress to users to determine their level of comprehension and comfort with what they see on screen. Users will also indicate which fields, databases, documents, and applications should be presented at each step of the workflow to make their jobs easier and more productive. The development process will then become a type of organizational role-playing exercise in which users assist in defining — and growing accustomed to — their workflow-enabled new job functions. Don't wait until after application deployment for this level of constructive hands-on input.

Pilot Implementation

After you have a reasonably bug-free, stable beta version of your workflow application, you are ready to roll it out to a pilot workgroup or department. Make sure you test it thoroughly in a laboratory environment before installing it in a real workgroup. Also be sure to have draft training materials and user manuals available for the pilot group to review. You will be ironing the bugs out of your workflow training approach at the same time you're perfecting the software.

> *Install software over the weekend and make sure it is running on all workstations by Monday.*

Choose the pilot group carefully. You want users who are committed to the objectives of the project and not resistant to new technologies. However, you don't want your application evaluated by people who will accept it sight unseen and tolerate flaws in the name of corporate solidarity. What your development team needs most is a quick, thoroughgoing, no-holds-barred critique of what works and what doesn't. You also want a pilot group with available computing resources — on both server and client machines — to run your workflow application.

Before the pilot gets underway, brief workgroup managers and users on project objectives, demonstrate the beta workflow application, and diagram the process on a flip chart or whiteboard. Try hard to control and moderate expectations for the pilot, letting the group know that what they see won't be perfect and that honest user feedback and communication is the point of the exercise.

Install software over the weekend and make sure the application is up and running on all client workstations by Monday morning, so that users' first impression is a good one. This 48-hour installation/debugging session may get fairly intense as your technical team struggles with hardware and software problems that weren't apparent during controlled laboratory testing.

Pilot-user trouble reports and suggestions should be fed back to the development team through any available channel. Encourage users to dash off e-mail *nastygrams* whenever they encounter an obvious bug, unfriendly feature, or confusing menu item or dialog box. Meet as often as necessary with users to hear their observations, concerns, and gut feelings. Walk around to see how people actually use the application — and determine whether they're muttering choice words that get filtered out of formal bug reports. Ask for written critiques and evaluations at the end of the pilot period. If this is too much to expect from users, you might try engaging them in one-on-one or group interviews.

Listen carefully to users involved in the pilot. They are the real experts on the business process in question and often have great ideas for improving it. Show users that their suggestions are being heard and incorporated in application changes. Perhaps you could post a list of bug reports and fixes to a shared departmental bulletin board. Keep a running total of bugs, complaints, and suggestions to determine whether these are increasing, staying constant, or, hopefully, decreasing as the application is refined.

A successful pilot will build support for your workflow application and possibly accelerate its introduction to other departments. Word of mouth from satisfied users is often the best advertising. If you can demonstrate immediate paybacks accruable to the pilot group (such as cost reductions and productivity improvements), the demand for your application will intensify. This may prove critical to the long-term acceptance of workflow technologies in your organization, especially if upper management has funded your project only on a provisional *demo or die* basis.

A successful pilot will encourage users to redefine their jobs to take advantage of the workflow application. Changing the way you work is often a painful exercise, forced upon you by insistent superiors and brute necessity. If users regard workflow as making their jobs easier — even in small but significant ways — they will eagerly change their mode of operation. They will spontaneously reengineer their business processes at the same time you're retooling their virtual workspaces. They will also spread the workflow gospel more readily to their colleagues in other workgroups.

Official Application Rollout

If all goes well in the pilot, you will be able to roll out the workflow application for keeps. This will require several concurrent activities.

IMPLEMENT FINAL BUG FIXES AND PRIORITY APPLICATION CHANGE REQUESTS

Before you roll out the permanent workflow application, you will need to define a baseline enterprise-wide software configuration. If you're managing several workflow pilot sites, it would be prudent to consolidate all of their feature requests and bug reports into a master list of priority changes. After these changes are made, freeze the application configuration and declare this Version 1.0. Institute a structured upgrade schedule under which changes (other than bug fixes) are introduced at regular intervals, such as every quarter.

PERFORM FINAL TESTING AND ACCEPTANCE

Define a suite of acceptance tests for users to certify that the workflow application performs as expected and meets all their documented requirements. For pilot sites, the acceptance tests may involve simply verifying that final software and hardware changes perform as expected and cause no undesirable side effects. For nonpilot sites, the acceptance tests will probably be more extensive, because users will be signing off on a broader suite of new software and hardware. Messaging-based workflow applications may require less rigorous acceptance testing than production workflow applications, because the former generally have less complex process models and user interfaces. Suite-based applications will usually require no acceptance testing at all, because they will usually involve a single run defined by a single user and are seldom repeated.

FINALIZE USER MANUALS AND PROVIDE INITIAL TRAINING

The best training occurs before cutover, during the design and pilot phases, when users are sensitized and educated on the changes to come. During the pilot phase, you should have received ample user feedback on user manuals and training materials. Roll these changes up into the final documents that will be distributed at cutover. Hold remedial training sessions to acquaint pilot users with the interface and features of the official for-keeps workflow application. Hold full-blown training sessions for nonpilot users who are encountering the workflow application for the first time. If users are also being introduced to new productivity applications (for example, spreadsheets and Web browsers) in the context of the workflow environment, they need to be trained in these as well. In addition, the workflow application may require some PC-illiterate users to start using the machines daily, which would require yet another level of training.

FINALIZE NEW OPERATING PROCEDURES

If it's part of a broader business-process redesign, the workflow application might entail some major or minor revisions to business procedures and forms. At the same time you bring users up to speed on the new application software, you will need to educate them on the ins and outs of the new operating procedure. With so much changing all at once, some users are bound to get a little flustered and resist the new workflow-enabled order of things. Be forewarned that some users will suspect a management plot to automate them out of jobs or subject them to intrusive workplace monitoring and surveillance. Respect these concerns and do your best to ease users' transition to the workflow-enabled business process. User comfort and understanding are critical to the success of any process redesign.

CUT OVER PROMPTLY TO THE NEW APPLICATION ON PUBLISHED DATE AND TIME

Give users one or two weeks prior notice of the workflow application cutover. This will give them time to prepare for the change and establish contingency procedures to keep business running as usual in case the new application runs into glitches during its first week or two of live operation. Publishing the cutover date and sticking to it will minimize work disruption. Phase out legacy systems and procedures at this time to avoid user confusion.

The ultimate criterion of user acceptance is whether the new workflow application makes sense to them and helps them in their jobs. They will resist the new workflow if learning it (and unlearning the old one) requires a significant investment of their time.

Fortunately, most workflow environments integrate with familiar components of users' existing environments, such as operating systems, applications, e-mail, and databases. The best way to position workflow in users' minds may be as a higher-level operating environment, one that better integrates existing tools and facilitates workgroup coordination. If designed and implemented properly, a workflow application should be no more radical or threatening than an e-mail inbox. A workflow application simply delivers new work to waiting users and routes it where it is supposed to go.

Operations

You will also need to give some thought as to how your workflow application will be administered, maintained, and modified as a part of normal MIS and telecommunications operations. This operations side of the project requires clear delineation of administration and maintenance, and the modification responsibilities.

Workflow applications can easily sprawl across many desktops, servers, directories, databases, messaging systems, departments, sites, and networks, making ongoing administration and maintenance about as easy as pushing a binding resolution through the U.N. General Assembly. One approach might be to designate business and technical administrators for each workgroup or workflow engine. The business administrator would set overall policy for his or her segment of the enterprise workflow and determine the official business process to be implemented in the software. The technical administrator would take direction from the business administrator, handling such mundane chores as creating user workflow accounts, establishing security profiles, modifying process definitions, loading and unloading application modules, monitoring system and workflow events, allocating work items among available queues, and archiving and logging workflow data. The technical administrator would have to define procedures for accomplishing these functions in league with administrators of all impacted systems.

Users will be clamoring for workflow software modifications almost from the day the application is implemented. Other users will be asking for the ability to suspend or reroute workflows on the fly to address exceptional business circumstances. You will be flooded with a steady stream of change requests that you will have to prioritize and queue up for controlled change administration. One approach might be to maintain the initial workflow project team as an ongoing reengineering control board. This board could evaluate change requests for their feasibility, cost, and alignment with business goals and objectives. It could also designate special individuals who have *manual override* privileges, such as the ability to redefine a limited set of workflow routes, roles, and rules as needed. Logs of workflow *manual overrides* should be kept so that the control board can determine the appropriateness of modifications or additional conditions in the underlying process model.

What's critically important is that your administration procedures not *freeze-dry* workflow applications in their current configurations, incapable of revision or optimization. Flexibility is the key to corporate survival. When workflows ossify, organizations die.

If simple process tweaks or forms redesigns require six months of intense lobbying, you might as well return to manual processes.

Summary

This chapter has presented workflow implementation and administration guidelines oriented primarily to complex, high-end applications, such as those associated with business-process reengineering projects.

You might consider these guidelines a bit on the overkill side if you're using any of the new breed of groupware and desktop application suites with embedded workflow capabilities, which make ad-hoc document routing features immediately available to any desktop in your company. As workflow capabilities become ubiquitous in all computing and networking environments, we'll take advantage of them more spontaneously and with less preplanning. We'll need to consult no one but ourselves before setting up a one-time, ad-hoc document-routing procedure.

One apt analogy is to the historical development of database management systems from yesterday's inflexible mainframe-based repositories managed by the high priests of MIS to today's client/server environments available to all desktops. New database query and report formats that used to take weeks or months to implement (because they had to be submitted to MIS for review and development) can now be executed on the fly by any user with a mouse and a clue. Likewise, new workflows can now be defined and implemented without delay by anybody who wants to get a document reviewed by a routing chain of his or her choosing.

Still, there will always be a need to automate complex, permanent business processes, which need to be planned, designed, and implemented carefully and professionally. When your ad-hoc workflows mature into company-wide standard operating procedures, you will return eagerly to the guidelines presented herein.

The next and final chapter of this book describes the human impacts of workflow technology. We as business and technical managers often assume that we can reengineer new business processes to the *n*th detail without thinking through the qualitative — but still very important — consequences on the workplace. We're building new collaboration environments that, like any ecology, may evolve in ways that are not entirely benign, at least as perceived by workflow participants.

If we can anticipate the human impacts of process changes (such as the possibility for increased workplace monitoring and privacy invasions) we can address them in application planning and design, before they explode into contentious issues.

CHAPTER SIXTEEN

ASSESSING HUMAN
DIMENSIONS AND
IMPACTS OF WORKFLOW
APPLICATIONS

W ork flows between human beings, and, quite often, it defines their position and purpose in life. You don't reengineer and automate work
processes without considering how these changes will contribute to —
or detract from — the quality of people's working lives.

This chapter points out the human context and consequences of implementing
production, messaging-, Web-, and suite-based workflow solutions. These concerns
range from a workflow application's ease-of-use to its impact on the workplace
power structure, staff monitoring, employee privacy, operational flexibility, and control over the speed and volume of work. Keep these considerations in mind as you're
selecting a workflow solution, mapping new business processes, and designing applications to bring these processes to life.

> *Human factors represent the greatest obstacle to acceptance of*
> *workflow applications.*

Human Side of Production Workflow

Having deconstructed the candidate process into its essential structure and media,
per the approach presented in Chapter 12, you're ready to consider how — or

whether — it can be supported by a production workflow application. It's a big step to move from a manual, paper-based workflow to one controlled by a ubiquitous network software environment.

Human-factors issues represent the greatest obstacle to the acceptance of workflow applications in more than 50 percent of cases, states Thomas Koulopoulos in his book *The Workflow Imperative*[1]. Workflow projects are often associated in the public mind with stepped-up corporate downsizing, reorganization, process speedups, work monitoring, procedural rigidity, and loss of individual worker autonomy. Workflow — defined as the flow of information and control in a process — is sure to be a touchy issue in many organizations, because it relates directly to the balance of power between management and staff, as well as between different workgroups and people within those groups.

Before committing serious corporate resources to workflow automation, you'll need to address a host of management, cultural, and technological issues, including the following:

- Has the process been documented fully and accurately?

- Is the process oriented primarily around structured document routing?

- Is the process performing poorly as currently constituted, taking staff, resource, and budget constraints into consideration?

- Is it important that the process always be followed to the letter, according to established corporate operating procedures?

- Is it feasible or desirable to provide all or most personnel with access to PCs and other terminals to participate in an automated workflow application?

- Are process participants open to procedural reengineering and unlikely to oppose workflow automation?

If you are able to answer yes to all of these questions, production workflow systems may represent a viable solution to your requirements. Otherwise, you run the risk of hard-wiring an overly structured solution to a process best left alone or tweaked around the edges.

Staff objections

Users will balk if a workflow solution deprives them of the flexibility and interpersonal give-and-take they feel is essential to their productivity. For example, consider some potential staff objections to automating the hypothetical procurement process introduced in Chapter 12.

DEFINING HARD-AND-FAST ROUTING AND HANDLING RULES FOR ALL CASES IS DIFFICULT

Originators are expected to specify the complete end-to-end routing path when a PR is generated, but this may be asking too much of the average staffer. Bureaucracies are too big, complex, and dynamic for most employees to know the proper routing procedure in all cases. One solution might be to define workflow rules that, for example, forward all PRs tagged as *information systems* to particular technical reviewers and procurement specialists. However, it would be difficult to define rules discriminating enough to know whether a particular request — based on its detailed technical content — better matches the expertise of specialist A or specialist B. Any such rules would constantly have to be updated to reflect new staff hires, departures, transfers, and training. Also, the rules would have to accommodate each staffer's current availability and workload.

Given the problems defining hard-and-fast routing rules, it might be easier simply to forward all PRs to the respective heads of information systems and procurement and let them assign the cases to whomever they want. However, reliance on ad-hoc routing would eliminate much of the rationale for a production workflow system.

THE PROCESS IS ORIENTED AROUND MEETINGS AND INTERACTION

The company's actual purchasing process (as opposed to the formal one defined in procedures manuals) may be more concurrent than sequential in nature. PRs may be written and reviewed at meetings that involve management, procurement, and vendor personnel, so that the actual formal routing chain is little more than a rubber-stamping exercise. If this is so, a production workflow application may be misguided overkill, because it automates the least important part of the process.

THE PROCESS ALREADY PERFORMS REASONABLY WELL ON AN END-TO-END BASIS

The paper-based purchasing process may already flow smoothly, not counting the occasional delays related to staff unavailability or crushing workloads. Barring a significant corporate reorganization, production workflow applications would hang on the same resource constraints, such as waiting for certain people to process case backlogs in their workflow inboxes.

PROCESS FACILITATORS ARE ALLOWED TO CIRCUMVENT STANDARD OPERATING PROCEDURES ON OCCASION

Standard operating procedures often may be observed in the breach. Unspoken rules may allow certain managers with clout to bypass the standard technical and legal reviews on some time-critical purchases. Management may be unwilling to give such flexibility to a production workflow application. In such cases, production workflow would rub against the grain of corporate cultures that never took formal procedures all that seriously in the first place.

PROCESS PARTICIPANTS HANDLE MOSTLY PAPER INFORMATION

Realizing value in the procurement process involves facilitating research and analysis of technical, market, financing, and sourcing alternatives. Most of the necessary information may be available in paper documents, which would be unavailable to production workflow applications unless scanned into the system (which may be more trouble than it's worth, especially on paper-heavy, short-turnaround procurements). The actual PR form might be routed electronically, but that alone could scarcely justify the cost of a production workflow application.

PROCESS PARTICIPANTS RESIST LOSS OF WORKPLACE CONTROL AND EXPOSURE TO PRODUCTIVITY MONITORING

Staff may see a production workflow system as a tool for management to increase its control over the office environment. Some employees might resist the very concept of workflow automation, because it involves letting an impersonal *process model* regulate their work schedules, pacing, and interlinkages. Many would suspect their bosses of using workflow tools to monitor staff activity, productivity, and errors behind the scenes — the Big Brother syndrome. Unfortunately, U.S. law does not require employers to inform staff when they are being monitored, though some other industrialized nations (such as France, Germany, and Canada) limit the types of information that employers may collect through workplace surveillance and the uses to which it may be put.

You will have to tread this minefield of management issues very carefully when selecting, designing, and implementing production workflow applications. If you're not careful, you could alienate staff and squeeze the creative, human spark out of your work environment. You will need to involve staff from the outset of the workflow project, educate them to the great advantages of workflow tools, and encourage them to rethink their jobs with a structured workflow in mind.

Potentially unpopular workflow innovations

Staff resistance could intensify if the workflow project dovetails with a foray into business-process reengineering. Some personnel may regard business-process reengineering as synonymous with downsizing, layoffs, and cutbacks. Alarms may ring in people's heads when they hear management even hint at the possibility of radical changes in staffing, procedures, roles, responsibilities, compensation structures, and incentives. In the purchasing process example, for instance, you should be sensitive to the potential for negative reaction to any of the following reengineering-style workflow innovations.

ADDING, MERGING, OR DELETING FIELDS ON THE FORM

The PR form may be too long or complex, a burden to fill out and review. It may be bogging down the process with unnecessary details or information relevant to only a handful of cases. But heaven help you if you try to prune this unsightly bush, because some reviewer, seven steps down the chain, may argue vehemently for each and every field, on the grounds that it is absolutely essential to some critical corporate concern.

ADDING OR DELETING WORKFLOW PARTICIPANTS

Reviewing the technical content of procurement documentation may be some people's core job responsibility, and they would not react kindly to being taken out of the loop. By the same token, they might take offense to inclusion of other reviewers whom they consider lacking in expertise or likely to cause processing bottlenecks.

ADDING OR DELETING PARTICIPANT PRIVILEGES

PR originators may have traditionally been able to specify the vendor for the desired goods and services. Try taking that away — limiting originators to defining functional requirements and relying on procurement staff to select vendors — and you might have a riot on your hands. By the same token, expect vehement opposition if you take away the MIS chief's ability to select the computer analyst or the facilities managers' ability to select the staff architect allowed to review a pending procurement.

RECONFIGURING TASK DEPENDENCIES AMONG WORKFLOW PARTICIPANTS

Some people enjoy being in the *critical path* for all procurements, which allows them unilaterally to delay or kill PRs. If you change the process and make such people's participation conditional on actions by prior reviewers, you've immediately weakened their clout. If you make their participation contingent on explicit invitation by someone who doesn't like them, you've hurt their pride and possibly derailed their careers.

Workflow-enabled corporate reengineering is bound to upset some people, so you will almost never achieve 100 percent consensus on a proposed process innovation. Your best tack is to remain sensitive to human-factors issues and obtain high-level executive sponsorship for the project, which allow you to weather any storms of grass-roots protest that may result.

Human Side of Messaging-based Workflow

Messaging-based workflow applications will probably rub fewer users the wrong way than a production workflow system. Messaging-based applications are usually implemented as productivity enhancers at the workgroup level, rather than as tools for enterprise-wide process reengineering. Consequently, staff may be less likely to balk at new messaging-based applications, because these tools are seldom associated with downsizing, process speedups, and work monitoring. Messaging-based applications are not liable to make staff feel controlled and manipulated by higher echelons.

Users may also feel less *locked into* messaging-based applications, because the process models can be modified more readily by users themselves. Users can easily design new forms and the business rules associated with them. Messaging-based workflow is a medium for continual, grass-roots process experimentation. Companies need not spend much money to acquire messaging-based workflow software and build prototype applications. Consequently, companies frequently have less at stake if a messaging-based workflow project fails.

Another advantage in favor of messaging-based workflow is its integration with users' existing e-mail systems. Users can retrieve workflow items from their familiar e-mail inboxes and build routing lists with an e-mail addressing dialog box. Many production workflow systems burden users with the need to check workflow-specific inboxes in addition to their familiar e-mail inboxes.

However, don't think that messaging-based workflow technology is an easy sell into all organizations and for all applications. You can anticipate any or all of the following objections to this technology.

Replacing a familiar paper business form with an unfamiliar electronic version

No matter how well rendered, an electronic form is not the same as the paper version it replaced. Some users may have grown so familiar and comfortable with the paper form that they see little value added in substituting bits for pulp. They may blanche when they see, for example, that an electronic form does not fit on a single computer display, but requires them to tab or page down to see the continuation. They may also resent their inability to scratch comments in the electronic form's margins, attach yellow-sticky notes, or file the form in an electronic folder with supporting documentation, much of which may remain in paper formats. Change-resistant users may be won over by some of the special capabilities of electronic forms, such as automated field entry, picklists, and calculation.

Adding business rules to processes that have traditionally depended on case-by-case user judgment

Some users may resent any attempts to limit their operational flexibility by imposing even rudimentary business rules and routing paths on processes that have traditionally been improvised on a case-by-case basis. Standard e-mail may suit them just fine, because it allows every document originator and recipient complete freedom in determining the subsequent routing path. In particular, deadwood middle managers may resist the introduction of codified routing rules, which they suspect as a ruse for cutting them entirely out of processes in which their current involvement is tenuous at best.

Providing a limited workflow solution for a process with more sophisticated requirements

Some users may be expecting a production workflow system and will be disappointed with an unsophisticated messaging-based solution that automates only a portion of the business process. Users may get frustrated with the messaging-based tool's simplistic routing models, lack of compound-document support, and limited document management and tracking capabilities. Network administrators may balk at messaging-based workflow's requirement that large documents be physically broadcast and routed as file attachments across the network.

Chances are, though, that most users will take messaging-based workflow in stride. They'll find it a logical synthesis and extension of familiar e-mail, electronic forms, and desktop applications. It will speed the flow and processing of routine administrative work, increasing users' productivity and freeing time for more interesting tasks.

Human Side of Web-based Workflow

Web-based workflow applications could run into the same type of cultural resistance that faces production workflow — from users reluctant to replace a familiar, manual process with an automated version handed down by some remote corporate authority.

Users may embrace Web-based workflow as an invaluable tool for coordinating complex processes.

Such reluctance could stem from the way in which Web-based workflow applications are developed and deployed: by application developers and *webmasters* associated with corporate or departmental MIS groups. Coordination with MIS is required by the simple fact that Web-based workflow software must be installed on a resource usually controlled by this group: Web sites.

Messaging-based workflow applications, by contrast, can often be developed by end users with minimal MIS involvement, because all the application software and data can be installed on user PCs. Servers function solely as message-transfer agents, passing workflow items as just another type of e-mail with file attachments. Consequently, messaging-based workflow applications may be perceived as more flexible, responsive, and aligned to grass-roots workgroup processes. The average user will probably not be able to go in and tweak a Web-based process model at all, or reroute processes dynamically, as they might be able to with other workflow technologies, including production workflow solutions.

However, users may very well embrace Web-based workflow as an invaluable tool for coordinating sometimes complex business processes over the wide area. In addition, Web-based workflow applications may be welcomed as another valuable service plugged into an increasingly familiar desktop application environment: the browser. From a usability standpoint, Web-based workflow is comparable to its messaging-based cousin in its reliance on electronic forms. And the increasingly multimedia-oriented capabilities of popular browsers makes this a potentially feature-rich, workflow desktop environment.

One distinct usability disadvantage of Web-based solutions (and production workflow products) is their requirement that users periodically log into servers (that is, Web sites) to retrieve and transmit work items. Messaging- and suite-based solutions are preferred because they can place work items in users' e-mail inboxes. The arrival of new work items can trigger beeps or other on-screen indicators if, as is often the case, people keep the mail client loaded through the work day.

Human Side of Suite-based Workflow

Suite-based workflow applications will fit quietly and effectively into the fabric of such desktop software as e-mail, word processors, spreadsheets, and desktop publishing systems.

Visible only as additional commands (typically, *add routing slip* and *send*) within menus of existing office productivity tools, workflow enablement will seem like a natural, logical extension to users' existing collaboration environment. Often a staff begins to use workflow capabilities immediately, without prompting, and with scarcely a moment's worth of training. Users may also be enticed to use embedded workflow features by the realization that they need not spend an extra penny to enjoy this functionality — it is bundled with many e-mail systems, groupware products, and application suites.

Suite-based workflow applications will almost certainly intensify the trend toward growing volumes of e-mail traffic. Popularity of these applications would make e-mail systems ever more critical in daily business operations, filling user inboxes with greater volumes of documents to be reviewed. Some users might resent the trend toward e-mail clutter.

Others might irritate their peers by relying too heavily on workflow-enabled applications, much as some e-mail users tend to exaggerate the importance of their messages by tagging every one *urgent* and always requesting receipt notifications. Overuse of workflow-enabled applications may reinforce hierarchical tendencies in some organizations, in cases where senior management route every document through the same rigid review chain.

Contrast this with more peer-oriented e-mail systems, which provide recipients with considerable freedom to reply to originators and forward messages to third parties of their choice. Many recipients feel that they are entitled to choose whether, how, when, and to whom they forward messages. Consequently, mandatory workflow routing — as defined by document/message originators — may reduce their control, as recipients, over their work environment. In such cases, they may feel that they are being manipulated and *yanked around* by overcontrolling colleagues concerned only with furthering their selfish agendas.

Conversely, some control-hungry users may get frustrated with the relatively simplistic process-definition capabilities of suite-based workflow products, which are seldom more sophisticated, often less so, than those included with messaging-based workflow solutions. For example, suite-based applications seldom allow document originators to specify conditional routing, which would send documents down different paths depending on data-values input or changes made at particular points in the review chain.

Summary

This chapter has presented the human dimensions of workflow applications, focusing on the different ways in which production, messaging-, Web-, and suite-based workflow solutions might be received and perceived by end users.

This now closes Part IV's presentation of management guidelines for justifying, planning, evaluating, implementing, and administering workflow applications in your organizations. This chapter ends on a humanistic note to remind the more technocratic readers that implementing workflow management systems successfully is a bit trickier — and calls on very different skill sets — than developing a Web page or installing a local-area network. You need to be one part management guru, one part coalition builder, one part business analyst, one part project manager, and one part systems integrator to get a workflow application off the drawing boards and into your organization's daily routines.

We have covered a lot of workflow and BPR territory in this book. To recap, the Introduction sounded the strategic keynote, underlining the connection between workflow-based process reengineering and success in today's fluid, dynamic, hyper-competitive global business environment. Part I presented the workflow paradigm, which enables you to conceptualize a reengineered organization and model it along three collaborative dimensions: platform, structure, and media. Part II described the basic architectures, features, and functions of workflow management systems and drew detailed distinctions between production, messaging-, Web-, and suite-based solutions. Part III presented a high-level survey of leading vendors and solutions in all workflow market segments. Part IV laid out a structured approach for you to find the right workflow solution, implement it properly, and maximize your return on this strategic investment.

Workflow management systems are powerful tools for business transformation. They can help you start small with incremental process innovations, or reengineer a new, sleek, globe-spanning, turbo-cruising corporate juggernaut that will roll over the competition — whatever new corporate form makes business sense.

PART V
Appendixes

This part provides supplementary material that will help round out your understanding of workflow technologies discussed in the body of the book, including lists of workflow vendors and consultants and a comprehensive workflow glossary.

APPENDIX A

WORKFLOW SYSTEM
RESOURCES

This Appendix provides comprehensive lists of vendors and products in each workflow market segment as of the date of publication, as well as lists of consultants, research firms, and publications in this market.

In the vendor list, product names are in parentheses alongside company names. Readers are encouraged to contact these companies at the phone numbers provided, or by checking out their Web sites. In cases where Web-site addresses are not listed, you may find these through querying Yahoo!, Alta Vista, Excite, or any of their counterpart search services.

Production Workflow Vendors and Products

Action Technologies Inc.
(ActionWorkflow System, including
Analyst, Builder, and Manager)
1303 Marina Village Parkway, Suite 100
Alameda, CA 94501
510-521-6190
800-WORKFLOW
http://www.actiontech.com

Adra Systems Inc. (CADRA, Matrix)
2 Executive Drive
Chelmsford, MA 01824
508-937-3700
http://www.adra.com

Application Partners, Inc.
(Workflow Innovation Toolkit,
the API Library)
379 Thornall Street, Third Floor
Edison, NJ 08837
800-603-7732
908-549-5464
http://www.application-partners.com

Applix, Inc. (Applixware)
112 Turnpike Road
Westboro, MA 01581
508-870-0300
http://www.applix.com

AT&T Global Information Solutions
(ProcessIT, Cooperation)
1700 South Patterson Boulevard
Dayton, OH 45479-0001
513-445-5000
http://www.att.com

Autodesk Inc. (Autodesk WorkCenter)
111 McInnis Parkway
San Rafael, CA 94903
415-507-5000
http://www.autodesk.com

BancTec Plexus Software Division
(FloWare)
4435 Spring Valley Road
Dallas, TX 75244
214-450-7753
http://www.plx.com

Blueridge Technologies Inc.
(Optix Workflow)
Flint Hill Square, P.O. Box 430
Flint Hill, VA 22627
703-675-3015
http://www.blueridge.com

Computron Technologies Corp.
(Computron Workflow, EPIC)
Meadows Office Complex, 301 Route 17
North (12th Floor)
Rutherford, NJ 07070
201-935-3400
http://www.ctronsoft.com

Diamond Head Software Inc.
(ImageBasic)
707 Richards Street, Penthouse 3
Honolulu, HI 96813
808-545-2377
http://www.dhs.com

Documentum Inc.
(Documentum EDMS)
5671 Gibraltar Drive
Pleasanton, CA 94588-8547
510-463-6850
http://www.documentum.com

DST Systems Inc.
(Automated Work Distributor)
1055 Broadway
Kansas City, MO 64105-1594
816-435-8600
http://www.dstsystems.com

EZPower Systems (PowerOffice)
1818 Market Street, 36th Floor
Philadelphia, PA 19103
215-496-1700
http://www.ezpower.com

FileNet Corp.
(WorkFlo Business System, Visual
WorkFlo, FileNet:WorkGroup,
Workforce, Saros Mezzanine, Saros
Document Manager)
3565 Harbor Boulevard
Costa Mesa, CA 92626-1420
714-966-3400
http://www.filenet.com

Fujitsu Open Systems Solutions Inc.
(Regatta Technology)
3055 Orchard Drive
San Jose, CA 95134
408-432-1300
http://www.ossi.com

Hewlett-Packard Co. (WorkManager)
West 120 Century Road
Paramus, NJ 07653
201-599-5776
800-826-4111
http://www.hp.com

IA Corp. (WorkVision)
1900 Powell Street, Suite 600
Emeryville, CA 94608-1840
510-450-7000
http://www.ia-us.com

IBM (IBM FlowMark, IBM ImagePlus)
Route 100, Building 1
Somers, NY 10589
914-766-1498
http://www.ibm.com

IdentiTech, Inc. (FYI)
100 Rialto Place
Melbourne, FL 32961
407-951-9503
http://www.identitech.com

I. Levy and Associates Inc.
(Navigator 2000/Document
Management System)
1633 Des Peres Road, Suite 300
St. Louis, MO 63131
314-822-0810
http://www.ilevy.com

**InConcert Corp., a Xerox New
Enterprise Company** (InConcert)
3400 Hillview Avenue
Palo Alto, CA 94304
415-424-0111
http://www.xsoft.com

**Information Management
Consultants Inc.** (ImageMover)
McLean, VA
703-893-3100
http://www.imcinc.com

Intelus Corp., a division of Sungard Data Systems (ProcessFlo)
9210 Corporate Boulevard, Suite 400
Rockville, MD 20850
301-990-6363
http://www.intelus.com

Intergraph Corp. (DM/Workflow)
Huntsville, AL 35894-0001
205-730-2700
800-345-4856
http://www.intergraph.com

International Computers Limited
(PowerFlow, TeamFlow, ProcessWise,
Case Manager Desktop, RoleModel)
Observatory House, Windsor Road
Slough, SL1 2EY UK
+44 (0) 1734 516000
http://www.icl.com

Keyfile Corp.
(Keyfile Enterprise Edition)
22 Cotton Road
Nashua, NH 03063
603-883-3800
http://www.keyfile.com

Logical Software Solutions Corp.
(FlowMan)
4041 Powder Mill Road, Suite 300
Calverton, MD 20705
301-474-0285
http://www.lssc.com

Lotus Development Corp.
(Lotus Notes:Document Imaging)
55 Cambridge Parkway
Cambridge, MA 01242
617-577-8500
http://www.lotus.com

Metafile Information Systems, Inc.
(Metaview FOLDERS)
421 First Avenue, SW
Rochester, MN 55902
800-638-2445

Network Imaging Systems Corp.
(1View: Workflow)
500 Huntman Park Drive
Herndon, VA
703-478-2260

Novasoft Systems Inc. (NovaManage)
8 New England Executive Park
Burlington, MA 01803
800-434-NOVA
617-221-0300
http://www.novasoft.com

Olivetti and Co., SpA
(X_Workflow, IBIsys, FlowMaster,
ICONDESK/Flow)
Via Jervis, 10015 Ivrea, Italy
+39 125 5200
http://www.olivetti.com

Optika Imaging Systems, Inc.
(FilePower, PowerFlow)
5755 Mark Dabling Blvd., #100
Colorado Springs, CO 80919
719-548-9800
http://www.optika.com

PaperWise, Inc. (ImageWise)
310 East 4500 South, Suite 480
Salt Lake City, UT 84107
801-261-8850
http://www.paperwise.com

PC DOCS Inc. (DOCS Open)
25 Burlington Mall Road
Burlington, MA 01803
617-273-3800
http://www.pcdocs.com

Portfolio Technologies Inc. (Office.IQ)
5600 Mowry School Road
Newark, CA 94560
510-226-5600
http://www.officeiq.com

PowerCerv Corp. (PowerFlow)
400 North Ashley Drive, Suite 1910
Tampa, FL 33602
617-248-1881
http://www.powercerv.com

Quality Decision Management Inc.
(Quality at Work)
200 Sutton Street, Suite 225
North Andover, MA 01845
508-688-8266
http://www.qdm.com

Reach Software Corp. (WorkMan)
872 Hermosa Dr.
Sunnyvale, CA 94086
408-733-8685
http://www.reachsoft.com

Siemens-Nixdorf Information Systems
(WorkParty)
200 Wheeler Road
Burlington, MA 01803
617-273-0480
http://www.sni.de

Staffware Corp. (Staffware)
70 Walnut Street
Wellesley, MA 02181
617-239-8221
http://www.staffware.com

Unisys Corp. (InfoImage)
P.O. Box 500
Blue Bell, PA 19424-0001
215-986-4011
http://www.unisys.com

Vidya Technologies Inc. (ThoughtFlow)
99 Erie Street
Cambridge, MA 02139-4534
617-497-7150
http://www.vidya.com

ViewStar Corp. (ViewStar)
1101 Marina Village Parkway
Alameda, CA 94501
510-865-7827
800-353-3517
http://www.viewstar.com

Wang Laboratories Inc.
(OPEN/workflow, OPEN/image,
FlowPath, ImageWorks, OmniDesk,
RouteBuilder)
One Industrial Avenue
Lowell, MA 01851
508-459-5000
800-639-WANG
http://www.wang.com

Workflow Incorporated (Doc-Flow)
7181 North Austin Avenue
Niles, IL 60714-4617
847-647-0444

Messaging-based Workflow Vendors and Products

Banyan Systems Inc. (BeyondMail)
120 Flanders Road
Westboro, MA 01581
508-898-1000
http://www.banyan.com

FileNet Corp. (Ensemble)
3565 Harbor Boulevard
Costa Mesa, CA 92626-1420
714-966-3400
http://www.filenet.com

Fischer International Systems Corp.
(EMC2/TAO, Workflow 2000)
4073 Mercantile Avenue
Naples, FL 33942
813-643-1500
http://www.fisc.com

IBM (FormTalk)
Route 100, Building 1
Somers, NY 10589
914-766-1498
http://www.ibm.com

JetForm Corp. (JetForm, FormFlow)
7600 Leesburg Pike, Suite 430
Falls Church, VA 22042
703-448-9544
800-538-3676
http://www.jetform.com

Lotus Development Corp.
(Lotus Notes, Lotus Forms)
55 Cambridge Parkway
Cambridge, MA 01242
617-577-8500
http://www.lotus.com

Microsoft Corp.
(Electronic Forms Designer)
1 Microsoft Way
Redmond, WA 98052
800-426-9400
http://www.microsoft.com

Novell Inc. (InForms)
155 North Technology Way
Orem, UT 84057
801-429-7000
800-451-5151
800-453-1267
http://www.novell.com

Verimation Inc. (Memo/Forms)
50 Tice Boulevard
Woodcliff Lake, NJ 07675
201-767-4795
http://www.verimation.se

Web-based Workflow Vendors and Products

Action Technologies (Metro)
1303 Marina Village Parkway, Suite 100
Alameda, CA 94501
510-521-6190
800-WORKFLOW
http://www.actiontech.com

Documentum Inc.
(Accelera, Virtual Document
Manager, EDMS)
5671 Gibraltar Drive
Pleasanton, CA 94588-8547
510-463-6850
http://www.documentum.com

JetForm Corp. (Web Connectivity Pak)
7600 Leesburg Pike, Suite 430
Falls Church, VA 22042
703-448-9544
800-538-3676
http://www.jetform.com

Novell Inc. (GroupWise Web Access)
155 North Technology Way
Orem, UT 84057
801-429-7000
800-451-5151
http://www.novell.com

OpenText
(Livelink Workflow, Livelink Intranet)
185 Columbia Street West
Waterloo, Ontario, CANADA N2L 5Z5
519-888-7111
http://www.opentext.com

Ultimus, Inc. (Ultimus)
4915 Waters Edge Drive
Raleigh, NC 27606-2460
919-233-7331
http://www.ultimus1.com

ViewStar Corp.
(InfoServer@Work, Process@Work,
InfoStore@Work, Internet
Transport Task)
1101 Marina Village Parkway
Alameda, CA 94501
510-865-7827
800-353-3517
http://www.viewstar.com

Suite-based Workflow Vendors and Products

Corel Corp. (PerfectOffice)
1600 Carling Avenue
Ottawa, Ontario, Canada K1Z 8R7
613-728-8200
http://www.corel.com

Digital Equipment Corp.
(TeamLinks, LinkWorks)
2 Results Way
Marlboro, MA 01752
508-493-5111
http://www.digital.com

Lotus Development Corp.
(Lotus Notes, Lotus SmartSuite)
55 Cambridge Parkway
Cambridge, MA 01242
617-577-8500
http://www.lotus.com

Microsoft Corp.
(Microsoft Exchange, Microsoft Office)
1 Microsoft Way
Redmond, WA 98052
800-426-9400
http://www.microsoft.com

Novell Inc. (GroupWise, Ensemble)
155 North Technology Way
Orem, UT 84057
801-429-7000
800-451-5151
http://www.novell.com

Workflow Research, Consulting, and Standards Organizations

Aberdeen Group
One Boston Place
Boston, MA 02108
617-723-7890
http://www.aberdeen.com

Andersen Consulting
1345 Avenue of the Americas
New York, NY 10105-0302
212-708-4000
http://www.ac.com

**Association for Information and Image
Management International**
1100 Wayne Avenue
Silver Spring, MD 20910
800-477-2446
301-587-8202
http://www.rrinc.com

Bruce Silver Associates
Weston, MA
617-237-6879

Burton Group
7050 Union Park Center, Suite 510
Midvale, UT 84047-4169
801-566-2880
http://www.tbg.com

Collaborative Strategies
1470 DeHaro Street
San Francisco, CA 94107
415-282-9197
http://www.collaborate.com

Connexus Consulting Group
6 Windsor Street
Andover, MA 01810-2605
508-474-9117
http://www.connexus.com

Coopers and Lybrand International
1 International Place
Boston, MA 02110-2621
617-478-5000
http://www.coopers.com

Creative Networks, Inc.
480 Lytton Avenue
Palo Alto, CA 94301-1536
415-326-9926

CSC Index Inc.
5 Cambridge Center
Cambridge, MA 02142
617-492-1500
http://www.csc.com

Datapro Information Services
600 Delran Parkway
Delran, NJ 08075
609-764-0100
http://www.datapro.com

**Dataquest Inc., a Gartner
Group Company**
251 River Oaks Parkway
San Jose, CA 95134-1913
408-437-8000
http://www.dataquest.com

Delphi Consulting Group
266 Beacon Street
Boston, MA 02116-1224
617-247-1511
http://www.delphigroup.com

Ernst and Young International
150 South Wacker Drive
Chicago, IL 60606-4202
312-879-2000
http://www.eyi.com

Gartner Group
56 Top Gallant Road
Stamford, CT 06902-7700
203-964-0096
http://www.gartner.com

Giga Information Group
1 Longwater Circle
Norwell, MA 02061-1616
617-982-9500
http://www.gigaweb.com

IDC/Avante Technologies
5 Speen Street
Framingham, MA 01701-4674
508-872-8200
http://www.idg.com

Meta Group Inc.
208 Harbor Drive
Stamford, CT 06912-0061
203-973-6700
http://www.metagroup.com

Patricia Seybold Group
148 State Street, 7th Floor
Boston, MA 02109
617-742-5200
http://www.psgroup.com

Rapport Communication
2721 N Street, NW
Washington, DC 20007
202-342-2727
http://www.rapport.com

**Workflow and Reengineering
International Association**
San Francisco, CA
800-476-8792
http://www.waria.com

Workflow Management Coalition
Avenue Marcel Thiry 204,
1200 Brussels, Belgium
+32 2 774 96 33
http://www.aiai.ed.ac.uk:80/WfMC

Yankee Group
200 Portland Street
Boston, MA 02114-1722
617-367-1000
http://www.yankeegroup.com

Workflow and Imaging Related Publications

Advanced Imaging
PTN Publishing Co.
445 Broadhollow Road
Melville, NY 11747-3601
516-845-2700

Delphi Report
Delphi Consulting Group
266 Beacon Street
Boston, MA 02116-1224
617-247-1511
http://www.delphigroup.com

Document Imaging Report
Phillips Business Information, Inc.
1201 Seven Locks Road
Potomac, MD 20854-2931
301-340-1250
http://www.phillips.com

GroupTalk
Collaborative Strategies
1470 DeHaro Street
San Francisco, CA 94107
415-282-9197
http://www.collaborate.com

Imaging Magazine
Telecom Library Inc.
12 West 21st Street
New York, NY 10010-6902
212-691-8215
http://www.telecomlibrary.com

Imaging Technology Report
Business Research Publications, Inc.
65 Bleecker Street
New York, NY 10012-2420
212-673-4700
http://www.brp.com

Imaging World
Cardinal Business Media, Inc.
1300 Virginia Drive
Fort Washington, PA 19034-3297
215-643-8000
http://www.cardinal.com

Workgroup Computing Report
Patricia Seybold Group
148 State Street, 7th Floor
Boston, MA 02109
617-742-5200
http://www.psgroup.com

Business Process Reengineering Vendors and Products

Antares Alliance Group (Rapid Re)
638 South Soda Creek Drive
Evergreen, CO 80439-9716
303-674-1776
http://www.antaresalliance.com

Cayenne Software, Inc.
(Bachman Analyst)
8 New England Executive Park
Burlington, MA 01803
800-528-2388
617-273-9003
http://www.cayennesoft.com

Digital Equipment Corp.
(DEC Model for Windows)
2 Results Way
Marlboro, MA 01752
508-493-5111
http://www.digital.com

High Performance Systems, Inc.
(ithink)
45 Lyme Road, Suite 300
Hanover, NH 03755
800-332-1202
603-643-9636
http://www.hps-inc.com

Imagine That, Inc. (Extend+BPR)
6830 Via Del Oro, Suite 230
San Jose, CA 95119-1353
408-365-0305
http://www.imaginethatinc.com

Interfacing Technologies Corp.
(FirstSTEP)
7575 Trans Canada, Suite 610
Saint-Laurent (Montreal), Quebec,
Canada H4T 1V6
516-856-9097
http://www.interfacing.com

Knowledge Based Systems, Inc.
(PROSIIM Process Modeling Software)
1500 University Drive East
College Station, TX 77840
409-260-5274
http://www.kbsi.com

Logic Works, Inc. (BPWin)
111 Campus Drive
Princeton, NJ 08540
609-514-1177
http://www.logicworks.com

Meta Software Corp.
(WorkFlow Analyzer)
125 Cambridge Park Drive
Cambridge, MA 02140
617-576-6920
http://www.metasoft.com

Oracle Corp. (Oracle Process Manager)
500 Oracle Parkway
Redwood City, CA 94065-1600
415-506-7200
http://www.oracle.com

Scitor Corp.
(Scitor Process Charter for Windows)
333 Middlefield Road, 2nd Floor
Menlo Park, CA 94025
800-549-9876
415-462-4200
http://www.scitor.com

Template Software
(Workflow Template)
45365 Vintage Park Plaza, Suite 100
Dulles, VA 20166
703-318-1000
http://www.template.com

Texas Instruments (BDF)
8405 Lemmon Avenue
Dallas, TX 75209-2645
214-995-2011
http://www.ti.com

APPENDIX B

WORKFLOW MANAGEMENT COALITION — THE WORKFLOW REFERENCE MODEL

Author: David Hollingsworth
Send comments to d.hollingsworth@wsr0104.wins.icl.co.uk

Workflow Management Coalition,
Avenue Marcel Thiry 204, 1200 Brussels, Belgium
Tel: (+32 2) 774 9633; Fax: (+32 2) 774 9690
Email: 10013.1555@compuserve.com

1. Introduction

1.1. Background

Workflow Management is a fast evolving technology which is increasingly being exploited by businesses in a variety of industries. Its primary characteristic is the automation of processes involving combinations of human and machine-based activities, particularly those involving interaction with IT applications and tools. Although its most prevalent use is within the office environment in staff intensive operations such as insurance, banking, legal and general administration, etc., it is also applicable to some classes of industrial and manufacturing applications

Many software vendors have WFM products available today which involve WFM technology and there is a continual introduction of more products into the market. The availability of a wide range of products within the market has allowed individual product vendors to focus on particular functional capabilities and users have adopted particular products to meet specific application needs. However, there are, as yet, no standards defined to enable different WFM products to work together, which is resulting in incompatible "islands" of process automation.

The WFM Coalition is a grouping of companies who have joined together to address the above situation. It has been recognised that all workflow management products have some common characteristics, enabling them potentially to achieve a level of interoperability through the use of common standards for various functions. The WFM Coalition has been established to identify these functional areas and develop appropriate specifications for implementation in workflow products. It is intended that such specifications will enable interoperability between heterogeneous workflow products and improved integration of workflow applications with other IT services such as electronic mail and document management, thereby improving the opportunities for the effective use of workflow technology within the IT market, to the benefit of both vendors and users of such technology.

1.2. Purpose

The purpose of this document is to provide a framework to support the development of the various specifications described above. It provides a common "Reference Model" for workflow management systems identifying their characteristics, terminology and components, enabling the individual specifications to be developed within the context of an overall model for workflow systems. The detailed specifications will be developed as separate documents.

1.3. Scope

This document covers the concepts, terminology, general structure of a workflow management system, its major functional components and the interfaces and information interchange flows between them. It identifies the areas appropriate for standardisation and illustrates the potential interoperability scenarios which may be supported through the use of common standards. It also discusses, where appropriate, the applicability of existing standards to workflow management systems and their integration with other standard IT services. It does not cover wider aspects of business process engineering which lie outside the use of information technology to support the business process.

1.4. Audience
The intended audience of this document is the workflow coalition membership as well as others that are interested in the efforts of the coalition and wish to understand the top level technical architecture which underpins the work of the Coalition. The document is intended for a moderately technical audience but extensive prior knowledge of workflow systems is not assumed.

1.5. How to Read This Document
Chapter 2 of this model provides a general introduction to the concepts of workflow systems technology, its evolution, the business context and background on the types of systems which may incorporate this type of technology. If you are unfamiliar with workflow technology you should start here; if you are already familiar with workflow management systems, consider starting at Chapter 3.

Chapter 3 of this model discusses the internal structure of workflow systems, the major functional components and the nature of their interactions. It introduces the top level architecture and identifies the various interfaces which may be used to support interoperability between different system components and integration with other major IT infrastructure components.

Chapter 4 of this model provides a general overview of the workflow application programme interface (WAPI), comments on the necessary protocol support for open interworking and discusses the principles of conformance to the specifications. It identifies those aspects of the specifications which are required to support various classes of interoperability. The detailed WAPI specifications are published as separate specification documents (see cross-references below).

1.6. Cross-References
WFMC SC00 — 1002   WFM Coalition Proposal Information
WFMC SC00 — 1006   WFM Coalition Technical Committee Operations
WFMC TC00 — 1008   Interoperability White Paper
WFMC TC00 — 1009   Client application API descriptions
WFMC TC00 — 1010   Workflow Definition Read/Write Descriptions
WFMC TC00 — 1011   Terminology and Glossary
WFMC TC00 — 1013   Workflow APIs — Naming Conventions

1.7. Revision History
This issue (1.1) is the second major version, incorporating the following changes from the previous version (0.6):

- Incorporation of updated terminology and glossary
- Incorporation of monitoring and metrics interface within the Reference Model

- Updated material on workflow interoperability (derived from the Coalition work on the Workflow Interoperability White Paper) and its associated interface operations, clarifying the various interoperability scenarios and proposed areas for open interoperability

- Incorporation of comments on the (optional) use of organisational roles within the basic model

- Incorporation of comments clarifying the use of workflow relevant data within the basic model

- Incorporation of minor changes to align with the output of other Coalition Working Groups, particularly the initial API specifications

- Improvements in clarification and consistency in various areas throughout the text, including amended document structure

Version 1.1 incorporates minor editorial changes as a result of the TC meeting in Vienna (10th Nov 94), plus revisions to improve consistency with other Coalition documentation.

2. Workflow Systems Overview

2.1. What is Workflow?

Workflow is concerned with the automation of procedures where documents, information or tasks are passed between participants according to a defined set of rules to achieve, or contribute to, an overall business goal. Whilst workflow may be manually organised, in practice most workflow is normally organised within the context of an IT system to provide computerised support for the procedural automation, and it is to this area that the work of the Coalition is directed.

Definition — Workflow

The computerised facilitation or automation of a business process, in whole or part.

Workflow is often associated with Business Process Re-engineering, which is concerned with the assessment, analysis, modelling, definition and subsequent operational implementation of the core business processes of an organisation (or other business entity). Although not all BPR activities result in workflow implementations, workflow technology is often an appropriate solution as it provides separation of the business procedure logic and its IT operational support, enabling subsequent changes to be incorporated into the procedural rules defining the business process. Conversely, not all workflow implementations necessarily form part of a BPR exercise, for example, implementations to automate an existing business procedure.

A Workflow Management System is one which provides procedural automation of a business process by management of the sequence of work activities and the invocation of appropriate human and/or IT resources associated with the various activity steps.

Definition — Workflow Management System

A system that completely defines, manages and executes "workflows" through the execution of software whose order of execution is driven by a computer representation of the workflow logic.

An individual business process may have a life cycle ranging from minutes to days (or even months), depending upon its complexity and the duration of the various constituent activities. Such systems may be implemented in a variety of ways, use a wide variety of IT and communications infrastructure, and operate in an environment ranging from small local workgroup to inter-enterprise. The WFMC Reference Model thus takes a broad view of workflow management, which is intended to accommodate the variety of implementation techniques and operational environments which characterise this technology.

Despite this variety, all WFM systems exhibit certain common characteristics, which provide a basis for developing integration and interoperability capability between different products. The Reference Model describes a common model for the construction of workflow systems and identifies how it may be related to various alternative implementation approaches.

At the highest level, all WFM systems may be characterised as providing support in three functional areas:

- the Build-time functions, concerned with defining, and possibly modelling, the workflow process and its constituent activities
- the Run-time control functions concerned with managing the workflow processes in an operational environment and sequencing the various activities to be handled as part of each process
- the Run-time interactions with human users and IT application tools for processing the various activity steps

Figure 1 illustrates the basic characteristics of WFM systems and the relationships between these main functions.

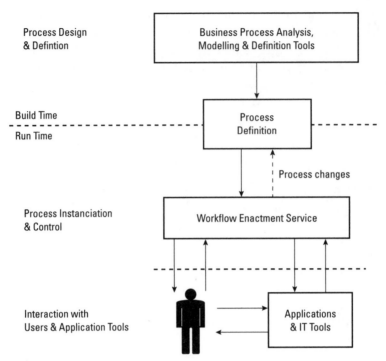

Figure 1
Workflow system characteristics.

2.1.1. BUILD-TIME FUNCTIONS

The Build-time functions are those which result in a computerised definition of a business process. During this phase, a business process is translated from the real world into a formal, computer processable definition by the use of one or more analysis, modelling and system definition techniques. The resulting definition is sometimes called a process model, a process template, process metadata, or a process definition. For purposes of this document, the term 'process definition' will be used.

Definition — Process Definition

The computerised representation of a process that includes the manual definition and workflow definition.

A process definition normally comprises a number of discrete activity steps, with associated computer and/or human operations and rules governing the progression of the process through the various activity steps. The process definition may be expressed in textual or graphical form or in a formal language notation. Some workflow systems may allow dynamic alterations to process definitions from the run-time operational environment, as indicated by the feed-back arrow in the above diagram.

Coalition members do not consider the initial creation of process definitions to be an area of standardisation. Rather, this is considered to be a major distinguishing area between products in the marketplace. However, the result of the Build-time operation, the process definition, is identified as one of the potential areas of standardisation to enable the interchange of process definition data between different build-time tools and run-time products.

2.1.2. RUN-TIME PROCESS CONTROL FUNCTIONS

At run time the process definition is interpreted by software which is responsible for creating and controlling operational instances of the process, scheduling the various activities steps within the process and invoking the appropriate human and IT application resources, etc. These run-time process control functions act as the linkage between the process as modelled within the process definition and the process as it is seen in the real world, reflected in the run-time interactions of users and IT application tools. The core component is the basic workflow management control software (or "engine"), responsible for process creation & deletion, control of the activity scheduling within an operational process, and interaction with application tools or human resources. This software is often distributed across a number of computer platforms to cope with processes which operate over a wide geographic basis.

2.1.3. RUN-TIME ACTIVITY INTERACTIONS

Individual activities within a workflow process are typically concerned with human operations, often realised in conjunction with the use of a particular IT tool (for example, form filling), or with information processing operations requiring a particular application program to operate on some defined information (for example, updating an orders database with a new record). Interaction with the process control software is necessary to transfer control between activities, to ascertain the operational status of processes, to invoke application tools and pass the appropriate data, etc. There are several benefits in having a standardised framework for supporting this type of interaction, including the use of a consistent interface to multiple workflow systems and the ability to develop common application tools to work with different workflow products.

2.1.4. DISTRIBUTION AND SYSTEM INTERFACES

The ability to distribute tasks and information between participants is a major distinguishing feature of workflow run-time infrastructure. The distribution function may operate at a variety of levels (workgroup to inter-organisation) depending upon the scope of the workflows; it may use a variety of underlying communications mechanisms (electronic mail, messaging passing, and distributed object technology, etc.). An alternative top-level view of workflow architecture which emphasises this distribution aspect is shown in Figure 2.

The workflow enactment service is shown as the core infrastructure function with interfaces to users and applications distributed across the workflow domain. Each of these interfaces is a potential point of integration between the workflow enactment service and other infrastructure or application components.

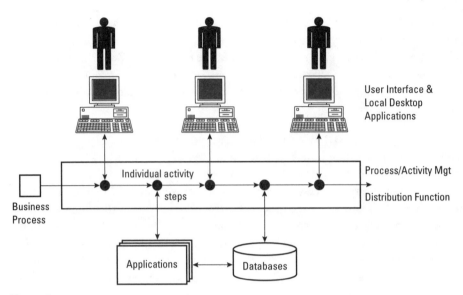

Figure 2
Distribution within the workflow enactment service.

The flow of work may involve the transfer of tasks between different vendors workflow products to enable different parts of the business process to be enacted on different platforms or sub-networks using particular products suited to that stage of the process. In this scenario the flow within the central box passes between two or more workflow products — for example activities 1, 2, and 5 may be executed by one workflow system and activities 3 and 4 by a different system, with control passed between them at appropriate points within the overall workflow. Standards to support this transfer of workflow control enable the development of composite workflow applications using several different workflow products operating together as a single logical entity.

The full range of interfaces being defined by the WFM Coalition therefore covers:

- specifications for process definition data and its interchange
- interfaces to support interoperability between different workflow systems
- interfaces to support interaction with a variety of IT application types
- interfaces to support interaction with user interface desktop functions
- interfaces to provide system monitoring and metric functions to facilitate the management of composite workflow application environments

These are further developed in Section 3.

2.2. The Evolution of Workflow
Many types of products in the IT market have supported aspects of workflow functionality for a number of years, yet it is only comparatively recently that its importance has

been recognised in its own right. The evolution of workflow as a technology has thus encompassed a number of different product areas.

2.2.1. IMAGE PROCESSING

Workflow has been closely associated with image systems, and many image systems have workflow capability either built-in or supplied in conjunction with a specific workflow product. Many business procedures involve interaction with paper-based information, which may need to be captured as image data as part of an automation process. Once paper-based information has been captured electronically as image data, it is often required to be passed between a number of different participants for different purposes within the process, possibly involving interaction with other IT applications, thereby creating a requirement for workflow functionality.

2.2.2. DOCUMENT MANAGEMENT

Document management technology is concerned with managing the lifecycle of electronic documents. Increasingly, this is including facilities for managing document repositories distributed within an organisation as a shared resource with facilities for routing documents (or even separate parts of documents) to individuals for information access or updating according to their specific roles relating to a specific document. The document may form part of a particular business procedure which requires access to the document by individual staff undertaking separate activities according to a particular sequence according to some procedural rules — i.e. a document-centric form of workflow.

2.2.3. ELECTRONIC MAIL AND DIRECTORIES

Electronic mail provides powerful facilities for distributing information between individuals within an organisation or between organisations; the use of directory mechanisms not only provides a way of identifying individual participants within an e-mail domain but also potentially recording information about individual user attributes, such as organisation roles or other attributes relating to business procedures. Thus electronic mail systems have themselves been progressing towards workflow functionality through the addition of routing commands to define a sequence of recipients for particular types of mail items in response to some form of identified business procedure.

2.2.4. GROUPWARE APPLICATIONS

The groupware industry has introduced a wide range of software applications designed to support and improve the interactions between groups of individuals. Initially many of these applications supported improvements in group working via informal processes, accessing group bulletin boards, or diary/scheduling applications on an ad-hoc basis. As the scope of such applications has spread towards more formal business-focussed group interactions, there has been an increasing requirement to provide a more formal and controllable procedural framework to support the use of groupware applications. Workflow technology provides a solution to this type of requirement.

2.2.5. TRANSACTION-BASED APPLICATIONS

For many years applications to support certain classes of business procedures ("transactions") have been developed using transaction management facilities within TP monitors and/or Database Management software. From the initial centralised style of working, such application software has increasingly enabled the distribution of transaction-based applications across a number of computer platforms. Transaction-based applications typically exhibit important characteristics of robustness and support for "atomic" properties of the transaction; however, they do not typically exhibit a separation between the business procedure logic and the invocation of the various application tools which may be required to support individual activities within the business process. Over time, this is leading to a requirement to consolidate workflow capabilities to control the business procedures with the ability to invoke traditional transaction application programs for appropriate parts of the business process, as well as other types of application (document- or office-based, etc.) for other parts of the business process.

2.2.6. PROJECT SUPPORT SOFTWARE

Software to handle complex IT application project development (e.g. IPSEs — "Integrated Project Support Environments") has often provided a form of workflow functionality within the project environment, for "transferring" development tasks between individuals and routing information between individuals to support these tasks. In some cases this type of software has been generalised to support a wider, business-oriented view of process and a wider range of application tools — offering a more general workflow capability.

2.2.7. BPR AND STRUCTURED SYSTEM DESIGN TOOLS

Business Process Re-engineering tools have provided IT based support for the activities of analysing, modelling and (re-)defining the core business processes of an organisation and the potential effects of change in such processes or organisational roles and responsibilities associated with such processes. This may include analysis of the process structure and information flows supporting it, the roles of individuals or organisational units within the process, and actions taken in response to different events, etc. A natural extension of such tools is to facilitate the implementation of the process with IT support infrastructure to control the flows of work and associated activities within the business process.

2.2.8. SEPARATION OF WORKFLOW FUNCTIONALITY

The market for workflow has evolved from requirements across a spectrum of the IT industry and is likely to continue to do so, with a wide range of products focussed on one or more particular aspects of the overall workflow requirement. Some may be provided in conjunction with other areas of technology, such as image processing or document management; others may be more general purpose. This multiplicity of products will allow wide choice for individual implementation circumstances and is recognised as something to be encouraged. However, it also increases the need for standards within the industry to enable different products to work together and integrate within a consistent overall architecture.

The reference architecture described in this document provides a framework which separates the various functions within a workflow environment and identifies various interface points at which product integration and interworking may be accomplished. It forms the template within which the individual interfaces and interchange specifications are being developed by the Coalition.

2.3. Product Implementation Model

OVERVIEW

Despite the variety in workflow products in the market, it has proved feasible to construct a general implementation model of a workflow system which can be matched to most products in the marketplace, thereby providing a common basis for developing interoperability scenarios.

This approach identifies the main functional components within a workflow system and the interfaces between them as an abstract model. It is recognised that many different concrete implementation variants of this abstract model will exist, and, therefore, the interfaces specified may be realised across a number of different platform and underlying distribution technologies. Furthermore, not all vendors may choose to expose every interface between the functional components within the model; this will be dealt with by the specification of a variety of conformance levels which will identify the particular interworking functions where open interfaces are supported for multivendor integration.

The main functional components of a generic workflow system are illustrated in Figure 3.

The generic model has three types of component:

- software components which provide support for various functions within the workflow system (shown in dark fill)
- various types of system definition and control data (shown unfilled) which are used by one or more software components
- applications and application databases (shown in light fill) which are not part of the workflow product, but which may be invoked by it as part of the total workflow system

The roles of the major functional components within this system are described below.

PROCESS DEFINITION TOOL

The process definition tool is used to create the process description in a computer processable form. This may be based on a formal process definition language, an object relationship model, or, in simpler systems, a script or a set of routing commands to transfer information between participating users. The definition tool may be supplied as part of a specific workflow product or may be part of a business process analysis product, which has other components to handle analysis or modelling of business operations. In this latter case there must be a compatible interchange format to transfer the process definitions to/from the run-time workflow software.

PROCESS DEFINITION

The process definition contains all necessary information about the process to enable it to be executed by the workflow enactment software. This includes information about its starting and completion conditions, constituent activities and rules for navigating between them, user tasks to be undertaken, references to applications which may to be invoked, definition of any workflow relevant data which may need to be referenced, etc.

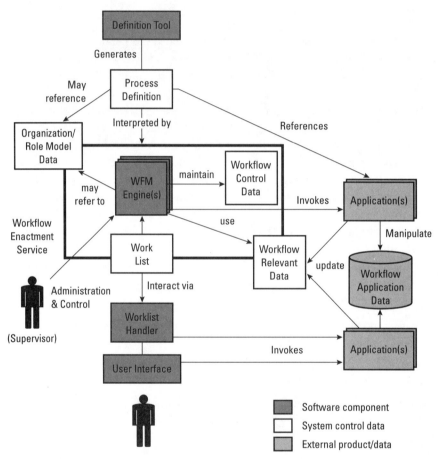

Figure 3
Generic workflow product structure.

The process definition may refer to an Organisation/Role model which contains information concerning organisational structure and roles within the organisation (e.g. an organisational directory). This enables the process definition to be specified in terms of organisational entities and role functions associated with particular activities or information objects, rather than specific participants. The workflow enactment service then has the responsibility of linking organisational entities or roles with the specific participants within the workflow run-time environment.

WORKFLOW ENACTMENT SERVICE

The workflow enactment software interprets the process description and controls the instantiation of processes and sequencing of activities, adding work items to the user work lists and invoking application tools as necessary. This is done through one or more co-operating workflow management engines, which manage(s) the execution of individual instances of the various processes. The workflow enactment service maintains internal control data either centralised or distributed across a set of workflow engines; this workflow control data includes the internal state information associated with the various process and activity instances under execution and may also include checkpointing and recovery/restart information used by the workflow engines to co-ordinate and recover from failure conditions.

The process definition, in conjunction with any (run-time) workflow relevant data is used to control the navigation through the various activity steps within the process, providing information about the entry and exit criteria for individual activity steps, parallel or sequential execution options for different activities, user tasks or IT applications associated with each activity, etc. This may require access to organisation/role model data, if the process definition includes constructs relating to these entity types.

The workflow engines also include some form of application tool invocation capability to activate applications necessary to execute particular activities. The generality of such mechanisms may vary greatly, with some simple systems only offering support of a single fixed tool such as a form or document editor, whereas others may provide methods for the invocation of a wider range of tools, both local and remote to the Workflow engine.

WORKFLOW RELEVANT DATA ANDAPPLICATION DATA

Where process navigation decisions, or other control operations within the workflow engine, are based on data generated or updated by workflow application programs, such data is accessible to the workflow engine and termed workflow relevant data (also known as "case data"); this is the only type of application data accessible to the workflow engine. Workflow application data is manipulated directly (and only) by the invoked applications, although the workflow engines may be responsible for transferring such data between applications (if necessary), as different applications are invoked at different activity points within the workflow process.

WORKLISTS

Where user interactions are necessary within the process execution, the workflow engine(s) place items on to worklists for attention by the worklist handler, which manages the interactions with the workflow participants. This process may be invisible to the workflow participants, with the worklist maintained within the workflow software and the user being presented sequentially with the next task to be performed. On other systems the worklist may be visible to the user, who has the responsibility of selecting individual items of work from the list and progressing them independently, with the worklist being used to indicate task completions.

WORKLIST HANDLER AND USER INTERFACE

The worklist handler is a software component which manages the interaction between workflow participants and the workflow enactment service. It is responsible for progressing work requiring user attention and interacts with the workflow enactment software via the worklist. In some systems this may be little more than a desktop application providing a simple in-tray of work items awaiting user attention. In other systems this may be far more sophisticated, controlling the allocation of work amongst a set of users to provide facilities such as load balancing and work reassignment. In addition to these worklist handling functions, workflow engines typically support a wider range of interactions with client applications, including sign-on and sign-off of workflow participants, requesting the commencement of an instance of particular process types, requesting workitems queued for particular participants, etc. Within the reference model, the term *workflow client application* is used in preference to "worklist handler" to reflect this wider range of potential usage, which includes process control functions as well as worklist manipulation.

In the diagram the User Interface is shown as a separate software component, responsible for the look and feel of the user dialogue and control of the local interface with the user. In certain systems this may be combined with the Worklist Handler into a single functional entity. It also expected that some client applications will interact with several different workflow services, enabling workitems from such services to be consolidated into a unified task list for presentation to participants via a common user interface.

Invocation of local applications may be necessary to support the user in the particular tasks to be undertaken. This may be done by the Worklist Handler, for example, at the time of presenting workitems to the user, or may be the responsibility of the user, using general facilities available at the User Interface software to load appropriate supporting applications. There is a distinction between application invocation at the Worklist Handler/User Interface (which is not directly controlled from the workflow engine and may not be visible to it) and direct application invocation by the workflow enactment software.

SUPERVISORY OPERATIONS

Within a workflow system there are a number of supervisory functions which are normally provided; these are typically supported on the basis of supervisory privilege to a particular workstation or user(s). These functions may enable supervisors to alter work allocation rules, to identify participants for specific organisational roles within a process, to track alerts for missed deadlines or other forms of event, to trace the history of a particular process instance, to enquire about work throughput or other statistics, etc. Where distributed workflow engines are used there may need to be specific commands to transfer such control operations or (partial) responses between different workflow engines to provide a single administrative interface.

EXPOSED AND IMBEDDED INTERFACES

Whilst the majority of workflow products can be related to the above structure, not all products offer exposed interfaces between the various individual system functional components; some products may implement several functional components together as a single logical entity with the interfaces embedded within the software component and not available for third party product use. The WFM specifications will identify, for each interface, the role of that interface in achieving interoperability, so that individual products can identify conformance against particular interoperability criteria. (For example, a particular product might offer an exposed interface for worklist manipulation but not for process definition interchange.)

2.4. Alternative Implementation Scenarios

The structural model of a generic workflow product identifies a series of software components and interfaces. In a concrete product implementation this structure may be realised in a variety of different ways; this is an important area of product differentiation. Major distinguishing factors between products include choice of platform and network infrastructure, as well as the inherent functionality of the workflow software itself. This section illustrates how the generic model copes with this variety of implementation approach, whilst retaining visible interfaces to facilitate multi-vendor product interworking.

A full discussion of all potential implementation design issues lies outside the scope of this document. Amongst the main alternatives considered are:

- centralised or distributed workflow enactment service
- worklist handler location(s) and distribution mechanism

WORKFLOW ENACTMENT SOFTWARE — ALTERNATIVE APPROACHES

The workflow enactment software consists of one or more workflow engines, which are responsible for managing all, or part, of the execution of individual process instances. This may be set up as a centralised system with a single workflow engine responsible for managing all process execution or as a distributed system in which several engines cooperate, each managing part of the overall execution. See Figure 4.

In the above scenario the two workflow services exhibit common properties at the boundary but follow different internal implementation architectures, whose characteristics may be product dependent.

Where several workflow engines cooperate in the execution of a process instance, the control data associated with the process instance must be accessible to the different engines. This workflow control data may be distributed across the engines, located at a master engine or held as a shared filestore resource, or some combination of these. The particular implementation approaches by which this data is made available to the engines is considered to be outside the current scope for standardisation. Similarly, the process definition data may be distributed across all engines or parts transferred to individual engines from some master source during process execution. Interfaces to handle supervisory operations or application invocation may be supported as distributed features or localised to particular engines. The implementation approaches to manage distribution of workflow across multiple engines are thus complex and numerous.

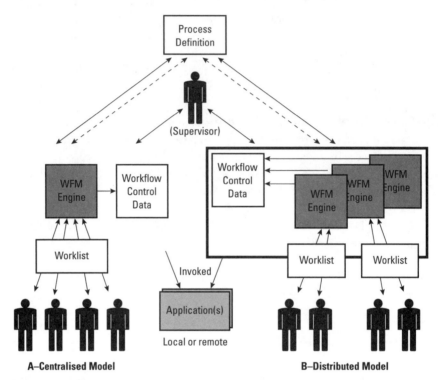

Figure 4
Standard workflow enactment service boundary.

The approach taken by the Coalition is to define a boundary around the workflow enactment service, which exhibits various standard functional attributes accessible via a set of common APIs. The internal mechanisms by which the enactment service delivers this capability are not defined and may include one or more homogenous workflow engines, communicating in a variety of ways.

To support interworking between different products, interfaces are defined for specific co-operative functions between different enactment services so that a composite multi-vendor workflow application may execute parts of a particular process on different enactment services (each comprising one or more specific vendors workflow engines). This is considered a more realistic approach (except perhaps in the long term) than attempting to standardise the internal interfaces and state data of a distributed workflow service.

WORKFLOW CLIENT APPLICATIONS — ALTERNATIVE APPROACHES

In the workflow model, interaction occurs between the worklist handler and a particular workflow engine through a well defined interface embracing the concept of a worklist — the queue of work items assigned to a particular user (or, possibly, group of common users) by the workflow enactment service. At the simplest level the worklist is accessible to the workflow engine for the purposes of assigning work items and to the worklist handler (i.e. the workflow client application) for the purpose of retrieving work items for presentation to the user for processing.

There are various possible product implementations of this worklist interaction model depending upon the nature of the product implementation and, in particular, on the type of infrastructure used to support the distribution of worklist handling.

Four possible approaches are illustrated in Figure 5, one supporting centralised worklist handling and three using a distributed worklist handler function.

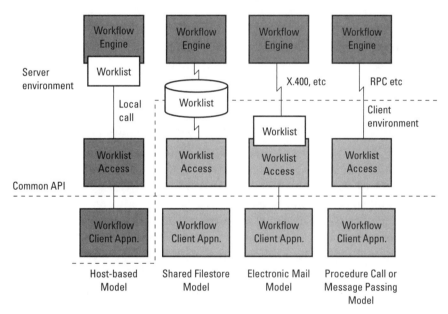

Figure 5
Alternative client worklist handler implementations.

The four example scenarios are as follows:

■ Host-based Model — the client worklist handler application is host based and communicates with the worklist via a local interface at the workflow engine. In this case the user interface function may be driven via a terminal or a remote workstation MMI.

- Shared filestore model — the worklist handler application is implemented as a client function and communication is via a shared filestore, which lies on the boundary between host and client platform environments and is accessible to both.

- Electronic mail model — communication is via electronic mail, which supports the distribution of work items to individual participants for local processing. In this scenario the worklist would normally lie at the client.

- Procedure Call or Message Passing model — communication is via procedure call, or other message-passing mechanism. In this scenario the worklist may be physically located on the workflow engine or at the worklist handler according to the particular implementation characteristics.

In each case it is feasible to construct a common API, which supports worklist handler access to the worklist and workflow engine functions, but which is located behind a specific worklist access function appropriate to the product implementation style.

2.5. The Need for Standardisation

The basic rationale to achieve standardisation of important workflow functional interfaces is driven by two major considerations:

- Ongoing support for business re-engineering & operational flexibility
- Integration requirements resulting from product specialisation and market variety

BUSINESS RE-ENGINEERING AND OPERATIONAL FLEXIBILITY

The strategic importance of business process re-engineering and associated workflow implementations will lead to the requirement for sufficient flexibility of product to cope with ongoing business change; indeed this is one of the key motivations behind the use of the technology. This will include cases where several separate business processes have been implemented using different workflow products, and require to be re-engineered into a single composite process involving interaction between existing workflows. These requirements may arise due to reorganisation, legislative changes, changing business objectives, etc. As the use of electronic data interchange develops, these workflows are likely to embrace inter-organisation communications as well as those internal to a single organisation.

In these situations it is extremely likely that different products will be in use within different organisations or departments and the inability of such products to interoperate will cause a significant potential problem in coping with business change. The market projections for the penetration of workflow technology suggest very widespread adoption during the next 5-10 years, leading to the potential incompatibility problems seen in previous generations of information technology unless appropriate interworking standards are developed.

The early availability of such standards with subsequent product implementations will provide a degree of confidence to the market, critical to the effective take-up of workflow technology.

SPECIALISATION AND MARKET VARIETY

There are currently estimated to be in excess of a hundred different workflow (and related) products in the market, focused on different aspects of functionality and data/application integration. The development of interworking standards will allow application choice of "best of breed" products for individual aspects of a workflow implementation. This may embrace process analysis and definition products from one vendor, coupled with workflow engine software from a different vendor, integrated with a client worklist handling application from a third.

An individual workflow may conveniently be broken down into several sub-processes each enacted on a specialist product suited to the specific data type, platform, or network environment related to that particular sub-process. The availability of interworking standards will provide the opportunity to implement composite solutions to business process requirements, linking several such specialist products to meet the precise needs of the process.

Furthermore, many workflow applications require to integrate with other, existing or emerging applications, ranging from desktop office functions to corporate transaction processing/database. The provision of a standard interface to support this will reduce product complexity and the amount of specialist integration skills necessary during implementation.

Members of the Coalition, both vendors and users, recognise the potential importance of standards in all these areas and are co-operating in their definition.

3. Workflow Reference Model

3.1. Overview

The Workflow Reference model has been developed from the generic workflow application structure by identifying the interfaces within this structure which enable products to interoperate at a variety of levels. All workflow systems contain a number of generic components which interact in a defined set of ways; different products will typically exhibit different levels of capability within each of these generic components. To achieve interoperability between workflow products, a standardised set of interfaces and data interchange formats between such components is necessary. A number of distinct interoperability scenarios can then be constructed by reference to such interfaces, identifying different levels of functional conformance as appropriate to the range of products in the market.

3.2. The Workflow Model

Figure 6 illustrates the major components and interfaces within the workflow architecture.

The architecture identifies the major components and interfaces. These are considered in turn in the following sections. As far as possible, the detail of the individual interfaces (APIs and interchange formats) will be developed as a common core set using additional parameters as necessary to cope with individual requirements of particular interfaces.

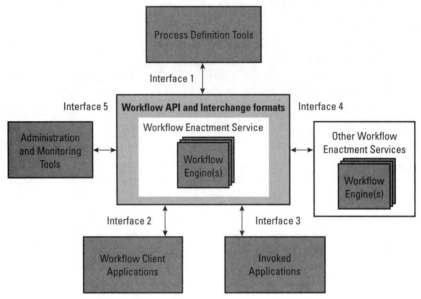

Figure 6
Workflow Reference Model — Components & Interfaces.

The interface around the workflow enactment service is designated WAPI — Workflow APIs and Interchange formats, which may be considered as a set of constructs by which the services of the workflow system may be accessed and which regulate the interactions between the workflow control software and other system components. Many of the functions within the 5 interface areas are common to two or more interface services hence it is more appropriate to consider WAPI as a unified service interface which is used to support workflow management functions across the 5 functional areas, rather than 5 individual interfaces.

3.3. Workflow Enactment Services

3.3.1. WHAT IS A WORKFLOW ENACTMENT SERVICE?

The workflow enactment service provides the run-time environment in which process instantiation and activation occurs, utilising one or more workflow management engines, responsible for interpreting and activating part, or all, of the process definition and interacting with the external resources necessary to process the various activities.

Definition — Workflow Enactment Service

A software service that may consist of one or more workflow engines in order to create, manage, and execute workflow instances. Applications may interface to this service via the workflow application programming interface (WAPI).

In the model adopted, there is a logical separation between this process and activity control logic, which constitutes the workflow enactment service, and the application tools and end user tasks which constitute the processing associated with each activity. This separation provides the opportunity for a wide range of industry standard or user specific application tools to be integrated within a particular workflow application.

Interaction with external resources accessible to the particular enactment service occurs via one of two interfaces:

■ The client application interface, through which a workflow engine interacts with a worklist handler, responsible for organising work on behalf of a user resource. It is the responsibility of the worklist handler to select and progress individual work items from the work list. Activation of application tools may be under the control of the worklist handler or the end-user.

■ The invoked application interface, which enables the workflow engine to directly activate a specific tool to undertake a particular activity. This would typically be a server-based application with no user interface; where a particular activity uses a tool which requires end-user interaction, it would normally be invoked via the worklist interface to provide more flexibility for user task scheduling. By using a standard interface for tool invocation, future application tools may be workflow enabled in a standardised manner.

These interfaces are described in sections 3.5 and 3.6 respectively.

Within this section, the workflow enactment service has been discussed as a single logical entity, although physically it may be either centralised or functionally distributed.

In a distributed workflow enactment service, several Workflow engines each control a part of the process enactment and interact with that subset of users and application tools related to the activities within the process for which they are responsible. Such an enactment service is considered to have common naming and administrative scope, so that process definitions (or subsets) and user/application names may be handled on a consistent basis. Distributed workflow systems make use of specific protocols and interchange formats between Workflow engines to synchronise their operations and exchange process and activity control information. Workflow relevant data may also be transferred between Workflow engines. Within a single homogeneous workflow enactment service, such operations are vendor specific.

Where heterogeneous products are involved, a standardised interchange is necessary between workflow engines. Using interface 4, the enactment service may transfer activities or sub-processes to another (heterogeneous) enactment service for execution. Within the Workflow Reference Model this is termed Workflow Engine Interchange and is considered under section 3.7.

Common administration and monitoring functions may also be required in such a heterogeneous environment; these are considered in section 3.8.

3.3.2. THE WORKFLOW ENGINE

A workflow engine is responsible for part (or all) of the run-time control environment within an enactment service.

Definition — Workflow Engine

A software service or "engine" that provides the run-time execution environment for a workflow instance.

Typically such software provides facilities to handle:

- interpretation of the process definition
- control of process instances — creation, activation, suspension, termination, etc.
- navigation between process activities, which may involve sequential or parallel operations, deadline scheduling, interpretation of workflow relevant data, etc.
- sign-on and sign-off of specific participants
- identification of workitems for user attention and an interface to support user interactions
- maintenance of workflow control data and workflow relevant data, passing workflow relevant data to/from applications or users
- an interface to invoke external applications and link any workflow relevant data
- supervisory actions for control, administration and audit purposes

A workflow engine can control the execution of a set of process, or sub-process, instances with a defined scope — determined by the range of object types, and their attributes, which it can interpret within the process definition(s).

In an enactment service consisting of multiple workflow engines, there is a partitioning of process execution across the constituent engines. This may be by process type, with a particular engine controlling a particular process type in its entirety, by functional distribution, with a particular engine controlling those parts of a process requiring user or resource allocation within its own control domain, or some other partitioning mechanism.

3.3.3. HOMOGENEOUS AND HETEROGENEOUS WORKFLOW ENACTMENT SERVICES

An homogeneous workflow enactment service comprises one or more compatible workflow engines which provide the runtime execution environment for workflow processes with a defined set of (product specific) process definition attributes. The mechanisms by which process execution is organised across the various workflow engines and protocols and interchange formats used to support this are product specific and not standardised.

A heterogeneous workflow enactment service comprises two or more homogeneous services, which follow common standards for interoperability at a defined conformance level. It is envisaged that a number of conformance levels will be defined to support increasing levels of common functionality.

These are expected to include (amongst other things):

- A common naming scheme across the heterogeneous domain

- Support for common process definition objects and attributes across the domain

- Support for workflow relevant data transfer across the domain

- Support for process, sub-process or activity transfer between heterogeneous workflow engines

- Support for common administration and monitoring functions within the domain

Support for common workflow control data and its interchange (e.g. shared process and activity state data) would be necessary to support totally open interworking between heterogeneous products; whilst an interesting standardisation challenge, it is considered unattainable in the foreseeable future, hence the emphasis on levels of interoperability governed by defined conformance criteria.

PROCESS AND ACTIVITY STATE TRANSITIONS

The workflow enactment service may be considered as a state transition machine, where individual process or activity instances change states in response to external events (e.g. completion of an activity) or to specific control decisions taken by a workflow engine (e.g. navigation to the next activity step within a process).

An illustrative basic state transition scheme for process instances is shown in Figure 7.

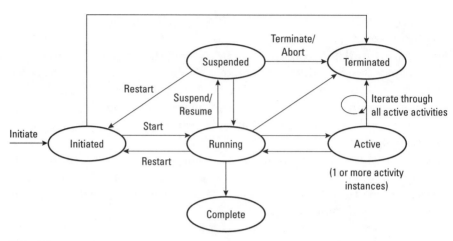

Figure 7
Example state transitions for a process instances

Within the above diagram, transition between states (represented by the arrows) take place in response to the particular WAPI commands identified; transition between certain states will also take place as a result of transition conditions within the process definition being met (e.g. as the result of an external event, or time or data dependent condition, etc.). The basic states are:

initiated — a process instance has been created, including any associated process state date and workflow relevant data, but the process has not (yet) fulfilled the conditions to cause it to start execution

running — the process instance has started execution and any of its activities may be started (once any appropriate activity start conditions have been met)

active — one or more of its activities has been started (i.e. a workitem has been created and assigned to an appropriate activity instance)

suspended — the process instance is quiescent and no activities are started until the process has returned to the running state (via a resume command)

completed — the process instance has fulfilled the conditions for completion; any internal post-completion operations such as logging audit data or statistics will be performed and the process instance destroyed

terminated — execution of the process instance has been stopped before its normal completion; any internal operations such as error logging or logging recovery data may be performed and the process instance destroyed

Activities may be non-interruptable; i.e. once a workflow service has started a particular activity within a process instance, it may not be possible to suspend or terminate that activity. This means that suspension/restart/terminate functions cannot be completed until all active activities have completed and the process instance returned to a running state. In addition, it may be required to mark a set of activities as an atomic unit, which are either executed in entirety or the process instance "rolled-back" to a restart point. The potential treatment of interruptable activities and atomic activity units with restart capability will require further consideration and is beyond the initial work of the Coalition.

Ignoring these additional complexities, a simple illustration (Figure 8) of the basic states and transitions for an activity instance is thus:

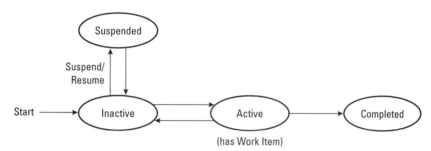

Figure 8
Example state transitions for activity instances.

The basic states of an activity instance are:

inactive — the activity within the process instance has been created but has not yet been activated (e.g. because activity entry conditions have not been met) and has no workitem for processing

active — a workitem has been created and assigned to the activity instance for processing

suspended — the activity instance is quiescent (e.g. as a result of a change_state_of_activity_instance command) and will not be allocated a workitem until returned to the running (inactive) state

completed — execution of the activity instance has completed (and any post-activity transition conditions will be evaluated)

A particular product implementation may, of course, support additional state types or use a different representation of the basic states and transitions shown above. The reference model does not attempt to prescribe standardised internal behaviour of workflow systems but the state transitions illustrate the basic underlying concepts which are necessary to scope the effects of the API command set which the Coalition is developing.

3.3.4. WORKFLOW APPLICATION PROGRAMMING INTERFACE AND INTERCHANGE

The WAPI may be regarded as a set of API calls and interchange functions supported by a workflow enactment service at its boundary for interaction with other resources and applications. Although this architecture refers to 5 "interfaces" within WAPI, a number of the functions within each of these interfaces are common (for example process status calls may be issued from the client application interface or the administration interface). The WAPI is thus being defined as a common core of API calls/interchange formats with specific extensions where necessary to cater individually for each of the five functional areas.

The majority of WAPI functions comprises of APIs calls with defined parameter sets/results codes. Where appropriate it also defines interchange data formats, for example, for the exchange of process definitions. The use of WAPI within each of the five functional areas is described within the following sections (3.4 — 3.8).

3.3.5. WORKFLOW CONTROL, WORKFLOW RELEVANT AND WORKFLOW APPLICATIONS DATA

The workflow enactment service maintains internal control data to identify the state of individual process or activity instances and may support other internal status information. This data is not accessible or interchangeable, as such, via the WAPI commands, but some of the information content may be provided in response to specific commands (e.g. query process status, give performance metrics, etc.). Homogeneous workflow enactment services may exchange such information between workflow engines by specific private dialogue.

Definition — Workflow Control Data

Internal data that is managed by the workflow management system and/or workflow engine.

Workflow Relevant Data is used by a workflow management system to determine particular transition conditions and may affect the choice of the next activity to be executed. Such data is potentially accessible to workflow applications for operations on the data and thus may need to be transferred between activities by the workflow enactment software. When operating in a heterogeneous environment, such data may need to be transferred between workflow engines, where the process execution sequence spans two or more workflow engines; this process may (potentially) require name mapping or data conversion.

Definition — Workflow Relevant Data

Data that is used by a workflow management system to determine the state transition of a workflow process instance.

Manipulation of application data may be required within each activity of a process definition, for example, by a particular tool or application, either under the direct control of the application or in conjunction with some form of user interaction. The work-flow model must, therefore, cope with any necessary interchange of case data between the various activities. In some circumstances this may also require some form of case data transformation between different tool data formats, for example, conversion of a document or spreadsheet from one application format to another. (In some systems this may be a function of the workflow enactment service; in others data conversion may be defined as an activity in its own right within the process definition.)

Definition — Workflow Application Data

Data that is application specific and not accessible by the workflow management system.

Workflow application data is not used by the workflow enactment software and is relevant only to the applications or user tasks executed during the workflow. As with workflow relevant data, it may need to be transferred (and/or transformed) between workflow engines in a heterogeneous enactment service, so as to be made available to the appropriate activities executed on the individual engines.

The relationship between an application and any workflow relevant or application data it needs to manipulate will normally be defined within the process definition. In some cases this may be an implicit relationship (for example, in those systems where case data is physically transferred to the next activity as part of the activity navigation within the process), whereas in others (for example, access to a shared object store) it may be an explicit relationship defining a specific object name and application access path. Within the reference model the former scenario will be called direct data inter-change and the latter indirect data interchange.

3.3.6. DATA INTERCHANGE

Interchange of workflow relevant and application data is (potentially) required across the WAPI to support interworking within three run-time functions:

- worklist handler (interface 2)
- invoked application (interface 3)
- workflow engine interchange (interface 4)

This section covers the general principles of data interchange; this area will require further specification work. The proposed API command set may include specific calls to accept/return workflow relevant data from/to the enactment service across the WAPI; variants of these could be defined for both direct and indirect case data interchange.

The direct interchange of application data is typified by e-mail driven workflow sys-tems in which the data is physically transferred between activities, either application or user-driven. In this situation there is no need to define an explicit relationship between activities and application data; the data is transferred as part of the standard workflow activity navigation and locally linked to the application on invocation. Where there is a requirement to provide data format conversion between activities, the model recognises that a particular application may define, as an attribute, the data type (or types) with which it is associated (this attribute information may be held local to a particular software environment or global to the entire workflow service — for example, in a directory). This enables systems which are constructed to use heterogeneous workflow applications to provide data conversion (where necessary) on the basis of attribute types defined for the respective applications. Conventions will need to be adopted (or developed) for transferring and retaining the data type information, for example, by the use of X.400 body part object identifiers or the Internet mail MIME mechanism (RFC-1341).

Some types of workflow system (for example, those implemented via a shared document store) do not physically transfer application data between activities. In these systems, data is accessed in situ by the application using an appropriate access path (which may be networked). In this case, the access path naming scheme must be global to all applications which may be invoked within the workflow service and appropriate access permissions must be available and controlled for each active process instance. Data format conversion in this scenario, if necessary, may be modelled as an activity in its own right, using an appropriate application tool (for example, a document converter).

Homogenous systems may use private conventions for object names and access permissions, but heterogeneous systems require a common scheme. In this case, either the (common) process definition must include access path references to the application data object storage, or the navigation between activities must include transfer of the necessary access path references for any data objects to be transferred between activities.

Where interworking between heterogeneous workflow products is planned, they must either follow the same approach to application data interchange or interwork through a gateway mechanism (section 3.7), which can map between the two approaches and/or handle any differences in object naming and data type conventions by appropriate conversion. Further work is required on the detail in this area, but it is possible that alternative interchange conformance criteria could be identified to cover the two cases.

The way in which application or workflow relevant data interchange is to be handled across the 3 interfaces is for more detailed study; the following notes identify some initial options.

Client applications — workflow relevant data may be embedded in the workitem and extracted from the worklist for presentation to the user or for linkage to a particular application tool (for example, by the worklist handler locating it in a particular local directory). Alternatively, the data may be indirectly passed to a specific application via some form of shared object store (for example, by the use of a common file for data in transit between applications, or by passing a specific file reference embedded as part of the workitem.)

Invoked applications — the data interchange will depend upon the nature of the application invocation interface (section 3.6) and may require the invocation service to embed the data within a specific application protocol. APIs for reading/writing workflow-relevant data are feasible for specific workflow-enabled applications or to construct generalised application agents.

Workflow engine interoperability — considerations are similar to the Client Application interface, although where the different systems support different application data interchange approaches, the use of a gateway function will be necessary to map between the two schemes and, possibly, handle name resolution.

3.4. Process Definition

3.4.1. PROCESS DEFINITION TOOLS

A variety of different tools may be used to analyse, model, describe and document a business process; such tools may vary from the informal ("pencil and paper") to sophisticated and highly formalised. The workflow model is not concerned with the particular nature of such tools nor how they interact during the build-time process. As noted earlier, such tools may be supplied as part of a workflow product or as a separate, for example, BPR product toolset.

Where a workflow product provides its own process definition tool, the resultant process definitions will normally be held within the workflow product domain and may, or may not, be accessible via a programming interface for reading and writing information. Where separate products are used for defining and executing the process, the process definitions may be transferred between the products as and when required or may be stored in a separate repository, accessible to both products (and possibly other development tools).

The final output from this process modelling and design activity is a process definition which can be interpreted at run time by the workflow engine(s) within the enactment service. For today's workflow products, each individual process definition is typically in a form specialised to the particular workflow management software for which it was designed. The workflow definition interchange interface will enable more flexibility in this area.

The process analysis, modelling, and definition tools may include the ability to model processes in the context of an organisation structure (although this is not a mandatory aspect of the workflow reference model). Where an organisation model is incorporated into such tools, the process definition will include organisation-related objects such as roles. These are related (typically) to system control data such as role: actor relationships (e.g. within an organisational directory) which may be referenced during process execution.

3.4.2. WORKFLOW DEFINITION INTERCHANGE (INTERFACE 1)

The interface between the modelling and definition tools and the run-time workflow management software is termed the process definition import/export interface. The nature of the interface is an interchange format and API calls, which can support the exchange of process definition information over a variety of physical or electronic interchange media. The interface may support the exchange of a complete process definition or a subset — for example, a set of process definition changes or the attributes of a particular activity within the process definition.

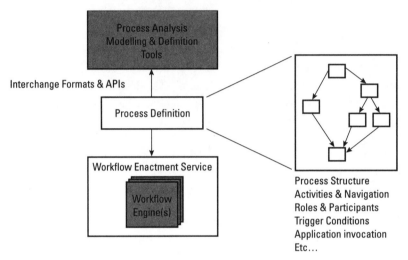

Figure 9
Process definition interchange.

There are clear benefits in using a standardised form for this definition.

Firstly, it defines a point of separation between the build-time and run-time environments, enabling a process definition generated by one modelling tool to be used as input to a number of different workflow run-time products. This enables user choice of modelling tools and workflow run-time products to be independent.

Secondly, it offers the potential to export a process definition to several different workflow products which could co-operate to provide a distributed run-time enactment service. (The ability to exchange process definition data is only one aspect of such a distributed service; there are other requirements in terms of run-time interactions between WFM-Engine, which are considered in section 3.8.)

There are two aspects to the Coalition's work in this area:

1. derivation of a meta-model which can be used to express the objects, their relationships, and attributes within a process definition and which can form the basis for a set of interchange formats to exchange this information between products

2. API calls (within the WAPI) between workflow systems or between a workflow system and process definition product, providing a common way to access workflow process definitions. Access may be read, read/write, or write only and may manipulate the set of standard objects defined within the meta-model or a product-specific set (for example, defined in a product type register).

A BASIC META-MODEL

The Coalition is developing a meta-model for the process definition, which identifies a basic set of object types appropriate to an initial level for the interchange of relatively simple process definitions. Further object types may be added, either by vendor specific extensions and/or by defining additional conformance levels with added functionality. See Figure 10.

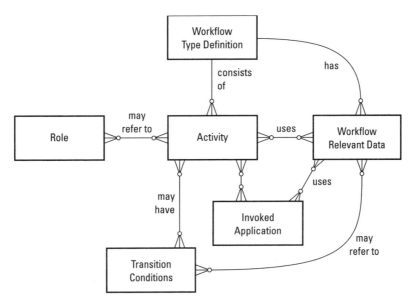

Figure 10
Basic process sefinition meta-model.

It is envisaged that particular attributes of the following types will be defined:

WORKFLOW TYPE DEFINITION

- Workflow process name
- Version number
- Process start and termination conditions
- Security, audit, or other control data

ACTIVITY

- Activity name
- Activity type (subflow, atomic flow, etc.)
- Pre- and post- activity conditions
- Other scheduling constraints

TRANSITION CONDITIONS

- Flow or Execution conditions

WORKFLOW RELEVANT DATA

- Data name and path
- Data types

ROLE

- Name and organisational entity

INVOKED APPLICATION

- Generic type or name
- Execution parameters
- Location or access path

In the case of distributed services, an allocation of activities to individual Workflow engines may also need to be made within the process definition, as an additional activity attribute. Process definition aspects affecting security and administration, for example, controls over privileged or supervisory activities within the process also require consideration in the longer term.

In defining interchange formats, it is assumed that a symbolic naming scheme would be supported which could be unambiguously mapped to real names and addresses in the run-time enactment service. This may be handled by dynamic address resolution mechanisms (for example, by the use of a directory service) or by other mechanisms external to the process definition. There are other industry groups working in related areas such as process modelling and CASE interchange tools; the proposed WFM Coalition approach in this area is to work with other groups to advance the definition of suitable interchange formats.

APIS TO ACCESS PROCESS DEFINITIONS

A set of API commands within WAPI is under development to support access to process definition data. It is expected that such specifications will cover a number of functions of the following general types. Commands are expected to be provided which operate on a list, or on individual objects or attributes.

SESSION ESTABLISHMENT

- connection/disconnection of sessions between participating systems

WORKFLOW DEFINITION OPERATIONS

- retrieval of lists of workflow process definition names from a repository or other source list
- selection/de-selection of a workflow process definition to provide a session handle for further object level operations
- read/write top level workflow process definition object

WORKFLOW DEFINITION OBJECT OPERATIONS

- creation, retrieval, & deletion of objects within a workflow definition
- retrieval, setting, and deletion of object attributes

3.5. Workflow Client Functions

3.5.1. WORKFLOW CLIENT APPLICATIONS

The worklist handler is the software entity which interacts with the end-user in those activities which involve human resources. The worklist handler may be supplied as part of a workflow management product or may be written by a user, for example, to provide a particular common house style for use with a number of different workflow applications utilising different vendor's products. In other cases, workflow may be integrated into a common desktop environment alongside other office services such as mail and work-in-progress folders to provide a unified task management system for the end-user. There is thus a need for a flexible mechanism of communication between a workflow enactment service and workflow client applications to support the construction of the many different operational systems which are expected to be encountered.

In the workflow model, interaction occurs between the client application and the workflow engine through a well defined interface embracing the concept of a worklist — the queue of work items assigned to a particular user (or, possibly, group of common users) by the workflow engine. At the simplest level the worklist is accessible to the workflow engine for the purposes of assigning work items and to the worklist handler for the purpose of retrieving work items for presentation to the user for processing. There are various possible product implementations of this worklist interaction (see section 2.4).

Activation of individual work items from the worklist (for example, launching application and linking workflow relevant data) may be under the control of the workflow client application or the end-user. A range of procedures is defined between the workflow client application and the workflow enactment service to enable new items to be added to the worklist, completed activities to be removed from the worklist, activities to be temporarily suspended, etc. These are described in section 3.5.2

Application invocation may also be handled from the worklist handler, either directly or under the control of the end-user. In general it is expected that the range of applications invoked from the worklist handler would be predominantly local to that environment, although it may place an unnecessary constraint on the generality of the model to assume that this will always be the case.

Part of the activity related data associated with the worklist is the necessary information to enable the worklist handler to invoke the appropriate applications(s). Where the application data is strongly typed, an association may be stored at the worklist handler and used for this purpose. In other cases an interchange of the full application name and address information may be necessary between the worklist handler and Workflow engine, in which case the workflow Client Application may also implement some functions from the invoked application interface (i/f 3) to obtain the necessary information.

A worklist may contain items relating to several different active instances of a single process and/or individual items from activations of several different processes. A worklist handler might potentially be interacting with several different Workflow engines and several different enactment services. (According to individual product implementation, separate physical worklists may be maintained for each process type, or the worklist handler may consolidate the various worklists items into a single representation to the end-user.) .

The interface between the client workflow application and Workflow engine must therefore be sufficiently flexible in terms of its use of:

- process and activity identifiers
- resource names and addresses
- data references and data structures
- alternative communications mechanisms

to contain these variations of implementation approach.

3.5.2. WORKFLOW CLIENT APPLICATION INTERFACE (INTERFACE 2)
The approach to meet the above requirement is to contain the variety behind a standard set of APIs (the WAPI), which may be used in a consistent manner for access from a workflow application to the Workflow engine and worklist, irrespective of the nature of actual product implementation.

The APIs and its parameters will be mapped onto several alternative communications mechanisms to fit the variety of workflow implementation models. (In the case of e-mail based communications, it is also possible, of course, for a worklist handler to directly access the incoming mailbox for incoming work items using any local mailbox access interface, rather than via specific WAPI calls. In this case the worklist handler application will take responsibility for filtering any nonworkflow e-mail items and handling them in an appropriate manner. Similarly commands or responses directed at the Workflow engine by the workflow application may be submitted directly to an outgoing mailbox handler. In this scenario a simple level of interoperability is achieved through the use of standardised mail interchange formats, rather than the full WAPI.)

The overall approach to the client application API is shown in Figure 11, following.

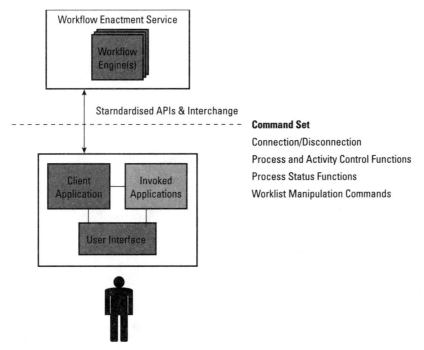

Figure 11
Client application Interface

The API specifications are published in a separate Coalition document; the following provides an overview of the intended APIs for client application use, grouped into various functional areas. Commands are provided for operations on individual or collective process or activity instances as well as worklist manipulation.

SESSION ESTABLISHMENT

■ connection/disconnection of sessions between participating systems

WORKFLOW DEFINITION OPERATIONS

■ retrieval/query functions (with optional selection criteria) on workflow process definition names or attributes

PROCESS CONTROL FUNCTIONS

- creation/starting/termination of an individual process instance
- suspension/resumption of an individual process instance
- forcing a state change within an individual process instance or activity instance
- assignment or query of an attribute (e.g. priority) of a process or activity instance

PROCESS STATUS FUNCTIONS

- Opening/closing a process or activity instances query, setting optional filter criteria
- Fetc.hing details of process instances or activity instances, filtered as specified
- Fetc.hing details of a specific (individual) process or activity instance

WORKLIST/WORKITEM HANDLING FUNCTIONS

- Opening/closing a worklist query, setting optional filter criteria
- Fetc.hing worklist items, filtered as specified
- Notification of selection/reassignment/completion of a (specific) workitem
- Assignment or query of a workitem attribute

PROCESS SUPERVISORY FUNCTIONS

(The following functions operate on all process or activity instances and are deemed to operate in the context of a supervisory privilege level, which may, or may not, be granted to a specific client application or user logged onto such application.)

- changing the operational status of a workflow process definition and/or its extant process instances
- changing the state of all process or activity instances of a specified type
- assigning attribute(s) to all process or activity instances of a specified type
- termination of all process instances

DATA HANDLING FUNCTIONS

- retrieval/return of workflow relevant or application data

ADMINISTRATION FUNCTIONS

Support for additional administration functions across the WAPI may be appropriate for certain client applications. A subset of the operations discussed in 3.8.2 may be included in a future conformance level.

APPLICATION INVOCATION

The functions outlined above provide a base level of functionality to support application invocation by the worklist handler function (e.g. by providing access to process/activity/workitem attributes and workflow relevant data). Some of the proposed commands for the application invocation function (section 3.6.2) may also be relevant to the client application environment.

It is possible that some product implementations may wish to support a subset of the full WAPI; further consideration will be given to identifying conformance levels to cater for the different interoperability requirements arising from the range of workflow products available in the market.

3.6. Invoked Application Functions

3.6.1. INVOKED APPLICATIONS

It may be assumed that any particular WFM implementation will not have sufficient logic to understand how to invoke all potential applications which might exist in an heterogeneous product environment. This would require the logic to cope with invocation across (potentially) all platform and network environments, together with a means of transferring application- or workflow-relevant data in a common format and encoding (or transforming it to the individual application environments).

However there are many workflow systems which deal with a more restrictive range of applications, particularly those where the data is strongly typed and may be directly associated (for example, via a directory) with a particular application tool such as a word processor or spreadsheet. In other cases invocation of an operation by a particular application may be accomplished through a standard interchange mechanism such as the OSI TP protocol or X.400. Some implementations use the concept of a "Application Agent" to contain this variety of method invocation behind a standard interface into the workflow enactment service. There is also the possibility of developing "workflow enabled" application tools which use a standard set of APIs to communicate with the workflow enactment service — to accept application data, signal, and respond to activity events, etc. Such APIs may be used directly by an application tool or by a application agent process acting as a front end for interaction with heritage or other applications written without a specific knowledge of workflow.

Some of the possible types of interface for application invocation are identified in the following Table 1.

Further discussion will be required on the full range of possible options for application invocation. The initial work of the Coalition is likely to focus on developing a catalogue of interface types, together with a set of APIs for use in future workflow specific applications.

3.6.2. INVOKED APPLICATIONS INTERFACE (INTERFACE 3)

Figure 12 shows the scope of this interface, which is intended to be applicable to application agents and (longer term) applications which have been designed to be "workflow enabled" (i.e. to interact directly with a workflow engine).

TABLE 1: APPLICATION INVOCATION INTERFACES

INTERFACE TYPE	WORKFLOW RELEVANT DATA ACCESS	STANDARDISATION CANDIDATE
Local Process Call	Local File	No
Shell Script	Local File	POSIX environments?
ORB Call (e.g. object linking and launch service)	Via reference (call parameters)	Yes
Remote Execution Call	Via reference (call parameters)	Yes
Message Passing (e.g. X.400)	Embedded or via reference	Yes
Transaction (e.g. OSI-TP)	Embedded or via reference	Yes

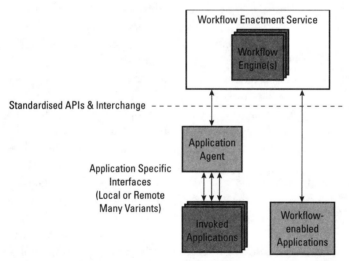

Figure 12
Invoked application interface.

In the simple case, application invocation is handled locally to a workflow engine, using information within the process definition to identify the nature of the activity, the type of application to be invoked, and any data requirements. The invoked application may be local to the workflow engine, co-resident on the same platform, or located on a separate, network-accessible platform; the process definition contains sufficient application type and addressing information (specific to the needs of the workflow engine) to invoke the application. In this case the conventions for application naming and addressing are local between the process definition and the workflow engine.

The detailed semantics and syntax of an API set for application invocation are for further study and will be documented as part of the Coalition specification set. Operation is envisaged over a variety of underlying interfaces, including a selection from the above table, some of which may operate synchronously and others asynchronously. The operation of the API is assumed at this stage to be potentially either single- or multi-threaded (in the latter case using an activity id handle for thread discrimination). The following provides an outline of a possible command set applicable to application invocation functions.

SESSION ESTABLISHMENT

- connection/disconnection of application (or application agent) session

ACTIVITY MANAGEMENT FUNCTIONS
(workflow engine to application)

- Start activity (workflow engine to application)
- Suspend/Resume/Abort activity (where an asynchronous application interface is available)

(application to workflow engine)

- Activity complete notification
- Signal event (e.g. synchronisation)
- Query activity attributes

DATA HANDLING FUNCTIONS

- Give workflow relevant data (pre-activity to application, post activity from application)
- Give application data or data address

More complex scenarios, involving interworking between heterogeneous Workflow engines, may require application invocation information to be transferred between Workflow engines, either as part of the run-time interchange or by importing (parts) of the process definition after the process development phase. This is considered under section 3.7 (workflow interoperability).

3.7. Workflow Interoperability

3.7.1. HETEROGENEOUS WORKFLOW ENACTMNENT SERVICES
A key objective of the Coalition is to define standards that will allow workflow systems produced by different vendors to pass work items seamlessly between one another.

Workflow products are diverse in nature ranging from those used for more ad-hoc routing of tasks or data to those aimed at highly regularised production processes. In its drive for interoperability standards, the Coalition is determined not to force workflow product vendors to choose between providing a strong product focused on the needs of its customers and giving up those strengths just to provide interoperability.

The work of the Coalition has therefore focussed on developing a variety of interoperability scenarios which can operate at a number of levels from simple task passing through to full workflow application interoperability with complete interchange of process definition, workflow relevant data, and a common look and feel. In this area it is expected that relatively simple interoperability scenarios will be supported initially, with the more complex situations requiring further work on interoperability definitions.

Although it is possible to consider the development of very complex interoperability scenarios in which a number of different vendor engines cooperate to deliver a single enactment service, this scenario is unlikely to be realised in the near future as it requires that all engines can interpret a common process definition and share a common set of workflow control data, in effect maintaining a shared view of process states across the heterogeneous workflow control engines. A more realistic target in the near term is the ability to transfer parts of a process for run-time support on a different enactment service.

Four possible interoperability models has been identified, covering various (increasing) levels of capability. The following sections describes these potential interoperability models; the illustrations use squares to indicate tasks or activities, with different shading to denote tasks co-ordinated by individual workflow enactment services.

3.7.2. SCENARIO I — CONNECTED DISCRETE (CHAINED)

This model allows a connection point within process A to connect to another point within process B. Although the illustration shows these connection points at the terminus and starting points of the processes, this is done for illustration purposes only. It is presumed that the connection points can be anywhere within the processes that makes sense for the meat-process created by the connection of the two. See Figure 13.

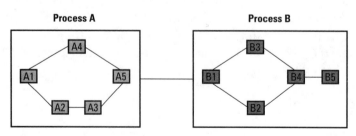

Figure 13
Chained services model.

This model supports the transfer of a single item of work (a process instance or activity) between the two workflow environments, which then operates independently in the second environment with no further synchronisation. In implementation terms it may be realised via a gateway application function, handling data format conversion, process and activity name mapping, etc., or may be subsumed into one of the workflow services, for example, when a standard API call is used between the two services.

3.7.3. SCENARIO 2 — HIERARCHICAL (NESTED SUBPROCESSES)

This allows a process executed in a particular workflow domain to be completely encapsulated as a single task within a (superior) process executed in a different workflow domain. A hierarchic relationship exists between the superior process and the encapsulated process, which in effect forms a sub-process of the superior. The hierarchic relationship may be continued across several levels, forming a set of nested subprocesses. Recursion within this scenario may, or may not, be permitted by individual product implementations. See Figure 14.

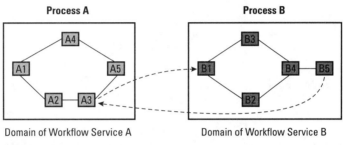

Figure 14
Nested subprocesses model.

In the diagram, Workflow Service A has an activity defined (A3) which is enacted as a complete process (B) on Workflow Service B, with control returned to Service A on completion. As in scenario 1 earlier, transfer of activity control may be via an applications gateway function or by direct API calls between the two workflow services. The diagram illustrates the simple case with a single entry and exit point in Process B, although activity navigation rules within B may permit other activity flow scenarios, for example, process completion conditions enabling the process to be completed prior to activity B5 and control returned to workflow domain A.

3.7.4. SCENARIO 3 — CONNECTED INDISCRETE (PEER-TO-PEER)

This model allows a fully mixed environment; the diagram indicates a composite process C, which includes activities which may be executed across multiple workflow services, forming a shared domain. Activities C1, C2, and C5 could be co-ordinated by server A (or even several homogenous servers within a common domain) and activities C3, C4, and C6 co-ordinated by server B.

In this scenario, the process would progress transparently from task to task, without any specific actions by users or administrators, with interactions between the individual workflow engines taking place as necessary. See Figure 15.

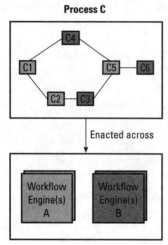

Figure 15
Peer-peer model.

This scenario requires that both workflow services support common API sets for communication and that both can interpret a common process definition, either imported to both environments from a common build process or exported between services during the run-time phase. Workflow-relevant and application data may also need to be passed between the various heterogeneous engines.

Whilst simply illustrated as an interworking scenario, there are various complexities within the peer-peer model which will require further study. As shown each particular activity is associated with a specific workflow domain, for example, predefined within the process definition. Further complexities arise where a specific activity may be executed on either of two independent workflow services or where a particular process instance can be created or terminated independently by either service. Systems administration, security, and recovery across co-operating workflow services will also need to be addressed. In the extreme, the two different workflow enactment services may be required to share much of the process state data normally maintained internally to each, in effect forming a single heterogeneous service. The Coalition intends to define a number of conformance levels, allowing earlier specifications to cope with simpler scenarios and additional functions to cope with more complex scenarios to be added in the future.

3.7.5. SCENARIO 4 — PARALLEL SYNCHRONISED

This model allows two processes to operate essentially independently, possibly across separate enactment services, but requires that synchronisation points exist between the two processes. Synchronisation requires that once the processes each reach a predefined point within their respective execution sequences, a common event is generated. This type of mechanism may be used to facilitate functions such as process scheduling across parallel execution threads, checkpointing of recovery data, or the transfer of workflow-relevant data between different process instances.

In the diagram following, Figure 16, synchronisation is shown between activity A3 within process A, and activity B4 within process B.

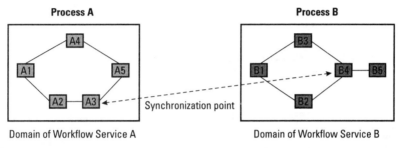

Figure 16
Parallel synchronised model.

Matching pairs of work can thus be synchronised at specific points in each process. This requires an event co-ordination and tracking mechanism, in addition to both services being able to recognise tasks from the two process definitions. It is included for completeness but is recognised as lying beyond the scope of the Coalition's current specification activity.

3.7.6. WAPI INTEROPERABILITY FUNCTIONS (INTERFACE 4)

The general nature of the information and control flows between heterogeneous workflow systems is shown in Figure 17.

There are two major aspects to the necessary interoperability:

- the extent to which common interpretation of the process definition (or a subset) is necessary and can be achieved

- run-time support for the interchange of various types of control information and to transfer workflow-relevant and/or application data between the different enactment services

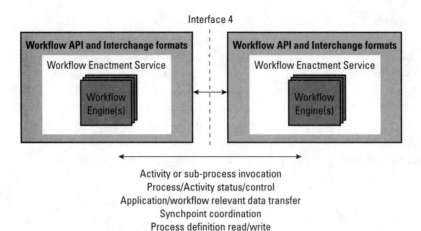

Figure 17
Workflow interoperability interface.

USE OF PROCESS DEFINITIONS ACROSS MULTIPLE DOMAINS

Where both enactment services can interpret a common process definition, for example, generated from a common build tool, this enables both environments to share a single view of the process definition objects and their attributes. This would include activity, application, organisation and role names, navigation conditions, etc. This potentially enables individual workflow engines to transfer execution of activities or sub-processes to heterogeneous workflow engines within the context of a common naming and object model. This approach is particularly applicable to interoperability scenario 3, where several systems are co-operating at peer level, although it can also be employed in simpler scenarios.

Where this shared view of a process definition is not feasible, the alternative approach of "exporting" details of a process definition subset as part of the runtime interchange may be possible. The process definition interchange APIs provide a means of requesting object and attribute data from a particular workflow service, thus enabling a workflow engine to obtain process definition data relevant to the execution of an individual activity or sub-process assigned to it in a co-operative enactment environment.

Where process definition interchange by either of the above approaches is infeasible, interoperability is constrained to a gateway approach, in which (typically a subset of) object names and attributes are mapped between the two environments via an application interworking gateway. In this simplest case, the two separate enactment services use their own process definition formats, with any mapping between the two handled within the gateway. This approach effectively constrains interworking to the simpler scenarios 1 and 2 or relatively trivial examples of scenario 4.

RUNTIME CONTROL INTERACTIONS

At run time, the WAPI calls are used to transfer control between workflow services to enact sub-processes or individual activities on a specific service. Where both services support a common level of WAPI calls and a common view of the process definition objects (including naming conventions and any workflow relevant or applications data), this will be done directly between Workflow engines — although this will require agreement on common protocol support for WAPI primitives.

Where this is not the case, the WAPI calls can be used to construct a gateway function providing interworking between the two workflow services by mapping the different object and data views between the two environments and (where necessary) supporting different protocol environments into each workflow service. This is illustrated in the following diagram, Figure 18.

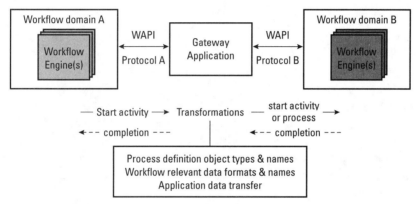

Figure 18
Gateway operation using WAPI.

The diagram illustrates the main principles of gateway operation; depending upon the particular interworking scenario an individual activity from one domain (A) may be mapped to a single activity or a new process/sub-process in the second domain (B).

A large number of WAPI commands are (ultimately) likely to be exploited to support interoperability either by direct call between the two workflow services or via a gateway function. Many of the WAPI commands discussed earlier (sections 3.4.2, 3.5.2 & 3.6.2) are also potentially applicable in workflow interoperability interactions:

- Session establishment
- Operations on workflow definitions and their objects
- Process control and status functions
- Activity management functions
- Data handling operations

A degree of common administration between multiple workflow domains will also be necessary using functions developed for interface 5 (section 3.8.2).

Once activities are being enacted on a separate (subordinate) service, interactions from workflow client applications with the original service (for example, query status of activity/process instance, or suspend/resume/terminate process instance) may need "referral" to the subordinate service. Some operations may thus need to be chained across several workflow engines (for example, where different activities within an active process instance are distributed across several machines). Some form of event notification service is also likely to be required to inform the initiating service of activity status changes and completion of activities and/or sub-processes. It is envisaged that a number of additional WAPI operations will be developed, over time, to support these and other functions arising from more complex interworking scenarios.

The range of possible interactions is relatively extensive and complex in terms of state transitions (including, for example, aspects such as failure containment and recovery); further study will be required to develop the necessary conformance levels which could form a practical basis for interoperability between different products.

3.8. Systems Administration

3.8.1. ADMINISTRATION AND MONITORING TOOLS

The final area of proposed specification is a common interface standard for administration and monitoring functions which will allow one vendor's management application to work with another's engine(s). This will provide a common interface which enables several workflow services to share a range of common administration and system monitoring functions.

Although process status commands are defined within the interfaces already described, there is a recognised requirement in some industries for a function to apply overall status monitoring and extract metrics information. The proposed interface is intended to allow a complete view of the status of work flowing through the organisation, regardless of which system it is in; it is also intended to present a comprehensive function set for administration purposes, including specific considerations of security, control, and authorisation.

The interface will include specific commands within the WAPI set to manipulate designated administration and monitoring functions. In addition, further review is intended to ascertain to what extent this interface can exploit existing protocol mechanisms such as CMIP and SNMP to set and retrieve management status and statistical information defined in an open MIB (Management Information Base).

3.8.2. ADMINISTRATION AND MONITORING INTERFACE (INTERFACE 5)

The interface as illustrated shows an independent management application interacting with different workflow domains, although alternative implementation scenarios are also feasible; for example, the management application may be an integral part of one enactment service, although capable of managing various functions across additional (heterogeneous) workflow domains. See Figure 19.

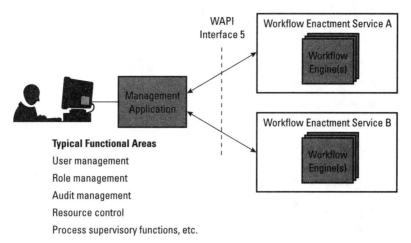

Figure 19
Systems administration & monitoring interface.

It is also feasible for the management application to take on other management functions, beyond those shown. For example, it may also manage workflow process definitions, acting as a repository and distributing process definitions to the various workflow domains via operations within interface 1.

The detail of this interface is for further study, but it is envisaged to include the following types of operation (some of which are common to other interface areas):

USER MANAGEMENT OPERATIONS

- establishment/deletion/suspension/amendment of privileges of users or workgroups

ROLE MANAGEMENT OPERATIONS

- define/delete/amend role: participant relationships
- set or unset role attributes

AUDIT MANAGEMENT OPERATIONS

- query/print/start new/delete audit trail or event log, etc.

RESOURCE CONTROL OPERATIONS

- set/unset/modify process or activity concurrency levels
- interrogate resource control data (counts, thresholds, usage parameters, etc.)

PROCESS SUPERVISORY FUNCTIONS

- changing the operational status of a workflow process definition and/or its extant process instances
- enabling or disabling particular versions of a process definition
- changing the state of all process or activity instances of a specified type
- assigning attribute(s) to all process or activity instances of a specified type
- termination of all process instances

PROCESS STATUS FUNCTIONS

- Opening/closing a process or activity instances query, setting optional filter criteria
- Fetc.hing details of process instances or activity instances, filtered as specified
- Fetc.hing details of a specific (individual) process or activity instance

4. WAPI Structure, Protocols, and Conformance

4.1 WAPI — Functional Overview of APIs

The WAPI is envisaged as a common set of API calls and related interchange formats which may be grouped together as required to support each of the five functional interface areas. Operations already identified across these 5 interface areas (and discussed in section 3) include those in the following groups:

API CALLS

- Session establishment
- Operations on workflow definitions and their objects
- Process control functions
- Process control supervisory functions
- Process status functions
- Activity management functions
- Data handling operations
- Worklist/Workitem Handling Functions
- User Management operations
- Role Management operations
- Audit Management operations
- Resource Control operations

DATA INTERCHANGE FUNCTIONS

Interchange formats are expected to be defined to cover:

- Process definition transfer
- Workflow-relevant data transfer

API CALL STRUCTURE AND NAMING

API calls will be defined initially in terms of their logical operations, the datatypes on which they may operate (i.e. as call parameters), and the supporting data structures referenced from such parameters. Language bindings are expected to be developed, initially for the C language and subsequently for other important development environments (both C++ and IDL are candidates for further study). Naming conventions are being specified for the call functions themselves, plus the supporting datatype definitions, parameter types and data structures (see document reference WFMC_TC00-1013 for API naming convention information).

4.2 WAPI Protocol Support

The WAPI calls will be able to function in two types of interconnection scenario:

1. Where an exposed WAPI interface is provided as a boundary function to a workflow enactment service (e.g. as vendor stub routines embedded in a client application or application agent), vendor specific mappings may be used to encode the call and associated parameters to the particular vendor protocol environment used to communicate with the workflow engines.

2. Where direct interworking between different products is provided (e.g. interoperability between different workflow engines), open (common) protocol support will be necessary. This will require a standardised mapping from WAPI calls onto one or, more likely, several interworking protocols.

The expected areas of standardisation relating to these two scenarios are as illustrated in the following diagram, Figure 20.

The details of protocol usage within WAPI are for further study, but it is expected that WAPI mappings will be developed onto important communications environments, i.e. those widely used by workflow products available in the market. Initial support for client application integration and workflow interoperability via an application gateway can be achieved using approach 1 (with vendor specific protocols); however, this approach has some inherent limitations, and the development of appropriate protocol usage specifications is a clear requirement in the medium term.

Implementations would be expected to identify the particular communications environment(s) which are supported, along with the specific API command set options being implemented for the particular interchange function. This subject will be further considered as conformance rules are developed (see following section).

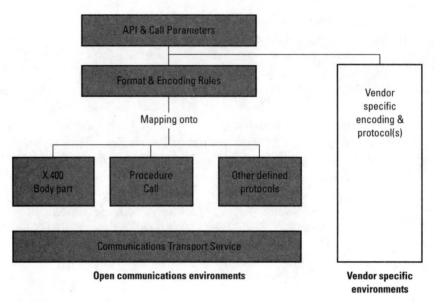

Figure 20
WAPI protocol support.

4.3. Conformance Principles

4.3.1. WHAT DOES CONFORMANCE MEAN?

Conformance will be defined against each particular functional area corresponding to one of the 5 interfaces, so that product vendors can offer an exposed interface for conformant interworking in one or more areas but do not have to implement all 5 functions to achieve interoperability.

For each interface it is expected that conformance will be classified at several levels, providing a minimum level of interoperability at level 1, with the option for more complex products to achieve conformance against a higher level of functionality for richer interworking, where appropriate. In the case of interface 4 functions, this will be particularly essential due to the potential complexities of workflow service interoperability. Products which achieve conformance at a particular level are expected to interwork with products at any conformance level below or equal to their own.

Conformance will need to be separately considered in terms of API support and protocol usage. It is likely that some form of matrix will need to be constructed indicating the particular API functions supported at a specific level and the protocol environments supported for interworking with other products.

It is possible that some form of interoperability testing or certification may be feasible, but this is an area requiring further investigation by the Coalition.

4.4. Interoperability Classifications and Conformance Levels

Conformance levels will be developed to assist in the classification of interoperable products.

The potential scope of workflow interoperability and application integration is very wide, and to develop a full range of APIs and interchange formats to cater for all potential interoperability scenarios is a major task. For these reasons it is considered essential that a set of interoperability scenarios is developed, ranging from the simple to the complex, so that interfaces for the simpler scenarios can be developed earlier. This will enable some of the benefits of interoperable systems to be realised in the nearer term, whilst further development work is done to develop the more complex interfaces. Various conformance levels can be defined to group the particular APIs, interchange formats, and protocol support necessary to meet specific interoperability scenarios. The remainder of this section documents a simple classification as a basis for further discussion in this area.

4.4.1. DEFINITION TOOL — WORKFLOW ENACTMENT SOFTWARE

Purpose — to allow separate choice of products for development tools (modelling, definition, etc.) and run-time workflow service delivery or to enable storage and retrieval of process definitions from a repository.

Interoperability — based on support for the Process Definition Import/Export Interface. The process definition is exported by the definition tool and imported by the workflow enactment software.

Conformance levels — based on a basic (minimum) set of process definition objects with optional extensions to cater for more sophisticated process definitions. File interchange formats and API call details to be discussed.

4.4.2. CLIENT APPLICATION INTEROPERATING WITH WORKFLOW ENACTMENT SERVICE(S)

Purpose

(1) to allow for the construction of a common worklist handler to provide worklist management for one or more workflow systems, for example, to provide a common house style for task management dialogue with the user, independently of the workflow management software in use. This enables the delivery of several different workflow services to be combined at the desktop, giving the appearance to the end user of a single service.

(2) to support simple interaction between the two workflow services controlled from the desktop environment (for example, workflow-relevant data interchange between two processes instantiated on different workflow services, or an activity within one process enactment causing the start of a new process on the second service — the activity gateway approach)

Interoperability — based on support for the WAPI calls and interchange formats from interface 2

Conformance levels — to support varying degrees of sophistication at the client application; details to be discussed; protocol usage options to be specified

4.4.3. APPLICATION AND TOOL INTEGRATION
Purpose

(1) to allow applications or tools to be workflow-enabled in a standardised manner (for example, to interact with a workflow engine via activity control functions or to accept/return case data, etc.)

(2) to allow the development of standardised application agents to interface non-workflow-enabled applications in a similar manner

Interoperability — based on support for the subset of WAPI calls to handle application invocation and access to workflow relevant data

Conformance levels — to be discussed, possibly classified by application type

4.4.4. WORKFLOW SERVICE INTEROPERABILITY
Purpose

(1) to support the development of process automation applications utilising different workflow enactment software products

(2) to enable existing (heterogeneous) workflow applications to exchange application or workflow relevant data, which is common to both processes, at an appropriate point within the processes

Interoperability — based on support for the WAPI calls and interchange formats using either the activity gateway or direct interfaces. The gateway model is of more immediate applicability; direct interoperability requires agreement on common process definition interchange and compatible protocol support.

Conformance levels and protocol support — to be discussed, reflecting the various interoperability scenarios described in section 3.7

4.4.5. COMMON WORKFLOW ADMINISTRATION AND MANAGEMENT
Purpose — to support common management, administration, and audit functions, across several workflow management products

Interoperability — based on support for WAPI calls from interface 5 to enable administration and monitoring functions to be supported by a common management application

Conformance levels and protocol usage — to be defined

Appendix — Glossary of Terms and Abbreviations

(Please refer to the WfMC Glossary Document for full terminology usage, including synonyms.)

Process Activity. A logical step or description of a piece of work that contributes toward the achievement of a process. A process activity may include a manual activity and/or an automated workflow activity.

Workflow Activity. The computer automation of a logical step that contributes toward the completion of a workflow .

Manual Activity. The manual steps that contribute toward the completion of a process.

Process Activity Instance. An instance of a Process Activity that is defined as part of a process instance. Such an instance may include a manual activity instance and/or a workflow activity instance

Workflow Activity Instance. An instance of a workflow activity that is defined as part of a workflow instance.

AND-Join. When two or more parallel executing activities converge into a single common thread of control.

AND-Split. When a single thread of control splits into two or more parallel activities.

Workflow Application. A software program(s) that will either completely or partially support the processing of a work item in order to accomplish the objective of a workflow activity instance.

Application Data. Data that is application specific and not accessible by the workflow management system.

Audit Trail. A historical record of the state transitions of a workflow instance from start to completion or termination

Business Process. A kind of process in the domain of business organisational structure and policy for the purpose of achieving business objectives.

BPR — Business Process Re-engineering. The process of (re-)assessment, analysis, modelling, definition, and subsequent operational implementation of the core business processes of an organisation, or other business entity.

Case Data. See Workflow Relevant Data.

CMIP. Common Management Information Protocol — an ISO standard (9596) for transferring mangement information across a network.

Iteration. A workflow activity cycle involving the repetitive execution of workflow activity(s) until a condition is met.

OR-Join. When two or more activity(s) workflow branches re-converge into a single thread of control without any synchronisation.

OR-Split. When a single thread of control makes a decision upon which branch to take when encountered with multiple workflow branches.

Parallel Routing. A segment of a workflow instance where workflow activity instances are executing in parallel and there are multiple threads of control.

Process. A co-ordinated (parallel and/or serial) set of process activity(s) that are connected in order to achieve a common goal. Such activities may consist of manual activity(s) and/or workflow activity(s).

Process Definition. The computerised representation of a process that includes the manual definition and workflow definition.

Workflow Definition. That part of the process definition that includes the automated aspects only versus the manual.

Manual Definition. That part of the process definition that includes the manual aspects only versus the automated (workflow).

Process Instance. Represents an instance of a process definition which includes the manual and the automated (workflow) aspects.

Workflow Instance. Represents an instance of a workflow definition which includes the automated aspects of a process instance only.

Manual Instance. Represents an instance of a Manual definition which includes all manual aspects of a process instance.

Process Definition Mode. The time period when manual and/or automated (workflow) descriptions of a process are defined and/or modified electronically.

Process Execution. The duration in time when manual and workflow execution takes place in support of a process.

Manual Execution. The duration in time when a human participant executes the manual definition of a process definition.

Workflow Execution. The duration in time when a workflow instance is created and managed by a Workflow Management System based on a workflow definition.

Workflow Relevant Data. Data that is used by a Workflow Management System to determine the state transition of a workflow instance. It may be typed (Engine may understand) or untyped (Engine will not understand).

Organisational Role. A collection of participants based on a set of attributes, qualifications, and/or skills.

Process Role. A mechanism that associates participants to a collection of workflow activity(s)

Sequential Routing. A segment of a process instance where activity's are executed in sequence.

SNMP. Systems Network Management Protocol — an Internet standard for network management

Sub-Process Definition. A process that is enacted or called from another process or sub-process that includes the manual and automated (workflow) parts of the process.

Tool. A tool is a workflow application that is invoked by the workflow management system.

Transition Condition. Criteria for moving, or state transitioning, from the current activity to the next activity(s) in a process instance, be it manual or automated (workflow).

WAPI. The application programming interface for workflow applications and tools in order to be able to interface to the Workflow Enactment System. WAPI is an acronym for **W**orkflow **A**pplication **P**rogramming **I**nterface.

WFM - Workflow Management. See Workflow Management System.

Workflow. The computerised facilitation or automation of a process, in whole or part.

Workflow Monitoring. The ability to track workflow events during workflow execution.

Workflow Engine. A software service or "engine" that provides the run-time execution environment for a workflow instance (individually, or in conjunction with other workflow engines).

Workflow Interoperability. The ability for two or more Workflow Engines to communicate and work together to co-ordinate work.

Workflow Participant. A resource which performs partially, or in full, the work represented by a workflow activity instance.

Workflow Management System. A system that completely defines, manages, and executes workflows through the execution of software whose order of execution is driven by a computer representation of the workflow logic. Such a system maps to the Workflow Coalition's reference model.

Workflow Enactment Service. A software service that may consist of one or more workflow engines in order to create, manage, and execute workflow instances. Applications may interface to this service via the workflow application programming interface (WAPI).

Workflow Control Data. Data that is managed by the Workflow Management System and/or a Workflow Engine.

Work Item. Representation of work to be processed in the context of an activity in a workflow instance.

Work Item Pool. Represents all work items.

Worklist. A list of work items.

Worklist Handler. Software component that manages and formulates a request to the workflow enactment service in order to obtain a list of work items.

The following materials are referenced in the text.

Introduction

1. Tom Peters, *Liberation Management: Necessary Disorganization for the Nanosecond Nineties* (Alfred A. Knopf, New York, 1992), 18.

2. Don Tapscott and Art Caston, *Paradigm Shift: The New Promise of Information Technology* (McGraw Hill, New York, 1993), xiii.

Chapter 1

1. Michael Hammer and James Champy, *Reengineering the Corporation: A Manifesto for Business Revolution* (HarperBusiness, New York, 1993).

2. D. Quinn Mills, *Rebirth of the Corporation* (John Wiley & Sons, 1991).

3. Rosabeth Moss Kanter, *When Giants Learn to Dance: Managing the Challenges of Strategy, Management, and Careers in the 1990s* (Simon and Schuster, New York, 1989).

4. Tapscott and Caston, *Paradigm Shift*.

5. Charles Savage, *Fifth Generation Management* (Digital Press, Burlington, Massachusetts, 1990).

6. Peters, *Liberation Management*.

7. Peter Drucker, "The Coming of the New Organization," *Harvard Business Review* (January-February 1988).

8. Thomas M. Koulopoulos, *The Workflow Imperative: Building Real-World Business Solutions* (Van Nostrand Reinhold, New York, 1995).

9. Peter G.W. Keen, *Shaping the Future: Business Design through Information Technology* (Harvard Business School Press, Cambridge, Massachusetts, 1991).

10. Michael Porter, *Competitive Advantage: Creating and Sustaining Superior Performance* (Free Press, New York, 1985).

11. William H. Davidow and Michael S. Malone, *The Virtual Corporation: Structuring and Revitalizing the Corporation for the 21st Century; Lessons from the World's Most Advanced Companies* (HarperCollins, New York, 1992).

12. Hammer and Champy, *Reengineering the Corporation*, 118.

13. Paul A. Strassmann, *Measuring Business Value of Information Technologies* (ICIT Press, Washington, 1988), 29-30.

14. Peter G.W. Keen, *Competing in Time* (Ballinger, Cambridge, Massachusetts, 1988), 3.

15. Peters, *Liberation Management*, 709.

16. William H. Davidow and Bro Uttal, *Total Customer Service: The Ultimate Weapon* (Harper & Row, New York, 1989), 196.

Chapter 2

1. International Data Corporation/Avante, *Work Management '94* (1994), vol. 1, no. 3.

2. Tapscott and Caston, 6.

3. Keen, *Competing in Time*, 88-89.

4. Davidow and Malone, 66.

5. Strassmann, 25-26.

6. N. Dean Meyer and Mary E. Boone, *The Information Edge* (McGraw-Hill, New York, 1987), 9.

7. Meyer and Boone, 9.

8. Koulopoulos, 4.

Chapter 3

1. Raymond L. Manganelli and Mark M. Klein, *The Reengineering Handbook: A Step-by-Step Guide to Business Transformation* (Amacom, New York, 1994), 8.

2. James G. Kobielus, *The Rapport Messaging Review* (Rapport Communication, Middletown OH, vol. 2, no. 1, October/November 1994), 6.

3. Jan Carlzon, *Moments of Truth* (Cambridgen, Massachusetts, Ballinger, 1987).

Chapter 5

1. Thomas M. Koulopoulos, *The Workflow Imperative*, 154.

Chapter 6

1. David Vaskevitch, *Client/Server Strategies: A Survival Guide for Corporate Reengineers* (IDG Books, San Mateo, California, 1993), 231-274.

2. Veda Catherine Storey, *View Creation: An Expert System for Database Design* (ICIT Press, Washington, DC, 1988) 6-7.

Chapter 11

1. Thomas Koulopoulos, *The Workflow Imperative*, 47.

2. David Coleman, *Grouptalk: Newsletter of Workgroup Computing*, "Groupware Tools for Business Process Reengineering," (Issue 21, June 1995, Collaborative Strategies, San Francisco, California), 1, 5.

Chapter 14

1. Rosemary Cafasso, "Kansas Governor's Office Puts Document Tracking On-Line," *Network World* (Framingham, Massachusetts, March 28, 1994).

2. Roger Sullivan, "Physical Plant Management Adopts Imaging and Workflow," *Imaging World* (February 1994).

3. Ronni T. Marshak, "Producing TV Guide: Using Workflow to Manage the Electronic Publication of 120 Regional Editions," *Workgroup Computing Report* (Patricia Seybold Group, Boston, July 1996), 1-7.

Chapter 16

1. Thomas M. Koulopoulos, *The Workflow Imperative*, 40-41.

GLOSSARY

Workflow Lingo Laid Bare

ActiveX: Object-oriented, multiplatform, multimedia application development tools for Microsoft's OLE/COM environment and the World Wide Web; formerly known as *OLE Controls (OCX)*.

Activity: A unit of work performed by a single workflow participant that has defined initiation and termination conditions. Upon completion of the activity, the resultant work product will generally be routed to other participants.

Address-driven modeling: Modeling a process as a routing path between predefined users, positions, or groups in the organization structure.

American National Standards Institute (ANSI): A nonprofit organization responsible for establishing U.S. standards in telecommunications, data-processing, and other industries.

American Standard Code for Information Interchange (ASCII): The standard coding method used to convert letters, numbers, punctuation, special characters, and hardware control codes into digital form.

ANSI: Acronym for *American National Standards Institute*.

API: Acronym for *application programming interface*.

Application programming interface (API): An external function accessed by programs through a well-defined programming statement.

Archiving: Transferring document files from on-line volumes to off-line media.

Ask: Synonymous with *activity*.

Authentication: Verification of a user's identity to a computer or network system.

Autolaunching: The ability to select a document by name or icon and thereby open that document and the application within which the document was created.

Biometric: Security technology that authenticates users based on some indelible and inimitable bodily feature or behavioral characteristic, such as fingerprints, retina scans, or voice prints.

Bitmap: An array of pixels (black and white or color dots), which together form characters or graphics on-screen.

Boolean searches: Searches that specify combinations or exclusions keywords, using such operators as AND, NOT, or OR.

Browser: Client software that facilitates on-line user access, viewing, and navigation of the World Wide Web.

Business process: A set of interdependent business activities.

Business process reengineering (BPR): The activity of reexamining, analyzing, modeling, simulating, and modifying business processes within a workgroup or organization.

CA: Acronym for *certification authority*.

Case: A single run of a workflow process.

Case management system: Synonymous with *production workflow system*.

Certification authority (CA): Organization or agency that publishes authenticated certificates binding user identifiers to public keys.

Chained workflow interoperability: Transfer of work items from one enactment service to another with control of the process being transferred entirely to the latter service.

Client: A software module or program that requests services from a separate module or program, which is referred to as a *server*.

Client/server: The partitioning of applications into separate software modules capable of operating on separate computers connected over a network.

CMC: Acronym for *Common Messaging Calls*.

Collaborative media: The work product and all raw and semifinished materials — including information and communications inputs — used to give products shape, substance, and coherence; includes information base, messaging, and conferencing media.

Collaborative platform: The geographic, physical, and technological environment in which work is performed, including infrastructure such as network access terminals, operating environments, and communications links.

Collaborative structure: The organizational apparatus and controls used to define, coordinate, and track workflows; includes chain of command, policies, operating procedures, project plans, schedules, budgets, standard practices, and automated information systems; also includes workflow routes, roles, and rules.

Common Messaging Calls (CMC): Master set of APIs that can be used by desktop applications to connect to MAPI, VIM, SMTP, MHS, or X.400 mail systems.

Common Object Request Broker Architecture (CORBA): Object management standard developed by the Object Management Group, an industry consortium.

Communications gateway: Hardware, software, or a combination of both that encapsulates, converts, or translates commands, messages, and information between dissimilar application environments to enable some basic level of service interoperability.

Component Object Model (COM): Microsoft's Windows-based object-management specification incorporating Object Linking and Embedding (OLE).

Compound document: Document that combines text, scanned images, bitmapped graphics, digitized voice, binary program files, and other electronic objects while preserving the integrity of the component documents.

Compression: The removal of redundant bits or information in a signal to make more efficient use of transmission or storage facilities.

Computer-aided software engineering: Application development tools that support development of database applications by enabling systems analysts to depict pertinent organizational interrelationships graphically.

Computer Graphics Metafile (CGM): An American National Standards Institute (ANSI) standard file format for exchanging graphical product depictions.

Computer output to laser disk (COLD): Hardware and software solutions that support storage, archival, and printing of computer data and files to laser disc.

Concurrency management: Synonymous with *version control.*

Concurrent route: A route in which activities share common predecessor and successor tasks and must end at the same time.

Conditional route: A route in which alternate paths can be taken, depending on the character of a triggering event.

Conferencing media: Network systems or services that support real-time communications among dispersed participants on a point-to-point or multipoint basis; includes plain old telephone service (POTS), audio conferencing, video conferencing, computer chat, and computer screen sharing.

Contextual search: The ability to locate a stored document by searching for text found in that document as opposed to searching by filename or other method.

CORBA: Acronym for *Common Object Request Broker Architecture.*

Cycle back to originator: Route in which the document returns to its originator after all other recipients have reviewed and forwarded it.

DASS: Acronym for *Distributed Authentication Security Service*.

Database: Structured set of computerized records organized in such a way as to facilitate input, updating, viewing, browsing, query, retrieval, reporting, sorting, indexing, joining, and manipulation by end users or application programs.

Database management system: Software designed to facilitate input, updating, viewing, browsing, query, retrieval, reporting, sorting, indexing, and manipulation of databases by end users or application programs.

Database server: A networked computer that performs all database management functions that require significant computing power, such as data retrieval, indexing, updating, sorting, joining, and query execution.

Data Encryption Standard (DES): A cryptographic algorithm designed by the National Institute of Standards and Technology to encipher and decipher data using a 64-bit key string.

Data models: Conceptual models (such as hierarchical, network, relational, and object) used to organize relationships among data.

DDE: Acronym for *Dynamic Data Exchange*.

Decision-chain modeling: Modeling a process as a chain of milestones and associated manual decision points.

Dependency: The temporal relationship of one activity to another, including start-to-start, start-to-finish, finish-to-start, and finish-to-finish relationships.

DES: Acronym for *Data Encryption Standard*.

Digital signature: String of bits that can be used to mathematically certify that a document was originated by a particular user and has not been altered or tampered during transmission or storage.

Digital Signature Algorithm (DSA): Digital signature specification adopted by the U.S. government as a Federal Information Processing Standard.

Directory services: Services that support naming, locator, address lookup and resolution functions for workflow applications, e-mail systems, network operating systems, and other distributed environments.

Directory System Agent (DSA): Software that manages the entirety or a well-defined component of a distributed directory.

Directory User Agent (DUA): Software that supports user query of Directory System Agents.

Distributed Authentication Security Service (DASS): An Experiment Internet Protocol, RFC 1507, that supports smart cards, single sign-on, credentials, mutual authentication, RSA public keys, X.500 directories, certification authorities, time-stamp-based replay protection, limited delegation, and user and node authentication.

Distributed System Object Model (DSOM): Object-management specification developed by IBM.

DMA: Acronym for *Document Management Alliance*.

DNS: Acronym for *Domain Name Service*.

Document: A file that has an author/originator, origination date/time, filename, and presentation format.

Document image processing system: Synonymous with *image management system*.

Document Management Alliance (DMA): Standard APIs for execution of file searches across multiple, heterogeneous document management systems, flat-file databases, file servers, network operating systems, and almost any other data store.

Document management system: Hardware, software, or combination environment that provides services to create, retrieve, view, edit, organize, and route text, graphics, and image files across one or more systems and applications on the network.

Document profile: A set of keywords associated with a document, such as filename, creator, date of last edit, and content-based descriptors manually entered by users.

Document server: Synonymous with *file server*.

Domain Name Service (DNS): Naming and address resolution service for the Internet and other TCP/IP-based networks.

DSA: Acronym for *Digital Signature Algorithm* or *Directory System Agent*.

DSOM: Acronym for *Distributed System Object Model*.

DUA: Acronym for *Directory User Agent*.

Dynamic Data Exchange (DDE): Cross-document data-linking capability included with Windows operating environments.

EDI: Acronym for *electronic data interchange*.

EDIFACT: Electronic data interchange (EDI) transaction-set standards developed by the United Nations' Electronic Data Interchange for Administration, Commerce, and Transport group.

Electronic commerce: Business transactions conducted over data networks, utilizing Internet, messaging, EDI, public-key cryptography, digital signature, encryption, and certification technologies.

Electronic data interchange (EDI): Electronic exchange of standardized business documents between companies and their suppliers, distributors, customers, and other trading partners.

Electronic forms: Computerized forms that replicate the layout of traditional paper forms while supporting value-added features such as autocalculation, mandatory field entry, database lookups, and structured routing.

Electronic mail: Application that supports interpersonal exchange of unstructured text messages and, sometimes, semistructured electronic forms and binary file attachments between networked users on a store-and-forward basis; also known as *e-mail*.

E-mail: Popular shorthand name for *electronic mail* or *electronic messaging*.

Electronic messaging: Services that support exchange of information between networked users; includes store-and-forward services (such as electronic mail, voice mail, and electronic data interchange), as well as real-time delivery services (such as paging and faxing). Sometimes used as a synonym for *electronic mail* or *e-mail*.

Embedded comments: Comments linked to the text upon which they comment.

Encapsulated PostScript (EPS): An image description format which translates graphics and text into descriptions that instruct a printer or typesetter on how to draw them.

Encryption: Algorithmic transformation of plain text into an unintelligible string of bits that can be returned to its original form — or decrypted — only through application of a special algorithm and key string.

EPS: Acronym for *Encapsulated PostScript*.

Event-flow modeling: Modeling a process as a chain of manual events (such as human decisions, and automated events, such as routing, collecting, printing, faxing, and archiving documents).

Execution conditions: Conditions or context within which a work item is processed manually within a particular activity, including the application tools invoked, information objects presented, and file access, input, and manipulation controls applied.

Extranet: Interorganizational network between the intranets of particular trading-partner organizations, running applications on top of Internet and World Wide Web protocols and formats, usually TCP/IP, DNS, HTTP, HTML, and Java.

Facsimile: Communications service that scans images at the transmitter, sending the constituent bits over the public telephone network, and reconstructs the image at the receiver, usually, but not always, printing the image immediately onto paper. Also known as *fax*.

Fax: Popular shorthand name for *facsimile*.

Field: Representation of a single attribute and data value in a database record.

File: A container of digital information that has a name and other attributes.

File management system: Software that supports organization, searching, retrieval, and administration of local or distributed files under the control of a computer or network operating environment.

File server: A networked computer that provides shared access to electronic files.

Filestore: Synonymous with *file server*.

File Transfer Protocol (FTP): An Internet service providing a family of commands for performing file and directory operations over the network, including the uploading and downloading of files.

Flow conditions: Conditions under which a work item is automatically transferred to the next user in the process.

Folder: A container of digital information that may include more than one file and be routed as a single object in a workflow.

Forms designer: Software that supports design of electronic forms.

Forms filler: Software that supports input, display, and routing of electronic forms.

Forms management system: A network application environment that supports origination, routing, filling, processing, and approval of electronic forms.

Fourth-generation language (4GL): Programming language that supports rapid application development through automated code generation and graphical definition of input screens, database structures, and report formats.

FTP: Acronym for *File Transfer Protocol*.

Full-text indexing: The ability to compile an alphabetical list of all or most words or character strings in a document as well as their offsets or positions within the document, thereby facilitating full-text searching.

Full-text searching: The technique of locating a document by searching for certain words, digits, sentences, or phrases.

Generic Security Services Application Program Interface (GSS-API): The specifications, defined in IETF RFC 1508, that support development of secure applications without the need to learn the particular architectures or functions of back-end authentication, confidentiality, integrity-checking, and other security services, such as Kerberos and PKCS.

GIF: Acronym for *Graphics Interchange Format*.

Gopher: Internet protocol supporting distributed, textual, menu-oriented library services.

Graphics Interchange Format (GIF): Raster image format standard; often used for in-line graphics on the World Wide Web.

Groupware: Collaborative application environments that integrate a wide range of media-oriented applications (e.g., electronic messaging, computer conferencing, document management, database management, image management, and object management) and structure-oriented applications (e.g., workflow management, time management, and project/task management).

GSS-API: Acronym for *Generic Security Services Application Program Interface*.

Hierarchical workflow interoperability: Transfer of work items from one enactment service to another service, with control of the process being returned to the original service at the same task where it left off, when the process managed by the latter service has completed.

HTML: Acronym for *HyperText Markup Language*.

HTTP: Acronym for *HyperText Transfer Protocol*.

HyperText: An information access method that allows users to peruse information associatively through linking of related blocks of information called *nodes*.

HyperText Markup Language (HTML): Standard for tagging a document's internal structure and links to external files, servers, and Internet sites; an extension to SGML that has become the standard for Web pages.

HyperText Transfer Protocol (HTTP): Standard communication protocol for connecting World Wide Web browsers to sites, using a standard addressing format referred to as a *Uniform Resource Locator (URL)*.

IDAPI: Acronym for *Independent Database Application Programming Interface*.

IGES: Acronym for *Initial Graphics Exchange Specification*.

IIOP: Acronym for *Internet Inter-ORB Protocol*.

Image: A computerized representation of a visual pattern, such as a photograph or graphic.

Image management system: System that manages creation, retrieval, viewing, editing, organization, and routing of scanned visual patterns.

IMAP4: Acronym for *Interactive Mail Access Protocol 4*.

Inbox: The location where inbound messages or work items are retained pending retrieval or completion by a user.

Independent Database Application Programming Interface (IDAPI): Borland-developed APIs for interfacing applications to SQL-compliant local or networked database management systems.

Index: An electronic file of keywords and other significant identifying information for documents (such as author, title, and date created) that text-retrieval software consults during a search.

Information-base sharing media: Network systems or services that support shared access to documents, records, files, databases, directories, designs, images, and other information objects.

Initial Graphics Exchange Specification (IGES): An ANSI standard for exchange of computerized graphical design models capable of modification and revision by the recipient.

Initiation conditions: The conditions under which the run-time enactment service will initialize a workflow and launch into the first activity.

In-line graphics: Bitmapped graphics transmitted along with an HTML-formatted page on the World Wide Web.

Integrated Services Digital Network (ISDN): A fully digital communications service, operating at rates between 144 kbps and 1.544 Mbps, designed to provide transparent end-to-end transmission of voice, data, video, and still image across the public switched telephone network.

Intelligent e-mail system: E-mail systems that provide such capabilities as sequential routing, cycle back to originator, and rule-based message management.

Internet: A worldwide network of packet data networks all connected using the TCP/IP suite of protocols, supporting application-level protocols such as SMTP (e-mail) and HTTP (World Wide Web), and functioning as a single virtual network.

Interactive Mail Access Protocol 4 (IMAP4): Internet standard protocol that supports a uniform, operating system-independent means for messaging user agents to manipulate and retrieve message data (e-mail or bulletin board) on remote message stores, on which the messages may be retained for future reference.

Internet Inter-ORB Protocol (IIOP): An open Internet protocol, based on the Common Object Request Broker Architecture (CORBA), for enabling applications to provide other applications, running under diverse operating environments, with access to selected functions and services across the Internet or an intranet.

Internetwork Packet Exchange/Sequenced Packet Exchange (IPX/SPX): Native protocol of Novell's NetWare network operating system.

Intranet: Internal corporate network running applications on top of Internet and World Wide Web protocols and formats, usually TCP/IP, DNS, HTTP, HTML, and Java.

Invoked applications: Software that is launched by the workflow enactment service, per the process definition, for the purpose of initiating or executing an activity.

IPX/SPX: Acronym for *Internetwork Packet Exchange/Sequenced Packet Exchange*.

ISDN: Acronym for *Integrated Services Digital Network*.

Iteration: Repetition of a workflow activity until a specified condition is satisfied.

Java: Dominant programming language for World Wide Web applications; Java, developed by Sun Microsystems, is a platform-independent, object-oriented language based on a simplified subset of C++; Java application components, called *applets*, are invoked from within HTML pages, either automatically upon page retrieval or manually through user commands and/or mouse-clicks; upon invocation, applets are transmitted from Web servers to the user's browser, where they are security-checked, interpreted, and executed on the fly, with results displayed within the current HTML page displayed.

JavaScript: Script language that allows programmers to control invocation, execution, and display of Java applets from within the Web browser or server, supporting a greater degree of application partitioning than is possible with the Java language alone.

JBIG: Acronym for *Joint Bi-Level Imaging Group*.

Joint Bi-Level Imaging Group (JBIG): Standard for describing, encoding, compressing, and decompressing black-and-white still images, supporting progressive image buildup on the receiving display.

Joint Photographic Experts Group (JPEG): Standard for describing, encoding, compressing, and decompressing continuous-tone, color still images, using an algorithm that achieves superior compression to Raster Groups III and IV by eliminating some redundant pixels from the original image.

JPEG: Acronym for *Joint Photographic Experts Group*.

Key: Secret information used to encrypt and/or decrypt other information.

Keyword search: The method of searching for files by querying keywords, or document descriptors, stored in a document profile.

LAN: Acronym for *local-area network*.

Laser disc: A storage medium written and read by laser.

LDAP: Acronym for *Lightweight Directory Access Protocol*.

Lightweight Directory Access Protocol (LDAP): A streamlined version of the X.500 Directory Access Protocol; supports anonymous browsing of directories, authenticated communications between a client and server directory, and referencing and replication between directory servers.

Local-area network (LAN): Geographically limited communications network designed primarily for high-speed data communications; most common technologies are Ethernet, Token Ring, and Fiber Distributed Data Interface.

Mail client: Desktop software that supports user origination, addressing, and submission of outbound items and retrieval, opening, display, and disposition of inbound items on electronic messaging systems.

Mail-enabled application: Application that can send and receive e-mail and file attachments through links to message handling systems.

MAPI: Acronym for *Messaging Application Programming Interface*.

MAPI Workflow Framework: APIs, developed by Microsoft and Wang, to support workflow-enabled applications over MAPI-compliant e-mail systems.

Message Handling Service (MHS): Specification, developed by Action Technologies and Novell, that provides standard procedures and formats for client software to send and receive messages.

Message Security Protocol (MSP): Specification developed by the U.S. government that allows a message and its digital signature to be contained within a single MIME or X.400 body part; allows support message classification by sensitivity and nonrepudiation of receipt.

Message store: Software that retains inbound and outbound messages temporarily, pending their subsequent delivery to intended recipients.

Message transfer agent (MTA): Server-based software that supports routing, delivery, forwarding, and communications functions on messaging systems.

Messaging Application Programming Interface (MAPI): Microsoft-developed APIs for interfacing Windows-based client applications to third-party message handling systems.

Messaging-based workflow systems: Workflow management systems that support definition and execution of simple process models, primarily provide an electronic-forms interface, and route documents as file attachments over users' existing e-mail systems.

Messaging media: Network systems and services that support exchange of messages on a store-and-forward basis; includes e-mail, voice mail, fax, paging, bulletin boards, electronic forms, and electronic data interchange.

MHS: Acronym for *Message Handling Service*.

Middleware: Software that provides run-time protocol and/or format translation services to support transparent deployment of distributed network applications.

Milestone-document modeling: Modeling a process as an integrated map of milestones, documents, roles, and dependencies.

MIME: Acronym for *Multipurpose Internet Messaging Extensions*.

MIME Object Security Standard (MOSS): Proposed Internet draft (RFCs 1847 and 1848) designed to succeed PEM; proposes adding PEM-based security services to MIME messages in a manner similar to S/MIME.

Modem: Device that modulates and demodulates signals transmitted over communications facilities.

MOSS: Acronym for *MIME Object Security Standard*.

Motion Picture Experts Group (MPEG): Standard for describing, encoding, compressing, and decompressing continuous-tone, color moving images.

MSP: Acronym for *Message Security Protocol*.

MTA: Acronym for *message transfer agent*.

Multimedia: A combination of two or more media, including voice, data, graphics, animation, scanned images, and video.

Multipurpose Internet Messaging Extensions (MIME): A standard for messaging over the Internet and other TCP/IP-based networks that supports transparent encoding, transport, and decoding of binary files alongside normal mail messages; supports descriptive tagging of binary file attachments and identifies the originating applications.

NDS: Acronym for *NetWare Directory Services*.

NetBEUI: Acronym for *NetBIOS Extended User Interface*.

NetBIOS: Acronym for *Network Basic Input/Output System*.

NetBIOS Extended User Interface (NetBEUI): LAN device driver and transport protocol originally developed by Microsoft.

NetWare Directory Services (NDS): Directory service supported in the Novell NetWare 4.X NOS.

Network Basic Input/Output System (NetBIOS): LAN protocol created by Microsoft and IBM.

Network File System (NFS): A machine and operating system-independent protocol developed by Sun Microsystems that supports transparent remote access to shared file systems.

Network News Transport Protocol (NNTP): Standard Internet protocol for connecting distributed, asynchronous, text-based discussion groups, referred to as *Usenet groups.*

Network operating system (NOS): Run-time software that allows LAN-connected devices to share files, disks, printers, communications links, and other facilities; it also supports centralized LAN administration, monitoring, and control.

NFS: Acronym for *Network File System.*

NOS: Acronym for *network operating system.*

NNTP: Acronym for *Network News Transport Protocol.*

Notification: A formatted message that is automatically sent to a user to report occurrence of a specific workflow event, such as receipt or forwarding of a work item.

Notification conditions: Conditions under which workflow events automatically trigger notifications to various users.

Object: Any digital representation of information that includes references or pointers to stored programs capable of manipulating the information.

Object database management system: Database management system that supports complex record structures, including data plus compact representations of repeating data, pointers to other records and files, and links to executable software associated with the record.

Object Linking and Embedding (OLE): A compound-document capability included with Windows operating environments.

Object-oriented programming: Programming techniques that support rapid application development and modification by reusing existing software modules, each of which performs a well-defined set of functions and contains executable program code plus the data that may be manipulated by this code.

Object request broker: Functional entity that performs registry, directory, and locator functions for distributed objects in a network environment.

Object store: Synonymous with *object database management system.*

OCR: Acronym for *optical character recognition.*

OCX: Acronym for *OLE Controls.*

ODA: Acronym for *Open Document Architecture.*

ODBC: Acronym for *Open Database Connectivity.*

ODMA: Acronym for *Open Document Management API.*

Office application suite: Specially priced, bundled groups of networked desktop applications that share a common user interface, functions, menus, icons, wizards, macros, and scripting languages.

OLE: Acronym for *Object Linking and Embedding.*

OLE Controls (OCX): Object-oriented development tools in the Microsoft OLE/COM environment.

Open Database Connectivity (ODBC): Microsoft-developed APIs for interfacing applications to SQL-compliant local or networked database management systems.

OpenDoc: Object management specification developed by Apple, Novell, and other companies, allowing many application modules (also called *applets*) and externally originated information objects to be invoked within a single electronic document.

Open Document Architecture (ODA): Standard for structural tagging, organization, and transfer of complex, compound documents.

Open Document Management API (ODMA): Platform-independent APIs that enable document management systems to be integrated with word processing, spreadsheet, desktop publishing, and other applications.

Open Systems Interconnection (OSI): A reference model developed by the International Organization for Standardization for a seven-layer network architecture used for the definition of network protocol standards.

Optical character recognition (OCR): The ability of a scanner to recognize and translate printed characters into machine-readable text.

Optical disk jukebox: A device that houses a number of optical disks and one or more drives, using robotics to move disks in and out of the drives as required.

Organizational entity: The project, workgroup, location, department, or company associated with a participant's role in a workflow.

OSI: Acronym for *Open Systems Interconnection*.

Outbox: The location where outbound messages or work items are retained pending forwarding to the next user, or where copies of forwarded items are retained for the user's files.

Paging: A radio service for transmitting short alphanumeric, numeric, beeping, or voice messages, either on a one-way receive-only basis or on a two-way basis with short acknowledgment or return messages.

Parallel routing: Routing in which duplicate copies of a workflow item are sent over two or more paths at the same time.

Parallel synchronized workflow interoperability: Transfer of synchronization messages but no work items between two workflow enactment services.

PDF: Acronym for *Portable Document Format*.

Peer-to-peer workflow interoperability: Transfer of work items between one workflow enactment service and another with control of the process flip-flopping back and forth between the services.

PGP: Acronym for *Pretty Good Privacy*.

PKCS-6: Acronym for *Public Key Cryptographic Services-6*.

PKCS-7: Acronym for *Public Key Cryptographic Services-7*.

POP3: Acronym for *Post Office Protocol 3*.

Portable Document Format (PDF): Adobe-developed document format supporting cross-platform high-fidelity document distribution between dissimilar operating environments and applications.

Post-activity conditions: Conditions that trigger the run-time enactment service to terminate an activity and initiate successor activities.

Post Office Protocol 3 (POP3): Internet standard protocol (RFC 1225) that supports a uniform, operating system-independent means for messaging user agents to retrieve message data (e-mail or bulletin board) on remote message stores, from which the messages are automatically deleted; requires that the messaging user agent have an IP address.

PostScript: Adobe-developed page-description language that is supported by the vast majority of desktop applications and laser printers.

Preactivity conditions: Conditions under which the run-time enactment service launches into a particular activity.

Pretty Good Privacy (PGP): Shareware public-key algorithm developed by Phillip Zimmermann.

Procedural programming language: Programming language that requires software developers to specify the precise procedural logic, user interface design, and environmental variables governing program operations.

Process definition: A flowchart or textual representation of a process that defines associated activities, routes, roles, rules, and documents.

Process-definition tool: Software that supports development of computerized representations, including both the automated and manual process components.

Process instance: A single run through a process.

Product data management systems: Production workflow systems designed to track the flow of computer-aided design, computer-aided manufacturing, and other engineering documents.

Production workflow systems: Workflow management systems that support complex process models and are built around the concept of a shared electronic filing cabinet, relying on network services — including database, file, directory, and security management — to ensure efficient task and document routing over the local or wide area.

Profile queries: Ability to locate a document by searching keywords or other descriptors contained in the document's profile, rather than by performing a full-text search.

Project management system: Application that enables managers to define a package of work to be performed by a group of people, including such details as participants, responsibilities, tasks, dependencies, resources, deliverables, outputs, hours, costs, and budgets.

Protocol: Framework for a dialogue conducted between network devices to establish, maintain, and terminate communications sessions and exchange information successfully.

Proximity searches: A method of searching text for each occurrence of one word within a specified distance from another word.

Public Key Cryptographic Services-6 (PKCS-6): Digital signature and public-key certificate standard developed and patented by RSA Data Security.

Public Key Cryptographic Services-7 (PKCS-7): The world's dominant public-key cryptographic standard, developed and patented by RSA Data Security.

Public-key cryptography: Cryptographic system that provides two different keys for encrypting and decrypting information; one key is held in private by a user and the other disclosed to other parties.

Raster: A bitmapped scanner or fax image.

Raster Groups III and IV: Standards for encoding, compressing, decompressing, and transmitting black-and-white document images over analog and digital telecommunications circuits, respectively.

Record: Repeating structure that represents two or more logically related fields in a computer database.

Relational database management system (RDBMS): Database management system that organizes information into one or more tables, each of which contains multiple rows (records) and columns (fields).

Relative distinguished name: Unique identifier for a network user or resource in an X.500 directory.

Relevance ranking: The ability of a text-retrieval system to sort the results of a search by their importance or interest to the user.

Remote procedure call (RPC): Programming technique for distributing application modules across multiple-networked devices while hiding the details of network connections from the applications.

Resource-utilization modeling: Modeling a process as linked subprocesses and activities, each of which is associated with a particular timeframe as well as human, equipment, and other material resources.

Role: The activities performed and privileges enjoyed by a specific workflow participant.

Route: The path that a workflow item takes through an organization.

Routing slip: An addressing format or dialog box that allows the originator to specify sequential routing of an outbound item on a messaging system.

RPC: Acronym for *remote procedure call.*

Rule: A statement of the conditions that will trigger automatic execution of one or more computer and network functions.

Scanner: An input device that uses light to examine patterns, which are then translated to bitmapped or rastered machine-readable data.

Script: A set of interdependent rules defined in a procedural computing language.

Secure Electronic Transactions (SET): Internet credit-card processing protocol.

Secure HyperText Transfer Protocol (SHTTP): Specification, proposed by Enterprise Integration Technologies, supporting secure connections between World Wide Web browsers and servers.

Secure Multipurpose Internet Mail Extensions (S/MIME): A standard, developed by the IETF, that adds digital signatures and encryption to Internet MIME messages described in RFC 1521; uses X.509 public-key certificates.

Secure Sockets Layer (SSL): Specification, proposed by Netscape Communications, supporting secure connections between World Wide Web browsers and servers.

Security conditions: The conditions under which workflow participants will be authenticated, authorized for various functions, and provided with workflow control and application data.

Security system: Hardware, software, or a combination of both that authenticates, access control, confidentiality, content integrity, and nonrepudiation services, or any combination of them.

Serial route: Synonymous with *sequential route*.

Server: A network-connected computer that provides shared access to resources such as applications, files, disks, printers, message transfer agents, and communications links. It is also a software module or program that provides services upon request from a separate module or program, which is referred to as a *client*.

Sequential route: A route in which there are no parallel paths and in which predecessor activities must be completed prior to initiation of their successors.

Session: User dialogue with an interactive computer system.

SET: Acronym for *Secure Electronic Transactions*.

SGML: Acronym for *Standard Generalized Markup Language*.

SHTTP: Acronym for *Secure HyperText Transfer Protocol*.

Simple Mail Transfer Protocol (SMTP): Standards, also referred to as *RFC821*, for electronic messaging over the Internet.

SMF 70 & 71: Acronym for *Standard Message Formats 70 and 71*.

SQL: Acronym for *Structured Query Language*.

SSL: Acronym for *Secure Sockets Layer*.

Standard Generalized Markup Language (SGML): Standard language used to tag the structural elements in a document to facilitate organization and formatting by external desktop publishing, layout, and other applications.

Standard Message Format (SMF) 70 and 71: Message formats supported by MHS-compliant e-mail systems.

Status: The current condition or state of a workflow item, such as awaiting retrieval, in process, or completed.

Storage management system: Hardware and software that provides access to and supports administration of hard disks, optical disks, tape drives, and other storage devices.

Store-and-forward: The process of receiving a message, retaining it in memory or on disk, and retransmitting it to its ultimate recipient or an intermediate point at another time.

StreetTalk: Directory service supported in the Banyan VINES NOS.

Structured Query Language (SQL): The dominant data query, retrieval, update, and administration language for relational database management systems.

Structured route: A route with predefined participants and dependencies.

Tagged Image File Format (TIFF): A bitmapped file format for describing and storing images that supports color and grayscale images.

TCP/IP: Acronym for *Transmission Control Protocol/Internet Protocol.*

Terminal: Any device capable of sending or receiving information over a communications channel.

Terminal emulation: Imitation of a specific terminal by a device through software or firmware.

Terminal-to-host communications: An application configuration in which data and programs are installed on a single computer and accessed, displayed, queried, and updated from dumb terminals or personal computers emulating such terminals.

Termination conditions: The conditions under which the run-time enactment service will terminate a workflow, notify the appropriate personnel, and process data to the appropriate storage systems.

Text retrieval: The ability to locate text documents containing the words and phrases specified by the searcher.

Throughput modeling: Modeling a process as activities that involve flows, accumulations, and rules for transforming inputs into outputs.

TIFF: Acronym for *Tagged Image File Format.*

Transactional modeling: Modeling a process in terms of customers, performers, and conditions of satisfaction for the process as a whole and/or for each milestone activity within the process.

Transaction monitor: Software that ensures the security and integrity of end-to-end database operations.

Transition conditions: Conditions that determine whether, when, and how an executing workflow advances to the next automated or manual activity, including flow conditions, execution conditions, and notification conditions.

Transmission Control Protocol/Internet Protocol (TCP/IP): A protocol suite for networking and internetworking that ensures that data packets are delivered to their destination in the order in which they were transmitted. Occupies the transport and network layers of the OSI Reference Model. Originally development for the U.S. Department of Defense.

Transparency: The ability of a system or service to maintain a consistent, logical interface, from the end user's point of view, shielding the user from complexity, reconfigurations, modifications, failures, and other distracting technical details in the serving platform.

Uniform Resource Locator (URL): Standard addressing format for accessing sites, pages, and other resources on the World Wide Web.

UNIX: A multiuser operating system initially developed by Bell Laboratories in the late 1960s and since modified and commercialized by many companies and organizations.

URL: Acronym for *Uniform Resource Locator.*

Value-added reseller (VAR): Resellers of computer hardware and software, adding value via custom applications, integration, add-on products, training, or support.

VAR: Acronym for *value-added reseller.*

Vendor-Independent Messaging (VIM): APIs, developed by Lotus and other e-mail vendors, for interfacing client applications to third-party message handling systems running in many operating environments.

Version control: The ability of a system to distinguish, track, and control separate versions of a document.

VIM: Acronym for *Vendor-Independent Messaging.*

WAN: Acronym for *wide-area network.*

WAIS: Acronym for *Wide-Area Information Services.*

WfMC: Acronym for *Workflow Management Coalition.*

Wide-Area Information Services (WAIS): Internet protocol supporting remote searching of indexed bibliographic databases.

Wide-area network (WAN): A data network that covers a larger geographic area than a single workgroup, facility, campus, or metropolitan area network.

Workflow: Flow of information and control in a business process.

Workflow administration and monitoring tools: Software that supports real-time surveillance, control, configuration, and optimization of workflow execution.

Workflow application data: Data that is used by workflow participants but not accessed by the run-time enactment service.

Workflow client application: Software that allows workflow participants to interact with workflow enactment services for the purpose of signing on and off the service, initiating processes, displaying worklists, invoking applications, and accessing workflow-relevant, application, and control data.

Workflow control data: Real-time data on work-item status and locations used by the workflow enactment service to control an active process.

Workflow definition: The subset of a process definition that describes activities, routes, roles, and rules that can be supported by automated computer and network tools.

Workflow-enabled application: An application that utilizes document routing and tracking services provided through APIs on a workflow enactment service.

Workflow enactment service: Software that provides a run-time environment for initiating, executing, sequencing, and controlling instances of a process definition, adding work items to user worklists and invoking application tools as necessary; includes one or more workflow engines.

Workflow engine: Server-resident software that provides the run-time execution environment for a workflow instance, either individually or in communication with other workflow engines; component of a distributed workflow enactment service.

Workflow management: The ability of a system to support structured routing and tracking of documents, folders, and other information throughout a workgroup or enterprise.

Workflow management system: A system that defines, manages, and executes automated workflows in accordance with a computerized process definition.

Workflow Management Coalition (WfMC): Industry consortium developing a Workflow Reference Model and associated technical standards.

Workflow Reference Model: A standard architecture, terminology, and technical interface for workflow management systems that has been proposed by the Workflow Management Coalition.

Workflow-relevant data: User-input application data that is read directly by the workflow enactment service for the purpose of triggering routing and execution rules.

Work item: An electronic document or folder currently involved in an active workflow.

Worklist: A list of work items pending completion by a particular user.

Worklist handler: Software that retrieves a list of work items from the workflow enactment service, displays items associated with particular users, and facilitates item retrieval, processing, and forwarding.

World Wide Web (the Web or WWW): Internet service that supports transparent, graphical, point-and-click navigation among distributed information services and resources, based on the HyperText Markup Language (for document hyperlinking), HyperText Transfer Protocol (for connecting browsers to servers), and Uniform Resource Locators (for naming and addressing resources).

WORM: Acronym for *Write Once Read Many*.

Write Once Read Many (WORM) drive: An optical storage medium that supports permanent, unalterable information storage.

WWW: Acronym for *World Wide Web*.

X12: EDI transaction-set standards developed by the American National Standards Institute.

X.25: Protocol standard developed by the International Telecommunications Union Telecommunications Standardization Sector for packet communications between user data terminal equipment and circuit-terminating equipment.

X.400 Message Handling Services: Electronic-messaging standards developed by the International Telecommunications Union's Telecommunications Standardization Sector.

X.435: Standards for EDI over X.400 electronic messaging system, developed by the International Telecommunications Union's Telecommunications Standardization Sector.

X.500 Directory Services: Directory-services standards developed by the International Telecommunications Union's Telecommunications Standardization Sector.

X.509 Public-Key Certificates: Public-key certificate standard developed by the International Telecommunications Union's Telecommunications Standardizaton Sector.

INDEX

(continued)

(continued)

(continued)

Colophon

This book was produced electronically in Foster City, California. Microsoft Word Version 6.0 was used for word processing; design and layout were produced with QuarkXpress 3.3 on a Power Macintosh 8500/120. The type face families used are Adobe Garamond and Myriad Multiple Master.

Senior Vice President and Group Publisher   Brenda McLaughlin

Director of Publishing   Walt Bruce

Acquisitions Editor   Ellen L. Camm

Marketing Manager   Jill Reinemann

Executive Managing Editor   Terry Somerson

Managing Editor   Andy Cummings

Administrative Assistant   Laura J. Moss

Editorial Assistant   Timothy J. Borek

Production Director   Andrew Walker

Supervisor of Page Layout   Laura Carpenter

Development Editors   Linda B. Laflamme, Susan Pines

Copy Editor   Judy Brunetti

Copy Edit Coordinator   Barry Childs-Helton

Technical Reviewer   Daniel Blum, Rapport Communications

Project Coordinator   Phyllis Beaty

Layout and Graphics   Mario F. Amador, Tom Debolski, Renée Dunn, Jude Levinson, Andreas F. Schueller, Mark Schumann, Elsie Yim

Quality Control Specialist   Mick Arellano

Proofreader   David Wise

Indexer   Ty Koontz

Production Administration   Tony Augsburger, Todd Klemme, Jason Marcuson, Christopher Pimentel, Leslie Popplewell, Theresa Sánchez-Baker, Melissa Stauffer

Book Design   Margery Cantor, Kurt Krames

Cover Design   Christine Cuccia

About the Author

James G. Kobielus is a contributing editor to *Network World,* the leading newsweekly of enterprise network computing. He is a recognized authority on strategic telecommunications and information systems topics. He has written extensively on workflow management systems, groupware, wireless communications, electronic commerce, network management, electronic software distribution, network security, messaging, and directory services.

Kobielus is a product planner and manager with LCC International Inc., a Virginia-based network design and engineering firm. Previously, he held telecommunications analysis positions with DynCorp Information and Engineering Technology Corp., Network Management Inc., Adeena Corp., MCI Telecommunications Corp., and the North American Telecommunications Association. He holds a Master of Arts in Journalism from the University of Wisconsin-Madison and a Bachelor of Arts in Economics (with High Honors) from the University of Michigan-Ann Arbor.

He lives in Alexandria, Virginia, with his wife Egidia and two children, Jason and Sonya. He also writes poetry.

IDG BOOKS WORLDWIDE REGISTRATION CARD

RETURN THIS REGISTRATION CARD FOR FREE CATALOG

Title of this book: **Workflow Strategies®**

My overall rating of this book: ❑ Very good [1]   ❑ Good [2]   ❑ Satisfactory [3]   ❑ Fair [4]   ❑ Poor [5]

How I first heard about this book:

❑ Found in bookstore; name: [6]   ❑ Book review: [7]

❑ Advertisement: [8]   ❑ Catalog: [9]

❑ Word of mouth; heard about book from friend, co-worker, etc.: [10]   ❑ Other: [11]

What I liked most about this book:

What I would change, add, delete, etc., in future editions of this book:

Other comments:

Number of computer books I purchase in a year: ❑ 1 [12]   ❑ 2-5 [13]   ❑ 6-10 [14]   ❑ More than 10 [15]

I would characterize my computer skills as: ❑ Beginner [16] ❑ Intermediate [17] ❑ Advanced [18] ❑ Professional [19]

I use ❑ DOS [20] ❑ Windows [21] ❑ OS/2 [22] ❑ Unix [23] ❑ Macintosh [24] ❑ Other: [25]_____
(please specify)

I would be interested in new books on the following subjects:
(please check all that apply, and use the spaces provided to identify specific software)

❑ Word processing: [26]   ❑ Spreadsheets: [27]

❑ Data bases: [28]   ❑ Desktop publishing: [29]

❑ File Utilities: [30]   ❑ Money management: [31]

❑ Networking: [32]   ❑ Programming languages: [33]

❑ Other: [34]

I use a PC at (please check all that apply): ❑ home [35] ❑ work [36] ❑ school [37] ❑ other: [38] _____

The disks I prefer to use are ❑ 5.25 [39] ❑ 3.5 [40] ❑ other: [41]_____

I have a CD ROM: ❑ yes [42]   ❑ no [43]

I plan to buy or upgrade computer hardware this year: ❑ yes [44]   ❑ no [45]

I plan to buy or upgrade computer software this year: ❑ yes [46]   ❑ no [47]

Name: Business title: [48]   Type of Business: [49]

Address (❑ home [50] ❑ work [51]/Company name:)

Street/Suite#

City [52]/State [53]/Zipcode [54]:   Country [55]

❑ **I liked this book!** You may quote me by name in future
IDG Books Worldwide promotional materials.

My daytime phone number is _____

IDG BOOKS

THE WORLD OF
COMPUTER
KNOWLEDGE